ALSO BY RACHEL POLONSKY

English Literature and the Russian Aesthetic Renaissance

MOLOTOV'S
MAGIC LANTERN

MOLOTOV'S MAGIC LANTERN

Travels in Russian History

❧

RACHEL POLONSKY

Farrar, Straus and Giroux

New York

Farrar, Straus and Giroux
18 West 18th Street, New York 10011

Some passages in this book were first published in
The Times Literary Supplement.

The Library of Congress has cataloged the hardcover edition as follows:
Polonsky, Rachel.
Molotov's magic lantern : travels in Russian history / Rachel Polonsky.—
1st American ed.
    p. cm.
"Originally published in 2010 by Faber and Faber Ltd., Great Britain as
Molotov's magic lantern : a journey in Russian history"—T.p. verso.
Includes bibliographical references and index.
ISBN 978-0-374-21197-4 (alk. paper)
    1. Russia (Federation)—Description and travel. 2. Moscow (Russia)—
Description and travel. 3. Polonsky, Rachel—Travel—Russia (Federation)
4. Molotov, Vyacheslav Mikhaylovich, 1890–1986—Homes and haunts—Russia
(Federation)—Moscow. 5. Molotov, Vyacheslav Mikhaylovich, 1890–1986—
Library. 6. Authors, Russian—20th century—Homes and haunts. 7. Authors,
Russian—20th century—Political and social views. 8. Moscow (Russia)—
History. 9. Communism and literature—Soviet Union—History. 10. Soviet
Union—Intellectual life. I. Title.

DK510.29.P65 2011
947—dc22

                                                                    2010023037

Paperback ISBN: 978-0-374-53320-5

Maps by András Bereznay; www.historyonmaps.com

www.fsgbooks.com

1 3 5 7 9 10 8 6 4 2

For Marc, in gratitude and love

Life . . . lives, people, revolutions, beloved faces have
appeared, changed and vanished between the Sparrow Hills
and Primrose Hill; already their traces have been almost
swept away . . .

ALEXANDER HERZEN, *Past and Thoughts*

. . . all our ideas have their origin in our idea of place . . .

OSCAR MILOSZ, *Les Arcanes*

la forme d'une ville
Change plus vite, hélas! que le cœur d'un mortel

CHARLES BAUDELAIRE, 'Le Cygne'

I can't feel you anymore, I can't even touch the books
you've read

BOB DYLAN, 'Idiot Wind'

Contents

MAPS

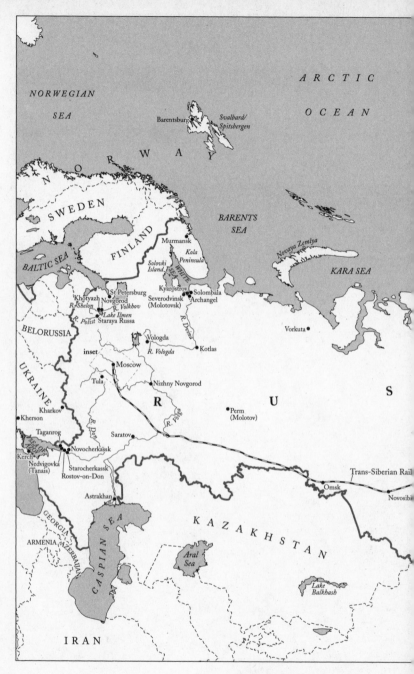

Map of Russia showing some of

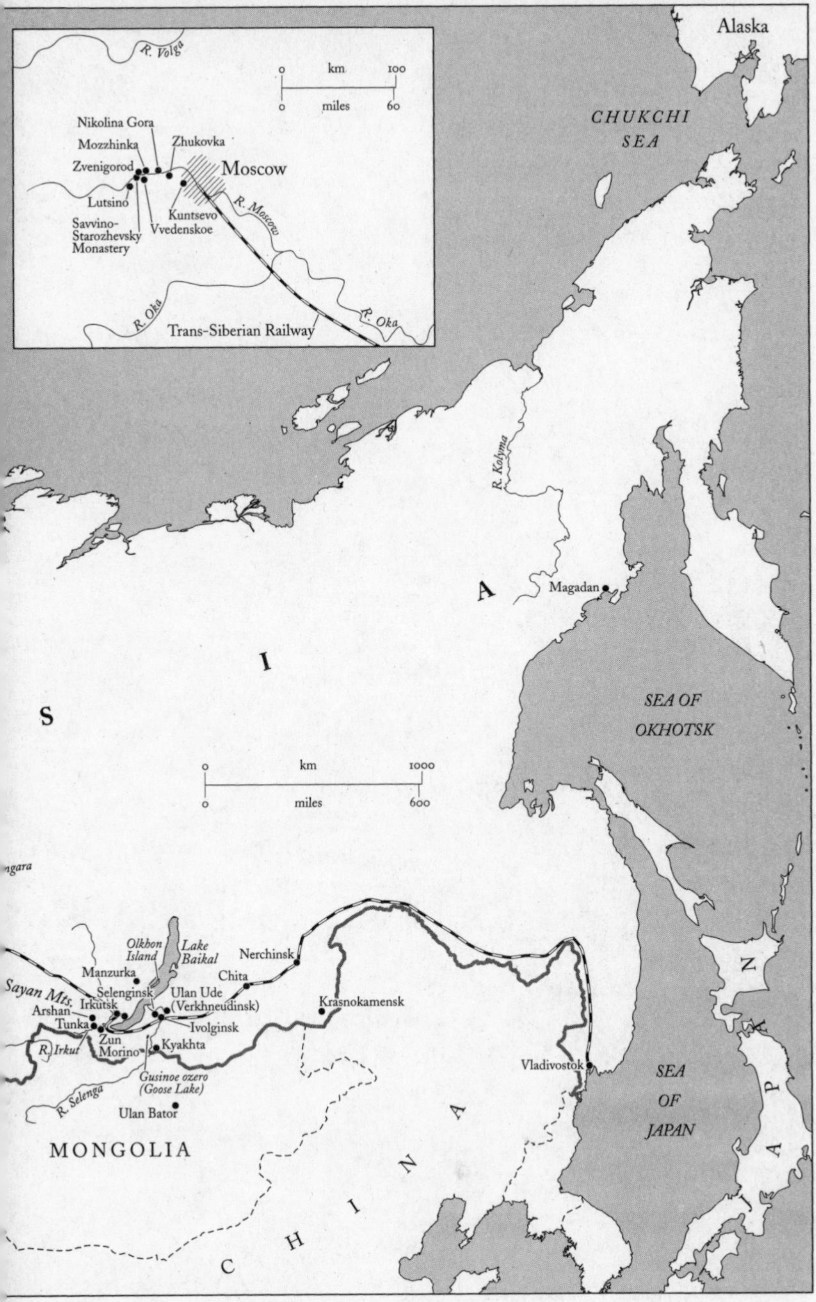

Alaska
CHUKCHI SEA
R. Volga
km
0
100
miles
0
60
Nikolina Gora
Mozzhinka
Zhukovka
Zvenigorod
Moscow
Lutsino
Kuntsevo
R. Moscow
Savvino-Starozhevsky Monastery
Vvedenskoe
R. Oka
R. Oka
Trans-Siberian Railway
R. Kolyma
Magadan
S
I
A
SEA OF OKHOTSK
km
0
1000
miles
0
600
ngara
Olkhon Island
Lake Baikal
Nerchinsk
Manzurka
Chita
Sayan Mts.
Selenginsk
Ulan Ude (Verkhneudinsk)
Irkutsk
Krasnokamensk
Arshan
Tunka
Ivolginsk
Zun Morino
Kyakhta
R. Irkut
Gusinoe ozero (Goose Lake)
R. Selenga
Ulan Bator
MONGOLIA
Vladivostok
SEA OF JAPAN
C H I N A
J A P A N

the places referred to in the book

Map of Moscow showing some of

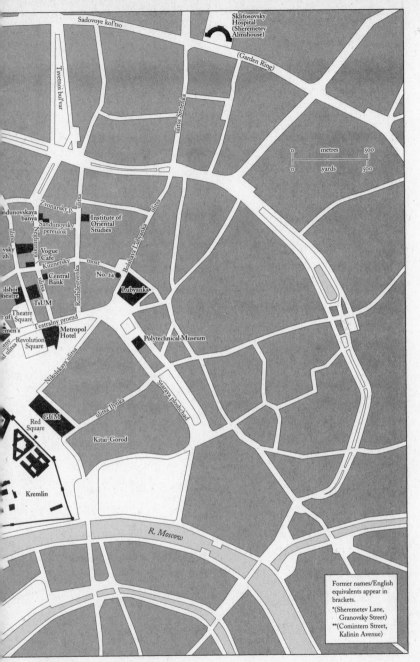

the places referred to in the book

Sadovoye kol'tso

Sklifosovsky Hospital (Sheremetev Almshouse)

Tsvetnoi bul'var

(Garden Ring)

ulitsa Sretenka

metres
yards

0   500
0   500

Zvonarsky p.

ndunovskaya banya

andunovsky pereulok

Institute of Oriental Studies

ulitsa

ulitsa

ysky zh

Vogue Cafe

Kuznetsky   most

Bolshaya Lubyanka

ulitsa

Central Bank

No. 24

olshoi heatre

TsUM

Rozhdestvenka

Lubyanka

Theatre Square

of men's

Teatralny proezd

Polytechnical Museum

Revolution Square

Metropol Hotel

Nikolskaya ulitsa

ov alitsa

Staraya ploshchad

GUM

ulitsa Ilyinka

Red Square

Kitai-Gorod

Kremlin

R. Moscow

Former names/English equivalents appear in brackets.

*(Sheremetev Lane, Granovsky Street)

**(Comintern Street, Kalinin Avenue)

MOLOTOV'S
MAGIC LANTERN

Prologue

In one corner of Molotov's drawing room stands a magic lantern.

With my back to the window that looks out over Romanov Lane, I wind the brass handle of the lantern, squinting down into the waist-high mahogany obelisk through a glass aperture as faint pictures click past on the revolving slide-carrier. A family group, ladies in old-fashioned bathing suits, smiles across from a rock on the Crimean seashore, hands shading eyes from the sun, then slips into the dark to make way for a staring shaman in torn trousers and a crooked hat; a circle of peasant women creaks past in a ritual dance, turning into three touched-up views of wooden houses and elegant public squares in the Siberian city of Irkutsk.

'Have at it,' the banker had said in his charming smoky drawl, dangling from one finger the keys to his apartment. He had rung our doorbell early as he passed on his way down the stairs. 'You're the scholar, you'll know what to make of it all.'

We had met the evening before at his welcome-to-Moscow party in one of the other Romanov apartments. Over my champagne and his Jack Daniel's, I told him, in my fumbling way, that I was some kind of fugitive academic, not really a journalist, working on a novel . . . He insisted, as certain investment bankers like to do, that he was not an evil capitalist and that he loved books. His true calling was politics, he said; for over a decade he had worked quixotically for the Democratic Party in his home state of Texas.

Our conversation picked up animation when he told me about Molotov's library. I already knew that the apartment he had moved into (immediately above our own) had been the Moscow home, in the last years of his long life, of Stalin's most loyal surviving henchman. I did not know that some of Molotov's possessions had remained in place – left there by the granddaughter who now let the apartment to international financiers – including hundreds of books, some inscribed to him or annotated in his hand, now apparently forgotten, on the lower shelves of closed bookcases in a back corridor.

My new friend the banker cannot have known what a gift he was making when he handed me those keys. In the first moments of my solitude in the grandeur of the Molotov apartment, with its spread of panelled rooms and its high stuccoed ceilings, I sensed that I had reached a destination. It was one of the destinations, even now obscure to me, for which I had made a sudden rush in that restless Cambridge spring, when the yearning to move had formed itself into a plan to come to Moscow. But a destination is rarely what we expect it to be, and destiny has a way of mocking our desires. That is one of the odd pleasures of thinking about history, including one's own, whether one believes it to be moved by chance, or providence, or the secret cunning of the dialectic.

How was I to regard Vyacheslav Molotov's abandoned library? I had not come to Moscow to pore over books like this. I was raised to value books, but these decaying volumes were residues of a malign force, not yet expired. For decades, their owner had been the second most powerful man in Stalin's empire, head of his government machine and his closest and most trusted comrade, a man who collaborated diligently in the tyrant's crimes, condemning millions to cruel deaths. As I lifted the books out of the shelves in soft crumbling piles, I found myself remembering a book that I had read in my teens, a gift from my father, called *Nightingale Fever*. It was a study by the Oxford scholar Ronald Hingley of the lives and works of four Russian poets – Anna Akhmatova, Osip Mandelstam, Marina Tsvetaeva and Boris Pasternak – 'nightingales' who would not stop singing, each persecuted, in ways that were brutal and exquisite, by the Soviet state that Molotov had been so active in building and sustaining in power. I was stirred then by the way in which, in Russia, the power of poetry is confirmed by politics, by the reactions to these four poets of the men in the Kremlin who thought they could command history. But those men were no more than shadow monsters in the story of the poets my father gave me.

I read their verse, seeing little through the veil of my meagre Russian, but compelled by sounds and rhythms, and the intimation of what Mandelstam called the 'monstrously condensed reality' which the modest exterior of lyric art contains. Some lines stayed in my head, like the first couplet of one of the poems in Mandelstam's first collection, *Stone*:

> *A body has been given to me, what am I to do with it?*
> *So single and so my own?*

I could only read that poem of 1909 – at once so simple and so sophisticated – through the knowledge of Mandelstam's death in a Gulag transit camp three decades later. 'For the quiet joy of breathing and living, whom, tell me, should I thank?' the poet asked:

> *I am both the gardener and the flower,*
> *in the dungeon of the world I am not solitary.*

History is sly, and shapes strange reciprocities. 'If Molotov did not exist', Stalin remarked, 'it would be necessary to invent him.' The nightingale poets, whose songs the Party could not silence, owed their tragic greatness to killers like Molotov. Mandelstam's widow, Nadezhda, says in her memoir *Hope Against Hope* that the image of 'thin-necked bosses' in the short poem that Mandelstam wrote about Stalin's tyranny (the poem that led to his first arrest in 1934) was inspired by the sight of 'Molotov's thin neck sticking out of his collar and the small head that crowned it. "Just like a tomcat", Mandelstam said, pointing at a portrait of Molotov.' In the course of things, Molotov even did Mandelstam a kindness. It was he who personally arranged a trip to the southern republic of Armenia for Mandelstam in the late 1920s (when his poetic gift had been dry for years), giving instructions to local Party organisations that the poet and his wife should be looked after properly. 'Armenia restored the gift of poetry to Mandelstam', Nadezhda remembered, 'and a new period of his life began'.

A look back at the past is a magic-lantern show. 'Memory is structured so that, like a projector, it illuminates discrete moments,' Akhmatova said, 'leaving unconquerable darkness all around.' I have a small set of images ready to be summoned at will to my mind's eye that illuminate moments on my way to the Molotov apartment.

I remember the gold letters on the spine of a black book on the shelves in my father's study – Nicolas Berdyaev, *The Meaning of History* – beneath which I slept on a camp bed for a few weeks in my childhood. I did not open the book (in which, as I later discovered, my grandfather had pencilled his name in Adelaide, South Australia, in the year 1937), but the assertion on its spine – history has a meaning – took root in my mind, conjoined with a Russian name.

I picture Moscow the first time, on a dry day in the spring of 1980, when I walked alone with a fifteen-year-old schoolfriend from the Pushkin Museum of Fine Arts back to the Hotel Bucharest on the far side of the river. We were unsure of the way. We bought ice creams from a stand. They were called *lakomki*, white columns of frozen cream wrapped in grainy chocolate paste that we told each other were the most delicious we had ever tasted. We walked through the Alexander Gardens beneath the Kremlin Wall, across Red Square and over the river, and we had a self-consciously intellectual conversation (the first of my life) about cubism and Soviet Communism, which we thought would never end, and found some crucial link between the two. The city was empty and hard and absolutely closed. I felt that Moscow was full of tightly locked mysteries and that we were invisible explorers, untouchable and free.

This was the first of several occasions when I came close to this place as I wandered in neighbouring streets. On our walk, my friend and I would have passed not far from the Romanov building, when its hundreds of apartments were still home to the highest ranks of the Soviet *nomenklatura*, the privileged elite of the state apparatus and the Red Army. It is as though memory had its own intuition, independent of my thinking mind, of this particular future out of the infinitude of possible futures. As though it carefully stored that image so that I could juxtapose it with my present view of the city, from a front window in the shadowed quiet of the Molotov apartment, looking across the Kremlin Hospital in the old Sheremetev Palace toward Mokhovaya Street (then called Marx Avenue), which we must have crossed that day. From the back windows, I can see the Voentorg, the Military Department Store on Vozdvizhenka Street, on whose bare shelves in the late 1980s I found a recording of Akhmatova reciting *Requiem*, her poetic cycle about Stalin's Terror. That was not long after the day in 1986 when Molotov's funeral party gathered for a wake in this apartment, from which the KGB had already removed all the private papers and photographs deemed important to the state. The vinyl trace of the old woman's cracked voice in the cavernous department store was a tiny improbable sign that the communist state was near withering, in a dialectic quite unlike the one that Molotov's tireless study of Marxism–Leninism had led him to expect.

I remember too a moment of bleak conflict with the man who is now my husband. We were standing with friends outside the Lenin Library metro station, below the high pillars of the Pashkov House. It was cold, everyone was hungry (there were no bright cafes in the city then), and we could not even agree on where to cross the street. I love the surprise that the future was holding secret: the home, with children in it, that we would share, just a few hundred yards from our destitution on that windy corner.

There are closer memories. The college rooms of the Russian don who had died a few weeks before I took up my Cambridge fellowship are certainly part of the story. He had learned the language in the armed forces, where he served on the Allied aid convoys to the Soviet Arctic ports, and after the war, when

Russian became a degree subject at the university, he had devoted his life to teaching Russian literature, and to his own reading. The old scholar had been known for his great height, his sarcasm, his erudition, and his particular interest in the mid-nineteenth-century conservative thinker Apollon Grigoriev. He had died intestate, having published nothing except an edition of Ivan Turgenev's *Fathers and Sons*, with the word stresses marked in. Why should he write, he would ask, when he could read fifty times as much in the time it would have taken him to produce some academic article of little worth?

The college did not know what to do with the chaos of books and papers – ruins of a private civilisation – piled in his rooms among old shoes and half-empty medicine bottles. The bursar asked me to take a look, and I spent several days inefficiently sorting through them, deciding which volumes should be kept for the library. I could take what I wanted from the rest, which were to be given or thrown away. What did it mean to be alone, making free with this dead man's books? Ask me for my biography and I will tell you the books I have read, Mandelstam said. The library of the Russian don revealed a man of the deepest cultivation, a true lover of books, who had lived half-secluded from the world, as scholars once could. He had acquired these books in many cities, their names – Archangel, Moscow, Helsinki, Paris, London – and the dates of acquisition inscribed in them in a light hand next to his own name: E. Sands. *The Jewish Problem*, a Penguin paperback, was dated 'Feb. 1939'. A Russian New Testament in black cloth, published by the Bible Society, was inscribed 'Cambridge Nov. 1942'. Did he take it with him on the convoys to Stalin's USSR? In it was a scrap on which he had transcribed, half in French, half in Latin, a line about marriage from St Paul's First Letter to the Corinthians: *'Mais s'ils manquent de continence . . . melius est enim nubere . . .* "But if they lack continence [let them marry]; for it is better to marry [than to burn]'. Left in their pages as bookmarks were scraps of ephemera, the outward events of a life slipped into the pages where the real dramas took place: the cards announcing the memorial services of deceased academics that come unbidden into college pigeon-holes each week; booksellers' invoices; notes from abject undergraduates about late essays and cancelled supervisions; holiday postcards from friends; racy tinted prints from a nineteenth-century satirical series by Gavarni called *The Gay Women of Paris*. There were the marks of his pencil in many of the books, mostly correcting typos, or noting factual errors; occasionally he would cross-reference, drawing readily from across the breadth of Russian literature and beyond. I imagined him in the dusty afternoon light on the chair by the window, buses grinding in the street below, his book resting on his crossed leg, his pencil vigilant. He had a large collection of French literature and French novels published in Soviet editions. In the late 1980s he had read a Russian translation of Marcel Proust's *Sodom and Gomorrah*, critically cross-checking passages, leaving a twisted scrap of an envelope as a bookmark in the page on which the narrator Marcel realises, after eighty pages of obsessional torment, that his jealousy of the various women whom Albertine may have loved has suddenly died. On it Sands had jotted a single phrase from Alexander Pushkin's verse novel *Eugene Onegin* (just three words in Russian): 'NB: "the science of the tender passion".'

Is there a set of secret maps to be found among a person's books, a way through the fortifications of the self? There is a scene in Chapter Seven of *Eugene Onegin*, after Onegin has departed on his wanderings, when Tatyana, who loves him, finds herself alone in his study. Reading avidly beneath the portrait of Byron and the statuette of Napoleon, Tatyana finds herself exploring a different world, trying to decipher the mysterious essence of the man from the traces of his fingernails in the pages of his books, the marks his pencil has made.

> *Everywhere the soul of Onegin*
> *Involuntarily reveals itself,*
> *Whether by a brief word, by a cross,*
> *Or by a question mark . . .*

Old books are objects of a mysterious and compulsive kind of desire, fed by a stubborn intuition that the past might yield its secrets to the touch, as though some further meaning or spirit dwells in their very matter. Books are the scene, the stage, of their own fate, Walter Benjamin says. As we look at them, we look through them at the distant past they contain. The books I looked at that afternoon in Sands's rooms formed the architecture of a biography, and though he left no will he had left me a legacy. I laid two books side by side on the carpet, two books with half a century between them: an orange-and-white Penguin paperback of Russian short stories selected by the political exile S. S. Koteliansky (Virginia Woolf's 'Kot'), with Sands's pen '*Do svidaniya*' – 'Goodbye' – on the cover, and a doodled profile, just like one of Pushkin's marginal scribbles, on the inside leaf, with the word '*ROSSIYA*' beneath it, and the date 1941. This was the year of the Anglo-Soviet Alliance, when the first-aid convoy, code-named 'Dervish', reached Archangel. Beside it I placed the most recent book in Sands's collection, a paperback of about the same size called *The Northern Convoys*, published in Archangel in 1991, the year the Soviet Union came apart.

For myself I kept a slim book by the dissident writer Lydia Chukovskaya on Alexander Herzen's philosophical memoir *Past and Thoughts*; a late Stalin-era anthology of the writings of the anti-tsarist rebel Ivan Yakushkin; a typed lecture on Anton Chekhov; a pamphlet explaining the rules of cricket in Russian; a battered set of Pushkin with one missing volume, inscribed 'Archangel, 1944', and a book of Soviet maritime songs about fighting for Stalin on the cliffs over the Barents Sea, into which Sands had slipped a copy of the Soviet anthem: 'unbreakable union of free republics, pulled together for ever by Great Rus'. Rather than leave them out for the prurient eyes of the college bursar, I buried inside random pages of his books the few love letters that I found in a box of papers, one written in several drafts to a woman in France whom he had seen again for the first time in decades – 'After all this time, you were just the same . . .' Did he ever send it? I also hid a sweetly witty monochrome postcard of Marilyn Monroe in nothing but a pair of Perspex platform heels, diamond earrings and a polka-dot scarf, dated 14 February (no year), from someone who hoped he 'would not be cross', and signed herself 'Dido D.'

I remember how I flushed when I found a passport-size picture, taken in Murmansk in 1942, of Sands in an astrakhan hat. (It was the winter after Molotov's secret May flight, as Soviet foreign minister, in a four-engine bomber over German-occupied territory, to formalise the Anglo-Soviet Alliance in Downing Street, where, at the garden gate, Winston Churchill gripped his arm and looked at his face, sure that for a moment he had seen the man appear 'inside the image'.) The photograph of the young Sands, in the brief time of action that came before the long years of contemplation in these rooms, stirred in me a desire to clean the dust of these unwanted lecture notes on Chekhov and Dostoevsky from my hands, and take a ship, without delay, to the Arctic ports.

Three years later, my husband, ever the rootless cosmopolitan, called me on a bad line from a Moscow street on his first visit to the city on legal business. He had not visited Russia since we had lived through the last dark winter of the Soviet system as graduate students in Leningrad.

'Moscow's a world city now.' Through the interference I could hear the excitement in his voice. 'It's become a real city.'

Then came the moment of consent to this adventure, in a vaulted windowless restaurant called the Boyars' Hall, made to look like ancient Rus, deep inside the art nouveau walls of the Metropol Hotel. We had spent an exhausting day making our way through the slush in a borrowed car, looking at strange apartments with bathrooms of black marble and entryways with the familiar Soviet redolence of tomcat pheromones. To an accordion, a chorus in fur-trimmed old-Muscovy gowns sang a folk song about passionate black eyes. How is it that banality can sometimes bring on a decisive kind of rapture? Is it because I watched too much bad Soviet TV on winter nights in Leningrad in 1990 that those minor chords and the yearning timbre of the Slavonic voice immediately summoned pictures of wide Russian rivers in the moonlight, snow-filled forests, grassy steppes in the sunshine of spring? I was on my second glass of wine, back in the fairy tale, and, without hesitation, as I knew I would, I said yes.

After I had packed up my treasured room in college, I left several cardboard boxes of my books and papers in the cellars there, telling myself and the fellowship that I would be back in eighteen months. I planned to spend my time in Moscow working in the great libraries of the city, studying orientalism in Russian poetry. Those eighteen months became ten years.

These years have not been spent in ordered study. I quickly strayed. Instead of the scholarly masterpiece on orientalism I had in mind, I have written this book, which recounts my wanderings among the muddle of past time that books and places make. On maps, the Kremlin looks like the round centre of a compass, with roads leading out from it to north, east, south and west into the spreading, never-quite-defined lands it tries to rule. I have travelled out from our home close to the Kremlin Wall whenever I have had the chance, following whims, hunches and bookish romances. I have made other journeys, just as full of random adventure, sitting among old men in grimy ill-fitting suits and thick plastic-rimmed spectacles at the desks in Reading Room No. 1 in the Lenin Library, as the Russian State Library is still familiarly known.

This great library, from which Lenin's name was removed by presidential decree in 1992, was once called the Rumyantsev Museum. Its most famous keeper, Nikolai Fyodorov, known as the 'Russian Socrates', was reputed to be familiar with the contents of all the books in its collections. In one story about the reach of the librarian's encyclopedic knowledge, a group of engineers working on the Trans-Siberian Railway came to show him maps of the projected route across the steppe, and Fyodorov, who had never been to Siberia, corrected their calculation of the altitude of some of the hills. Fyodorov believed, quite literally, that books were animate beings, because they expressed the thought, the souls, of their authors. At the heart of his library work and his philosophical writings (which were published posthumously in 1903 as *The Philosophy of the Common Task*) was a refusal to be reconciled with the fact of death. Man's task on earth was the material resurrection of the dead ('not as crazy as it sounds', Lev Tolstoy remarked), who were present, unconstituted in the library dust, souls waiting in books for the systematic returning of past generations to life. ('There was no man on earth who felt such sorrow at the death of people,' Berdyaev said.) He spent the last quarter of the nineteenth century living inside the catalogue of the Rumyantsev Museum, hardly eating or sleeping, reluctant even to sit down. Russia's greatest thinkers came to find him in the library to discuss ideas. Tolstoy, Fyodor Dostoevsky and the philosopher Vladimir Solovyov (who called Fyodorov his 'teacher and spiritual father') all regarded him as a philosopher of genius. Boris Pasternak's father, the artist Leonid Pasternak, who was another devotee, once hid behind the bookstacks in the reading room to make secret sketches of Fyodorov, who was philosophically averse to the idea of his image being taken, believing that the icon, in which the human countenance is sanctified and presented in its transcendent aspect, is the only genre worthy of the human face.

Fyodorov was a pioneer in the practice of librarianship. He believed that the keeping of books was sacred work. A library catalogue, he thought, should be arranged by the authors' dates of death, like a calendar of saints' days. The book, he believed, is the most exalted among remains of the past, for it represents that past at its most human, the past as thought. For him, only the struggle against the common enemy death, the task of resurrecting the 'fathers', would unify mankind. 'To study', for Fyodorov, meant 'not to reproach and not to praise, but to restore life'.

Now the librarians in the Lenin Library are working to restore the names of the dozens of their predecessors who were 'repressed' – arrested, shot, lost without trace – in the 1920s and

1930s. In October 1928, the *Red Evening Newspaper* reported that the library had become 'a refuge for groups of counter-revolutionary intelligentsia', and descendants of the nobility. The great librarian, bibliographer and editor Vladimir Nevsky, who was director of the library after the Revolution and laid the first stone of the new library building in 1927, was arrested in 1935, denounced the Old Bolshevik Nikolai Bukharin under interrogation, and was shot in 1937, the bloodiest year of Stalin's Great Terror. In his later years, Molotov, who was answerable for innumerable similar deaths, often passed his days in Reading Room No. 1. Disgraced by the Party he had served, he pored over the past, building up fortifications around the ideas that had controlled his life, still believing that they could direct the future.

The reading room's vast side windows look out over Mokhovaya, across the old Comintern headquarters, where in the 1920s communists from abroad like Antonio Gramsci, Béla Kun, Georgy Dimitrov and Ho Chi Minh worked for world revolution, towards the Trinity Gates and the towers and golden domes of the Kremlin on the hill. On the forecourt beneath the library on the Vozdvizhenka side is a giant statue of Dostoevsky, unveiled in the year we arrived in Moscow to replace a statue of Lenin (who hated the novelist). Recently young supporters of Vladimir Putin have sometimes gathered at his feet in made-for-TV manifestations of loyalty. Dostoevsky, now a co-opted prophet of Putin's 'new Byzantium', is sculpted with hunched shoulders and a scoliotic spine, a man who sacrificed the last of his health bent over a desk, barely enduring the torture of his calling to write.

As Dostoevsky knew, it is the thoughts and desires of real people that give towns their contour and shape. 'The form of a town changes, alas, more quickly than the human heart,' wrote Baudelaire; and the form of a town is no less bewildering, or full of secrets and traces of loss. Each place I have explored has beckoned me towards the next, towards some further arrangement of landscape, politics and myth, which I have reassembled in this book of travels. All my expeditions have been half-blind shadow-ings of the pursuits of others, sometimes tracing lines leading to places of exile, quest or crime, out of the rotting pages of Molotov's books, sometimes following stories that began or ended in this grand apartment building on Romanov Lane.

I went north by train when the nights were white, in homage to the unsung military and intellectual service of Sands, whom I knew only through his books, a few scraps of leftover paper and a photograph. To the west of Moscow, around Zvenigorod, and fur-ther north on the shores of Lake Ilmen, where Christianity first challenged and accommodated the pagan deities of the rivers, the thunder and the trees, I visited ruined places – monasteries, research stations, dachas, sanatoria – where science has tangled with religious belief, where biochemists and nuclear physicists, suffering under ideological tyranny or working deep inside its twisted structures, turned for light and healing to the writings of Chekhov and Dostoevsky, to the powers of sacred water, or the teachings of dissident priests.

On the Siberian steppe, south of Lake Baikal, in the vast expanse of dry grass and earth, of light and cold, space itself has been made into an instrument of political repression. Yet this space has never lost its power to conjure the hope of liberty. State and the individual personality seem at once to dissolve in the vistas of deep time, and simultaneously, outlined against the blank horizon, to become more defined, more real and present, more evidently fated to collide. Men and women sent to the furthest limit of Russian territory in punishment for their defiance of authoritarian rule have created in words a vivid, though often hid-den, landscape of 'inner freedom'.

The magic lantern in Molotov's apartment has furnished my imagination. Like the magic lantern that the anxious child Marcel is given at the beginning of Proust's *In Search of Lost Time*, it replaces the 'opaqueness of the walls' with an impalpable irides-cence, momentary vacillating scenes from legend, reflections of history. In my reading and my travelling, images of distant times and places have flashed into view, illusions leading beyond the limits of understanding into receding interiors of the human mind, into the essences, which we sometimes think we catch, of material things. Russian history and the Russian present have revealed themselves to me in glimpses, through a narrow lens, like the faded images waiting for light in this antique slide projector: moments of my own past, and moments considered worthy of record by people I shall never know, summoned as if by magic out of the surrounding dark.

ONE

Romanov

I need some corner . . . In my memory, I go through the apartments
abandoned by the bourgeoisie.
ISAAC BABEL, 'An Evening at the Tsarina's', 1922

The luxury of this house makes a false promise.

Its windows are set deep among ornate columns, projecting
cornices, scrolled and floriate mouldings. From the upper storeys,
between wrought-iron balconies and overhanging chambers
raised on tendril-wound columns, tiers of sculpted faces wearing
Phrygian helmets and animal skins look out over the street, hinting at higher mysteries of domestic comfort contained within.
The façade is designed to emphasise the extreme thickness of the
outer walls, and the shadowed warmth of their recesses, as though,
in the inmost part of this city, in this street of many names, a
house could offer a refuge from history.

Ulochki-shkatulochki, ulochki moskovskie: 'The streets are little
caskets', go the words of a love song to old Moscow. Before I lived
here, I knew that Romanov Lane was not a little casket but a great
chest of secret treasure. The men who lived in No. 3 had metro
stations, institutes, cities, battle cruisers, tractors, auto-plants,
warhorses, lunar craters and stars named after them. On my walks
down to the Lenin Library from our first Moscow apartment on
Tverskaya Street, I would choose to come this way, to get closer, I
liked to think, to the hidden lives of those men. I was one of those
passers-by who walk haltingly along the front of No. 3, pausing to
look at the memorial plaques in granite or dark marble fixed at eye
level on the earth-pink wall, then gaze up past the wilted carna-
tions laid on top of the plaques to the plaster hammers and sickles
that crest the pediments over the doorways, wondering quite what

it meant for all those Stalin-era field marshals and Party apparatchiks to 'live here', as the inscriptions say they did.

Who is in the *nomenklatura* of No. 3, the building that old
Muscovites still refer to as 'the House of the Generals' or, less reverently, as 'the Party Archive' or 'the Mausoleum'? What intricate
conspiracies of fate and human intention in the bloody political
drama of the twentieth century worked to keep these particular
names in view? The hidden logic and direction of the 'struggle', as
the Party piously called it, are impossible to follow in the series of
names and faces on the wall of this house. Among them are heroes
of the Civil War who moved into its apartments in the first years
of Soviet power, fighting men who defeated the White armies in
Siberia and the Russian south, and pressed the Revolution deep
into Central Asia: Mikhail Frunze, briefly Trotsky's successor as
Commissar of War, who moved here in 1924 and died the following year after a simple operation for a stomach ulcer, leaving
the suspicion that he had been assassinated by his physicians
on Stalin's orders; Semyon Budyonny, Kliment Voroshilov and
Semyon Timoshenko, cavalry generals who survived and flourished as their comrades-in-arms were purged in the years before
the Second World War; General Alexander Vasilevsky, who
moved into the building in the first winter of the war and reas-
sured a concerned Stalin that he had been 'provided with an excel-
lent apartment'. Further along the wall is a sparse remnant of Old
Bolsheviks: Pyotr Smidovich, who staffed the legendary 'special
train' from which Trotsky and his leather-wearing entourage
administered the Red Army throughout the Civil War; Dmitri
Manuilsky, a good storyteller and joker, as Molotov later remembered, but 'confused' and 'mixed up with Trotskyists'; and Emilian
Yaroslavsky in his porthole spectacles, Siberian-born son of a
Jewish political exile, long-standing head of the League of
the Militant Godless, graphomaniac Party historian, and one
of the very few of his kind to die a natural death.

Not far from Yaroslavsky on the wall is Andrei Andreev, a former waiter and (that rarity in the higher reaches of the Party)

genuine proletarian, who served Stalin with implacable loyalty through the forced collectivisation of agriculture and the Great Terror. As you walk down Romanov from Bolshaya Nikitskaya Street, just beyond the wide gateway to the courtyard with its tall trees and its gaudy painted fountain, you come face to face with Alexei Kosygin, the small-eyed puffiness of his countenance caught for ever in the granite. Kosygin rose in the Party under Stalin. He replaced Nikita Khrushchev as Soviet Premier in 1964, and Khrushchev, fallen from grace, immediately moved back to his apartment in No. 3. Later Kosygin assisted in the quiet abandonment of the utopian dream that the state would one day wither away under communism. With future General Secretary Leonid Brezhnev he worked to contrive that outwardly static but secretly moribund phenomenon known as 'actually existing socialism', for which so many still pine. Last of all, at the Vozdvizhenka end of the building, under our bedroom window, is a plaque to Marshal Ivan Konev, the son of a poor peasant from the Vologda region. His chiselled gaze, straining out over some imagined battlefield, meets the blank side wall of the Kremlin Hospital. 'So who is going to take Berlin, we or the Allies?' Stalin asked Konev and Marshal Zhukov at the beginning of April 1945. 'We will take Berlin,' Konev replied. Eight years later, in the months after Stalin's death, though he had never been anything but a soldier, Konev acted as head of the Special Judicial Panel at the brief and vicious trial of Lavrenty Beria, at the end of which the reviled former chief of secret police and sadistic sexual predator was sentenced for 'treason against the Motherland' and 'secret links with foreign intelligence' and shot the same night in a cell fitted for that single purpose.

There are many more names in the invisible *nomenklatura* of No. 3, names without plaques, erased by state murder or sullen disgrace from the charmed list during every decade of Soviet power: Trotsky, Beloborodov, Sokolnikov, Frumkin, Furtseva, Malenkov, Rokossovsky, Togliatti, Zhukov, Vyshinsky, Kosior, Tevosyan, Khrushchev, Molotov . . . And before them, playing a cameo part in the history of this house, which has always been so uniquely intimate with the destiny of the nation, a group of young actresses from the Moscow Art Theatre who shared an apartment high above the courtyard. In the hot summer of 1918, they gave aid, shelter and love to the British agent Sidney Reilly, 'ace of spies', as he plotted to overthrow Lenin and Trotsky. Elizaveta Otten, 'Reilly's chief girl', may have been the first of the many inhabitants of this house to be arrested at night by the secret police.

In that year, in which the Bolsheviks moved the capital to Moscow and took over the major buildings of the city under the Marxist slogan 'expropriate the expropriators', the actresses were still living *la vie de bohème* among the families of advocates, physicians and university professors for whom No. 3 had been built twenty years earlier. Some of those members of the small and high-minded professional class of the late tsarist era remained in their now 'communalised' apartments after the Bolsheviks took over No. 3 as the most prestigious residence for the Party elite outside the Kremlin. The street was renamed Granovsky after a politically liberal Moscow University historian, 'the ideal professor' of the nineteenth century (and prototype for the ridiculous Stepan Verkhovensky in Dostoevsky's novel *Demons*), and the building became known as the 'Fifth House of the Soviets'. (The first four 'Houses of the Soviets' – grand Moscow buildings appropriated by the Bolsheviks – were the National Hotel, the Metropol, an Orthodox seminary and the Peterhof Hotel on the corner of Vozdvizhenka and Mokhovaya Streets opposite the Lenin Library.) Many of the lawyers, doctors and academics in No. 3 were dubbed 'people of the past', and sent to labour camps or shot in the 1930s, leaving no trace of their lives except in private memory, old issues of the *All Moscow* telephone directory and the scattered annals of their professions. To my knowledge, none of their descendants is among the well-to-do heirs of Red Army generals and Communist Party magnates who now own the apartments, though I have come across several people from the old Moscow intelligentsia who recall with pride that long ago, before Stalin's purges, this great house was their family home.

❦

In the Soviet period, this one-way street was closed to ordinary traffic. Militiamen would check documents. The most privileged members of the *nomenklatura* came to Granovsky to visit the Kremlin Hospital polyclinic and its pharmacy, and to use their state-issued coupons in the Kremlin *stolovaya*: worth a purely symbolic two roubles ten for lunch, and two fifty for an evening meal, or the equivalent in take-out or groceries from the well-stocked food store. The *stolovaya* was reserved for the highest ranks of the state apparatus; the coupons were a mark of the highest social prestige. Before big public holidays cars would draw up and sleek men would load them with parcels of meat, caviar, fruit and vegetables, delicacies unavailable to the mass of the population. Under Stalin, the *nomenklatura* was driven around the city in American cars – Packards and Cadillacs, Buicks and Lincoln Town Cars. Later the elite turned to Soviet-produced ZILs and Volgas.

Now, Hummers, stately Maybachs and Bentleys with curtains that concertina electronically shut when you look into their windows, and even a few last Russian-made Zhigulis are parked up on the pavements all day, and the flow of traffic is rarely broken. The economy, financiers say, is afloat on a sea of liquidity. The 'automobile-and-harem' culture of the elite that Trotsky so despised now displays itself with libertine flagrance on Romanov. To walk down the street is to weave back and forth between bumpers and the walls of buildings, except on those stretches, outside office buildings, where the pavement and the kerb have been unofficially privatised and security guards patrol, the ubiquitous shaven-headed sentinels of central Moscow, in pointed shoes and bulky black jackets half-concealing guns. Yet Romanov retains an air of cloistral seclusion. This is a feature of the relationship among its narrowness, the height of the buildings and its cradling bend. From the courtyard of No. 3, halfway along, a tall oak, an aspen and a poplar rise to the height of the buildings and shadow the middle of the street. Elsewhere in Moscow the skies seem to extend endlessly: 'in no other metropolis do you have so much sky overhead', Walter Benjamin observed when he came to Moscow in 1926; 'in this city you always sense the vast horizon of the Russian steppes'. Here, the façades of two museums at either end enclose Romanov within the city's vast spaces like doors in a palatial enfilade.

At one end, on the turquoise-and-white face of the 1902 Zoological Museum on Bolshaya Nikitskaya, the plasterwork seems to have evolved into a rampage of shape and line. Stone monkeys, rams' heads, owls and hares writhe free of a cornucopia of looping and twisting lower life-forms: reptiles, insects and plants. The interior of the building is a labyrinth of laboratories, offices, a library, auditoria and long back corridors lined with rooms of study for many professors. When he was living in the Herzen House of Writers on nearby Tverskoi Boulevard, Mandelstam liked to visit the museum. He was grateful to the great biologists Linnaeus, Buffon and Pallas for awakening his 'childish astonishment at science'. He loved the museum's dark-painted galleried halls crowded with stuffed animals staring from behind vitrines – night predators with glass eyes, *Bubulcus ibis*, *Delphinus delphis* – and cabinets stacked with bottled creatures from the sea. 'Lying around unsupervised in the dark vestibule of the zoological museum on Nikitsky Street is the jawbone of a whale, like a huge plough', Mandelstam wrote in *Journey to Armenia*, an exuberant piece of travel prose that thrills to the drama of evolution. The museum's curator Boris Kuzin ('anything but a bookworm, he studied science on the run') was a friend and inspiration to Mandelstam, and the poet would sit drinking Georgian wine in his vast office in the depths of the museum. Sometimes Mandelstam would rise and pace round the room, composing poems that came suddenly, like 'Cherry Brandy', datelined 'March 1931, Moscow, Zoolog. Museum', which Nadezhda wrote down right there in the museum as he spoke it: 'I will tell it to you straight . . . everything is just brandy, cherry brandy, my angel'.

In a symmetry unusual for a contemporary Moscow street, low curving buildings stand on opposite corners at either end of Romanov: the University History Faculty building on Bolshaya Nikitskaya, and the Sheremetev Corner House on Vozdvizhenka, once the home of the serf opera singer Praskovia Kovalyova, 'the Pearl', secret wife of Count Nikolai Sheremetev, scion of one of Russia's greatest aristocratic dynasties. At the northern end, where Romanov meets Vozdvizhenka, the Schusev Museum of Architecture, once the 'State Chamber', seals the street with restrained classical grace.

> *Where to the Hellene shone*
> *Beauty,*
> *To me, from the black holes gaped*
> *Shame*

Mandelstam writes in 'Cherry Brandy'. The city's finances were once administered from the State Chamber. When Vozdvizhenka became a street of government buildings in the first years after the Revolution, this three-storeyed palace was turned over for use as headquarters of the Central Committee. Every day, Stalin and Molotov would walk the few hundred yards to their offices in No. 5 Vozdvizhenka from their apartments in the Kremlin – without bodyguards, as Molotov remembered with nostalgia. In 1923 the Central Committee offices moved to Staraya Ploshchad', Old Square, on the other side of the Kremlin, closer to the Lubyanka. It was only at the end of 1930 that the Politburo, acting on a report from the secret police, resolved that 'Comrade Stalin be immediately required to cease travelling around the city by foot'.

This spread of land on the crest of the hill above the now-buried Neglinnaya River lay within the 'White City', an extensive region on the north side of the Kremlin, enclosed for two centuries by fortified walls of white stone and brick, built in the late sixteenth century, whose curving line is still traced by Moscow's ring of boulevards. The land on which Romanov Lane stands was once known as Romanov Court, and belonged to the seventeenth-century Moscow boyar Nikita Romanov, who had been given it by his cousin the Tsar. Over the centuries, the loosely arranged estates, stone palaces, courts and monasteries were rectified into streets. Before the revolutionary remaking of Russian culture, street names were anecdotal and popular. In former centuries this land was known variously as the 'Romanov Palaces', 'Nikitsky' (after the well-liked boyar) and also by the names of other landowners, Razumovsky and Khitrovo, whose demesnes were on this ground before Count Nikolai Sheremetev bought it, as an act of generosity, from his cash-strapped brother-in-law Count Alexei Razumovsky. After that, the street became Sheremetev Lane.

Perpendicular to it are Bolshaya Nikitskaya Street (known in ancient Moscow as Novgorod Street) and Vozdvizhenka, one of Moscow's oldest roads, which radiate out from the gates of the Kremlin in the direction of the ancient city of Novgorod three hundred miles to the north-west. In 1471, Tsar Ivan III was greeted ceremonially on Vozdvizhenka, on the Trinity Bridge, just beyond the Kremlin's Trinity Gates, which once crossed the wide Neglinnaya, on his return from a military campaign to subdue the republic of Novgorod. The names Vozdvizhenka and Bolshaya Nikitskaya were taken from local monasteries – the Krestodvizhensky Monastery (Monastery of the Elevation of the Cross) and the Nikitsky Convent – founded in the fifteenth and sixteenth centuries when Moscow had risen to power as the centre of the unified Russian state. The Elevation of the Cross is a Byzantine feast traditionally associated with the glory of Orthodox Christian empire, which commemorates the recovery from the Persians by Heraclius of the 'true cross', unearthed in Jerusalem by Emperor Constantine's mother, Helena, while her son was building the Cathedral of Hagia Sophia. On the mid-September feast day of the Elevation, which is once again celebrated in the surviving churches of the neighbourhood, 'Lord have mercy' is sung again and again, as the Cross is raised high. In 1934, the Church of the Elevation (all that remained of the monastery after the great fire that greeted Napoleon's army in 1812) was demolished during Stalin's massive reconstruction of Moscow; its parish priest, Father Alexander Sidorov, had been murdered in a labour camp three years earlier. The Nikitsky Monastery had been demolished the previous year. Before its demolition, the Bolsheviks who lived on this street could see the nuns from the back rooms of their apartments, heads bowed over their quilting. In 1935, an electricity station for the new metro system was erected in the place of the convent, a windowless temple of power in heavily massed dark grey stone, with friezes of hero workers, their giant muscled bodies hewing, welding, drilling.

On Romanov, images of Moscow's past and present and dreams of its future arrange themselves for contemplation. On one side of the street at the Bolshaya Nikitskaya end is the two-storey rear wing of a small classical palace, once the possession of a succession of Russia's noblest families – Golitsyns, Orlovs and Meshcherskys – and now the premises of Moscow University Press. The rebel poet Vilgelm Kyukhelbeker worked in the palace as a private tutor in the years immediately preceding the Decembrist uprising against tsarist autocracy in 1825, in which he played a crucial part. An opulent, rarely patronised 'Antiques Salon' now occupies the corner of the palace on the Romanov side, its windows displaying gilded porcelain urns, a stuffed Siberian tiger, model ships, eighteenth-century landscapes. Bright Perspex signs are pinned like wings on the walls of the palace, advertising new restaurants called Tesoro and Papillon, and the Avant-garde Floristry Boutique. As the windows run along what was once a low side-wing of the palace, the building slips free of the commercial logic that drives the changes on Romanov and sinks back into the cosy shabbiness of a more stagnant era. The windows of the communal apartments are dusty, some of their panes cracked, the attic spaces derelict. Large areas of pale yellow paint and plaster have come away from the outer walls. In one room, icons are clustered on a shelf, a man works under a bare lightbulb, sickly-looking spider plants and jars of marinated cucumbers stand in the space between the double window panes, rags and dirty cloths are tumbled halfway up the glass.

On the opposite side of Romanov, in No. 4, a brokerage house sells mutual funds and shares in the extractive industries in Siberia and the far north from an office fronted in gleaming floor-to-ceiling glass. As in a high room, sounds and scents are intensified in the street. Late each afternoon, outside No. 4, a man in a dark suit stands at the kerb in a cloud of vanilla-scented pipe smoke, reading the pink business papers. Lawyers and stockbrokers cluster under the arches above the polished granite steps of the building, drawing on their cigarettes, gossiping, clutching their coats about them. The slender heels of Moscow's loveliest *demimondaines* tap the pavement as they make their way, shining for the evening in diamonds and air-soft sable skins, on a narrow pathway of granite flagstones set with green cat's eyes, from the luxury health club in the basement of No. 4 to the opened doors of their chauffeur-driven cars.

Until the dilapidated building next to No. 4, known as the Professors' House, was scaffolded and shrouded for evisceration and *remont* (renovation), the sound of invisible wind chimes would float teasingly down on the air from somewhere on the upper floors. This street is sheltered from the coarser winds that move capriciously about the city. In deepest winter, the gales blow across the Neglinnaya valley below the Kremlin's western wall and husk the snow, fine as smoke, off the roof of the Kremlin Hospital. Sometimes, in the weeks when everything is melting and pedestrians walk in the middle of the streets, or nervously along the pavements, looking up frequently, choosing between the perils of cars that might run them down or large icicles that might fall from the eaves of high buildings, the ice in the drainpipes explodes into fragments and cascades in a noisy rush to the pavement.

On one of the balconies of No. 5 Romanov Lane, where communal apartments are still being converted for foreign bankers, oil executives and Moscow's new tycoons, Tajik labourers in poor

clothes take the air, laughing, speaking their own language, looking down on the street. They live in the apartments while the work
is done. Below them, in a black jeep, four men in bullet-proof
vests and blue-grey urban camouflage that makes them look like
shadows in the twilight wait for the tycoon who occasionally
visits his apartment in the building, ready for sudden violence.
The large apartments in No. 5 (which was built fifteen years after
No. 3, in a more restrained style but on a comparable scale) were
communalised in the 1920s. Bolsheviks of lower rank than those in
the 'Fifth House of the Soviets' next door moved in with the 'people of the past': manufacturers, doctors and professors with Jewish
names. In 1928 the future dissident V. S. Zhukovsky, son of a
young communist from the Ukraine who had once raised his
hand for Trotsky at a Party meeting, moved with his parents into
two rooms of a five-room apartment, shared by four families, on
the second floor of No. 5. People still called the street 'Sheremetev'
then. In his memoir, *Muscovite from Granovsky Street,* he recalls his
mother's parties in their small living room, the Blüthner piano, the
expression on his father's face as he read Hitler's *Mein Kampf*
(which he left face-down on the table) and the timetable for
weekly use of the single bathroom. One of the residents of the
kommunalka, the irritable, uxorious Professor Himmelfarb, was
arrested one night in 1931 and died in prison before standing trial.
Even after Stalin's death, his widow was too afraid to appeal for
his rehabilitation. Another resident, a working-class Party member, a former miner, shot himself at the height of the Terror.
Zhukovsky's own father was arrested (how could he have survived
that vote for Trotsky?) and shot in the Lubyanka in 1940, as his
son learned only after the death of Stalin.

⚜

When I have left No. 3 and its inner doors are closed to me again,
I know that the memories of my years here will collapse, as memories do, into a collection of moments, with their own curious

logic, cut free from the sense of duration, the aspect of time which can never be reclaimed. I cannot, for all my efforts, remember through which of the many doors I entered the house for the first time, or even whether the entrance was through the 'black entrance' from the courtyard or from the street. In my recollections, the interior, which was remarkable, has entirely detached itself from the exterior. It is as though I was led in and out in a blindfold. (Perhaps it was the same spatial vagueness that allowed the families of Politburo members and top generals to live as neighbours here through the years of night-time arrests and show trials.) It was the last autumn of the Yeltsin presidency, rents were still down after the national default and the currency crash of the previous year, and we were exhausted by the louche and noisy environs of Tverskaya, where drug addicts came to the stairwell of our building at night and left their used needles in the elevator. At that time, I still thought of No. 3 as an unattainable dream house. I came to see the smaller of the two apartments that were advertised to let. I remember the smell of alcohol on the breath of the blowsy middle-aged woman who greeted us, the pale outstretched hand of the long-haired exquisite in velvet slippers and a silk Chinese jacket who stood behind her. I remember the drops of coloured crystal on the delicate eighteenth-century chandelier in the front hall, the Karelian birch curves of the Biedermeyer chairs in the main room, and in the gilt mirrors, the reflected colours and lines of oils by Picasso, Braque, Matisse and the Russian avant-garde painters Natalia Goncharova and Mikhail Larionov. 'Not suitable for a family . . . the antiques . . . we were looking for a bachelor, an *aesthete*,' the woman told me as she showed me through the rooms. She pointed to a chaise in the corner: 'It belonged to Napoleon's aide-de-camp. He didn't take it back to France,' she laughed. 'Your collection is extraordinary,' I murmured. 'It was my late husband who was the collector.' Her rheumy eyes fixed me with a brief light. 'He was a diplomat.'

When we first moved into apartment 59, the view from my study window was clear all the way to the Voentorg. This 'Military

Department Store', built five years before the Revolution as premises for the Military-Economic Society of Moscow Officers,
became one of the grandest department stores in Soviet Moscow,
the equal of GUM on Red Square and TsUM by the Bolshoi
Theatre. Families of the generals in No. 3 had special access to the
Voentorg, and in the first years after the war they could sometimes
find on its shelves delicious Lend-Lease conserves sent from
America. My view was a tranquil, scarcely inhabited and private
one, truly a luxury in the centre of a city. The ex-KGB colonel who
ran a security firm from the mews building behind the house
rarely came into his office. Wind-sown birch saplings grew on the
brick wall outside, their silky fraying bark catching the tonalities
of the old buildings in the neighbourhood: dull white, ochre, pink
and rust; shades of plaster, light earth, northern skies and snow.
Crows came to promenade the length of the yellow-painted gas
pipe that ran along the wall.

One of the first books I read in my efforts to excavate Romanov
was *Year of Victory*, the memoir of Marshal Konev, which I borrowed from Molotov's collection for a day and brought downstairs
to our apartment, in which he had once lived. Twice hero of the
Soviet Union, once commander of the First Ukrainian Front,
famed as a master of military surprise, camouflage and the art of
encircling cities, the Marshal lived in No. 3 from 1947 until his
death in 1973. (The year Konev moved into apartment 59 was the
year Marshal Zhukov fell out of favour with a jealous Stalin.
Zhukov's apartment in No. 3 was searched by the secret police,
and every item of furniture was noted.) As I read Konev's memoir,
I tried to conjure an image of the comfortable old survivor of
Stalin, sitting in his study, sharing my view, as he recollected the
race to take Berlin. But ghosts have no flesh and no dimension, so
all I could imagine was the broad-jawed granite hero on the street
façade beneath the bedroom window. I tried to superimpose on
my urban view Konev's surreal description of a snowy Polish battlefield swarming with Red Army tanks camouflaged in white
tulle requisitioned from a nearby factory. 'I see in my mind's eye',

he writes, 'the standing chimneys of Silesia, the gun flashes, the grinding caterpillar tracks, the tulle-covered tanks . . .' Long after these images had dissolved, I was told by an acquaintance who knew the Marshal's daughter that my study had been her bedroom, and that the long corridor leading to it had been lined with trophy art in heavy gilt frames brought back after the Soviet victory from the ransacked castles of east Prussia.

Before long the view from my study window began to change. I lost the birch tree, my view of the Voentorg and most of the sky. Construction workers began to raise a new building for the Moscow city government's dubiously titled Department of Extra-Budgetary Construction Policy on the land next door. The building site was theatrical as well as cacophonic, a rising stage on which workmen moved about all winter long in padded jackets, felt boots and canvas helmets laced at the back like old-fashioned corsets. Night and day for months they worked, shouting, grinding, crashing, raining showers of sparks over the brick wall. As the new building went up, the Corner House, which had been allowed to decay in the Soviet period, underwent *kapitalny remont*, complete renovation. In the gutted stucco shell of the house, shadow workmen moved about at night on a wooden scaffold, lit by naked bulbs hung from the rafters. For a few weeks I could see in through the back windows and out the other side. The house was quite hollow, no wall or floor or ceiling left intact. 'What are you muttering, midnight? / . . . Parasha is dead, The young mistress of the place . . . / Incense streams from every window, the beloved lock has been cut, / And the oval of her face darkens', Akhmatova wrote in a draft of *Poem Without a Hero*, her great attempt to arrange past time through poetry, when she was living in another Sheremetev Palace in what was then Leningrad. Her 'Parasha' was Praskovia, the serf girl who married Russia's richest bachelor, lived briefly in the Corner House and died in childbirth, and who by the late nineteenth century had become a sentimental heroine of folklore, a paragon of charity and innate gentility.

When the renovation of the Corner House was almost complete, the interior was closed from view. Then the palace was painted deep yellow. A relief of classical heads set in medallions was coloured bright blue to match the PVC window frames, the pipework and the stripes on the city bureaucrats' smart new building. Ruched nylon curtains were hung in the windows, which radiated nothing now but fluorescent light. The courtyard was paved and fitted with a *shlagbaum*, an electronic barrier, and with it came a detail of thickset guards with their own booth. Beneath the iron railings, up against the wall of No. 3, an ornamental garden was laid, a stiff arrangement of evergreen shrubs, white gravel and a rococo plaster water feature.

To appreciate the beauty of Moscow, one must settle down and live here, the art critic Pavel Muratov wrote in 1909. Moscow's 'genius of place' lies not in the extrovert, premeditated beauty of grand public spaces or harmonious architectural ensembles, but in its haphazard, intimate, muddled beauty, a beauty made by people and their money, not by the state. There is nothing one can do to unify Moscow, Muratov said, it is always 'incoherent, disconnected, inconsistent'. To learn to love the city is to become familiar with its little lanes and side streets. Its charms can be discovered either through careful study or quite by chance, at the very moment when one's attention strays. Yet to learn to love Moscow is also to become familiar with a certain kind of grief, for it is not a city whose authorities are much given to its conservation. Moscow advances architecturally in sudden rushes of new prosperity or state ideology after bursts of frenzied destruction, from without or within, or long periods of stagnation and neglect, leaving all those who love 'old Moscow' to their quiet laments. I wanted to melt away the accretions on the Corner House, to replace them with an image of some absolute Moscow, beautiful and undefiled, so I crossed under Vozdvizhenka, through the dank pedestrian tunnel lined with kiosks that in those days still ran from one side of the street to the other from the foot of the Voentorg, and went to the library.

I leafed through the 1917 city directory, *All Moscow*, the last telephone book to be published in imperial Russia. How would this thick book, with its lists of names and numbers that will never ring, fit into librarian Fyodorov's scheme for resurrection of the dead through books? Beside No. 8 Vozdvizhenka, the address of the Corner House, is the name Count Sergei Dmitrievich Sheremetev. Among the many civic affiliations listed after his name, the Count includes his membership of a committee dedicated to the establishment of a museum of 1812, the year in which Moscow was saved, by its own destruction, from Napoleon's dream of conquest.

I ordered the writings of the Count. The slender books that the librarians cranked up from the stacks two hours later appeared to have been little touched in the century since their writing. In their pages, I found the city that I had searched for in the hollows of the Corner House. 'All these buildings of the "New Moscow" are without a future,' the Count wrote defiantly in the summer of 1902 in *Moscow Recollections*, as though on one appointed day the new buildings would disappear and give him back the vistas he had once loved and owned. 'Old Moscow' will survive them, he promised, for without it there could be no Russia. In an orgy of 'intoxicated capitalism' in which the city no longer knew itself nor called itself by its own name, the heart of Moscow was being transformed, filled up with 'shameful' and 'degenerate' new buildings hiding from view its ancient churches, which were left to fall into ruin.

Count Sergei was in late middle age when his native city began to change from the feudal city of noble estates, ancient monasteries, churches and Eastern-style bazaars into a European-style capitalist metropolis. It was in his time, the age of the 'investment property', the *dokhodny dom*, that Sheremetev Lane was transformed from a loosely arranged set of palaces and attendant buildings facing in different directions into a modern street of apartment houses for rent. The Count's family had been the wealthiest in serf-owning Russia, giving rise to the expression 'rich as a Sheremetev'. Yet by the late nineteenth century Russia was no longer the possession of the aristocracy. Money reshaped the city.

Count Sergei served in the Cavalry Guards during the Russo-Turkish War of 1877–8, a conflict with the Islamic Ottomans over 'sacred' lands and the rights of Christian Slavs in the Balkans which aroused a crescendo of heartfelt public patriotism and pan-Slavic Orthodox nationalism. After the war the Count retired from military service to devote himself to history. He was an anti-quarian and a conservationist, a curator of his family's and his nation's past. He was made an honorary member of the Imperial Academy of Sciences, published historical journals and pam-phlets, headed cultural commissions, established learned societies and museums in Moscow and St Petersburg, and supported tradi-tional Russian arts and crafts, such as the decorative painting of small lacquer boxes.

In his writings and civic activities the Count found a new role for the Russian aristocrat, no longer surveying his limitless mate-rial demesnes in the present, but turning over salvaged fragments of memory as a curator, a melancholy nostalgic researching lost time, a collector assembling and reassembling objects from the past for display. He made public the private, domestic history of the aristocracy, as though preparing for the catastrophic loss of property that, even in his quiet defiance, he seemed to perceive on the near horizon.

In *The Romanov Court on Vozdvizhenka*, the Count records that in the early seventeenth century the quiet and remote lane 'on the white earth between Nikitsky and the Arbat in the parish of Dionysus the Areopagite' in the walled White City to the west of the Kremlin was the demesne of Boyar Romanov. He reconstructs the eighteenth-century street from old architectural plans, filling in the family homes of a collegiate assessor and a lieutenant gov-ernor of the City of Moscow among the grander buildings of Romanov Court, as well as all the arrangement of store rooms, barns, awnings, outhouses, wells, cellars, vegetable plots, summer houses and fruit orchards.

By the end of the eighteenth century, as the Count writes, the street contained two palaces: an older, larger palace (now part of the Kremlin Hospital) on one side, and the Corner House on the other, which had been built in 1790 for Count Razumovsky. Count Nikolai Sheremetev bought all these properties in the last year of the eighteenth century, and the exquisite 'Moscow baroque' brick-and-whitewash Church of the Sign behind the first palace, which became the domestic church of the Sheremetev family. Count Nikolai and Praskovia 'the Pearl' began their married life in the Corner House after their secret nuptials in St Simeon the Stylite, a tiny onion-domed church a little further up the street.

In *Old Vozdvizhenka*, Count Sergei pores over the inventories of the sale of the Corner House, in which, he observes, Praskovia's name is never mentioned. He gives precise descriptions of the layout of the rooms, their shapes and dimensions, refurnishing them one by one. He describes the ceremonial staircase with its ornamented balustrade, which led up to a front reception room with four long windows. Next to this was a dining room with yellow walls and a sky-blue ceiling, two fireplaces and a portrait of the great Russian saint Sergius of Radonezh. Columned Venetian windows gave an unbroken view of the Kremlin. On the orange walls of the drawing room hung an icon of the Vladimir Mother of Tenderness, the Eleousa, one of Russia's most sacred images. Room by room, the Count lists musical instruments, folding screens, icons, wall-coverings, oak tables, red and green morocco armchairs, brass and mahogany commodes. From its furnishings – a clavichord, a prie-dieu, an icon of the Mother of God of Smolensk and a portrait of Praskovia in a gold frame – he deduces that one particular room was the bedchamber of the hidden 'Pearl'.

Reading these pages in this library, in whose collections his contemporary Fyodorov conceived the systematic work of bodily resurrection, I sensed that there was more at work in the Count's researches than aristocratic family nostalgia and an antiquarian sensibility. This was a religious activity, like icon painting. The Count was finding access to the dead city of his ancestors as an icon painter creates a portal into the transcendent world, controlling the viewpoint, adding golden light. 'A recollection is a lightning flash of the past, which shines and lights up the path we have travelled,' wrote Pushkin's friend the poet Prince Pyotr Vyazemsky, lines which Count Sergei uses as an epigraph to his memoirs. He was using that light to look for his ancestors and their world in heaven, which, according to his Orthodox beliefs, is made of the material of this world, redeemed. All past time is present. Everyone returns, called by name, transfigured.

In the redeemed world of the Russian aristocracy as Count Sergei paints it, social divisions are a sweetly ordered hierarchy. Ascetic piety and humility of spirit are possible, indeed made all the more sincere and beautiful, within the conditions of limitless wealth in which the family lived before the abolition of serfdom and the rise of the money economy. The Count's mother died too early for him to have any recollection of her. Family affection came in abundance from his father, various pious aunts and his two adored grandmothers, Varvara Petrovna and Ekaterina Vasilievna. 'Each room contains such precious memories', he wrote, invoking beloved names, tenderly remembered personalities: the servant girls, Aksyusha, Cristina, Polya and Persida the Serb, who sang and could write; Matvei Yermolaev, the ancient footman whose sole duty was to sit at the top of the great staircase that led up from the street, ready to announce the arrival of guests.

The Count's own childhood rooms were in the larger palace, in the fourteen-windowed *piano nobile* of the side wing that looked over the street, which always lay clean when it snowed because so little traffic passed. He could see all the way to the Church of Christ the Saviour, away down the Moscow River. The quiet was broken only when new recruits lined up outside the State Chamber on Vozdvizhenka. There were snowball fights in the courtyard and Christmas trees full of lights and toys, and an organ that his mother had ordered from abroad before her death, around which the family would gather to sing.

The Count remembers the jubilee of Tsar Nicholas I in 1850,

when both palaces shone with magnificent illuminations organised by his father. Loyalty to the Tsar was not unmixed with liberal sensibilities in the lives of the Sheremetevs. The democratic
ideas of the Decembrists had once been discussed in a serious literary circle in the Corner House in the years before the aristocratic uprising against the Tsar in December 1825. The group
stayed together after that fateful date, and its members remained
sympathetic to republican ideals. After the jubilee one of the
conspirators, Ivan Yakushkin, who had married into the Sheremetev family, came to stay in the Corner House, still under careful watch by police spies, after the amnesty by Alexander II in
1856 and his return from over thirty years in Siberian exile, to repair his broken health and spirit.

The Count's grandmothers embody the virtuous spirit of the
aristocracy. Their submission to providence and quietism in the
face of history become the spirit of the memoir itself, which, for
all its devotion to the past and lamentation at the spectacle of
urban change, is a self-schooling in detachment, in the acceptance
of loss, with the hope of redemption. Varvara Petrovna, a famous
beauty in her youth, held the family together. He pictures her at
her desk in a white peignoir, writing letters to her grandchildren,
her long braid reaching almost to the floor. Ekaterina Vasilievna,
who lived out her days in the Corner House, always referred to it
as 'le réfuge des Chéreméteff'. Her humbly furnished room was
known as her 'cell'; she ate plain food, always with a bunch of dill
beside her plate. (Food at the Corner House was always poor, the
Count notes, except for the famous 'Sheremetev liqueur', made by
the servant girl Marisha, as the family was too kind to reproach or
dismiss their incompetent cook.) Every day, the family doctor,
Karl Karlovich Pfel, would call on the old lady for a glass of coffee. 'You would sit for a while in her room', Count Sergei remembers, 'and your soul would become quiet'. He remembers her odd
pronunciation, her fear of half-open doors, which reminded her of
yawning mouths, and her dislike of the dusk hour before the
lamps were lit. She loved spiritual reading and poetry, and would

quote the poet Mikhail Lermontov's lines on the fleetingness of life. Among her guests were the melancholic Kachalov, returned from a pilgrimage to Jerusalem; the tiresome rattle-trap Varvara Raevskaya, who published her own book of pieties; and Dr Popandopulo, author of a treatise on the subject dearest to his heart, the maladies of Napoleon.

When Ekaterina Vasilievna died, 'half of Moscow' came out in the streets to mourn. She had worried that she would look a fright in her coffin, but she looked calm and holy, with a palm branch in her hand. After four days, her body was carried across Vozdvizhenka to the Church of the Elevation. The words 'Blessed are the Peacemakers' were engraved on her tomb. In her world of peace, serfs all love their masters and mistresses, the Decembrists have come home to heal, there are no bomb-throwing 'nihilist' terrorists in the streets, ready to assassinate members of the nobility, and Napoleon, who destroyed Moscow, is of concern solely on account of his ailments.

In the final paragraphs of *The Vozdvizhenka Corner House*, written in 1903 (the year of Fyodorov's death), the Count writes that the past becomes 'clear and bright' before his mind's eye as he records it. The house 'was always a refuge for our family, each of its rooms is filled with memories of far-off times of happiness'. He senses that he is not just sitting in the same house, but in the very same setting, with the same view on to the street and the Kremlin. 'I thank God that the house is still intact', he writes, 'and that its view has not been built up, that the rooms are all just as they were and all the old things in them still preserved.' The State Chamber 'is still there, the same noise comes from the road, the same sounds of blessing and prayer rise on the morning air from the same Church of the Elevation, whose ancient tombs still grace the wide street'. The Count basks in the deep silence of the winter, seeing how the sled tracks in the snowy street shine in the sun, revelling in the bright air and the view of the Kremlin domes, 'from where the sounds of bells spread out across stone Moscow and Holy Russia, a ringing which will only cease when Russia herself ceases'.

Count Sergei's last great project was to have been the transformation of the Corner House into a repository for private archives. In 1918, according to his son, who was also a historian and museum curator, Count Sergei 'willingly and almost joyfully' handed over to the 'new Russia' all his palaces and estates, and thanked Lenin, without irony, for freeing him of the burden of property. He died the same year.

⤳⤲

While our front windows frame a perfect view of the palace in which Count Sergei spent his childhood, the kitchen windows look directly across into the mews where the *dvorniki* who maintain the building live with their families. Since long before the Revolution, to be a *dvornik* has been a traditional calling of Tatars. The Tatar *dvorniki* in our building drink alcohol, often to excess, but on the Muslim feast of Miram-Biram one year I watched as they pulled the carcass of a cow from the back of the car and divided it into three in the dusty courtyard. Electricians, plumbers, guards and concierges work in shifts night and day, many of them living in the building, all under the command of a *komendantka*, who is feared by everyone in No. 3, regardless of rank. One of the plumbers is a highly educated man who speaks beautiful English, goes three times a week to concerts at the Conservatoire on Bolshaya Nikitskaya and likes to talk about poetry; he chooses to work as a plumber, he says, for the peace it gives him for his thoughts. Every day of the year, without exception, he spends an hour sitting outside with his shirt off, 'air bathing' for health. Through their net curtains we can see the TV playing each evening in the mews, Putin's tight face glowing into the room, mouthing silently. Early each morning a thin grey cat steps out through the open window and a man leans on the window ledge in his vest, smoking. One morning, an ambulance and a militia car were parked below our kitchen window. A shrouded body was carried out of the mews on a stretcher. Later the

concierge said that the stepson of one of the *dvornik*
and murdered him in a drunken rage, then slit his
'*Gadost*',' she murmured, 'Filth', and not a further wo
horror was ever spoken.

All the apartments in No. 3 have two entrances: one grand
entrance from the street or the courtyard (there are eight main
entrances); another, called the 'black entrance', from a caged back
staircase, which in our case leads out into the space between the
main house and the mews. In the past, the back staircase was used
for bringing up fuel for the dutch stoves from the basement, where
each apartment had its own numbered store of firewood, and for
the spacious attics, which were once used for airing laundry. From
her basement room between the two staircases, the concierge can
hear when either the back or the front door is opened. For a long
time it was understood that all the maintenance workers at No. 3
were agents of the secret police. Later, after Stalin, it was assumed
that only some of them, in particular the female concierges who sit
in each entryway, were obliged to report on the private affairs of
the residents. The widows of Red Army commanders who still
live in No. 3 tend to scoff at the notion that their homes were
under constant surveillance. They prefer to reminisce about their
knitting circle. The children of the house always played together
in the courtyard, whether their parents were marshals, disgraced
members of the Politburo or *dvorniki*.

From the back corridor (which is above the travel agency in the
basement, Intertour Luxe) we look across at the windows of the
'court artist' who once painted the Politburo. To walk on Romanov he wears a green velvet frock coat, waistcoat and silk
cravat, and has his own lavish state-bestowed gallery in a small
palace on Znamenka Street, down the hill from the Ministry of
Defence buildings, just across the road from the Pashkov House.
The artist has been married more times than anyone can count.
Before she and her mother were moved out to make way for
a younger paramour, his little daughter, who sometimes visits,
coming out to play in the courtyard in a silky ballgown, invited

.ny children to tea. She gave them, as a gift for me, a little com-
pact mirror with the artist's painting of her mother dressed as a
nineteenth-century *devitsa*, a country maiden. When the artist
arrived home unannounced, the little girl took fright and hurried my daughters out into the courtyard through the black entrance. His windows are the only ones in the house that the
komendantka has allowed to be replaced, front and back, with
PVC trimmed with fancy anachronistic arches in brass. The
komendantka is an aged coquette who loathes women and children, has a preternatural sensitivity to the subtleties of *nomenklatura* status, and takes bribes from residents for all concessions
in brown envelopes of cash and bottles of cognac.

While Count Sergei Sheremetev was at his desk in the Corner
House, creating his idyll-city of aristocracy and faith, his contemporary the journalist Vladimir Gilyarovsky was exploring a
Moscow of slum-dwellers and criminals, prostitutes, entertainers,
petty traders and newspapermen. Born of Cossack stock in the
northern town of Vologda, Gilyarovsky had served in the Russo-
Turkish War and hired himself out as a factory hand, a barge-
hauler, a private tutor and a provincial actor before coming to
Moscow to make his name as a crime reporter. A well-loved
eccentric, he was known as 'Uncle Gilyai'. He was a friend of
Anton Chekhov, and of the performers and directors of the
Moscow Art Theatre, whom he memorialised in his book *Theatre
People*. In *Moscow and Muscovites*, a fond portrait of the city and
its inhabitants first published in 1926, Gilyarovsky describes the
populous, gossiping, raffish city at whose existence Count Sergei's
memoirs never hint. He wanders the streets, the boulevards and
public squares, narrating tales of life in Moscow's taverns and
gambling dens, its bathhouses, newspaper offices, nightclubs,
theatres and student digs.

One of the chapters in *Moscow and Muscovites* is set in the interior of the Sheremetev Palace across the street, Count Sergei's
childhood home. When the Count was a young adult, the elegant

mid-eighteenth-century palace became the City Duma, a parliament whose seats were increasingly occupied, as the nineteenth century progressed, not by noblemen, but by members of the merchant class. When the Duma moved out to purpose-built premises next to Red Square, the Sheremetev Palace was let to the Hunting Club, whose previous accommodation had famously burned down one night around a group of wild and oblivious card-players.

Gilyarovsky describes how the 'lordly chambers' of the Sheremetev palace that the city administrators had left in tatty disarray were luxuriously renovated and transformed into the most prestigious private club in Moscow. 'Bourgeois fast-livers of both sexes gathered for dinners, exhibitions, and masquerades,' at which the prizes were of fabled extravagance, Gilyarovsky recounts. Wealthy Muscovites hosted intimate Sunday suppers in the great hall of the palace, at which choirs of young girls sang serenades. Gilyarovsky describes scenes from evenings at the Club, where exquisites in smoking jackets play baccarat and a hunting gentleman, a great lover of 'cards, women, and horses', has his hair slicked down in an 'English parting'. A boisterous nouveau riche from the Volga region comes up to Moscow to play cards all night. A cool young gambler with the 'manners of an Englishman', whose face displays no expression, cannot endure the tragedy of losing.

In one vignette, Gilyarovsky presents a dark man, a gambler and celebrated raconteur, who spent all his money on cards and women. He had the 'most beautiful beard in all Moscow', and all the ladies at the Hunting Club desired him. The dark man places on the baccarat table an intriguing piece of treasure – a large gold snuffbox with a huge gleaming letter N chased across its lid – and tells the other gamblers that he paid an insane price in Paris for his little conversation piece. He shows them all a certificate of authenticity, proving that it had once been the snuffbox of Napoleon. Indeed, the dark-bearded gambler says, it is a snuffbox with an epic history. Napoleon had just snorted a huge pinch of tobacco from the beautiful gold box at the very moment his adjutant was making a battlefield report, and had missed what the adjutant was saying. On account of this, the great general moved his cavalry into an area where they were cut off from the foot-soldiers fighting on the plain. And so, Gilyarovsky muses, the world can be turned upside down by a pinch of snuff. Perhaps, he adds in one of his melancholy asides, the dark man had some fore-boding of hungry days to come in Monaco or on the Riviera.

The Hunting Club was not just the setting for decadent card games and light-hearted masquerades. Every week the Society of Art and Literature would put on a show, and a group of amateur players, who would later become the Moscow Art Theatre, would perform. According to Gilyarovsky, the director Konstantin Stanislavsky's company was somewhat too artistically sophisti-cated for the *demi-monde* that frequented the Hunting Club. The play they most enjoyed was *The Drowned Bell*, in which a hairy wood demon jumped over stones and ruts while a water sprite in the form of a huge frog croaked and paddled about in a brook.

On one 'significant and never-to-be-forgotten day' in Sep-tember 1898, another of the actresses whose intimate lives are bound up with this street fell in love. It was at the Hunting Club that Olga Knipper first met Chekhov. 'I will never forget the anx-ious palpitating agitation which overcame me when I was told that the great playwright would be attending our rehearsal of *The Seagull*,' the actress records, 'nor the unusual state of mind in which I made my way, on that day, to the Hunting Club.' It was there, she said, that the 'fine and tangled knot' of her life 'began to lace itself'.

When Gilyarovsky wrote *Moscow and Muscovites*, the city he was describing had vanished into memory just like the pious feu-dal city of the Count. After 1917 the Sheremetev palace was occu-pied by a military academy and a museum of the Red Army and Navy. Next to the Kremlin Hospital pharmacy's low doorway, a granite plaque cut into the side wing of the palace commemorates a speech that Lenin gave to the Red Army recruits in 1919 before they were sent to the southern front to fight the Whites. On May

Day of the same year, Lenin stood on Red Square, his arm upraised in a pose that would be replicated in thousands of monuments all over the Soviet empire, and promised the crowd that their grandchildren would be unable to imagine that public buildings had once been someone's property.

❦

Lenin's Revolution shone a new historical light on the treasures of the past. For two hot months in the middle of 1918, this investment property that the Sheremetevs had built between their palaces twenty years before became the centre of conspiratorial drama on which the fortunes of Russia turned. A secret war played out within the walls of No. 3 between the Bolsheviks and the would-be saviour of the Russian bourgeoisie, British agent Sidney Reilly, who found this a perfect setting in which to plot the counter-revolution.

That summer, when the large barometer next to the grand courtyard entrance was showing temperatures above thirty-five degrees Celsius, Lenin warned that the Bolshevik Revolution was in its 'direst period'. Russia was in a paroxysm of class war. The Soviet republic had contracted to the size of the fifteenth-century Grand Duchy of Muscovy. The British had occupied the northern coast from Murmansk down to Archangel and Kem and proclaimed a 'Government of Northern Russia'; the Germans held Pskov and Minsk, and occupied the Ukraine to the west; Czechoslovak forces controlled important cities along the Volga River and the length of the Trans-Siberian Railway, while Vladivostok in the farthest east was under the rule of the Japanese. To the south, in the Cossack domains around Rostov-on-Don, White forces were in command, the French had landed a naval garrison in Odessa and the Turks were moving on the frontier of the Russian Caucasus. Closer to Moscow, counter-revolution was ascendant in Yaroslavl, Kostroma, Rybinsk and Nizhny-Novgorod.

In Moscow itself, only recently reinstated as the capital, the revolutionary struggle played out with particular symbolic intensity. The Revolution had 'raised its flag in Moscow', the Bolsheviks proclaimed, in order 'graphically to manifest the link between Russia's being and the fate of the whole world'. Moscow, the Party newspaper *Izvestiya* declared, was the 'last sanctuary of the loose, lazy bourgeois spirit' of the Russian past, a city of priests, merchants and idle nobility. 'Knock the bourgeoisie out of their nests!' ran the slogan. The year 1918 saw an extreme chiliastic rejection of all the institutions of private property, the spoils of exploitation. Owners were enemies of the future order. It was not just the exigencies of civil conflict but also revolutionary utopianism that led to 'war communism', the Bolshevik policy of extreme communisation of property, nationalisation of land, economic centralisation and compulsory requisitioning. In November 1918, Molotov, who was charged with nationalising the economy of the north, published an article admitting that the 'expropriation of the expropriators' was 'in reality occurring less smoothly . . . than those who call themselves followers of Marx thought it would occur . . .' After more than nine months of socialist rule, he said, the hour had 'not yet struck for all the property of capitalists'. Inflation was encouraged as a way of ruinously destabilising any market economy. Trotsky's principal economist ally, Evgeny Preobrazhensky, talked of the 'machine gun of the commissariat of finance, attacking the bourgeois system in the rear and using the currency laws of that system to destroy it'. Banks were abolished and a plan to replace money with 'labour units' was devised. In an attempt to exert total control over the allocation of goods, all private trade was banned. To some, 'war communism' was a heroic period, a time of moral elation, when the 'bourgeois had become a contemptible and rejected creature . . . a *pariah*, deprived not only of his property but also of his honour'.

All the while, lightly roosted in what he called his 'theatrical safe house' just a street away from the gates of the Kremlin, Sidney Reilly mapped out a counter-revolutionary conspiracy so intricate that, as *Izvestiya* later remarked, it 'transports us back to the atmosphere of the Venetian republic, the medieval Italian states, or the barbarous lands of the East'. Reilly's plan was to overthrow the Bolshevik government and draw Russia back into the First World War. He planned to place the entire revolutionary government under arrest at a meeting of the Council of People's Commissars in the Bolshoi Theatre at the beginning of September. Reporting on the plot later, the Soviet press claimed that Reilly's intention was to kill them, but his solution to the problem of their power was more theatrical. He planned to parade Lenin and Trotsky trouserless through the streets of Moscow with their coat-tails flapping so that 'everybody should be aware that the tyrants of Russia were prisoners'. He assured his superiors in London that 'beneath their national apathy the great mass of the Russian people longed to be delivered from their oppressors'. For the denouement, Reilly cast himself as 'master of Moscow'.

I have read numerous accounts of the Reilly affair, in Russian and English sources, and (as is usually the case with spy stories) the facts seem impossible to establish. Reilly's true role in the conspiracy has never been fully understood. One book suggests that he may have been a double agent, the 'First Man', working for the Cheka, Lenin's secret police. It is hard to find any continuity of conviction or allegiance in his strange life, except to his desire for adventure and the logic of his own audacity and cunning. He remains half out of sight, keeping secrets to the end. He collected and discarded identities, wives, mistresses, homes, passports, false beards, tall tales, putative origins, cash fortunes and fine possessions. In reality 'Sidney Reilly' was an illegitimate Odessa-born Jew named Sigmund Rosenblum, sharing social origins with many of the Old Bolsheviks. Another of the anti-Bolshevik conspirators, the head of the British diplomatic mission in Moscow, Robert Bruce Lockhart, described him as 'cast in the Napoleonic mould'.

What intrigues me about this resonant tale of espionage and high political intrigue, known in the Soviet press as the 'Lockhart plot', is the role played in it by No. 3 and Elizaveta Otten, one of the pretty occupants of apartment 85. Otten must have valued her good name and her place in the order of the city. She is the only one of the young artistes who shared the apartment to have her name and address listed in the Moscow directory of 1917: 'Otten, Eliz. Emil., Sheremetevsky 3'. She was twenty. A photograph in her personal archive, which is kept in Moscow's main puppet theatre, shows her in stage paint, with a cupid's bow pencilled beyond the edges of her lips, lowered false eyelashes, a gentle gaze and a scarf tied around her fair hair. Her father, the manager of a tea company, had disapproved of her dreams of the stage. Yet Otten had recently made her debut at the Moscow Art Theatre Studio in a play called *The Green Ring* by the Symbolist poet Zinaida Gippius.

Sharing the apartment with Otten was a dancer from the Art Theatre, known as Dagmara K., who also took an active part in the anti-Bolshevik conspiracy. She was the mistress of Count Alexander Sheremetev, composer, conductor of the Imperial Court Choir until 1917, and half-brother of Count Sergei. Perhaps it was through Count Alexander that Reilly, who had connections in elite Moscow society as well as in its lower depths, first made the acquaintance of the actresses in No. 3.

Known to the actresses as Sidney Georgievich, the practised seducer Reilly had been a 'frequent visitor' in the apartment before Elizaveta Otten became his 'chief girl' in Moscow and he moved in to stay. Throughout the summer, Otten and her friends served as resourceful go-betweens as he spun his plot. Every morning another young dancer, the charming Maria Fride, would come up the staircase to deliver written intelligence from inside the Kremlin, copies she had made overnight of all the documents that had passed through the hands of her brother, Colonel Alexander Fride, on the previous day. The colonel, a Latvian Rifles officer, worked for the Bolsheviks as chief of military communications. Otten couriered secret letters between Reilly and the acting British consul, and received deliveries of documents from the Kremlin mole. Reilly, meanwhile, accumulated hundreds of thousands of roubles, mainly from the personal donations of Muscovites, which he secreted in a bureau drawer in the apartment: cash to bribe the Latvian mercenaries who guarded the Kremlin. In a city which had sunk, as he writes in his self-heroising memoir *Britain's Master Spy*, 'into a state of putrescence and stagnation beyond recall', the young performers were no doubt grateful for his material largesse. Whatever their motives or real convictions, Reilly considered them to be 'entirely' on his side, and among his 'most loyal and devoted collaborators'.

Perhaps it was not just the charms of the obligingly conspiratorial young women from the Art Theatre but also the perfect aptness for his counter-revolutionary phantasmagoria of the despoiled building in which they lived that drew Reilly to make this his principal 'safe house' in Red Moscow. The home of 'Mlle S.', as he calls Elizaveta Otten, was a most fitting address at which to conspire to save the bourgeoisie as a class. 'The house in Cheremeteff was a large place containing no fewer than two hundred flats, and some of these were of the largest size', Reilly says, adding that the apartment of the 'interesting young ladies' was so spacious that they had spare rooms to let to an ex-government official and a professor of music. Many of the other apartments, he notes, already accommodated several families. It was as though his mission could be distilled into the importance of saving this particular house and its inhabitants from the ravening Bolsheviks who were poised to claim it as their own.

Even the name of the street seems to have possessed evocative power for Reilly, who calls it 'Cheremeteff' again and again. The lineaments of his proclaimed cause and of the emblematic importance to him of No. 3 emerge in his apocalyptic portrait of the city under Red Terror. The city is 'paved with desolation, filth, squalor, fiendish cruelty, abject terror, lust, starvation'; Moscow has become a vision of hell, 'baptised in the blood of the bourgeoisie'. In this 'city of the damned', 'Cheremeteff' represents a tableau of almost allegorical pathos. Reilly describes a gang of men and women under guard, weakly attempting to clear refuse from the streets which reek of the carcasses of abandoned horses. The forced labourers have 'well-bred scholarly faces', the women are dignified and refined: 'they were members of the bourgeoisie; they had been stockbrokers, lawyers, schoolmistresses, when there had been stocks, laws, and schools in Russia'. Meanwhile, Reilly adds, former servants refuse to work, and spend their days carrying off 'from the flats of their erstwhile masters and mistresses such furniture as they coveted for the better decoration of their own apartments'. In his fantasies Reilly becomes the agent of conservation, as the city is ripped violently by the proletariat from the gentle bourgeoisie. The house in 'Cheremeteff' is a last citadel. The mission of Moscow's new Napoleon is to deliver the fallen class from its dispossession, to restore the plunder.

It is true that none of the *maisons à loyer* that were inserted into the empty spaces on the old patrimonial streets of Moscow as the moneyed bourgeoisie rose suddenly to prominence at the end of the nineteenth century quite equals No. 3 in extravagance and allure. Its buildings display a reckless confidence in prosperity, as though the heavy opulence of a bourgeois interior had been projected onto the façades, flagrant and over-ripe, inviting violation. The architect, Alexander Meisner, a native of Novgorod and member of the conservationist Archaeological Society, was one of the most prestigious in Moscow. Meisner worked for the Sheremetevs on another Moscow property, and in 1903 remodelled the façade and interiors of the late-eighteenth-century Noblemen's Club, an assembly for the aristocracy close to Red Square, adding a third storey. In his design for No. 3, Meisner gave grand emphasis to the front entrances and staircases, which have an aristocratic air of ceremony. In the density of its textures and the fluidity of its ornamentation, both inside and out, the style of the house is more Viennese *moderne* than Parisian belle époque. Yet in the way that it sinks back from the street behind ornate iron railings into a deep and shaded courtyard, the house manifests an indulgence in the superfluity of space that is peculiarly Russian.

Reilly moved about Moscow on false papers as 'Relinsky of the

Cheka', or Mr Constantine, a Greek businessman. In the first of many conspiratorial set-pieces in his memoir, narrated with an eye to the stock gestures of his calling, the 'legendary master spy' turns round on 'Cheremeteff' to check that nobody is in the street. Unobserved, he slips into No. 3 and ascends the 'abominably stinking' staircase. The building is 'deathly silent'. He stops at a door, listens, looks up and down the stairs. He knocks. The door opens half an inch. 'Is that you, Dagmara?' There comes the sound of a chain being removed, the door opens, and the agent slips in: 'M. Constantine, Chief of the British Secret Intelligence Service in Soviet Russia'.

Days before the planned *coup d'état*, the plot was exposed. A failed assassination attempt on Lenin at the end of August was followed by mass arrests, summary executions and an intensification of class war in Moscow's grandest apartment buildings. In a routine raid on the apartment of 'Reilly's girls', the secret police stumbled on the conspiracy, so it is said. When the Cheka arrived at the door, Dagmara K. later told an admiring Reilly, she grabbed a bundle of thousand-rouble notes from the bureau drawer and thrust them between her legs, keeping them in her underwear until the agents left. Otten was arrested. Maria Fride was picked up on her way upstairs with a portfolio of secret documents. For unknown reasons, Dagmara K. was spared.

Reilly was in Petrograd (as St Petersburg had been renamed in the First World War) when he saw the news of the 'mighty English conspiracy' in the press. 'The name of Cheremeteff . . . caught my eye. For a moment the paper swam before my eyes, the walls rocked and surged towards me. The window seemed to advance and recede . . .' Reilly regained his bearings and hurried to Moscow in disguise, waiting to make his escape from Russia. With his Colt in his inside pocket, 'ready to put the last bullet into my own head, rather than fall into the hands of that scum', he disappeared into obscure depths of the city, far from 'Cheremeteff', the guest of indigent enemies of the regime and understanding prostitutes in fashionable bordellos which the Cheka did not touch.

Under interrogation in the Butyrka prison, Elizaveta Otten method-acted for her life. Though she had been schooled to play in less hackneyed dramas, what Konstantin Stanislavsky would have called the 'inner reality' of her plight drew from her a convincing portrayal of the broken-hearted ingénue, seduced and betrayed by a double-dealing stranger. 'From the very beginning of our acquaintance he could bind me to himself,' she wrote in an appeal to the Red Cross. Reilly had lived with her, 'paying court', and she had been 'very fond of him'. It was only at her interrogation, she claimed, that she discovered that he had been 'foully deceiving' her for political purposes, taking advantage of her 'exclusively good attitude'. Like all recorded details of the plot, accounts of her incarceration vary. Reilly says that her health was gravely weakened by eight-hour cross-examinations in which she was allowed neither to eat nor to sit down. Lockhart reported that the torments devised for her were more psychologically refined. She was kept in a cell with dozens of other women, including seven who claimed to be married to Reilly. All young and beautiful, the spy's putative wives ranged from 'an actress' to 'the daughter of a concierge', and the 'jealousy and fighting between them had to be seen to be believed'.

At the end of November Otten appeared before a revolutionary tribunal in a mass trial of the alleged conspirators. *Izvestiya* dubbed them 'dirty servants of a dirty affair'. In 1918, jurisprudence had been distilled to the single question of whether or not a given act was 'committed with a view to restoring the oppressor class to power'. When asked to explain why she had destroyed a letter addressed to Reilly when the Cheka came to search her apartment, Otten defended her move as 'instinctive', quite oblivious of the interests of the oppressor class. Her performance (or if Reilly is to be believed, a fifty-thousand-rouble bribe for her 'investigator') gained Otten an acquittal, but her write-up in *Izvestiya* was ignominious. The newspaper described her as 'a former actress of the art theatre' and misspelled her name.

Reilly's fascination with Napoleon was one of the only continuities in his biography. Over twenty-five years, he assembled a precious collection of books, paintings and artefacts relating to Bonaparte's life, which financial difficulties finally obliged him to sell for near $100,000 at auction in New York in 1921. Did the sale include the snuffbox that once lay on the baccarat table at the Hunting Club on 'Cheremeteff'?

⤗

'The two of us could not have been called friends,' the writer and labour-camp survivor Varlam Shalamov writes in the Gulag story 'Dry Ration', 'we simply loved to remember Moscow together – her streets and her monuments, the Moscow River covered with its thin layer of oil glistening like mother-of-pearl . . . we were ready to talk endlessly of Moscow'. In the Gulag, talking of Moscow was one of the ways of forming bonds for prisoners, like talking about food or remembering sex and fantasising about women. Women, food, Moscow. 'A Muscovite?' asks the Gulag doctor Lunin in 'Descendant of a Decembrist'. The young medical student in the story is the great-grandson of the famous rebel Mikhail Lunin, a noble hussar with an exquisite columned palace decorated with lyres on Nikitsky Boulevard, whom Pushkin called 'a friend of Mars, Bacchus, and Venus'. 'You know, Muscovites are a people who, more than any other, like to talk about their city – the streets, the ice rinks, the houses, the Moscow River . . .' Lunin muses. He craves another educated person to talk to in the camps, so, as his eyes wander the surgeon's shelves in search of bread, Shalamov forces himself 'to remember Moscow's Kitai-gorod district, and the Nikitsky Gates where the writer Andrei Sobol shot himself, where Stern shot at the German ambassador's car . . . that history of Moscow's streets which no one will ever write down'. 'Yes, Moscow, Moscow. Tell me, how many women have you had?' Lunin replies. Shalamov had come to the city from Vologda, to 'seething Moscow', to study Soviet law, in the days when Andrei Vyshinsky was expounding the new revolutionary jurisprudence that would send him to the Gulag twice for the same thought crime.

The nomadism of seething Moscow, the refusal of settled bourgeois life, was part of the lure of the Russian Revolution for foreign sympathisers. Walter Benjamin perceived something unsettled, provisional and wild about Moscow itself. It seemed an 'improvised metropolis that had fallen into place overnight'. All this appealed to the American reporter Louise Bryant, lover of the communist John Reed. At Reed's beckoning, she hurried to Petrograd by train from Finland to take her part in the events of October 1917, to absorb the philosophy of revolution into her sensory world. In *Mirrors of Moscow*, published six years later, she promised to show the real people behind the 'screen of smoke and flame', the revolutionaries – Vladimir Lenin, Lev Kamenev, Felix Dzerzhinsky, Anatoli Lunacharsky, Mikhail Kalinin, Alexandra Kollontai and Lev Trotsky – 'as they really are, as I know them in their homes, where the red glare does not penetrate and they live as other men'. She did not see what Trotsky already saw. Even as the romance of revolution stirred Bryant's Greenwich Village bohemian sensibility, its leaders were acquiring bourgeois tastes. 'Here, then, they are,' she reported to her American readers from Bolshevik Moscow, 'the Russians of today. Close to the Tartar and the Cossack of the plain, children of serfs and Norsemen and Mongols – close to the earth and striving for the stars.' She was photographed in a Russian peasant *sarafan* (a pinafore dress) with the sidelong gaze of a demure village girl, and again, in a contrasting pose, in Cossack boots and a fetching fur hat, smoking and smiling mischievously into the camera lens.

Ivy Litvinov, the English wife of the Soviet commissar (and future Commissar of Foreign Affairs) Maxim Litvinov, who came to Moscow in the early 1920s, wrote home that she had assumed that in revolutionary Russia 'ideas' would be everything and 'things' would matter little, 'because everyone would have what they want without superfluities', but when she walked about the city streets, 'peering into ground-floor windows', she saw 'the *things* of Moscow huggermuggering in all the corners and realised that they had never been so important'.

'War communism' led to shortage, famine, the breakdown of civic life. In 1921 Lenin announced the New Economic Policy. Economic life was dramatically liberalised while factions and freedom of discussion within the Party were suppressed. The broken city quickly returned to life. Rubble and sewage were cleaned from the streets, public services reinstated and housing rationalised. A state bank was founded. Currency was reformed and a new partly gold-backed currency unit known as the *chervonets* was introduced. On his way out of Russia during the NEP, Walter Benjamin bribed an official with a *chervonets* to ensure safe passage for the trunkful of toys and children's books he had haggled over in the street markets of Moscow. Smaller-scale private property was handed back to former owners and for a few years foreign concessions were allowed. A new Moscow directory was published in 1922, advertising innumerable 'Trust' companies, and giving the telephone numbers of the offices in the Kremlin and along Vozdvizhenka of Bolshevik commissars, including Lenin and Trotsky. 'The Viy is reading the telephone directory in Red Square,' Mandelstam wrote in his angry NEP prose-piece *The Fourth Prose*. 'Lift up my eyelids . . . Connect me with the Central Committee'. (The Viy is an arch-goblin from Russian folklore with iron eyelids and a glance that kills.)

If settled dwelling was the ideal of the nineteenth-century bourgeois order, unsettled living was the condition of the 1920s. 'The wretched city of Moscow, why does it not want to give me a place in its bosom?' the young Petersburg-born composer Dmitri Shostakovich complained when he came to Moscow in 1925, at the beginning of his career. He could find nowhere to stay in the destabilised city, though he strained towards it, he said, with all his soul. Shostakovich found refuge in No. 3, conveniently located just around the corner from the Moscow Conservatoire, as the guest of the writer Galina Serebryakova, ex-wife of the revolutionary

Leonid Serebryakov; she had just married her second Old Bolshevik, Grigory Sokolnikov, Commissar of Finance, deviser of the *chervonets* that made the economic recovery of the NEP possible. Sokolnikov, whose true name was Hirsh Brilliant ('diamond'), was a graduate in economics from the Sorbonne, an old-guard revolutionary who had returned to Russia with Lenin in the sealed train in April 1917, and signed the peace treaty with Germany at Brest-Litovsk. In Moscow, Shostakovich was befriended by Marshal Tukhachevsky, a connoisseur of music who made violins in his spare time, and who would act as his protector for the next decade. Arrested in 1936, Sokolnikov and Serebryakov were tried together as members of the 'Anti-Soviet Trotskyite Centre'; Andrei Vyshinsky was prosecutor. Among the many crimes of which the 'Centre' was accused was a fictional attempt on the life of Molotov. Serebryakov, who had 'confessed' to everything he was accused of after his investigators told him they were bringing his daughter into the Lubyanka for a 'meeting', was shot. Sokolnikov, who had likewise 'confessed' to save Galina, was sentenced to ten years and murdered in a labour camp. Galina was arrested in 1937. She came back to Moscow from Siberia after almost twenty years, her Party loyalty unbroken. Mikhail Tukhachevsky was shot in 1937, without the honour of a 'show trial'. Shostakovich's Fifth Symphony, which was performed at the end of that year, is heard by many as a bitter requiem for lost friends, including the friends he stayed with in this house in 1925.

Like Shostakovich, Benjamin found himself searching for a refuge in Moscow at the height of the NEP. He came in the deep winter of 1926, a time of profound personal and intellectual strain. He was in love with a Latvian revolutionary, the theatre director Asja Lacis, who was recovering from a nervous breakdown in a sanatorium near Tverskaya. At the same time he was trying to decide whether to join the German Communist Party. He wanted to see the city of Marxist revolution, where the 'continuum of history' had been exploded, where, as he put it, 'all factuality is already theory'. The revolution's potential for success or failure was 'brutally visible' on the streets, among the people. (Benjamin could not see the brutal struggle that was taking place in the Kremlin that winter as Stalin moved against his rivals.) He told his editor, Martin Buber, that he would write a 'physiognomy' of Moscow for the journal *The Creature*, an essay which would allow 'the creatural to speak for itself', seizing and rendering the 'very new and disorienting language that echoes loudly through the resounding mask of an environment'.

In my years here I have often returned to Benjamin's *Moscow Diary*. Of all the European magi of what was known as 'theory' among the gatekeepers to the world of ideas who taught me in Cambridge twenty-five years ago, Benjamin is the only one I have read since with pleasure. His prose is febrile with curiosity about real places and real people; with his obsessive love for the beautiful and strange, his fascination with physical things and the complexities of human relationships with physical things, from rare books to handmade toys, fur coats and cream cakes.

Benjamin began work on his *Arcades Project* immediately after his return from Moscow. The vast never-finished collage of suggestive quotations and fragments of insight was an attempt to characterise Second Empire Paris, the 'capital of the nineteenth century'. Rather than using the inventory style of traditional histories of civilisation, he tried to capture the city in all its changing manifestations, revealing how the riches of civilisation are passed on and 'strangely altered by the constant efforts of society', both conscious and unconscious. He grasped at history by stealth, exploring the crepuscular city, radiating artificial light, refracted in glass, from ever-changing angles, looking for correspondences, gathering random scraps and traces that could be assembled and juxtaposed to make a picture of its inner life, which he called a 'dialectical fairyland'.

I have been drawn back to the *Diary* for precise historical reasons too. Benjamin found Moscow 'an exact touchstone for the foreigner'. Its reality drove off the abstractions that 'so effortlessly come to the European's mind'. No theory would hold. Everything was material fact. Life leapt out at him, 'combative, determined, mute', from the arches of gates, the frames of doors, the lettering on street signs, the images of boots or freshly ironed laundry, a worn stoop or a stairway's solid landing. He registered acutely the disorientation of the city as it was transformed by the communist dream of a leap out of the history of things, as the bonds of ownership were broken and private life 'withered'.

'It has to do with fashioning a shell for ourselves', Benjamin noted of the verb 'to dwell'. He saw 'indwelling' as the condition of the nineteenth century, the century of the bourgeoisie, when the residence 'was conceived as a receptacle for the person, encasing him with all its appurtenances so deeply . . . that one might be reminded of the inside of a compass case, where the instrument lies embedded in deep, usually violet folds of velvet'. Like so many foreign onlookers, Benjamin thought the Russian Revolution was the beginning of the end of that world. He believed that Marxian dialectical thinking was the 'organ of historical awakening'. With this new organ of perception, he believed one could see history at its secret work: 'with the destabilising of the market economy, we begin to recognise the monuments of the bourgeoisie as ruins even before they have crumbled,' he wrote. When he came to Moscow, he was convinced that everything in the new collectivist society contrived against the bourgeois 'melancholia of cosiness'. The bourgeois city centred on the distinction between work and home had been shaken up. Living arrangements were 'a difficult question'. People had abandoned domesticity; they lived in the office, the club, the street. As part of the communist credo, love and marriage had become a 'bagatelle'; sex should be like taking a glass of water, declared People's Commissar Alexandra Kollontai. The idea of the completed bourgeois interior – wall-coverings, pictures, sofa cushions, antimacassars, coverlets, knick-knacks on the consoles – had been discarded. Of all Moscow institutions, only the street children on Tverskaya, sitting in rags against the wall of the Museum of the Revolution, refused to be budged. Everything else in the city was 'under the banner of the *remont*'.

Now, in the twenty-first century, since the sudden official abandonment of the communist dream, the city was back under the banner of the *remont*. As the price of oil and gas, Russia's great sources of wealth, rose on global markets, the transformation of Moscow took on a quality of frenzy. It was dialectical, I suppose. Things revolved and became their opposite. It was certainly loud. Through the mask of the environment, the *embourgeoisement* of Moscow resonated day and night, echoing from building sites on every side. It was hard to sleep. I lay in bed and thought of a phrase in Mandelstam's *Fourth Prose*, 'the hound-dog nights of Moscow'. Yes, the nights were hound-dogs. Everyone was restless, busy fashioning a shell, searching out a new interior in which to work or dwell.

Moscow Diary is a record of homelessness and erotic failure. Benjamin's longing to find a place of rest with Lacis, to possess her, threads its way from the first pages when he sights her standing in the slush on Tverskaya Street in a fur hat, to the end, where he is carried away from her through the twilit streets, clutching on his knees a suitcase full of possessions, weeping tears of loss. There is no interior space in the city in which the lovers can find comfort together. The only time they are alone in the dark is in a horse-drawn sleigh on the Arbat, where they embrace. Instead he spends money, buying things for his collection, gifts for Asja: three little houses made of coloured paper from a stall on the far side of the Moscow River, 'for the enormous price of thirty kopecks', which he carries awkwardly in his arms in the bitter cold; hand-painted lacquer boxes (he is captivated, of course, by small closed caskets); sweets, blouses, stockings. The only fully furnished interior he finds in the city is in an odd little museum dedicated to daily life in the 1840s, where he sees a room full of Louis-Philippe furniture: chests, candelabras, pier glasses, folding screens, even writing paper and shawls draped over chairs. In a tender moment alone in a room, Benjamin reads Lacis his translation of the lesbian scene in Proust's *Du Côté de chez Swann*. 'Asja grasped its savage nihilism', he writes, how Proust in a certain fashion ventures into the tidy private chamber within the petit bourgeois that bears the inscription *sadism* and then mercilessly smashes everything to pieces, so that nothing remains of the untarnished clear-cut conception of wickedness, but instead within every fracture evil explicitly shows its true substance – 'humanity', or even 'kindness'.

He can only experience Moscow through Asja, he says. Animosity and love shift in him 'like winds'. He imagines her conquest of his heart as a feat of urban engineering; she has laid a street through him. Sometimes, when he catches sight of her, she does not look beautiful: wild beneath her fur hat, her face puffy from time spent bedridden. He reads a passage from his new book *One-Way Street*, filled with metaphors of home, of the longing for refuge in a great and populous city, for the mysteries of the interior, out of sight of passers-by. Benjamin fails to grasp Moscow, just as he fails to possess Asja Lacis: 'nowhere does Moscow really look like the city it is'. Buildings seem to be holding something back. He wants to find a way in, to touch their spirit, their combative, determined life, to ambush them with his eye, from above, from the height of an aeroplane. He tries to work out how best to take a place in, from 'as many dimensions as possible'. 'The same thing with houses. It is only after having crept along a series of them in search of a very specific one that you come to learn what they contain.'

⤔

Until Stalin's death, V. S. Zhukovsky remembers, there were carpets on the outer steps of each entryway at the 'Fifth House of the Soviets'. As a young boy growing up next door, he could see into the courtyard of No. 3 from his friend Slava's kitchen window. One day he watched four Packard limousines sweep into Granovsky; sitting together in the back of one of the cars were Stalin's henchmen Lavrenty Beria and Georgy Malenkov. The cortège turned into No. 3, where Malenkov got out, and Beria was driven off round the corner, in the direction of his mansion on the Garden Ring. Molotov moved into the house later, after his expulsion from the Central Committee. Zhukovsky occasionally saw him in the street, walking with his wife, Polina Zhemchuzhina. Molotov was always painstakingly well-dressed, Zhukovsky recalls, with a sleek, healthy appearance that belied his age, and a penetrating glance. Polina (who was seven years younger than her husband) was small, withered and bent. (She had been beaten in the Lubyanka and spent three years in exile in Kazakhstan, where she was officially referred to as 'Object No. 12'.) It was admirable, Zhukovsky says, the solicitous way Molotov led his wife down the street, holding her by the arm.

The Stalinist poet Felix Chuev, who, with a tape recorder hidden in his pocket, conducted 140 long conversations with Molotov in the last two decades of his life, remembers him on the threshold of No. 3 on a wet day in March 1977. Chuev had driven him into town from his dacha at Zhukovka outside Moscow. In the car Molotov sang an old Soviet fighting song: 'in the struggle for the power of the Soviets, we will die as one! . . . Who knows why we should all die as one', he mused at the end of the song. Chuev drew up at Molotov's entrance and, observed by astonished passers-by, the old man stepped out over the puddles. Molotov hid behind the outer door of the house, then suddenly came out into the street again for a few seconds and waved his hand . . .

'In a quarter-century we have not tracked anyone down', Alexander Solzhenitsyn wrote in *The Gulag Archipelago*: 'We have not brought anyone to trial. It is their wounds we are afraid to reopen. And as a symbol of them all, the smug and stupid Molotov lives on at Granovsky No. 3, a man who has learned nothing at all, even now, though he is saturated with our blood and nobly crosses the sidewalk to seat himself in his long, wide automobile.'

TWO

Apartment 61

You should not live in the Kremlin . . .
ANNA AKHMATOVA

On the morning the banker gave me the keys to the Molotov apartment, I went upstairs. To avoid detection by the concierge who sits in her small room in the *sous-sol* listening for the sounds of doors, I took off my shoes and stayed close to the outer wall. For when she comes out and peers round the door jamb, wrapping her shawl about her, and calling out '*Kto?*' ('Who?'), she can see through the wrought iron of the banister that curls in leafy arabesques beneath the polished handrail, all the way up from the tiled entrance hall to the fifth-storey landing.

Of course, there was no serious reason to be wary of the natural curiosity of a warm-hearted babushka, but why oblige her to wonder why I was letting myself into a neighbour's apartment? There was also something that invited furtive behaviour in the way the light was thickened by the dust scaled on the double panes of window glass, funnelling into long beams on the worn stone steps. 'Security' has traditionally been a term with wide application here. The concierge still has a duty to report on the residents of the building, particularly on the citizens of 'imperialist' foreign powers. Though the apartments were privatised at the end of the Soviet period and are now owned by the people who happened to be living in them at the time, the 'freehold' belongs to the *apparat* of the President. No. 3 is Kremlin property. The *komendantka* is proud of the fact that she still reports to the security services. As she declared loudly to the nannies of the foreign children in the courtyard one day: 'This house is listened to. It always has been, and always will be.' Stalin hired a Czech engineer to plant listening devices in the offices of his comrades in the early 1920s, and he and Molotov opened files on them, with their life stories and particular weaknesses carefully documented for future use. As Molotov himself remarked when reflecting on the fact that his own homes had been bugged, 'as long as classes exist, that's life'. Or, as his enemy Trotsky put it, 'the state is not pure spirit'. Eighty years ago, 'organs' of the young Soviet state stood at the door of apartment 62 and at this entrance to No. 3, watching Trotsky come and go, reporting every move to Stalin.

Apartment 62 is now the home of a well-known TV producer and his fourth wife, an arrogantly sexy blonde who spends much of the year in Tuscany. Their doorway is the grandest on the staircase, faced with bullet-proof glass and a fancy iron grille. But through it a distant past is still visible. As though in a magic lantern, or a diorama, in which nineteenth-century spectators looked at glowing images of exciting or macabre historical scenes set in the innermost rooms of the city, picture Trotsky being carried through it by the secret police on a frigid winter night in 1928.

Trotsky, who had made the Revolution with Lenin in 1917, had become an oppositional figure by the mid-1920s. In June 1926, Stalin wrote to Molotov that it was time to 'smash Trotsky's mug', turn him into a renegade. At the XIVth Party Congress six months earlier, at which Molotov had been promoted to full membership of the Politburo and become one of the USSR's most prominent politicians, he spoke against the opposition, advocating fanaticism and the liquidation of all genuine political argument among Bolsheviks. The outcome of the struggle, Molotov declared, will be decided by 'a genuine conviction about the correctness of one's line'. The 'ideology of unbelief' undermines everything: 'doubt makes a communist waver, makes his hands shake'. At a plenum that autumn, Molotov introduced a Politburo resolution stripping Trotsky of his full membership of the Central Committee.

Molotov's hatred for the intellectually flamboyant Trotsky dated back to the early years of the Revolution, when Lenin had laughingly told him that Trotsky considered him a plodder. When

Molotov was made a full member of the Central Committee of the Party at the Xth Party Congress in 1921, Lenin famously dubbed him the 'best filing clerk in Russia'. Molotov remained faithful to Lenin despite these slights, fashioning himself as a standard-bearer of his ideological legacy after Lenin's death in 1924, but he turned his hatred on Trotsky, calling him a 'revolutionary narcissist', an 'individualist', a 'despiser of the masses'. Trotsky, for his part, sneered openly at Molotov at one Party meeting, calling him 'mediocrity incarnate', to which Molotov responded, 'It is not given to everyone to be a genius. I only flatter myself that I have willpower and energy.'

In October 1927, as Trotsky made a final speech at a meeting of the Central Committee, warning about the violence behind Stalin's growing power and the coming Thermidor, Emilian Yaroslavsky threw a heavy book of statistics at his head. 'Behind the extreme organisation-men there is a resurgent internal bourgeoisie,' Trotsky shouted over the catcalls of other Central Committee members at the October plenum, 'and behind that is the world bourgeoisie.' Stalin sat quietly drawing wolves on the margins of the speech he was about to deliver, which denounced Trotsky as a traitor to Lenin's legacy. Was it at this meeting that one of Trotsky's supporters drew the caricature recently discovered in a strange collection of sketches (some of them violently obscene) in the Party archives? Dated 1927, 'artist unknown', the cartoon depicts 'Yaroslavka' as the sleuth-dog of the 'All-Party oppressor and gendarme Stalin'. Behind Stalin and Yaroslavsky is a prison labelled 'party apparatus' and a miserable prisoner labelled 'Great Communist Party'. With the resolutions of the XVth Party Congress rolled up in the top of his boot, Stalin is trampling on 'party democracy'.

Trotsky's isolation from the Party was soon complete; he was expelled from the Central Committee and moved out of the Kremlin. 'Until I find permanent accommodation, I shall be living temporarily at the apartment of Comrade Beloborodov (3 Granovsky Street, Apt. 62)', he wrote to the titular head of the government. (He was destined to live as a nomad, in true revolu-

tionary fashion, until Ramón Mercader's ice pick opened his skull
in Mexico thirteen years later.) Moving to No. 3 made Trotsky a
neighbour of Semyon Budyonny, the moustachioed cavalry general from the Cossack steppes who had, by then, been living in
the house for three years. Two weeks before Trotsky's eviction,
Budyonny had overseen the pogrom-like break-up of a street
demonstration held by Trotsky and his supporters. Molotov, meanwhile, continued his attacks in print and on the streets, denouncing
'Trotskyism' in an article commemorating the tenth anniversary of
the Revolution, and personally breaking up Trotsky's speech to a
meeting of Moscow workers at the Paveletsky Station, demanding
in the name of the Central Committee that the 'illegal gathering'
be disbanded. In a rage, Trotsky denounced Stalin and his henchmen as 'grave-diggers' of the Revolution. The following day,
Pravda accused Trotsky of forming an illegal party.

During his two-month stay at No. 3, Trotsky tried to settle
down to book work. No state publisher would take his writings, so
he appealed to an independent-minded old comrade David
Ryazanov, founder-director of the Marx–Engels Institute, who
commissioned him to translate the classics of 'scientific socialism'.
At night, wearing felt boots to keep out the cold, Trotsky would
rise from the pages of Marx to pace the room like a prisoner. At
the end of the year he was given notice that he was to be exiled to
Kazakhstan. His host, Alexander Beloborodov (the man who had
sent out the command to murder the imperial family in July 1918),
was informed at the same time that he was to be sent into exile in
Komi in th : north.

The Sc iet caricaturist Boris Efimov remembered visiting
No. 3 in F :bruary 1928, just after the announcement of Trotsky's
impendin ; deportation. The well-known critic and art historian
Vyachesl v Polonsky, who had suggested the visit, had given
Efimov s)me books for Trotsky, telling him to take no notice of
the secret policeman in the stairwell. Trotsky opened the door
himself, and graciously took Efimov's coat. He showed him into a
small study off the hallway, and they sat down to talk. Trotsky

encouraged Efimov to keep up his work – caricature was of vital importance in such 'odd' times, he said – and lamented that Efimov's brother had gone over to the 'Thermidoreans'. The apartment smelled strongly of borscht, and soon a woman's voice from the kitchen summoned Trotsky to the table. As Trotsky helped him on with his coat, Efimov was so overcome by embarrassment at the attentions of the great man that he could not get his arm into his sleeve. 'Safe journey, Lev Davidovich!' Efimov said, 'safe return . . .' and they embraced. When the secret police guard at the bottom of the stairs saw the young caricaturist leaving without his parcel of books, he reached for the telephone. Trotsky carefully packed up all his books and papers for the journey. Stalin soon regretted having allowed him to take them with him into exile.

When Trotsky reaches the scene of his deportation in his autobiography, *My Life*, to frame the historical pathos of the moment, he turns the narrative over to a spectator: his wife, Natalya Sedova. When the men from the OGPU (the secret police) came to take him to the railway station, Trotsky refused to go quietly; he would not allow Stalin to present his exile as voluntary. The family locked itself inside one of the rooms in the apartment. (On this particular night, Trotsky was wearing indoor slippers rather than felt boots, emphasising the violation of his temporary home.) The agents shouted orders through the door, telephoned their masters for instructions and finally smashed their way in, reaching uniformed arms through the broken door glass. One of them shouted, 'Shoot me, Comrade Trotsky, shoot me,' and Trotsky told him to calm down and stop talking nonsense. The agents rammed on his boots, fur coat and shapka and lifted him through the door and down the stairs, locking his two grown sons inside the apartment. They forced their way out, and one of them, Lyova, ran up and down the staircase ringing doorbells, shouting, 'They are carrying Comrade Trotsky away.' 'Frightened faces flashed by us at the doors and on the staircase,' Sedova recalls; 'in this house only prominent Soviet workers were living.'

In the course of the next decade, 'prominent Soviet workers' would learn to keep the doors closed, not to look out when they heard the heavy tread of boots on the common staircase at night, the commotion of arrest in a neighbouring apartment or the sound that Mandelstam's wife remembered all her life, the sound of the 1930s, the heave and whine of old lifts in 'the hours of love and peace'.

Thinking about the meaning of the scene on the staircase, I sense that this house was not merely a setting for history, but a player in the drama. These apartments were velvet cases fashioned for the families of the bourgeoisie, for love and peace and the accumulation of possessions. Years later, Trotsky decided that the deep cause of his loss of power was the rapid development of bourgeois tastes among the revolutionaries. After the Civil War, the 'philistine in the Bolshevik' had been liberated. Unlike Trotsky, in his own image of himself, the others had not 'absorbed the philosophy of revolution into their flesh and blood, so that it dominated their consciousness and co-ordinated with their sensory world'. Even before Lenin's death, Trotsky observed, the leading Bolsheviks had begun to behave like a social elite: 'the nomads of revolution went over to settled living, the philistine characteristics, sympathies and tastes of self-satisfied officials were aroused and developed'. They began to attend the ballet and hold drinking parties in their homes, at which they would pull to pieces anyone who happened to be absent. 'Gossiping over a bottle of wine or returning from the ballet, one smug official would say to another: "He can think of nothing but permanent revolution."' Amid the splendours and comforts of No. 3, the prospect of permanent revolution stimulated little more than defensive ennui in the nomads of 1917.

Though for Trotsky Molotov embodied the apparatus of the totalitarian-bureaucratic dictatorship, he gave his opponent credit for revealing 'a little more freedom from the ritual phrase than other Soviet leaders'. They shared a revolutionary appetite for the category of future time, free of the clutter of the present and the past, in which their weaker comrades had learned to take pleasure like 'the most finished snobs' of the world bourgeoisie. 'Human personality begins for socialism not with the concern for a prosperous life', Trotsky wrote in *The Revolution Betrayed*, 'but on the contrary with the cessation of this concern.' Trotsky's acute denunciation of the byzantinism and police rule of the mid-1930s in that book persuaded Stalin that it was time to solve with murderous finality the problem of 'Trotskyite' opposition within the Party. Both Trotsky and Molotov professed belief in Marxist revolution as a threshold in history, a doorway to a bright future, to which Lenin's vanguard party held the keys. History was moving inevitably in a certain direction, according to internal laws that could be discovered through the study of 'scientific socialism'. Over the threshold, led by the Party, mankind would leap, as Engels had promised, from the 'kingdom of necessity' to the 'kingdom of freedom'. In that coming kingdom, the 'extraneous objective forces that have hitherto governed history pass under the control of man himself', who will become at last the master of history, no longer its victim, in control of himself, and in control of external nature. When society seizes the means of production from the property-owning class, the production of commodities is done away with and, simultaneously, the mastery of product over producer. There will be no more need for money or the state. Only then, according to Engels, would the dehumanising struggle for individual existence disappear. The bourgeois order is anarchy. It must be replaced by the systematic organisation of communism, when man will at last emerge into full humanity, as conscious lord of nature, no longer dominated by dead matter, by things. For dependence on things, and human relationships based on things, Marx taught, were the greatest threats to 'mastery over one's destiny', unworthy of a rational creature. For Trotsky and for Molotov, despite all their lethal disagreements, Marxism was not only a map of the future, but a moral system, a guide to personal virtue. 'Marxism is an objective science,' Molotov said, 'it calls bad things bad and good things good. It demands genuine uncompromising struggle for the good.' He had always chosen revolutionary duty over his family, whom he loved 'body and soul', he reflected late in life, and though he thought objectivity about his own life a 'theoretic impossibility', his conscience was satisfied.

Molotov was still living close to Stalin in a Kremlin apartment when Trotsky was forced into exile. He was busy that year purging the Moscow City administration of 'right deviationists' and organising the forcible requisitioning of grain from peasants in the Ukraine. Decades later, at the end of his life, Molotov's family occupied both apartments on the third floor of this house, 61 and 62 on the other side of the staircase, Trotsky's last refuge in Russia. Molotov still enjoyed recalling the humiliation on the landing of his longtime adversary, the 'rightist adventurer'. 'Trotsky was carried out of his apartment,' Molotov reminisced with a discernible fondness for the scene; 'two men carried him out. One was my chief of security, Pogudin . . . Pogudin was strong.'

❧

The true revolutionaries wanted to break down the door of history and burst out of it. Their historical materialism 'leads inevitably to the crumbling away of historical reality', Berdyaev writes in *The Meaning of History*, and historical reality is 'above all a concrete and not an abstract reality'. Beyond the outer door of the Molotov apartment, which was eight feet high and padded in black leather, was a heavy wooden inner door, elaborately carved on one side, lined on the other with more studded leather. (These are double doors, with a wide space between them, as in the college rooms, known as 'sets', of Cambridge dons.) Just inside, a closed-circuit security camera held tremulous black-and-white images on a split screen of the street entrance and the staircase. Leaving the lights off, I wandered through the rooms. Each of the apartments on the staircase is laid out differently, but, like the others, this one was divided into two halves: vast 'ceremonial' rooms for entertaining at the front, with intricately moulded cornices, and rooms of slightly lesser grandeur leading off back corridors for family life. On the right of the entry hall was a door leading into the family rooms, where a dim T-shaped corridor led to four large bedrooms, their walls lined in floral synthetic fabrics, patterned in dull oranges and browns. At the junction of the corridor was a revolving bookstand, which contained art books and a Russian translation, bound in cloth, of Winston Churchill's multi-volume *History of the Second World War*, published in a tiny numbered edition, for restricted use, by the Soviet Ministry of Defence. I took a volume from the bookstand and leafed through its pages, stopping at a sentence which had prompted an exclamation mark in the margin: 'If Hitler invaded hell, I would make at least a favourable reference to the devil in the House of Commons.' I sat down on an armchair beside the bookstand and turned the pages slowly, stopping at passages marked by their attentive earlier reader. 'Vyacheslav Molotov was a man of outstanding ability and cold-blooded ruthlessness,' recorded Churchill.

He had survived the fearful hazards and ordeals to which all Bolshevik leaders had been subjected in the years of triumphant revolution. He had lived and thrived in a society where ever-varying intrigue was accompanied by the constant menace of personal liquidation. His cannon-ball head, black moustache, and comprehending eyes, his slab face, his verbal adroitness and imperturbable demeanour, were appropriate manifestations of his qualities and skill. He was above all men fitted to be the agent and instrument of the policy of an incalculable machine . . . I have never seen a human being who more perfectly represented the modern conception of a robot.

In the front half of the apartment were a drawing room, a dining room and a study. The drawing room was panelled two-thirds of the way up to the high ceiling in honey-coloured wood, inlaid with delicate marquetry, set with narrow polished columns. In the dining room, a two-tone marble fireplace, heavy and baroque, had been set into the original ceiling-high tiled dutch stove. Against one wall was a staid 1930s-style buffet which looked as though it should have a brass number plate on its back, like all the state-issued *nomenklatura* perquisites that once furnished No. 3. My landlord, a genial man, well satisfied by life (he was high up in the Supreme Soviet under Brezhnev and loved to tell tales of the alcoholism and domestic violence of the children of the Party elite), later told me that this dining room had been Molotov's study. 'He was a legend,' he told me with a chuckle, pointing up at our ceiling, 'but he was a coward. All Stalin's men were cowards.'

Covering the old parquet in the drawing room was a large carpet – muted gold, pale pink and grey, figured with cypress trees, roses and gazelles – given to Molotov, I had been told, by the Shah of Persia. The chandeliers in the Molotov apartment were the hypertrophied black, bronze and sculpted-glass designs of the Stalin era, now sought after by collectors of Soviet 'antiques', though I was not able to tell whether they dated from the mid-1930s, when the Party said that life had become 'happier and more beautiful', and encouraged the acquisition of wallpapers, lampshades and phonograph recordings of jazz, or from the period of high Stalinist baroque after the war. Oil paintings in gilt frames hung on the walls: late-nineteenth-century sentimental genre scenes of peasant children sleeping in a huddle, fishermen on a seashore. Arranged in a display case was a collection of ivory and lacquer ornaments that the banker had told me were gifts to Molotov from Chairman Mao. In her memoir, *Only One Year*, Stalin's daughter Svetlana Alliluyeva remembered with distaste the richly decorated homes of her father's henchmen, 'crammed with fine rugs, gold and silver Caucasian weapons, valuable porcelain'. After the Second World War (when Molotov was foreign minister), 'waves of gifts began arriving from other, especially fraternal socialist countries and from China. Jade vases, carved ivory, Indian silks, Persian rugs, handicrafts from Yugoslavia, Bulgaria, Czechoslovakia . . . it is hard to imagine valuables that did not decorate the abodes of these "veterans of the Revolution".'

The tendencies to personal accumulation were not spectres of the capitalist past in Soviet society, as Trotsky lamented in *The*

Revolution Betrayed, but 'new, mighty and continually reborn'. After the austerities of 'war communism', the NEP quickly brought these tendencies back into play, to the dismay of true believers. The one idea of the ascetic librarian Fyodorov that the Soviet writer Maxim Gorky liked was the idea that in capitalist societies women drive consumerism, with their endless desire for 'toys'. In a letter of 1926, he invoked Fyodorov ('an original thinker'), who argued that 'not only all industry but that all civilisation was women's stuff': '"The woman and the sexual forces she unleashes" create effeteness and consumption which in turn lead to degeneration and extinction. Such a domination by the woman was not just burdensome but destructive.' Human beings are like birds, Fyodorov observed: 'beautiful plumage and cosy nests have become fashionable clothes, plushy boudoirs and soft furniture, but they still serve in the same capacity as sexual stimulant'. The Soviet journalist 'Zorich' published a feuilleton with the title 'Lady with a Little Dog' (borrowed from Chekhov), in which he criticised Party boss Sergei Kirov's pampered wife, who, when her husband was called up from Baku to Moscow in 1926 to rout the Trotskyites in the Party, commandeered a whole railway carriage for her pet dogs. Stalin reacted to the article by declaring Zorich guilty of spreading slander and falsehood. (In 1937 Zorich, whose real name was Vasili Lokot, was shot.) As the Soviet elite established its world of privilege, Trotsky denounced the 'automobile-harem factor' which, he said, shaped the morals of the ever more acquisitive bureaucracy. He scoffed at the Soviet discovery of the word *luxe*, and saw the wives of highly placed Party members, with their love of furs, jewellery, perfumes and soft furnishings, as chief culprits in the degeneration of the Bolsheviks into a 'new aristocracy', a caste committed to nothing so much as the protection of its own material privilege.

Old-fashioned femininity, both commodified and expressed through commodities, soon became incorporated, overtly and covertly, into the Party's programme for the development of Soviet society. Molotov's wife, Polina Zhemchuzhina, played a leading role in the fashioning of Soviet femininity. While Molotov, who was born Vyacheslav Skryabin, had adopted a suitably revolutionary pseudonym in 1915, from *molot* meaning 'hammer', his wife, the daughter of a Jewish tailor from a Cossack village in Zaporozhe in the Russian south, had changed her name from Perl Karpovskaya to Polina Zhemchuzhina, which means 'little pearl'. Before joining the Communist Party in 1918, Zhemchuzhina had worked in a cigarette factory and as a cashier in a pharmacy. According to official Party mythology, Molotov met Zhemchuzhina, who was said to be 'popular with the peasants', on a farm, where she was supervising experiments with methods of sowing sugar-beet. In fact, the two met in a Moscow hospital in the summer of 1921, when Zhemchuzhina had been taken ill at an International Women's Conference, to which she had come as a Party delegate from the south. As one of the organisers of the conference, Molotov paid her a courtesy visit. They fell in love and were 'married' within months, in de facto Bolshevik fashion. By all accounts, their mutual devotion was lifelong. Molotov treasured his pearl in memory as 'beautiful, intelligent, and a genuine Bolshevik'; he had always loved her, he said, 'with all his soul'.

The year after their marriage, Zhemchuzhina travelled to Czechoslovakia for further medical treatment, and Molotov made his first trip abroad to visit her, travelling on to Italy under a false name to observe 'the rise of Fascism'. ('Mysterious ailments' were a constant feature of Zhemchuzhina's life, Alliluyeva remembers, and when she became the 'first lady' of the Kremlin after the suicide of Stalin's wife in 1932, she would often visit spas in Berlin and Karlovy Vary with a huge retinue of attendants.) After studying economics, Zhemchuzhina became director of a perfume factory called New Dawn in 1930. The factory soon changed its name to the Essential Oils Trust, and was known affectionately as 'The Secret of Woman'. (At that time, Molotov was already head of the Council of People's Commissars [Sovnarkom], and was engaged in the more serious Party business of directing the industrialisation

of the First Five-Year Plan and the collectivisation of agriculture.)
Throughout the 1930s, when she and Molotov were sharing quarters in the Kremlin with Stalin, Zhemchuzhina worked in light
industry: in food and fisheries, cosmetics and perfumes, textiles,
haberdashery and fancy goods. During and immediately after the
Great Terror, her career advanced conspicuously. And after the
head of the secret police, Genrikh Yagoda, was arrested at a meeting of the Council of People's Commissars presided over by
Molotov in the spring of 1937 (he was a 'skunk . . . a filthy nobody . . . a reptile', he told Chuev), the Molotovs took over his fine
state dacha. In 1938 Zhemchuzhina launched a new toothpaste
called Sanit, advertised with a poster of the beautiful smiling face
of the female pilot Shura Kuvshinova. (In June of that year, just
before the poster appeared, the Moscow artist who had designed
it, Israel Bograd, was arrested and shot as an 'English spy'.) In
1939, the year Molotov replaced Litvinov as Commissar of Foreign
Affairs, Zhemchuzhina became Commissar of Fisheries and a
'candidate member' of the Central Committee.

Zhemchuzhina prided herself on being the best-dressed
woman in the Soviet Union; she studied techniques for the production of silks and synthetics, and organised permits for
European fashion houses to open branches in Moscow and
Leningrad. Defying the tradition of female Bolshevik puritanism
exemplified by Lenin's fiercely plain wife, Nadezhda Krupskaya,
Zhemchuzhina encouraged Soviet women to use cosmetics: nail
varnish, lipstick, powder and scent. She proudly invited foreign
diplomats, like US Ambassador Joseph Davies, to visit the cosmetics factories, perfumeries and beauty salons opened under her
auspices. Alliluyeva remembers that the Molotovs' apartment and
dacha 'were distinguished by good taste and luxurious furniture
(by Soviet standards, of course)'. Zhemchuzhina's visits to Paris,
Berlin and America when Molotov was Commissar of Foreign
Affairs made her forget her humble past and her revolutionary
ideals, Alliluyeva writes, and she hosted lavish diplomatic receptions at her dacha and in other official residences, delighting her

guests with elaborate cuisine, elegant tableware and bountiful arrangements of lilac and cyclamen (her favourite flower). She ran her family like an aristocrat, hiring the best tutors in languages, music and gymnastics for her daughter, who, like Stalin's, was named Svetlana. She even fostered the daughter of kitchen workers whom she had noticed one day in the Fourth House of the Soviets, and raised the little girl, whose name was Sonia, as Svetlana's sister in their Kremlin apartment. Sonia (known as 'Molotova' at school) remembers that when Molotov telephoned Zhemchuzhina in the Crimea on 22 June 1941 to tell her that Hitler's armies had invaded the USSR, her first reaction was to summon a hairdresser. Freshly coiffed and ready to leave for Moscow, she listened to Molotov's midday radio declaration of war. 'This unheard-of attack on our country is a perfidy unparalleled in the history of civilised nations . . .' Molotov told the people of the USSR, failing for a moment to overcome his habitual stammer, as Zhemchuzhina's manicurist worked on her nails.

How much interest did Molotov take in the acquisition or preservation of all the beautifications, knick-knacks and *objets d'art* that came to rest here, in the melancholy interior of his last Moscow home? Accounts of his feeling for material possessions vary greatly. Zhukovsky relates the Moscow rumour that when Molotov moved from his apartment in the Kremlin to a mansion on the scenic Lenin Hills, after Stalin's death (Khrushchev's new residences for Party bosses, built in 'Stalin Empire' style, were nicknamed 'Lenin's Testaments'), he demanded that his study be painted in the colours of a sunset. Alliluyeva remembers that these mansions had walls upholstered in silk, expensive wood panelling, marble mantels, massive pieces of state-owned furniture (and terrible plumbing). 'We all had our weaknesses', Molotov told Chuev, 'and acquired some of the ways of the gentry. We were seduced into that lifestyle, there is no denying that.' Yet Molotov looked down on the bon viveur and aesthete Voroshilov, whose homes were famously the most opulent and festive of all. And other members of the Party looked down on Molotov as a dreary killjoy, nicknaming him 'stone arse' because he spent so much time at his books. At his death, Molotov left only five hundred roubles to pay for his funeral; the housekeeper, Tatiana, who took care of him in his widowerhood at his last dacha in Zhukovka (which he had been granted in 1966 after much petitioning of the Party by Zhemchuzhina), claimed that his need for comfort was minimal, that he lived simply, as befitted a good communist, and never left lights on. Chuev describes his small attic study at the dacha: one window, a small desk with a volume of Chekhov and a couple of journals on it, and on the wall a political map of the world, under cellophane. 'He asked for nothing . . . he did not need or like luxury, he owned neither carpets or chandeliers,' remembered the woman who looked after the furniture storeroom in the dacha compound. After his death, she kept a reverent watch over his writing desk. Here in this vast Moscow apartment, an uncrumbled monument of the bourgeoisie, possessions seem to have closed around Molotov's communist virtue with a sneering, combative gleam: dead things, though not mute, like the death-lists that remain in the archives with his signature (and epithets in his hand like 'scum' and 'bastard') all over them: the material legacy of a life in power, of the consequences of theories he took from books and turned into the divining rod of virtue, and his own dogged work of survival.

⁓᪥⁓

One of the greatest privileges of political power under Stalin was the possession of a private library. Stalin's closest henchmen – Voroshilov, Molotov, Lazar Kaganovich, Anastas Mikoyan – 'had the same libraries as the one in father's apartment in the Kremlin', Svetlana Alliluyeva records. By regulation, publishers were obliged to send free copies of all newly published books to these men. After the purges of 1937 and 1938, she says, the most valuable books in these private libraries were the Soviet publications of the 1920s and 1930s, which had been completely withdrawn from public circulation. In these few collections alone, the 'works of authors who later had been arrested and perished still stood on the shelves'. There were 'Party publications reflecting struggles among its various factions and trends – Trotsky and Bukharin – publications that had vanished leaving no trace in public libraries'. After 1930, to own such books was to be guilty of a crime punishable by execution or the Gulag.

According to Alliluyeva, Voroshilov's library was utterly destroyed when his splendid three-storey dacha burned to the ground one day after the war (his grandson had been playing with matches under the New Year tree). 'The government decided to confiscate my father's library,' Alliluyeva says, 'disposing of it at its discretion.' As it turns out, Stalin's library was kept as part of his personal archive in the institution now known as RGASPI – the Russian State Archive of Social Political History on Bolshaya Dmitrovka Street, which had begun as David Ryazanov's Marx–Engels Institute. Stalin's library was recently opened to researchers, and revealed Stalin to have been a responsive reader, passionately engaged with the contents of his books on political theory (there were no other kinds of book in the library). He marked everything he read abundantly: underlining, annotating, arguing in the margins, exclaiming. 'Stop it, Koba, don't make a fool of yourself. Everyone knows that theory is not exactly your field,' Ryazanov had once said contemptuously to Stalin (whose Party nickname was 'Koba') at a Party meeting. For the rest of his life, Stalin, who hated Ryazanov for his bookish superiority, studied political theory late into the night, attacking his books with his pen, striving for mastery.

What happened to Molotov's precious library? Alliluyeva says that 'after being kicked out of the Politburo and the Kremlin', Kaganovich and Molotov were allowed to keep their libraries as personal property, and that they 'sold the most valuable and rare items, taking the rest with them . . . to their new modest dwellings'. Chuev continues the story. When Molotov and his 'anti-Party group' of Stalinists were defeated by Khrushchev at the Central

Committee Plenum in 1957, Molotov was driven out of his mansion on the Lenin Hills. He took almost nothing with him from there or from his dacha, Chuev records, leaving everything, 'including an enormous library, which was packed into fifty-seven large boxes and transported to the cellars of the Ministry of Foreign Affairs'. The cellars flooded and Molotov's books 'perished'.

Were the books that I found in No. 3, the home Molotov moved into after his disgrace, an especially treasured few, saved from the flood? The bookcases in the study looked as though they should contain multi-volume sets of Marx and Engels, Lenin and Stalin. The same kind of bookcase appears in a 1949 painting of Stalin, a Soviet icon – 'The Great Stalin is the Light of Communism!' – now sold, in postmodern spirit, as a curiosity in Moscow bookshops. The Generalissimo stands, pipe in hand, a sage expression in his eyes, staring into the middle distance (where the communist future, which only he can see properly beyond the frame, is laid out), a volume of Lenin open in his hand. In the glass-fronted bookcases behind Stalin, in descending order, are the works of Marx, Engels and Lenin. On the lower shelves are his own works, including the *History of the Communist Party* (rumoured to have been ghosted by Emilian Yaroslavsky). The painting, with its arrangement of bookcase, eyes, hand and pipe, captures all the aura of the nineteenth-century book, the whole paradox of Marxism–Leninism. For how can this ideology solve the problem at its own heart? If all thought is just a reflection of economic relations, how is it that these few men of books – prophets and carriers of light – can see through the illusion into the true mystery of the historical process?

Instead of these prophets, what I found in the shelves of the Molotov apartment was a rich and civilised eclectica of books to which a *nomenklatura* family would have had access by closed sub-scription in the later Soviet period, when good books were in deficit and the only affordable ones on general sale were the unreadable memoirs of Red Army generals and Party officials, and 'table books' of scientific atheism. Here, by contrast, were the

Russian classics – Pushkin, Nekrasov, Dostoevsky, Chekhov – in fine editions; a reprint of Vladimir Dal's classic *Dictionary of the Great Russian Language*; an 1877 edition of Guizot's *History of France as Told to My Grandchildren*, each of its five volumes hand-inscribed in Greek; a life of Edgar Allan Poe; a translation of Thomas Malory's *Morte d'Arthur*; a large volume in glossy colour on the work of the great medieval icon painter Andrei Rublev; a book on the émigré Ivan Bunin (Varlam Shalamov's sentence in the far northern Gulag was extended after a stool-pigeon overheard him praising Bunin's prose); the works of the 'foreign sympathisers' George Bernard Shaw and H. G. Wells; and an illustrated edition of Dante's *Divine Comedy*, translated, in his final illness, by Akhmatova's lifelong friend the scholar Mikhail Lozinsky, in which the pages of *Inferno* had been stuck together by damp.

Books like this were once a precious commodity, a black-market currency. Before trips to the USSR in the 1980s, my friends and I would visit a small white house in Pimlico in London. Its front room was filled with Russian Bibles published in the West, and Soviet editions of literary works, including the four nightingale poets, whose works the state publishers now grudgingly put out in small print runs to be exported for foreign currency. The bookstore, which gave out these books for free, wanted them smuggled back into Russia to play their subtle part in the winning of the Cold War. This cultivated undercover operation was funded, we supposed, by MI6 or the CIA. The woman who handed over the books (as many as we could carry) once pressed on me a Russian translation of *Brideshead Revisited* with the assurance that Evelyn Waugh ('Ivlin Vo'; she thought he was female) was extremely popular in the USSR.

'Let us talk of the physiology of reading,' Mandelstam wrote in *Journey to Armenia*. 'It is a rich, inexhaustible and, it would seem, forbidden theme. Out of the whole material world, of all physical bodies, a book is the one object that inspires man with the highest degree of confidence. When a book is firmly established on a reader's desk it is like a canvas stretched on a frame.' The wide leather-skinned desk standing among the bookshelves of this once most exalted of apparatchiks still had the aura of confidence in the Marxist ideology of the book, of the opening of books for the discovery of firm knowledge. I took down from the shelf the first volume ('A to Actualism') of the *Great Soviet Encyclopedia* and opened it on the desk.

'The date of publication and the format of books is the only exact knowledge there is,' Anatole France once remarked. The dates of publication of this edition of the encyclopedia were 1949–58, years full of event in Molotov's life: the arrest of Zhemchuzhina; Stalin's death; Zhemchuzhina's release from the Lubyanka by Beria on the day after Stalin's funeral (Molotov's birthday); Beria's execution; the testing on the Kazakh steppe of the Soviet H-bomb; Khrushchev's 'secret speech' to the XXth Party Congress denouncing the crimes of Stalin and the 'cult of personality'; Molotov's demotion to ambassador to Mongolia and expulsion from the Central Committee with his comrades in the Stalinist 'anti-Party group' which had opposed Khrushchev's leadership in the hope of reinstating the 'harsh unquestioning discipline' that they believed necessary for the triumph of communism. By the time the last volume of this encyclopedia appeared, history had conspired to disintegrate the claims to 'exact knowledge' that its entries embodied.

I read the entry on the medieval philosopher Abelard, savouring the poised and surely intended irony of these few sentences, written perhaps by some remnant of the *ancien régime* or secret Trotskyite at the height of the Stalin cult: 'Abelard's autobiographical work, *The History of My Misfortunes*, was widely known (Russian translation 1902), describing the cruel fanaticism of the Catholic Church and the merciless persecution of the smallest manifestation of free thought'. On the opposite page, under the entry for the Soviet republic of Adzharia in the Caucasus, was a picture of the young Stalin as a member of the revolutionary underground, posing, in 1902, with the workers of Batumi.

I looked up 'Molotov' in the 'M' volume, which came out the year after Stalin's death. The encyclopedia related that he was born in 1890 into the family of a shopkeeper and joined the Party in 1906. Then the prose began to swell and roll in waves of hypnotic totalitarian cliché: all Molotov's strength, knowledge and vast experience had been dedicated to the great aim of building communism in the Soviet Union; as faithful disciple and comrade-in-arms of the great Lenin and comrade-in-arms of Stalin, he had faithfully served the cause of the workers, the cause of communism, all his life long, earning through his fruitful work for the good of the socialist Motherland the ardent love and respect of the Party, the workers of the Soviet Union, strugglers for peace, democracy and socialism, and so on and on. I turned the page, and there were more Molotovs: cities, towns, villages, streets, river ports, theatres, libraries and schools, pharmaceutical and medical institutes, across the length and breadth of the mighty Soviet Union, to south, north and east across the vastest territory on the planet. Even as this volume was printed, these names were about to change again: the city of Perm in the pre-Urals which had been renamed to commemorate Molotov's fiftieth birthday in 1940; the industrial port Molotovsk, named for him in 1938, a creation of the war, where most of the Lend-Lease materiel was unloaded, at the mouth of the White Sea near Archangel; Nolinsk, his father's town, where there was a house museum dedicated to Molotov; four villages named Molotova in the Ferghana Valley; and the towns of Molotovobad in Kirghizia and Tajikistan, one of which lay on the river Isfaram on a branch of the Kokand–Andizhan line, on the road to Stalinobad. I carefully unfolded a pull-out map of the Molotovsk region; curled in one of the folds lay a grey hair.

I closed the encyclopedia, leaving the single hair in its paper mausoleum, relic of an old man's physiological need to read of the greatness his beloved Party had so abruptly confiscated. Next I took down the most dilapidated books on the shelves. As I touched the pages of Lemke's famed edition of the works of

Alexander Herzen, pieces of decaying paper, worn to tissue, came away from their edges onto my fingers. Many of the twenty volumes of this sought-after rarity were published during the period of 'war communism' after the Revolution, when market relations (and even, briefly, money) had been abolished and the state controlled every aspect of the economy. The introduction to the first volume likens the hunger for books among the people to their desperate hunger for food. Herzen, a bitter opponent of tsarist autocracy, was taken up and canonised by the Bolsheviks as a worthy forebear. In 1920, a commission charged with ideologically appropriate nomenclature for the main thoroughfares of Moscow renamed Bolshaya Nikitskaya (the wide street off which Romanov leads) Herzen Street. A note in the first volume of Lemke warns that anyone who tries to sell it for anything above the marked price will do so 'under terror of the law'.

Books have their fates, and here was one that heroically staged its own drama. This was what I had been hoping to find in here: ink markings. (Shalamov, who learned in the Gulag that a graphite pencil was a 'greater miracle than a diamond', associated ink with the evil powers of the state. 'What kind of ink is used to sign death sentences . . . ? No death sentence has ever been signed simply in pencil.') Dozens of entries in the index were marked in different-coloured ink. Here was the fierce hunger of the autodidact, who craves all knowledge, and wants no end to the feast. 'Emperor Augustus' was underlined in green ink; 'Agrippina', 'Addison', 'Bach', 'Balzac' and 'Beethoven' in faint lead pencil; the Decembrist 'Bestuzhev', 'Shelley', 'Shakespeare' and 'Count Sheremetev' in blue. Besides the index, only volume 13 contained any markings. This volume, which contained Herzen's *Past and Thoughts*, was published in 1921, the year the Civil War ended, when the national hunger for books was at its most acute. Shalamov remembers the arrival that year in his native Vologda of a single copy, one for the whole town, of the poetry of Nikolai Nekrasov, printed faintly on paper as fragile as gift-wrapping tissue.

Against a passage on page 15, the reader had drawn two long

parallel lines in purple ink that had bled deep into the porous browned paper. From a chapter titled 'Return to Moscow and Intellectual Debate', the passage was a long complaint by Herzen against Hegel, father of the idea that history has its own inner direction, its own secret cunning. Hegel was afraid of the light of day, writes Herzen; he 'confined himself within the sphere of abstractions' in order to avoid 'practical applications'. The only area in which Hegel dared to apply his theories in practice, Herzen complains, was in the realm of aesthetics. The philosopher came out into the light like an invalid, and even then, he left behind in the 'dialectic maze' all questions of most interest to modern man. His disciples were feeble, complacent and limited in outlook. Dialectics should have been about 'the development of reality itself', Herzen railed, but Hegel left it as nothing more than a system of logical gymnastics, like the philosophical pursuits of the Greek Sophists or the medieval scholastics. If these purple ink lines were made by Molotov, their point is clear. They register the fear of all those who face the prospect or the memory of years spent over books: the fear that their reading might be no more than a sterile game, an escape from life, leading nowhere, as thought dissolves to nothing with the passing of time. The purple lines mark the defiance of a bookish revolutionary in the face of that quiet terror. Dialectics, that magical art, was not to be kept in libraries, as a scholastic matter, applied only to the realm of art and beauty. Books and thoughts should change the world. The fulfilment of history itself is at stake in dialectical theory, though it may rely on pen, paper and print. Dialectics serve political action, revolution, 'necessary' bloodshed.

❧

As he describes the pleasures of book collecting in his beguiling short essay 'Unpacking My Library', Walter Benjamin quotes Hegel: 'it is only when it is dark that the owl of Minerva begins its flight', to which Benjamin adds that it is 'only in extinction that the collector can be comprehended'. In the intimate relationship of ownership, a person lives inside his possessions, makes of them a dwelling place for his spirit.

Aside from the Lemke Herzen, the books in the apartment that had clearly belonged to Molotov (rather than to his intellectually accomplished daughter, Svetlana, an academic historian, and her husband, Alexei Nikonov, also a historian as well as an agent of the secret police) had been pushed into the tomblike obscurity of the bottom shelves of one of those tall glass-fronted bookcases that can be found in so many Russian apartments, where books on the upper shelves are turned to display their faces like pictures. I knelt down, slid the wooden flap back into the bookcase along its metal runners, and pulled out handfuls of books, laying them in piles on the parquet around me, arranging and rearranging by date, author and subject matter, never finding an ordered system, overwhelmed by their number and the dust that soon filled the airless back corridor. Many of the books contained traces of intimate habitation. In the front page of one of the oldest of them, *The Tasks of Socialists in the Battle with Hunger in Russia* by Georgy Plekhanov, the 'father of Russian Marxism', published in St Petersburg in 1906, the year in which Molotov was officially said to have joined the Bolshevik Party (in fact, he probably joined in 1908 or 1909), was the name 'V. Skryabin'. The pages of the book on the battle with hunger were uncut, as were the pages in his many editions of Plekhanov, all edited by David Ryazanov, inscribed 'To Molotov'. 'I was raised on Plekhanov, not on Lenin,' Molotov told Chuev; 'it was with good reason that Lenin valued him so highly . . . and Stalin too, when he said that Hitler wanted to wipe out the country of Plekhanov and Lenin, and named Plekhanov first'.

Though many were in a state of extreme decay (particularly those published in the early 1920s before the revival of the market economy under the NEP), the books had clearly once been objects of careful preservation. All the signs suggested that Molotov had possessed these books as a true collector possesses: poring over

them, ordering them, living in them. The library had been cata-
logued, and later recatalogued, the numbers marked in purple ink
on the inside covers and middle pages – 5651, 5652, 7366 – and
many of the books had been rebound in cardboard dust-jackets
(also dark purple). If I followed the system correctly, his library
had once contained well over ten thousand books, of which a few
hundred were left here. As the uncut pages of his considerable
Plekhanov collection attest, Molotov must have had multiple
copies of many works. Besides, the non-reading of books, as
Benjamin said, is characteristic of collectors, who can become
invalids if they lose their books and, in order to acquire them, can
quite easily turn into criminals.

Chuev confirms that Molotov was a diligent reader, though a
slow one. He read a 'striking amount', he says, not only works of
political and economic theory, but also (unlike Stalin) imaginative
literature. He subscribed to periodicals, regularly visited Moscow's
main bookshop, 'House of the Book' on the Arbat, spent many
hours in the Lenin Library (where his own collected speeches had
been removed from the catalogue) and would always ask what he
should read next. He talked about poetry, including the early-
twentieth-century Symbolist poets Valery Bryusov and Alexander
Blok, and knew a great deal by heart, quoting Pushkin and
Pasternak's lyric verse. 'Everyone should read poetry,' Molotov
told Chuev. He tried hard to restrain his pleasure in verse, he said,
limiting the time he devoted to reading it, turning back to prose
because 'one does need to get hold of facts'.

Here were the treasures that Svetlana Alliluyeva remembered
from the libraries of her father's henchmen: the publications of the
1920s and 1930s, the works of men who had been arrested and
shot. Publications from the earliest years of Soviet rule gave a dim
image of a new regime in the process of being theorised into existence at urgent speed. From the 'war communism' of 1918 was a
book on 'tax entitlements of local Soviets' published by the
Commissariat of Internal Affairs in the new capital, Moscow, out-
lining 'extreme revolutionary taxation', and from 1919, a heavily

annotated book on *Syndicates and Trusts in Russia*. There were precious books from the NEP period with brilliant constructivist designs on their covers. The addresses of their publishers – Petrovka Street, Vozdvizhenka, Kuznetsky Lane – drew a map of Moscow in the early 1920s, the Moscow of the first post-revolutionary edition of *All Moscow*, its streets vibrant with small shops, 'trusts', and publishing houses employing the most inventive graphic designers in the world to create their books. There were textbooks and courses of lectures on the history of the revolutionary movement, works of legal theory – *Basic Questions of the Theory of the Soviet State* and *The Revolutionary Role of Law and the State*, published by the People's Commissariat of Justice; a course of *Political Literacy*, edited by Nikolai Bukharin, its binding gone, its pages tied together with string, and Bukharin's *Theory of Historical Materialism*, a popular textbook of Marxist sociology, published in 1923. A book of articles and lectures by Mikhail Frunze, entitled *On New Paths*, had been published in 1925, the year the Red Army commander died under the surgeon's knife. *Towards the Question of the Stabilisation of World Capitalism*, also published in 1925, had the names of three authors on the cover: Trotsky, Karl Radek and the economist Evgeny Varga. By 1947, when Molotov, as foreign minister, commissioned Varga to write him a report on America's Marshall Plan, the other two authors had been murdered: Radek by a common criminal in an Arctic labour camp, Trotsky in Mexico by an assassin sent by Stalin.

There were a few works of literature in lovely editions from the NEP years. In the cover of a 1923 edition of Joseph Conrad's novel *Within the Tides* (all pages cut), the publisher Frenkel advertised a list of popular works of literature and philosophy, including a new edition of Oswald Spengler's *Decline of the West*. There were two novels by Anatole France, one inscribed to Molotov, either by its translator, P. S. Neiman, or by its editor, B. V. Himmelfarb (the ink had faded almost to invisibility), published in 1925 by a small press called Contemporary Problems at No. 40 Sivtsev Vrazhek Lane. Among four editions of the stories of the popular Indian writer

Rabindranath Tagore was one with a placid blue Buddha on its cover. The graphomane Yaroslavsky's name appeared on the covers of dozens of books, few of which had their pages cut. As well as the tenth edition of 1938, Molotov possessed early NEP-era editions of Yaroslavsky's classic, *The Bible for Believers and Unbelievers* (first published in 1922 as a series of articles in the journal *Atheist*), which declared that the proletarian revolution had exposed the 'harmful role of the Bible' and the 'deception of religion', and that the peasants on Soviet collective farms were the true 'inheritors of the earth'. I leafed through the decayed pages of a seven-volume magnum opus entitled *Christ* by the revolutionary elder Nikolai Morozov. This veteran of tsarist prisons, cherished by the Bolshevik regime, had spent the later part of his life on a scientific refutation of the Christian story, based on 'astronomical' analysis of the Gospels and the Book of Revelation. According to Morozov, it could be demonstrated beyond any possible doubt that Christ had been nailed to the cross on 20 March AD 368, and survived. Morozov sent each large, magnificently illustrated volume to Molotov, tenderly inscribed: 'To dear Comrade Molotov, with heartfelt greetings . . . November 1925'; 'To deeply respected and dear Vyacheslav Mikhailovich Molotov, with all my heart . . . January 1933'. The first pages of the first volume were heavily marked in purple ink, with abundant marginal question marks beside passages on early Christian heresies and schisms. In the later volumes, the pages had not even been cut.

There were documents of recent history. *The End of Russian Tsarism: Memoirs of a Former Commander of the Gendarme Corps* (Petrograd, 1923), dense with pencil markings, had almost entirely deteriorated, but in the fold between pages 162 and 163 lay another single hair. Molotov also possessed two volumes of the fond and utterly mundane correspondence, conducted in English, of the last Tsar and his wife, Alexandra, from 1914 to 1917, as well as *Monarchy Before the Fall, 1914–1917: The Papers of Nicholas II*, and the letters exchanged between Tsar Nicholas II and his cousin Kaiser Wilhelm (who addressed the Tsar as 'Dearest Nicky') between 1894 and 1914. There was a report on the First International Communist Women's Conference of 1921 (all pages cut), a personal memento perhaps of the event that brought Polina Zhemchuzhina to Moscow from the south, with an introduction by the free-love advocate Alexandra Kollontai (who once described Molotov as the 'embodiment of greyness and servility').

With a soft pencil, Molotov had restored the titles on a set of proceedings of the Xth Party Congress of 1921, its fragility a testimony in itself to the need for the Party to restore the market economy by introducing the NEP. The majority of the men whose names appeared on the books' covers were killed in the 1930s: Trotsky, Bukharin, Preobrazhensky, Serebryakov, Sokolnikov, Georgy Pyatakov, Mikhail Tomsky, Grigory Zinoviev, Kamenev, Yan Rudzutak. Rudzutak, the Latvian Party member who had once been Molotov's deputy, was the highest member of the Party (and a candidate member of the Politburo) to be arrested when he was taken to the Lubyanka in 1937. It marked a new stage of the Great Terror; now no one was safe. Rudzutak had been a close associate of Molotov's, his assistant in the Council of People's Commissars and an ally in the struggle against the 'Trotskyites'. He had written the introduction to the 1927 one-volume edition of the discussions of the Xth Party Congress that I held in my hands, saying that the reason for reopening the debate was to show the inadequacy of Trotsky's theoretical positions and his political differences with Lenin. Molotov was coolly intrigued by the courage Rudzutak showed under torture, by the fact that he never confessed. Hitherto, he had been known for his laziness. 'I personally knew him well,' he remembered; 'a very nice fellow . . . by the end of his life, however, I got the impression that he was too interested in feathering his own nest . . .' Echoing Trotsky's appeals to Bolshevik virtue, Molotov says that Rudzutak was 'no longer waging the struggle as a true revolutionary', that he was too mixed up with women. He remembered visiting the Lubyanka with some other Politburo members and hearing Rudzutak's allegations of torture: 'he seems to have been cruelly tortured', Molotov remarked, 'but one must not act just on personal impressions'.

There were inscriptions to Molotov in the front pages of many of the books: 'to dear Comrade Molotov'; 'to dear Vyacheslav Molotov'; 'to much respected Comrade Molotov'; 'to Vyacheslav Mikhailovich, with all my heart . . .'; 'to the closest colleague of the Great Stalin, Vyacheslav Mikhailovich Molotov, as a sign of sincere love and deep respect from the author, F. Konstantinov'; '*to Dear Vyacheslav*, to the most brilliant comrade-in-arms of dear Ilyich from a grateful disciple – your brother, Victor German'; 'to the Great Molotov with expressions of hope and Party credentials, A. K. Azizyan (CP member since 1917)'. Azizyan's book was sent with a letter, signed 'with communist wishes', dated December 1927, the month in which Molotov delivered a report on the collectivisation of agriculture at the XVth Party Congress. Azizyan, who describes himself as a 'mouthpiece for the farmer' at the Congress, makes some anxious corrections of minor slips, and worries about whether the copies of his book have arrived in Moscow in time to be of use. There were a number of books on farming and the peasantry dating from the late 1920s, when fierce debates in the Party about the pace of the collectivisation of agriculture were under way. One of these, A. Bolshakov's *The Countryside: 1917–1927*, with a preface by the Bolshevik Mikhail Kalinin and an introduction by the great orientalist S. F. Oldenburg (whose name I knew well from past research on quite unrelated themes), had a slip of foolscap tucked inside the cover bearing the words, 'Respected Comrade Molotov! Knowing your deep interest in questions relating to the contemporary countryside, I beg you to accept my book, with comradely greetings, A. Bolshakov, April 1927, Moscow, 1st House of the Soviets, Room 402'.

'I myself come from a village, but I didn't know rural life well,' Molotov said much later of that time of lethal struggle in the Soviet countryside. After the XVth Party Congress, Molotov was sent to visit villages in the Ukraine. He spent the nights on a special train, guarded by the OGPU. 'I applied the utmost pressure to extort grain,' he remembered, 'all kinds of rather harsh methods.'

In the campaign of forced collectivisation and the 'liquidation of the kulaks [richer peasants]' which led to many millions of deportations and deaths, Molotov played as zealous a role as anyone in the upper reaches of the Party. A book in his library published in 1928, entitled *The Collective Farm Movement: its Past, Present Tasks and Significance*, had been inscribed by its author in red ink in a very shaky hand, 'Vyacheslav Mikhailovich! I will be very grateful if you will read this . . . and set down your opinion of it. A. Mitrofanov, 17/vi/28'. Eighty out of its 132 pages have been cut. In the summer of 1928, Moisei Frumkin, Deputy Commissar for Finance, wrote a letter of protest to the Politburo, in which he attacked Molotov's extreme hostility towards the kulaks. (Another Jewish Bolshevik from the Russian south, Frumkin had moved into apartment 73 in this house in 1922. He liked to amuse Lenin with politically apposite Jewish jokes.) 'The countryside, with the exception of a small section of the poor peasants, is against us,' Frumkin warned the Central Committee. 'I do recall a man by the name of Frumkin,' Molotov told Chuev more than four decades later, 'a very straightforward man. I knew him well. A man of integrity who confronted the Central Committee openly . . .' 'What became of him?' Chuev asked. 'He too got mixed up with right-wingers, I think,' Molotov replied, suddenly vague on details. (Frumkin was arrested in October 1937 and shot in 1938.) Another work in Molotov's collection, personally dedicated by Azizyan (only 9 of its 204 pages have been cut), on *Rent Relations in the Soviet Countryside*, had been edited by Yakov Yakovlev, then chairman of the All-Union Collective Farm Council, who accompanied Molotov to Tambov in January 1928 to urge more extreme grain requisitioning and more merciless repression of kulaks. When Molotov was appointed head of the Council of People's Commissars in 1930, the ardent collectiviser Yakovlev was his Commissar of Agriculture. By the end of the decade Yakovlev had been implicated in the elaborately fabricated case against Bukharin. He was shot in March 1939.

'The soul of the collector is intelligible only by having regard to his conception of Time,' Spengler wrote. Molotov revealed the true collector's woe, long after the fact, at the loss of part of his collection, even, or perhaps especially, when the cause of that loss had been his own generosity. Remembering how the bourgeois city of Moscow had resisted the Bolshevik Revolution in 1917, how extremely slowly the 'uprising' had proceeded, Molotov's mind turned to a man called Alexander Arosev, 'a very close friend of mine'. Molotov had met Arosev (a member of the recently founded Socialist Revolutionary Party) in 1905 in Kazan, where his parents had sent him from his native north to attend a technical school, a *realschule*. Molotov (then still called Skryabin) had just begun to take an interest in radical politics after the Russian defeat in the Russo-Japanese War and the strikes and insurrections of 1905. He and Arosev shared a sentence of exile in the Vologda region from 1909 to 1911. Arosev 'became an author', Molotov remembered. They remained friends until the late 1930s, spending leisure time together with their families. Just before his arrest in the summer of 1937, Arosev telephoned Molotov. Hearing his voice on the line, Molotov twice put down the receiver. Arosev called a third time, and told Molotov he could hear him breathing. After several more calls, Molotov uttered just two words, communicating to Arosev that he would help his children. 'I kept some of his books with his autograph,' Molotov mused. 'Some time ago at a jubilee party in his honour, I was foolish enough to give all these books to his eldest daughter ...' It appears that it was not so much the loss of his 'very close friend' to the purges, but the loss of part of his own book collection, after Arosev's rehabilitation in 1955, to a 'foolish' emotional impulse that Molotov continued to regret.

'We will kill every enemy,' Stalin had promised in a toast in November 1937; 'if he is an Old Bolshevik, we will destroy his relatives, his family. We will destroy anyone who with his deeds or *thoughts* strikes a blow against the unity of the Soviet state.' Of the small group of men who signed almost four hundred execution lists during the Great Terror, which lasted, at its peak, from the summer of 1937 with Politburo Order no. 00447 against 'anti-Soviet elements' until the early winter of 1938, Molotov signed the greatest number: 373 (eleven more lists than Stalin himself signed), bearing the names of 43,569 people. On one day in December 1937, Molotov, Stalin and Andrei Zhdanov signed away 2,274 lives. It was Molotov who had suggested sentencing by list. On some lists, he personally changed verdicts from imprisonment to death, but he made a habit of underlining numbers, not names.

Whenever Molotov spoke about the purges of his comrades in the Party in later life, he revealed an indifference to facts quite out of keeping with his punctilio when it came to numbering and renumbering the library catalogue that I was putting together in fragments on the floor of his apartment. 'I'm not interested in who said what and where, who spat on whom . . .', he retorted when asked why he did not write a memoir. 'Was he repressed . . . ?' he replied when asked about another Bolshevik he had once known well. 'I don't remember. Who cares? . . . You can't remember everything.' Stalin's men cultivated this kind of rejection of memory, of the concrete reality of the past.

David Ryazanov, many of whose publications of the 1920s were in Molotov's collection, was exiled to Saratov, he did not know when: 'he was knowledgeable and well-read. But, as Lenin used to say about him, "This man is a topsy-turvy library." Everything was mixed up in his head, everything was a muddle . . . What use could he be?' Someone must have told Molotov how Ryazanov (who had looked with such scorn on Stalin's clumsy attempts to use the language of Marxist theory) had turned to bitter mockery at the end of his life. 'I would like to see how socialism is going to be built in a single town, in a single apartment,' Ryazanov would say. 'What use could he be?' Ryazanov was arrested in 1937 and shot in 1938.

Elsewhere Molotov reveals the obsessional book collector's indifference to the ownership rights of others, casually admitting that he secured permission to remove from the Lenin Library a large collection of thin booklets, works by Marshal Tukhachevsky, many of which he then kept. Benjamin characterises the obsessive bibliophile of real stature as one for whom 'the borrowing of a book with its attendant non-returning' is the mode of acquisition most appropriate, and who will guard his treasures, turning a 'deaf ear to all reminders from the everyday world of legality'. Molotov took out the books by Tukhachevsky because he disapproved of Khrushchev's rehabilitation of the brilliant and charismatic General, who had been tried for Trotskyite conspiracy in proceedings led by Marshal Budyonny and summarily shot along with the elite of the Red Army in the summer of 1937. It was a tacit directive from Molotov – speaking of the need to root out 'wreckers' in the army – that had led to the arrest of Tukhachevsky and other senior officers. Like anyone else, Molotov found it very hard to keep track of all his purged comrades – so many stories to remember – but he did recall that Beloborodov had been tortured for many months for information about Tukhachevsky. The orders to torture came from the highest levels of the state; though he denied it to the end of his life, Molotov had counter-signed a decree approving torture in 1937. Nikolai Yezhov, head of the NKVD (as the secret police was renamed in 1934), had sent to Stalin the 'unsatisfactory' confession of Beloborodov, who had once been head of the Russian NKVD, and Stalin ordered torture to get a 'real confession' out of him. 'There is a story that he was dragged down a prison corridor, screaming, "I am Beloborodov. Pass the word to the Central Committee that I am being tortured."' Three decades after all this, Molotov looked through Tukhachevsky's writings, which he had not read before, for evidence of guilt, and because, as he remarked, 'the works of a genius are always exciting to look through'. He was hoping to enjoy the books even as he hoped that the man who wrote them would stay firmly condemned as an 'enemy of the people'. To his regret, he found 'nothing revealing' or even exciting, noting with a hint of cynical disdain that the 'booklets' were full of eulogies to Party leaders, the usual promises that the Germans would be smashed, and long italicised quotations from Stalin, Voroshilov and himself. For Molotov, the brilliant Tukhachevsky's 'conspiracy' was no more than a possibility that had to be pre-empted with a bullet. 'Tukhachevsky did not know where he was going,' Molotov convinced himself. 'It seems to me that he would have veered to the right . . . 1937 was necessary'.

A weary impatience with the unknowability of other people is sometimes a characteristic of the bibliophile, who loves with fervour publication dates and catalogue numbers, all the categories of exact knowledge that a book can be made to represent. Just such a weariness emerges when Molotov allows himself to speak of all the killing that history had seemed to demand of him and his comrades, the difficulty of maintaining the 'harsh unquestioning discipline' that dictatorship requires. 'Who is to maintain it?' he asked, expressing what appears to be rare and genuine bewilderment. 'People do not always want it, down deep, oppose it . . . we do not have ready-made pure people, purged of all sins . . .'

Only one book in the remains of Molotov's library, the text of his own speech to the Supreme Soviet after his diplomatic mission to London in the summer of 1942 on the ratification of the Anglo-Soviet agreement to ally against Hitler (catalogue number 11531), had been inscribed by Molotov himself, in fine hand, in faded blue ink: 'To Polinochka, Your Vyacheslav'. From a man whose first vocation was to history, this must have been a particularly significant conjugal token.

In some books, traces of domestic life were still more intimate and cryptic: a scrap of paper with a fir tree, with boxed gifts under it (it was Molotov's idea to bring back the banned tradition of the fir tree – to celebrate New Year's rather than Christmas), and the words 'C-R-I-S-I-S O-F F-A-S-C-I-S-M' blocked out in squares like a solution in a crossword puzzle; a torn-off bookmark bearing the single word 'borscht' (in later life, Zhemchuzhina always chopped garlic into the beetroot soup, the way Stalin had liked it); and pencilled on the back page of his comrade Vyshinsky's 1952 speech to the UN General Assembly on how to avert the threat of a thermonuclear world war, the words, 'door handles, shelf with mirror, pegs for the bathroom'.

꙰

After my first hours with Molotov's books, I went into the street, to take a little of what passes for air in this city. A cheery cleaning lady named Lena had broken in on my solitude in the late morning. She wanted to vacuum the parquet in the corridor, the bookdust-soultrace from which Fyodorov would have hoped to resurrect the dead, so I put the books carefully back in their shelves. I stood at the corner of Romanov and Vozdvizhenka, outside the Corner House, and looked up at the windows of the study in the Molotov apartment, my throat full of dust, my head full of catalogue numbers marked in purple ink above the names of men who had begged Molotov for their lives. Cars surged up around the Kremlin wall from the Stone Bridge, powerful German cars built for the dramatic acceleration that this turn in the rising road invites.

I looked across at the Lenin Library. It is said that a large fragment of the skull of Adolf Hitler, carried back to Moscow from the Führer's bunker in Berlin in 1945, is still hidden somewhere inside. In May 1939, Stalin, who had been preparing him for the role for two years, appointed Molotov Commissar of Foreign Affairs, replacing the cosmopolitan Jew Litvinov. Litvinov learned of his dismissal when NKVD troops surrounded his office at No. 24 Kuznetsky Most, and Beria, Malenkov and Molotov arrived together to take over. Following Stalin's orders, Molotov's first move was to purge the commissariat of the many sophisticated Jews, practised at diplomacy and good at languages, who worked there, and replace them with monoglot Russians who knew nothing of the diplomatic arts and had never dealt with foreigners. In his fruitless negotiations with the Triple Alliance, Molotov received the ambassadors of Britain and France seated at a vast desk on a dais, his interlocutors far below him, balancing their papers on their knees. By the end of August, Molotov and his German counterpart Ribbentrop had signed (in Stalin's presence) a non-aggression pact. The pact between Nazi Germany and the USSR contained a 'secret protocol' (whose existence Molotov denied to the end of his life), demarcating 'spheres of influence' for the two powers over the Baltic states and Poland. In September, the USSR invaded Poland, and, the following March, Molotov (with the rest of the Politburo) approved a request from Beria to execute the entire Polish officer corps – approximately 22,000 men – in the Katyn forest.

Later that year, Molotov dined with Hitler in Berlin. Well, 'the state is not pure spirit'. Toasting Hitler? 'That's diplomacy,' said Molotov. Hitler proposed to Molotov that they 'divide the whole world'. He ranted about England ('some miserable island, owns half the world and wants to grab it all . . . it's unjust!'), and took no meat or coffee or alcohol. 'It seemed to me a rabbit was sitting next to me eating grass', Molotov remarked; 'an idealistic man'. He formed his own opinion of what was going on inside the skull that would within a few years end up inside a box in the great library across the street. Like Napoleon, Hitler had dreamed of destroying Moscow and entering its ruins as conqueror. 'Movies and books portray him as a madman, a maniac, but that's not true,' Molotov reflected; 'he was very clever, though narrow-minded and obtuse at the same time because of his egotism and the absurdity of his primordial idea.'

THREE

The Banya

With light steam!

It was in a spirit of dedicated scholarship that, in my first years in Moscow, I would end my Fridays among the odalisques at the Sandunovskaya Bathhouse. In the scented dark, the accumulated book-grime of a week's research in the library of the Institute of Oriental Studies steamed gratefully from the pores. And after all, since the time of Muscovy, English travellers have relished uncovering in the recondite rituals of the Russian bathhouse a cultural gravitation towards the sensual, unhistorical and easeful East of Western imagination. In time, my purposes in that library faded. My research into Russian orientalism had taken me into a mirrored hall with infinite regressions leading in every direction. I was no longer borne up on what Mandelstam called the 'ambassadorial winds of Persian poetry'. I let go of my dream of reading the ghazals of Hafiz in the original like some nineteenth-century scholar-traveller, but my bathing habits lingered on.

It was likewise a kind of scholarly *déformation professionelle* that led me to peep, one Friday evening, at the jacket of the thick red book that the beauty opposite me was reading as she reclined between steamings on a leather divan, legs waving languidly in the air, in nothing but a pair of plastic beach slippers and a turban. She had a Barbie-doll figure, a sunbed tan and a butterfly tattooed on one hip. She was reading Oswald Spengler's *The Decline of the West*. And why not? The dust-jacket on the hardback edition of the same work that I had recently bought from a makeshift bookstand in the Kuznetsky Most metro station did advertise its appeal to a wide circle of readers.

While Europe immolated herself in the First World War, Spengler, the autodidact son of a postal worker, laboured at his writing with a burning sense of destiny in a cramped apartment in Munich. As the survivors returned and Russia collapsed into revolution, his work of historiographical prophecy, *The Decline of the West*, captured the zeitgeist and a wide readership. In Russia, the book was received with public enthusiasm and scholarly solemnity, and immediately translated as *The Sunset of Europe*. Spengler's vision of Russia was drawn from Dostoevsky and a poetic apprehension of the role of the steppe in the formation of the Russian soul. His 'morphology of history', which hinged on a distinction between organic, religious 'culture' and mechanical, international 'civilisation', gave Russian messianism a shining new edge. The decline of the West is an inevitable part of its organic historical lifecycle. The primitive soul of Old Russia was never capable of adapting to Western civilisation with its individualistic notions of justice and personal fulfilment, its materialistic world cities. Russian love grows out of the boundless plain; it is the mystical love of brothers 'under equal pressure all along the earth', self-oblivious, sharing in collective guilt and redemption. Capitalism and parliamentarism are alien to the national organism: 'the primitive tsarism of Moscow is the only form which is even today appropriate to the Russian world'. From Russia, European culture demands only the reverence due to the beloved dead. The next thousand years will belong to Dostoevsky's Christianity, Spengler promised.

Early in my time here, in a fever of acquisitiveness, I purchased in cheap popular editions the works of many prominent Russian cultural thinkers of the late nineteenth and early twentieth centuries, who, like the 'reactionary and Nietzschean' Spengler (as he was labelled in Soviet times), went unpublished for seventy years. In Russian intellectual life, a conversation that was cut off and redirected after the Bolshevik Revolution had resumed its course. Its theme: East, West, whence and whither Russia?

Spengler was promptly dropped on the divan when a large woman, naked and shining, swung open the door from the wash-

ing room and shouted, 'Steam, girls! Under the steam, my beauties!' Women rose from all corners of the opulent changing room,
winding linen sheets around themselves, tucking damp strands of
hair into felt cloche hats, as they followed one another through
the swing door. At the far end of the washing room, the *parilshchitsa*, who wore a felt hat modelled on the *budyonnovka*, the Red
Cavalry hat, held open a low wooden door, ushering everyone into
the steam room. A skinny child in flip-flops, tipping her head
back to see out from under her hat, moved forward with the rest
and was told sharply by her mother to sit down on the marble slab
outside among the tubs of soaking birch twigs, and come in after
the steam had dropped. 'What a brave little girl!' an elderly
woman exclaimed. 'Teach them to steam when they're little.' The
young woman in the turban was already lying, fully wrapped in
her sheet, on the floor of the raised wooden platform, as the other
women climbed the steps, chattering and sighing, bending double
under the pressure of the heat. One by one, they arranged themselves on the floor, drawing the linen sheets over their heads.

'Ready, beauties?' the *parilshchitsa* asked, closing the door of the
hot room and making the sign of the cross. 'It's going to be strong
steam.' From under the sheets came murmurs of assent. The iron
hatch squeaked heavily as she levered open the stove. 'God be with
you,' she said, and the next sound was the slap of cool water hit-
ting the incandescent stones, exploding into a hiss of steam. As
ladlefuls of water flew at the stones in steady rhythm, the heat
thickened. 'Is it moving yet?' someone asked. 'Oh, wonderful, it
smells of kvass!' 'Enough, girls?' the *parilshchitsa* called. 'No, still
too little,' came a general reply. 'It's ready to drop, girls,' the *parilshchitsa* finally announced, pushing shut the aperture; 'it's kind
steam, good steam.' '*Oi oi*, so good, so good, thank you, and the
Lord have mercy on you,' murmured the elderly woman, uncovering her veiny legs, as the blanket of steam that had risen
to the vaulted plaster ceiling descended through the shrouded
bodies laid side by side along the wooden boards. 'So that you will
be soft and real, my beauties, and never unkind . . .', replied the

parilshchitsa, flicking a last ladleful on to the ceiling. 'My next steam will be gentle steam!'

⋘⋙

'The transparent steam gathers above them', Pushkin rhapsodised in a piquant scene in his long poem *Ruslan and Lyudmila*. A young khan is attended by enchanting maidens – gentle, silent, half-naked – who disarm him of his dusty shield, helmet, sword and spurs, and lead him to a 'marvellous Russian banya'. They lay him on luxurious carpets among cool fountains; one soothes his tired limbs with rose essence, another scents his dark curls and a third waves over him branches of young birch, burning with hot fragrance. The khan quite forgets his quest for the Russian princess Lyudmila.

Composed before Pushkin first travelled to the exotic south, the light iambics of *Ruslan and Lyudmila* overlay the reality of the Russian banya with a lavish fantasy of oriental rest and pleasure. The poet visited the newly luxurious Sanduny with his friends whenever he came to Moscow, though according to the oral lore of the Sanduny his visits were more about male drinking feats than soft maidens and essence of rose. In those days, Catherine the Great's protegée Elizaveta Sandunova, whose diamonds had paid for the building of the bathhouse, was still alive. The Sanduny was a place for glamorous literary Moscow to congregate. The society that gathered at the English Club and Zinaida Volkonskaya's salon on Tverskaya would come to be steamed and scrubbed by the practised *banshchiki*, to relax on clean sheets spread over the soft divans in its palatial mirrored changing rooms, and refresh themselves on vodka, kvass or chilled Moët. There was even a fashion then for dousing the hot stones with champagne. Pushkin, who lived for a time in a 'pretty filthy two-roomed apartment' in the Hotel Europe on Tverskaya, where he spent the days in a 'silvery Tartar dressing-gown with a bare chest, without the slightest of comforts around him', 'loved a good hot steam', the centenarian actor Ivan Grigorovsky told Gilyarovsky decades later. Like many Moscow theatre people, Grigorovsky came regularly to the Sanduny. Never without his hip-flask of vodka, he was taught to drink by the 'hussar-poet' Denis Davydov, who limped out of the steam room one day, settled on a divan opposite the actor and in characteristically heroic style downed a mix of arak and whortleberry vodka, while reciting verses by his friend Pushkin on the joys of alcohol.

❧

When the steam had softened, women shook off their damp coverings and moved into new poses, cross-legged on the floor, crouching with arms wrapped around themselves, or full length on the higher benches, stretching, and gently scratching their limbs. A few made their way out of the steam room, muttering and exhaling heavily, as the little girl appeared at the bottom of the steps. After the dim hush of the steam room, the high-ceilinged washing room was full of white light, unrestrained chatter and the sound of free-flowing showers. Women scooped basins of icy water from a marble bathtub and poured it over themselves, climbed gasping in and out of a barrel, or pulled a chain to release a sudden gush from a wooden cask suspended high on the wall. Half visible behind a plastic curtain, an attendant leaned over a marble slab, scrubbing an outstretched figure with a foamy loofah. My changing-room neighbour was daubing her limbs with gritty brown paste. Among the battery of French cosmetics on the slab before her were a carton of cream and a jar of fresh coffee grounds from which she had contrived her pungent scrub.

What would Spengler have made of her? What would her washing rituals represent in his great scheme? Since the time of Peter the Great, according to Spengler, the primitive Russian soul had been forced, like molten volcanic matter, into the alien moulds of the baroque, the Enlightenment and the urban culture of the nineteenth century. Russian cities are of 'alien type', like ulcers on the 'townless' land, 'false, unnatural, unconvincing'. 'Moscow had no proper soul,' he wrote. The city that grew up around the Kremlin, ringing the ancient fortress, was an 'imitation city': 'the spirit of the upper classes was Western, and the lower had brought in with them the soul of the countryside. Between the worlds there was no reciprocal comprehension, no communication, no charity.'

Spengler had not been to the Sanduny. Here, the primitive practices of townless ancient Russia survive within the elaborate stone structures of the nineteenth-century city. Throughout the history of this bathhouse, the city's Europeanised upper classes have communicated, in intimate reciprocal touch, perhaps even in charity, with the Russian countryside. The practice of steam bathing grew out of the landscape itself, the rivers and woods, fire and snow. In pagan Slavic myths, gods drew magic power from baths of steam. Steam scented with fragrant grasses was believed to banish the evil spirits that bring disease. The eleventh-century Spanish-Arab geographer Abu Ubayd Abd Allah al-Bakri described the stone stove in a house of wood on to which the ancient 'Rusichi' poured water, agitating the air with switches of dry branches to draw it towards their bodies. The *Primary Chronicle* of Nestor, written in the early twelfth century, relates how the Apostle Andrew (according to Orthodox tradition, the 'first-called' disciple came this far from Jerusalem in the first century) observed the ancient Slavs lighting wooden banyas, throwing kvass on the fire, whipping themselves with branches of young birch until they wept, before reviving themselves with freezing water, calling it 'washing', not 'torture'.

Across the social classes, every important event in Russian life was preceded by a visit to the banya. Primitive country banyas were called 'black banyas'; sometimes peasants would fling water on to the stoves in their huts to turn them into steam baths. Princes and boyars traditionally washed on Saturdays to prepare for the sabbath. Royal banyas were fitted with smooth planks of lime, an unscented softwood that does not splinter. A boyar could prove himself by enduring the extreme heat on the top shelf of the banya, for which he might gain the privilege of beating the prince with birch twigs. In the sixteenth and seventeenth centuries, foreign diplomats and travellers observed, and sometimes adopted, the bathing practices of their hosts. An English envoy at Vologda remarked that, in this land of long winters and no doctors, the steam bath was the only means of preventing illness. In 1720, Peter the Great issued an *ukaz* authorising the building of banyas for all ranks in society. In his 'artificial' city of St Petersburg, public baths were free of tax if built in stone (Spengler's emblem of the timeless become space). The Tsar, who had taken the waters at Baden-Baden and Karlsbad, considered a policy of banya-building sufficient for improving the nation's health. 'No, no, for Russia banyas are enough,' he responded when asked to increase the number of doctors serving the common people.

By the middle of the eighteenth century, the immemorial practice of steam bathing had metamorphosed into an established urban custom. The spread of public banyas provoked concern in the senate about standards of public morality. Under Tsarina Elizabeth, mixed bathing was forbidden. The widely ignored edict was reinforced four decades later under Catherine the Great, in a detailed decree which specified, to general dissatisfaction, that women should bathe in the mornings and men in the evenings.

It was a Portuguese Jewish doctor, educated in six European cities, who transformed the scarcely recorded folk rituals of the Russian steam bath into a subject of Enlightenment medical science. 'In the concluding days of my life, dedicated to the service of the Russian Empire,' António Nunes Ribeiro Sanches wrote in his treatise on the banya, 'I cannot, it seems, do anything that would be of greater use to others, than to demonstrate the properties of the baths used by its inhabitants since the times of deep antiquity.' Sanches had studied at Leiden under the Dutch humanist and physician Herman Boerhaave (who had briefly tutored Peter the Great in Holland in 1715). In search of qualified doctors, the Russian government turned to Boerhaave, who recommended Sanches. He entered state service in 1731 as 'physicus' to the medical chancellery. Sanches was soon working for the military, accompanying the army on campaigns. He took note of the Turkish baths in the southern city of Azov, when Russian troops entered the city in 1736. His reputation grew, and he moved to St Petersburg, where he attended the imperial family. At the age of forty-eight, Sanches was afflicted with an eye disease, and left Russia with a court pension and honorary membership in the Imperial Academy of Sciences. He settled in Paris to a life of study. A year later, he was summarily stripped of both his Academy membership and his pension. His friend Count Kirill Razumovsky, head of the Academy (and father of the Razumovsky count who sold the Corner House to Count Nikolai Sheremetev), explained in embarrassment that this sudden disgrace was because the conscience of Tsarina Elizabeth would not allow her to tolerate in her Academy anyone who lived 'under the banner of Moses and the Old Testament prophets'. Sanches continued to devote himself to scholarship, treating the poor out of charity, kept from destitution by quiet donations from Russian aristocrats in Paris. The only work he published in these years was an influential study on the origins and treatment of syphilis. Aside from dozens of unpublished manuscripts on medical themes, he left a treatise entitled 'The Origin of the Persecution of the Jews'. Catherine the Great (whom he had cured of a life-threatening illness when she was fifteen) restored Sanches's pension, but not his membership of the Academy. He never returned to Russia.

Sanches's book, *About Russian Banyas*, is a work of wounded love. Published in Paris in 1774, and soon translated into many European languages, including Russian, it lauds the customs of the empire that had rejected him as alien. Catherine read the book and handed it round her court, which shared a sense of pride in his insistence that a Russian peasant custom should become an exalted feature of European civilisation. Far from Russia, the doctor's one consolation, he wrote, was to visit the banya in his thoughts, to reflect scientifically on its virtues. In the steam, Sanches was sure he had discovered a secret of alchemical power that would dispense with the need for three-quarters of the medicines known to science, and most of the concoctions of apothecaries. According to Sanches, the unique power of the Russian banya lies in the constant renewal of steam. When water is thrown into the stove, the elements of fire and earth in it are liberated. The naked body, stretched full length, is touched, penetrated, nourished; the skin relaxes, vital juices multiply and circulate, unwholesome vapours are expelled, blood and breath flow freely. The bather begins to sweat, experiencing the most pleasant relaxation in all his limbs and organs, and inclines towards the sweetest possible sleep. The banya alleviates every ailment – from eye infections, digestive and menstrual disorders, to rabies, smallpox and venereal disease (which Sanches believed to be the most widespread health problem in the Russian empire). Fresh steam can even alleviate insomnia, anger at the loss of property, depression and aggrieved honour; the body is calmed, order restored, bad thoughts driven away. Birch twigs, honey, vinegar and kvass are essential to the curative rituals of the banya. The great classical and renaissance physicians, Hippocrates, Galen and Paracelsus, understood the strengthening and healing powers of steam, but since the rise of the power of Christian bishops determined to abolish pagan practices, Sanches writes in a firm spirit of Enlightenment anti-clericalism, bathing has died out in Europe. Only in Russia, where the climate is hard, doctors are few and pagan practices survive intact, is the custom alive in its most beneficial form. As the power of the imperial state depends on the vigour of the population, Sanches suggests that the establishment and maintenance of clean and affordable banyas in every town and village should be one of the responsibilities of the police.

Amid the eclectic luxury of the Sanduny, the practices that Sanches described are still dogmatically observed. After the 'second steam' women emerged gleaming into the washing room, grey leaves clinging to their heat-mottled skin, rustling birch switches now limp and bruised. 'Your health, girls,' the *parilshchitsa* said as the last woman left the sanctum of the steam room. In the changing room, the radio quietly played Italian pop. The masseuse and the hairdresser smoked Vogue cigarettes in the mirrored anteroom. Attendants in slippers brought glasses of beer, bowls of shrimps, dumplings in broth, green tea and honey. My neighbour had inclined to that sweet sleep that Sanches remembered so fondly, lying on the divan, ankles neatly crossed, Spengler serving as her pillow.

'Intelligence is the replacement of unconscious living by the exercise of thought, masterly, but bloodless and jejune,' Spengler wrote in a visionary chapter on 'Cities and People'. The city means eye and intellect, money, tension and causality; the countryside means blood and instinct, mother-wit, cosmic pulsation and destiny. History, to Spengler, is the history of the town, which grows and declines organically, moving in a majestic evolutionary arc from primitive barter-centre to 'Culture-city' and at last to world-city, 'and so, doomed . . . on to final self-destruction'. The giant towns of civilisation are detached from the soul-root of culture, which is always tied to the landscape. Spengler imagines looking down from a tower upon a sea of houses overflowing in all directions, the noble aspect of old time destroyed by clearances and rebuildings. He discerns in the scene the exact epoch in the life-cycle of a town that 'marks the end of organic growth and the beginning of an inorganic and therefore unrestrained process of agglomerations'. If the peasant, who is historyless, should find himself in the city, he 'stands helpless on the pavement, understanding nothing and understood by nobody, tolerated as a useful type in farce and provider of the world's daily bread'.

In the story of the Sanduny, though, there is as much instinct, blood and destiny as money, eye and intellect. Indeed it is hard to say which epoch in the life-cycle of Moscow Spengler would have recognised if he had looked down in 1810 and seen the large brick building newly risen on the land where, to the mystification of the neighbourhood, the actor Sila Sandunov had recently demolished so many old houses. Was this a culture blossoming or beginning to die?

Sandunov's real name was Silvio Zandukeli. He was born in Moscow of noble Georgian stock and raised in Bolshaya Gruzina, a new Moscow neighbourhood that had grown up after King Vakhtang VI of the Georgian province of Kartli was dethroned by the Iranians and his followers emigrated to Russia. The first 'gentry banya' in Russia, accessible to any citizen who could afford its charges, had opened in Bolshaya Gruzina in 1790. Clean and expensive, with its heated changing room, it felt as cosy as a club. Sandunov's grandfather Moisei Zandukeli, like the other Georgians in exile, would reminisce about the Tiflis Baths, and the healing iron-sulphur water that ceaselessly bubbled hot from the ground. Before a talent-hunter lured him to the Hermitage Theatre in St Petersburg, Sandunov worked for an English manager named Murdoch at a theatre near the Petrovsky Gates. Agile and bold on stage, Sandunov excelled in the stock role of the cunning servant.

The money on which Sandunov's banya was founded came from his even more talented wife, Elizaveta (known as 'Lizanka'), a mezzo-soprano with an astonishing range, an actress of brilliant versatility and a favourite of Catherine the Great. The Tsarina had heard the beautiful dark-eyed Lizanka's debut in 1790 in the role of Amor and sent her a diamond ring in a velvet case with a note saying, 'As you sang yesterday about a husband, this ring is to be given to none other than your groom.' She nicknamed the singer 'Uranova' after the newly discovered planet Uranus. When Lizanka married Sila Sandunov (after rejecting the attentions of a number of scheming older men), Catherine gave the beautiful couple a grand wedding and abundant gifts, including a nuptial song composed by herself and a collection of diamonds.

Sila and Lizanka Sandunov returned to Moscow to continue their careers on the stage, settling in the area where the Metropol Hotel now stands. Each of them was engaged by Count Nikolai Sheremetev to train actors and singers for his serf theatre; Lizanka gave acting and voice lessons to Praskovia. After Praskovia's tragic death, she would perform for her wealthy audiences a peasant folk song, learned from Sheremetev's serfs, about the actress's love affair with the Count. With money from the sale of the diamonds, the Sandunovs speculated on the property market, buying up an area between the Neglinnaya and the recently drained and buried Samotyochny Canal. After a visit to Georgia (some provinces of which were now governed by Russia), Sila Sandunov decided what to do with the land. He had read Sanches in his days at court; Moscow did not need the healing springs of the Caucasus. Since 1802, when Alexander I had decreed that stone bathhouses be built all over the empire, numerous banyas with heated changing rooms had appeared near the banks of the Moscow River and the Yauza, or by ponds, streams and smaller rivers (long since buried) like the Nishchenka, the Khapilovka or the Neglinnaya. Sandunov decided to establish the finest, most expensive establishment in the city, with rituals and luxuries modelled on the cultures of the East. Unassuming from the outside, the interior of his bathhouse was palatial, with gilt-framed mirrors and marble-columned halls. In place of the hard benches found in other Russian banyas were soft divans answering the body's desire for gentle sleep after steam, with tables set out for food and drink. Attendants provided clean sheets, and expert washing and grooming. Moscow's rich, already admirers of the theatrical talents of the Sandunovs, were delighted. Generals, police chiefs and powerful city bureaucrats came first to bathe, as their guests. Rich men could be scrubbed and beaten by their own servants in the innovative private 'numbered' banyas. Brides took to visiting the numbered banyas to be washed from silver tubs before their wedding rites. The real profits, however, came from the unadorned two-kopeck section for the ordinary people of the city.

The pleasure-seeking spendthrift Sandunov left soon after the opening of the banya to take the waters in the Caucasus, leaving Lizanka in Moscow. On his return, their marriage disintegrated amid rumours of domestic violence and infidelity, professional rivalry and bitter disputes over money. The merchant woman Avdotya Lamakina, whose slovenly bathhouse on the other side of the Neglinka had suffered a loss of profits, observed the feud eagerly until, in early 1812, a court ruled that their property be sold and the proceeds divided. The coarse and illiterate Lamakina, with a shrewd commercial eye for the borrowed lustre of the stage, bought the banya and named it Sanduny.

For Spengler, the burning of Moscow as Napoleon's army entered in 1812 was the 'mighty symbolic act of a primitive people', an 'expression of Maccabaean hatred of the foreigner and heretic'. Russia was not ready for cities. Russia's 'destiny should have been to continue without a history for some generations', but after Alexander I's triumphal entry into Paris in 1814, the nation 'was forced into a false and artificial history that the soul of Old Russia was simply incapable of understanding'. Built of stone, as the Tsar had decreed ten years before Napoleon's invasion, the Sanduny survived the flames of 1812, a sanctuary, taken for granted in the nineteenth-century city, for the body of the citizen and the primitive practices of old Russia, reinvented by the medical investigations of a Sephardic physician and the fantasy and enterprise of a Georgian actor.

Naked at the banya, ethnicities and social classes mixed, differences blurring in the steam. Gilyarovsky describes the commerce in bathhouse attendants, *banshchiki*, between country and town in the nineteenth century. *Banshchiki* traditionally came from the same few villages in nearby districts: Ryazan, Tula and Zaraisk. *Banshchiki* made good would return to their villages, wearing caps with shiny peaks and fob watches, to pick out boys to serve in the bathhouses of the city. The barely literate youths would be given new bast shoes, two sets of rough undergarments, and official papers, often with faked ages. Relatives and friends from the village who had already established themselves in Moscow would wash and trim the boys, and teach them the ways of the city. They would learn to decant kvass, prepare loofahs and tie *veniki*, switches of leaves. Later they would assist the barbers in the changing rooms, learning to trim nails, cut off corns, address the city gentry and play their parts in the banya's elaborate system of tip-sharing. A few would progress to the hard role of *parilshchik*, working barefoot from dawn till midnight in nothing but a short apron, cleaning out the washing room, raising and refreshing the steam.

After Pushkin's *Journey to Arzrum*, a further attempt was made to orientalise the Sanduny by hiring Asiatic *banshchiki* and adopting new washing rituals with woollen gloves and soap lather. On his way through Georgia during the Russo-Turkish War of 1829, Pushkin had visited the luxurious Tiflis Baths on ladies' day, where, to his delight, the 'lovely Georgian maids', oblivious of their nakedness, carried on laughing and gossiping as he passed. The poet was washed by a noseless Tatar named Hassan, who laid him on the stone floor, cracked his limbs, stretched his joints and beat him fiercely. 'Asiatic *banshchiki* are sometimes transported into ecstasy,' Pushkin reported; 'they jump on your shoulders, slide their legs across your thighs, and do squatting dances on your back, *e sempre bene* . . .' But non-Russian *banshchiki* were a passing fashion at the Sanduny; for their beatings, Muscovites preferred birch twigs to Tatar fists.

❧

As my neighbour slept, the woman beside me ate cherry dumplings with sour cream; the best in Moscow, she said. An Armenian woman with a perfect nose, whom I had often seen before at the Sanduny, demonstrated to her companion (who was in the grandeur of late pregnancy) a circular scrubbing motion with the loofah. 'Steam and then scrub, then steam and miss one scrub,' she instructed, mimicking the abrasions in the air; 'then your skin will be clean and perfect, just like mine.' An attendant sat down beside me and proposed, in a stage whisper, various services off the books: especially good tea with fresh mint, a scalp massage, or perhaps a vigorous beating by the *parilshchitsa* with the thickest *veniki* of birch and oak. The Sanduny's new computerised accounting system had upset the generally agreeable traditions of casual hand-to-hand cash payments, and the employees were still figuring out ways round it.

'Every culture has its own way of thinking in money,' Spengler observed. Founded on the sale of Lizanka's imperial diamonds, the Sanduny was soon caught up in the city's rapidly growing web of self-made fortunes, speculation and graft. In the middle of the nineteenth century, Moscow's banya king was the merchant Pyotr Biryukov, once a *banshchik* at Lamakina's Sanduny, whose wealth had been founded on tips for his skill in soaping, beating and scrubbing the bodies of the rich. Some of Biryukov's bathhouses were notorious as places of disrepute. Streetwalkers would pick up men on Tsvetnoi Boulevard or Rakhmanovsky Lane and take them to the numbered banyas at the Samotyochny Baths, where Biryukov had whitewashed the windows. Biryukov rented the Sanduny from its new owner, the firewood magnate Ivan Firsanov, and, with his intimate knowledge of the banya and hard eye for revenue, did away with Sila Sandunov's romantic luxuries. Silver basins were replaced with wood, curtained booths disappeared, mirrors came off the walls. Biryukov's economies allowed him to acquire more bathhouses around the city, and he vied with other proprietors for permission to build on open ground near the Kremlin, driving in his carriage to the Duma in its palace on Vozdvizhenka to deliver applications to build, which filled the files of the city administration with 'opinions', 'outstanding matters' and 'investigations', and the pockets of its bureaucrats with bribes.

For the 1860s liberal poet Pyotr Shumacher, the banya embodied cherished ideals of freedom and brotherhood. His body was uncomfortably large and gout-ridden, but the steam and the birch switch elicited from him verse in rich Russian of a passionate physical intensity. He described laying his tired bones on the high shelf, soft and free, in the berry-scented steam, as the *venik*, 'boyar of the banya', became fragrant and swollen. He would sleep at the Sanduny for hours at a time and then take home his *venik* to use as a pillow. Ennui and spite would evaporate from his spirit, and he would emerge from the bathhouse feeling light and kind. His poem about the equality with men he found in the simple Volkovsky Baths on the Yauza River was so politically piquant that it could not be printed, and was passed hand to hand at illegal gatherings. For all his radical sentiments, Schumacher lived the last years of his life on the charity of the Sheremetevs, spending the winters in the magnificent almshouse on Sukharevka (built in honour of Praskovia) and summers as a guest of the Count in the 'Dutch House' at the Sheremetev estate Kuskovo.

The young Chekhov, who would one day live by the Sanduny, used the banya, with its blurrings of social identity, as a setting for comic prose. 'In the Banya', first published in 1885 under the writer's alias, A. Chekhonte, is composed of two self-contained miniatures of Moscow life. The steam room is a chamber for the immediate spoken life of the city. Merchants, priests, Tatars and gentry wash and groom together, discussing money, marriage, contemporary manners and ideas. Hard to identify, they are reduced to their speech and the facts of their nakedness. Mikhailo, the savvy barber, applies blood-drawing cups to the crimson body of a fat man, while a gaunt man with long hair, whom Mikhailo takes for some kind of 'anti-Christian' writer 'with ideas', beats himself with a *venik* on the top shelf. The gaunt man tells Mikhailo in a wheezing bass that there have been many writers in Russia 'who have brought enlightenment and should be honoured, not profaned'. When he descends, Mikhailo sees that the unclothed speaker is in fact a man of the cloth. 'Father Deacon,' Mikhailo begs, 'forgive me, for the sake of Christ, for the fact that I thought you had ideas in your head.'

In Chekhov's time, the Sanduny continued to be a place in which money, art and the commerce between cultures combined around the simplest desires of the body. Romantic dreams of Eastern pleasure and theatrical glamour returned to the banya in the last decade of the nineteenth century, when the Sanduny was rebuilt. Firsanov lived in grand style in a noble mansion on Prechistenka with chandeliers and lackeys, and owned a country estate, Srednikovo, which had once belonged to Lermontov. His daughter, Vera Voronina, heir to his fortune in Moscow property, was a highly cultivated young widow who hosted a salon in the

Prechistenka mansion. Voronina married Alexei Gonetsky, a disinherited cornet with an eye for fashion, an invented past and an ardent interest in steam bathing. The Gonetskys decided to rebuild the Sanduny as a place of unsurpassed luxury, a pleasure palace blending East and West.

The couple read everything on the subject, from the then-fashionable *Letters* of the English traveller Lady Mary Wortley Montagu to dissertations by students at the Imperial Military Medical Academy on the banya's effects on digestion and stomach acid, haemoglobin levels, breastmilk yield and weight regulation. Gonetsky made a tour of European bathing spots and invited a Viennese architect, B. V. Freidenberg, who had read Sanches and specialised in bathhouses, to come to Moscow.

After numerous bureaucratic objections and delays, the governor of Moscow admiringly approved Freidenberg's lavish plans for the new building in 1894. Vera, who provided the money, graciously pretended that her husband was financing the venture. The proposed ensemble of two- and three-storey buildings included a luxury bazaar and furnished apartments. There were to be arches and columns, grille-work, bas-reliefs of horses and female figures leaping out of the sea foam, cupolae, three closed courtyards and a fountain. Inside would be swimming pools with glass roofs. A separate building would house an electricity generator, steam boilers and oil supplies. It was to be the first large building in the city completely illuminated by electricity. Within a week of the governor's signature, workmen began to demolish the old Sanduny, in which Pushkin had bathed. It was early spring. Passers-by stopped to look as brick dust blew down Neglinnaya.

Gonetsky hurried the building work, quarrelling with Freidenberg, who deplored his haste, his ignorance of architecture and the eclectic vulgarity of his tastes. Gonetsky demanded a chaotic temple of colliding influences, composed without restraint: rococo and Gothic, mosaic panneaux, murals of the Neapolitan coast and marquises in French parks, Byzantine icons, nude sculptures in the Roman style holding up lamps, Louis XIV mirrors, halls decorated in the styles of Turkey and Arabia, and a Renaissance reading corner. In February 1896, the boilers were heated for the first time, hot water ran through the pipes and the generator was switched on, flooding the surrounding streets with an unfamiliar new radiance.

The Gonetskys moved from Prechistenka to an eleven-room apartment in the new building, looking out over Zvonarsky, a narrow lane on the hill where black jeeps now ride the pavements while their owners steam in the Sanduny. The building was blessed in a grand service with a monastery choir. A priest doused the steam rooms with holy water. A shop selling the best musical instruments and its own editions of sheet music opened on the ground floor of the building on the Neglinnaya side. Soon Chekhov, who had always loved to visit the original Sanduny with his artist brother Nikolai, moved into a large apartment on an upper floor with Olga Knipper. He was a sick man by then, and rarely came out into the streets.

The new Sanduny was frequented by actors, musicians, writers and journalists, as well as by Moscow's merchant nouveaux riches. The attendants wore pink and purple silk and satin. Water that had rinsed the bodies of the rich sluiced down through the plumbing system to the five-kopeck baths on the ground floor, where poorer people washed. The composer Sergei Rachmaninov and the opera singer Fyodor Chaliapin came to make music in Vera's apartment and steam in the baths, where Chaliapin, big and handsome as a *bogatyr*, a medieval Russian knight, said his voice sounded better than in any theatre. Meanwhile, Gonetsky, enterprising as ever with his wife's fortune, had developed a passion for glass-roofed trading arcades, and engaged Freidenberg, who had returned to Russia for the coronation of Nicholas II, to design a grand *passage* to link Neglinnaya and Petrovka Streets.

Like the marriage of the Sandunovs, the partnership between Vera and Alexei Gonetsky fell apart amid recriminations over money and fidelity. Vera borrowed one of Chaliapin's bodyguards to protect her from her husband, whom she had barred from all her homes, and changed her name back to Firsanova. She took charge of the Sanduny. Whether their owner knew it or not, the numbered banyas soon became notorious again as places of indecency, frequented by prostitutes and their clients. In 1918, the Sanduny was expropriated and stayed open throughout the Soviet period as Gosbani No. 1. Vera Firsanova remained in Moscow until 1930, when Chaliapin helped to organise her emigration to Paris.

৵

The pleasures of the banya go deep. I walked out on to Neglinnaya, a street whose name remembers a buried river, in the cold of the March evening. Clear-headed, gentler of spirit, I felt the heat of the steam room still softening inside, my body guarded against the hardness, dirt and chill of the city by the hours passed, out of the light, inside one of the city's own stone sanctuaries. 'With light steam,' Russians say to a person who has just finished at the banya. It is impossible to convey its meaning, but this is a benediction of the utmost precision. The banya has its own complex grammar, caught by Chekhov's acute ear for speech, a pattern of verbs and prepositions which evoke immediately and untranslatably the dynamic relationship between flesh and hot vapour.

I walked past the Central Bank, a yellow palace of finance already newly in place when Gonetsky asked the city authorities for permission to rebuild the Sanduny. Light snow was falling, twirling slowly in the pink-yellow light of the streetlamps, turning to slush under walking feet and the wheels of the cars. Electricity gives them an aura at this time of day, these buildings of stone, Spengler's time become rigid space, with their strange languages of ornament. Across the street, the shops in the trading *passage* that still runs between Neglinnaya and Petrovka glowed with furs, lace and jewels, caught in spotlit scenes of frozen mannequin swagger in the windows, to lure the city's living dolls, through whose bodies and material desires money flows around the city. Beyond Gonetsky's arcades, cars with black windows were parked three deep outside the Vogue Cafe, chauffeurs sleeping on the reclined leather seats.

At the corner I turned up Kuznetsky Most, walking dreamily up the long rising street of banks and luxury shops which runs from Bolshaya Dmitrovka Street to Bolshaya Lubyanka, crossing Petrovka, Neglinnaya and Rozhdestvenka on its way. There have always been beautiful shops on Kuznetsky Most, whose name means 'blacksmith bridge', remembering a bridge that crossed the Neglinnaya River when it still ran above ground. Before 1812, the best French shops in Moscow lined the street; it was part of the city's French colony, known as a 'sanctuary of luxury and fashion'. When Napoleon's troops entered Moscow, they protected the French parfumeries, furriers, couturiers, diamond boutiques and patisseries from the great fire. I crossed Rozhdestvenka Street, where the Institute of Oriental Studies of the Academy of Sciences now occupies the pillared mansion that was once the Anglia-Paris Hotel. I thought about the orientalist S. F. Oldenburg, the internationally renowned scholar of Buddhism who wrote the introduction to the Bolshevik book on the countryside that I had found, to my surprise, in Molotov's library. Oldenburg was a Constitutional Democrat who served in Kerensky's short-lived Provisional Government as Minister of Public Education, and, after October 1917, co-operated with the Bolshevik regime in its task of public enlightenment, working for the Institute of Oriental Studies from 1930 until his death in 1934. His introduction expressed the hope that the primitive Russian countryside (which he compared to rural India) would, under the new political order, at last awaken from its primordial sleep and come to share in the historical life of civilisation.

At No. 24 Kuznetsky Most, on the corner of Bolshaya Lubyanka Street, every kind of art and business flourished in centuries past. When No. 24 was called the 'Golitsyn House' (after the prince who owned the land), biscuits, sweets and medicinal vinegars were on sale here. After 1812, a Moscow University professor named Reiss opened a pharmacy specialising in curative mineral waters.

I. P. Vitali, sculptor of the fountain outside the Bolshoi, lived in the house in the early nineteenth century, and received Pushkin as his guest. In the 1850s, plants and seeds and English metal goods were sold in shops on the ground floor, and, later in the century, the firm Shwabier, Russia's largest retailer of optical, geodesic and medical instruments, set up for business alongside a photographer's studio, a rose shop, an underwear boutique called 'The Jockey Club' and the sweet counters of Landrin, the 'caramel king'.

In 1918, No. 24 was taken over by the new government. Until the giant Stalin 'wedding cake' was built for the Ministry of Foreign Affairs at Smolenskaya in 1952, the four-storey building was the premises of Narkomindel, the People's Commissariat of Foreign Affairs. As Commissar (renamed 'Foreign Minister' after 1946), Molotov worked sixteen-hour days at his enormous mahogany desk. Visitors to his office in No. 24 remember the neat arrangement of pens, pencils, rulers and notepads on the desk, and his battery of telephones. On the wall were portraits of Marx, Lenin and Stalin, and three great generals of Russian imperial history, Suvorov, Kutuzov and Nakhimov.

In the 1920s, the building was shared with the Berlitz language courses and an official organisation called the 'Political Red Cross', which gave assistance to the families of prisoners. Later, during the purges of the 1930s, relatives of political prisoners would come to the 'reception' of the NKVD in No. 24 to ask about the fates of their arrested loved ones. From the night of his father's arrest until 1948, V. S. Zhukovsky would come here regularly from Granovsky Street to ask his whereabouts. 'He's with us,' he was always told, which meant that his father was in the Lubyanka. But after a few years, the young lieutenant at the desk would just smile and say, 'We can't tell you anything.' 'Why not?' 'That's just the way it is.' It was only after Stalin's death that Zhukovsky learned that his father had been shot in 1940, convicted for 'counter-revolutionary activity' under Article 58 of the Criminal Code.

The Lubyanka, an old insurance company headquarters in whose deep interior the body of the citizen has known terrible attentions, is just across the street. In 1937, Stalin's secret police uncovered 'Trotskyites' and 'saboteurs' among the staff at Gosbani No. 1, and brought them the short distance up the hill, into its darkness. Polina Zhemchuzhina spent many months in the cells of the Lubyanka, where she was interrogated day after day, accused of every kind of treachery against the state, from 'criminal contacts with Jewish nationalists' to orgies with workers in the Ministry of Light Industry. In her secret police file, there is a letter from her friend Galina Serebryakova, written to Zhemchuzhina from the Gulag, and a letter to her brother, who emigrated to America after the Revolution, changed his name to Sam Karp and made good. Zhemchuzhina had been accused, among other things, of having once attended a memorial service at a synagogue. In her four-volume file, there is also a scrap of paper with her handwriting on it: 'with these four years of separation four eternities have flowed over my strange and terrible life', she wrote to an unnamed addressee; 'only the thought of you forces me to live, and the knowledge that you may still need the remnants of my tormented heart . . .' 'Security had done a thorough job on her,' Molotov remembered; 'they had outdone themselves.' Beria would walk past him at Politburo meetings and hiss in his ear, 'Polina is alive!' 'She was in the Lubyanka prison in Moscow,' Molotov said, 'and I didn't even know she was there.'

Gigantic and immoderate, as closed and featureless as an Egyptian pyramid, the second secret police building, raised in dark granite, iron and black marble on the site of the demolished buildings of No. 24 Kuznetsky Most in the last years of Yuri Andropov's long tenure as Chairman of the KGB, expresses nothing but its own massing of adamant power. When Andropov (whose memorial plaque on the wall of the Lubyanka former KGB agent Vladimir Putin unveiled in one of the first acts of his presidency) became General Secretary of the Party in 1982, he chose to initiate a grand reform of the whole Soviet system by ordering a clean-up of the corruption at the Sandunovskaya Bathhouse down the hill.

FOUR

Lutsino

Zvenigorod (I still rejoiced at that wonderful name) . . .
MARINA TSVETAEVA

After several years in Moscow, we acknowledged the good sense
of the way in which Russian life, across the social classes, is clearly
divided into work time in the city and 'rest' *na dache*. We found
a dacha to rent in the Academy of Sciences colony above the
Moscow River at Lutsino, a village close to the ancient town of
Zvenigorod, an hour's drive west of the city. When we first saw
dacha No. 3, its paint was blotched and flaking, its verandahs
draped with dead creepers. Nina Balandina, our landlady, used our
first month's rent to have the dacha painted greeny-blue and the
former chauffeur's quarters, in which she lived, pale yellow. When
October came she asked us to rake and burn the fallen leaves and
pine needles and feed the ash from our slow bonfires to the shrubs
that she had planted with her mother when Academician
Balandin came back from the Gulag. We sat outside till late,
drinking wine and roasting potatoes in soft caverns beneath the
flames, and left the fire, fragrant with damp pine bark, twisting
smoke till morning. We pulled up nettles behind the dacha, and
cut back the rowanberry branches that had crossed Nina's narrow
path through the garden to the fenced boundary of the colony,
where the forest ends. She laughed with good humour at our
unruly dog, who had no feeling for property rights and treated her
as an intruder, barking and running frantic circles round her as she
limped across the garden every morning and evening, to and from
the village church of St Nikola the Miracle-Worker. Nina had
spent most of her childhood summers here, apart from the
interval in her early teens between 1949 and Stalin's death in 1953,

lost years her father (like so many Gulag survivors) never discussed, when, after his second arrest, he was an 'enemy of the people' and his dacha was confiscated.

Alexei Balandin was first arrested, as a 'socially dangerous element', in the summer of 1936, and taken from Butyrka prison to a former monastery at Voronovo, at which high-ranking members of the NKVD interrogated, tortured and shot political prisoners. It was a miracle, believes Nina (who traces a pattern of miracles in her family's past), that her father was not arrested a year later in 1937, when the bacchanal of state murder was in its frenzy. Two of Balandin's graduate students, the 'anti-Soviet terrorists' Vadim Usinin and Vasili Agapov, denounced their professor, under torture, as part of a Trotskyite terrorist group, alleged to be using the laboratories of the Chemistry Faculty of Moscow University to make explosives. Balandin was sentenced to 'administrative exile' in the distant city of Orenburg. Eminent colleagues petitioned Molotov in person; but by then, Nina says, Comrade Molotov was indifferent to name or scientific prestige. (In conversation Nina referred to Molotov and Stalin as 'Comrade'.) The intercession of the Chief Prosecutor, Andrei Vyshinsky, was another miracle. Vyshinsky personally ordered Balandin's release from exile in 1939, allowing him to return to his research in organic catalytics, for which, in the 1940s, he was made a member of the Academy of Sciences and awarded a Stalin Prize and the title to dacha No. 3.]

When the KGB archives opened in the early 1990s, Nina read the protocols of her father's interrogations. During his months in Butyrka and the Lubyanka, charged with 'crimes against Soviet power', the only thing for which Balandin admitted guilt was concealment of his social origins. If he had signed any other 'confession', Nina's mother would never have been able to secure his amnesty so soon after Stalin's death, and he might never have known rest in the golden light of Lutsino again. Her mother found a good advocate who saved him, as Nina told us more than once. Though he had only done a few months of 'black work' in the nickel mines at Norilsk before being moved, along with several atomic physicists and flying aces, into the metallurgical plant, his health was broken. He had shared freezing barracks with common criminals, his fur hat was stolen in winter, and he took a knife wound in the stomach in a fight over a rouble. While he was in the Arctic, fellow scientists were forbidden to use his name or mention his theories in publications, or even at conferences on the subject of his work.

You never recover, Nina said. Her father was always on her mind. He left her wealthy in real estate, with a dacha in a good colony and a large Moscow apartment on the Garden Ring opposite the US Embassy, but she lived ascetically in her barely furnished yellow house, sleeping little, ordering her days to the practice of the Orthodox faith, which she had come to in the last years of Soviet power through the teachings of the priest Alexander Men. When the weather turned cold, her face became red and chapped. In November, at the edge of winter, the grass was laid flat and matted with fine frost, the nettles darkened and wilted, expiring elegantly on a couch of papery dead leaves. Woodpeckers tapped urgently, high on the bare trunks of the pines. Nina put galoshes over her shoes and wore her dirty turquoise anorak, the ragged synthetic fur on its hood mingling with her wispy grey hair. Her step across the garden became slower, more pained.

As the protocols from the Lubyanka confirm with all the legalistic rancour of class struggle, Nina's father's origins were bourgeois. Indeed, by 1917, his mother, Vera Balandina, was a self-made millionairess who owned railroads, coal mines and steamboats that plied the great Yenisei River, from Krasnoyarsk to the Arctic seas. Nina is free now to celebrate this Siberian matriarch for all that her enlightened capitalism was able to catalyse in the peasant lands of her native region. Against her father's wishes, Vera Balandina had gone to St Petersburg to enrol in the Bestuzhev Higher Courses for Women, graduating in 1893 with a Master's degree in chemistry. She socialised with revolutionary-democratic *kursistki* like Olga Ulyanova, Lenin's sister, whom she greatly admired, and Zinaida Nevzorova, wife of the Bolshevik Gleb Krzhizhanovsky (who worked with Molotov in the Party secretariat on Vozdvizhenka in 1922 and was later one of his deputies in the Council of People's Commissars). Vera married another natural scientist and travelled with him to Paris, where she attended lectures at the Sorbonne and worked at the Institut Pasteur. Back in Siberia, true to the progressive convictions that had formed in her student days, Balandina founded a non-fee-paying girls' school, a 'people's library', a theatre and a bookshop which stocked the latest publications in the arts and sciences. She set up chemistry laboratories and organised prospecting expeditions. She discovered diamonds in eastern Siberia, and rich seams of coal on the wide Abakansky steppe. There she founded mines and a town, naming it Chernogorsk, Black Mountain. Her mines were electrified above and below ground, connected by canal and rail with wharfs on the Yenisei River. She built a hospital, a grain mill, a school, a library for the miners and mutual credit associations that soon spread over all parts of Siberia. In 1912, Vera Balandina was the only woman to serve on the railway-building committee of the Ministry of Finance. Poor babushka, Nina lamented one spring afternoon as we stood on the back verandah of the dacha looking out at the lily of the valley blooming among the resurgent nettles, what would she have said if she knew that under Comrade Stalin the town she created had become a Gulag, with prisoners working the mines?

For her own children, Vera set up a chemistry laboratory at home. Alexei Balandin later reflected that, although intellectual life was sparse in Siberia, it offered a rich natural environment which he hoped to understand and turn to the use of his people. He had completed his education in Moscow, in a liberal gymnasium on Znamenka, the first mixed school of its kind in Russia, a serious and exciting institution in which he was confirmed in his scientific vocation. In one lesson, an eccentric geography teacher, forgetting that he was addressing schoolchildren, had agitatedly

tried to explain Ernest Rutherford's discovery of the structure of
the atom: 'a remarkable event, an event of the highest significance,
my dear gentlemen . . .' The 'philosophy of chemistry' is the
'foundation of the contemplation of the world', the eighteen-year-
old Balandin wrote, as he prepared to enter Moscow University's
Faculty of Medicine. Chemistry is a 'penetration into the secrets
of nature' which will 'broaden our understanding of the mysterious phenomena associated with radioactive substances'.

Some minds penetrate further into the secrets of nature than
others, achieving hard understanding as well as delight. The
people for whom the Lutsino dachas were built in the late 1940s
have theories and natural effects named after them. Though
Academician Rebinder, father of Nina's neighbour Mariana at
dacha No. 2, is more fondly remembered in Lutsino for his love of
mushroom-hunting, his style on the tennis courts, and for the rare
and decorative trees that he planted in the colony, a certain process
of reduction in the solidity of heavy bodies is still known as the
'Rebinder effect'. When I was told that the first enquiries into the
influence of atmospheric turbulence on the diffusion of light rays
were conducted close by, in the laboratories of the Zvenigorod
Research Centre, I could think only of the brilliance of the rainbow over the cemetery last spring. The description of the 'intensification of falling light dispersed by objects in its path' evokes in
my mind nothing more than the sunshine finding its way through
this dense forest, moving from tree to tree, flushing the snow balanced on the branches, and coming to rest at midday in radiant
hoops in the tops of the pines.

The Lutsino colony lies along a hill above the Moscow River.
We often took the hour-long walk through the colony, down a narrow path to the riverbank and back along the *opushka*, as the edge
of the forest is called, under the steepening slope. Light and matter often changed roles here. In late summer the river water would
look glazed, exhausted in the last heat, in some places no colour at
all, just a surface of light with a dull beaten sheen. Downriver, a
rowing boat lay motionless on the water, its fisherman a silhouette

in the haze. After the violent rainstorms of the night, the earth still steamed. Thousands of spider-spun threads webbed the grass, trembling. The lush clover was weighted with large globes of rainwater. Vapour hung in the rushes on the opposite bank. The villages across the dark ploughed fields were lost in mist.

Andrei Sakharov, who looked deeply into the mysterious workings of the material world, spent long summers in the villages around the ancient town of Zvenigorod during his childhood, first at Dunino with a 'large, warm-hearted family of Russified Germans', the Ulmers, doctors, engineers and lawyers, most of whom were arrested and killed in the 1930s. Later at Lutsino, he would wander for hours alone on the *opushka* by the river. Summers in this serene lyrical countryside left deep impressions on him, he wrote in his memoirs. All his life, his greatest joy was to lie on his back and look up through the branches at the sky, listening to the hum of insects, or to roll over on his stomach the way he had as a suntanned child, and observe their tiny life in the grass and the sand. His glancing memories of childhood summers include a recollection of newspaper reports of the Zinoviev–Kamenev trial, and Vyshinsky's summation for the prosecution, 'filled, as always, with cruel and affected rhetoric'. Sakharov grew up to become an atomic physicist. In 1948, when German prisoners of war were still building the dacha colony at Lutsino, he joined an elite Academy of Sciences research team, under the supervision of Beria (who had taken over the project from Molotov, who was not up to the subtleties of the task), investigating the possibility of creating thermonuclear weapons.

Five years later, Sakharov found himself lying on his stomach again, far from Lutsino, near the settlement of Kara-Aul in Kazakhstan, watching in awe as the Soviet H-bomb was tested. He tore off his goggles to see better the streamers of purple dust that were sucked up into the stem of a vast and shimmering mushroom cloud, as the earth rumbled and the sky turned a sinister blue-black. Working on the project, Sakharov said, he suddenly became old and grey.

'For seven years or so, the Soviet Union had to live with the fact that America had the capability of inflicting very great destruction on Russian cities, without the Soviet Union being able to reply in kind,' the reader underlined in thick hard pencil, with a firm tick in the margin, in P. M. S. Blackett's *Studies of War: Nuclear and Conventional* (London, 1962), one of the more heavily annotated books in the Molotov library. 'To justify to the tender consciences of Western peoples the deliberate plan, in certain military circumstances, to annihilate tens of millions of Russian men, women, and children,' he marked with a double line in the margin, 'it was necessary to believe the USSR to be innately aggressive and wicked. Once a nation pledges its safety to an absolute weapon, it becomes emotionally essential to believe in an absolute enemy.'

⊰❦⊱

Lutsino, named after Lucina, daughter of Jupiter and goddess of childbirth, had been associated with the biological and medical sciences since the late nineteenth century. Anton Chekhov spent the wet summer after his graduation from Moscow University in 1884 working as a doctor in a country hospital in the nearby monastery town of Zvenigorod, whose name means 'town of ringing bells'. His friend the painter Isaac Levitan was also working in Zvenigorod that year, rendering in paint the infinite greens of the local landscape, mixing white and gold for the meadow grass, and a shade for the *opushka* so dark it is almost black. The artist Maria Yakunchikova, daughter of the entrepreneurial Moscow merchant and philanthropist Vasili Yakunchikov (who financed the building of the Moscow Conservatoire), also spent summers painting near Zvenigorod. At Vvedenskoe, the noble estate that her father had acquired in the mid-1860s, Maria Yakunchikova hosted Levitan, Chekhov and the composer Tchaikovsky. In 1884, Vvedenskoe was bought by Count Sergei Sheremetev, as a dowry for his daughter Maria.

In the early 1900s, three of Chekhov's classmates from the Faculty of Medicine acquired plots on the wooded hill above the river, where the colony now stands, and built dachas on its sandy soil. They shared the humane culture of the late-nineteenth-century Moscow intelligentsia, in which the natural sciences, liberal politics and the arts were closely integrated. This culture, which flourished in leisured conversation on small country estates, found its lasting expression in Chekhov's life and writing. The estate of S. S. Goloushev, a well-known physician, lay furthest upriver of the three. Under his pseudonym Glagol, he published theatre and fine arts criticism in Moscow journals, and was among the first to identify Levitan's talent, devoting two articles to the painter's 'Zvenigorod period'. Grigory Rossolimo's estate occupied the highest position above the river. A pioneering child psychologist and neuropathologist, Rossolimo published articles on the 'individuality of the child', 'musical talent in children' and 'children of the near future'. In 1922, he was summoned to Lenin's country estate at Gorki to treat the ailing Party leader. Russia's greatest writers, painters and musicians were among Rossolimo's close friends; Tolstoy, Maxim Gorky, Konstantin Balmont, Tchaikovsky and the painter Valentin Serov were guests at his home. Chekhov, Mikhail Zoshchenko and the poet Teffi read their work at his soirées.

Rossolimo's stepson and heir Sergei Skadovsky, a hydrobiologist and founder of the 'new science' of physico-chemical biology, married the daughter of N. S. Speransky, a professor of dermatology, the third of Chekhov's contemporaries, the original Lutsino *dachniki*. Skadovsky was known for his acting skills. Once, when he read one of Chekhov's short stories aloud, the writer Mikhail Bulgakov told him to drop biology and head for the Moscow Art Theatre. In 1910 Skadovsky purchased a large piece of the remaining land and founded a private hydrobiological station, with several laboratories dedicated to the study of freshwater organisms. The Biostation, as it is now known, later became part of Moscow University, and a centre for Russian genetic science.

Of the buildings that burned down in the winter months of 1941, when the Red Army faced the Germans on the opposite bank of the river, some were later rebuilt, including Rossolimo's dacha, No. 37 in the present colony, where his descendants still live. Only the lime trees, the tennis courts, the gateposts and a woodland stream named after Chekhov remain of the original estate. Skadovsky is buried in the cemetery on the hill behind Nina's dacha.

Within months of the war's end, Stalin decreed that, as reward for their contribution to the victory over Hitler, Russia's most eminent professors and academicians should be given summer homes designed by Alexei Schusev (architect of the Lenin Mausoleum and many other Moscow landmarks) with rights of ownership, in the loveliest parts of the Moscow region. To the lasting pride of their owners, the dachas, all alike, were made up in Finland, placed at irregular angles on the contoured land among the trees by German prisoners of war, and fitted with East German sanitary ware. A few years later, more dachas were built for scientists who had contributed to the development of the Soviet atomic bomb. There was once a sculpture in the colony of Lenin seated on a bench, his head turned towards the standing figure of Stalin. Stalin's greatcoat lay along the back of the bench. Mariana Rebinder has kept the letter to her father of July 1950 announcing the order by Sergei Vavilov, President of the Academy of Sciences, instructing the *dachniki* to deposit five hundred roubles in the colony *kassa* or the Zvenigorod branch of Gosbank within a week to pay for the sculpture of their leaders. After Khrushchev's 'secret speech' to the XXth Party Congress in 1956, Stalin was removed, leaving Lenin with the greatcoat and the mysterious trace of a single jackboot. Thirty years later, the sculpture disappeared altogether, unlamented.

The Biostation, a more charming and enduring relic of another time, is carelessly preserved, but still loved by the *dachniki*. I skied to it one cold day in late February. The sky was deep unbroken blue. The snow had become heavy on the groined branches of the firs, which had lost their mournful aspect in the brilliance of the sunshine. Bare white birch trunks gleamed among them. Occasionally, a gentle wind picked up the snow from the trees and blew it, sparkling, into the air. At the water tower, which stands tall above the treetops on rusted iron legs, two of the colony dogs came out, exhilarated by the frost, to lead me along the road with their tails aloft. Where the snow was deep they would canter into it, playfighting, the sandy mongrel biting the neck of the stud-collared Alsatian until he was barked into submission. I stopped at the colony's roadside notice-board to catch up on the latest turns in the great dispute between factions in the Academy of Sciences about the property rights of the *dachniki*. (Mariana Rebinder was deeply involved in the intricate politics of the colony, which reflected the wider politics of the nation, in which issues of property seethe unresolved.) A public meeting had been announced for Saturday evening in the garden of one of the dachas. A tough-looking old woman in an astrakhan coat was clearing the snow from her driveway; a few elderly *dachniki* in Soviet winter coats with beaver collars and felt boots were out walking in the thrilling silence of the morning. The dachas showed their colours in the purity of the winter light: palest yellow green, turquoise, golden ochre and ash pink. Further along were some new brick houses, but the wooden dachas were more unkempt, unpainted, with broken fences and woodsheds in rot and disarray. Combs of icicles hung from their corrugated iron roofs, crooked fangs, five feet long. Smoke came from the chimney of Skadovsky's dacha, the last property before the Biostation. A sign on its iron gates – bearing its emblem, a woodpecker on a pine trunk – forbade unauthorised entry, but there was no one about, so I skied in and down the steep hill in the deepening snow, among the green-painted dormitory buildings. Their windows were dark, hung with torn nylon curtains; some had panes of glass missing. The WC huts leaned awkwardly in the snow, their doors swinging open, almost off their hinges. I followed the narrow winding path down to the river, uneasy on my skis in the deep drifts among the trees. The

Lower Dachas of the Biostation occupy a secluded bend in the river. The dilapidated buildings, half buried in snow, told of summers past and the companionable pleasures of biological research. A Lada van lay rusting behind a half-collapsed shed with a ladder leading up to a hayloft. There was a row of iron huts, different sizes, in corroding shades of blue and green, and tanks mounted on platforms with pipes and taps. In the centre of this seemingly haphazard ensemble was a large wooden building with tables and benches in front of it, facing a smaller three-sided structure housing a *mangal* grill.

Here, where biology once grew freely as a natural science, Stalin's favourites degraded it into an ideological farce. Not all the Lutsino *dachniki* were natural scientists: some were in the social sciences. On the way back from the Biostation, I took the loop in the road that leads past dacha No. 7, whose grounds are grander than most in the colony. Said to have a parquet floor, the dacha was given to Academician Andrei Vyshinsky to mark his years of scholarly service to the Soviet state. However, after the arrest of the Old Bolshevik Leonid Serebryakov (Galina Serebryakova's first husband) in 1936, Vyshinsky had acquired Serebryakov's state dacha at nearby Nikolina Gora, which he had long coveted openly, so the smaller Lutsino dacha was merely a 'reserve' dacha, and the Chief Prosecutor's visits were rare.

I had found Vyshinsky in Moscow, among Molotov's books, and here he was again, at his property in the country. When he replaced Molotov as foreign minister in 1949 (a few weeks after Zhemchuzhina's arrest), Vyshinsky took over his second-floor office at No. 24 Kuznetsky Most. Vyshinsky was sensitive, it seems, to the accusation that he was attached to comfort and property. After his death, a red file was found in his safe, with a loaded Browning pistol lying on top of it. In the file was a letter to Stalin from the former head of the Comintern, Dmitri Manuilsky, written in 1948, which had been forwarded to Vyshinsky by Stalin, who loved to set his men against each other. Manuilsky and Vyshinsky had worked as comrades for years, sitting side by side as

Soviet delegates to the UN; their books lie crammed together in the dark of the bookcase in the Molotov apartment. In the letter, Manuilsky told Stalin that Vyshinsky was a coward and a traitor, a man of petit-bourgeois tastes, loyal only to his own craving for luxury and security.

Recorded in the annals of the colony as a 'lawyer, historian, and state activist', in suit and tie, with his high brow, square face and dark-rimmed spectacles, Vyshinsky was made an academician (the highest title for a Soviet scholar) in 1939, not long after the conclusion of the Moscow show trials. He was a learned man. The son of a pharmacist, he taught Latin at a gymnasium, an elite school with a classical curriculum, before the Revolution. In the 1920s, before he set his mind to questions of jurisprudence in the dictatorship of the proletariat, he wrote popular books charting the primordial human longing for a just and beautiful world: from the Garden of Eden, through Hesiod, Virgil and Plato, Thomas More's *Utopia* and Tommaso Campanella's *City of the Sun*, to Engels and Marx. The Stalin Constitution of 1936, which Vyshinsky had a hand in drafting, guaranteed citizens freedom from arbitrary arrest and the right of defence in a public trial before an independent judge 'subject only to the law', but Vyshinsky skilfully turned law into an instrument of state power, at once brutal and subtle. He demolished the 'bourgeois' concept of advocacy with all its 'false pathos', and defined the signed confession (even extracted under torture) as the highest form of evidence. Law was the state and the state was the law. At the trial of his former comrades Bukharin and Rykov, he screamed, in words which Andrei Sakharov could not forget: 'Our people demand that we crush the accursed vermin . . . the graves of the hated traitors will grow with tall weeds and thistles, covered with the eternal contempt of honest Soviet people.' They 'tried with their dirty feet to stamp out the best, most fragrant flowers in our socialist state'; they should be shot like 'mad dogs'. Summing up in the last of the trials, Vyshinsky described the accused as 'a foul-smelling heap of human garbage . . . the last scum and filth of the past'.

Dusya Fetisova, who lived in the chauffeur's quarters of Vyshinsky's dacha, serving its inhabitants from the late 1940s until her death in 1994, would have known nothing of her landlord's role in the corruption of Soviet jurisprudence. She is remembered in Lutsino for her good heart, her skill in making plants grow in poor soil, and her freely told tales of life at No. 7. Hard as she tried to please them, tidying the house and arranging rowanberry branches in vases, Dusya received from Vyshinsky's widow and his daughter Zinaida neither money nor thanks. They withdrew from other people, she said, always resenting their eviction from Nikolina Gora after Vyshinsky's death. After the death of Vyshinsky's widow (who was gentler and more sociable than her daughter), Zinaida, a legal scholar like her father, came only for short spells in the summer. She was afraid of sleeping in the dacha alone, and, as Dusya put it, it was hard for someone so proud and suspicious to find companionship. Dusya always wished that the little chauffeur's cottage in which she lived should be bequeathed to her, but Zinaida, she said, did not want to bequeath anything to anyone. Despite the rumours of its opulence, Dusya says that the dacha was sparsely furnished and some of its rooms quite empty. One of Nina's friends in the colony has some battered cane furniture bought from the Vyshinsky family. To Nina Balandina, Vyshinsky will always be the agent of her father's deliverance from exile.

Dusya's previous mistress at No. 7 was no kinder than Zinaida Vyshinskaya. Academician Olga Lepeshinskaya, to whom Vyshinsky lent No. 7 at the apex of her career in biology, lived there between 1949 and 1952. When I asked Nina what she knew about Lepeshinskaya, she blinked and shook her head. It was hard to remember her father's lost years, she said; it was painful to think of what happened. Dusya's recollections were fluent. Lepeshinskaya, an 'Old Bolshevichka', had known Lenin in exile in Siberia and Geneva. She boasted that when she was pregnant with her daughter, Lenin had asked her what she craved, and when she replied, 'My baby wants lobster,' he found her a tin of conserved crabmeat. Lepeshinskaya was so shrewish, mean and untrusting, Dusya remembered, that she would poke through the garbage to check that her servant had not stolen any leftovers for her animals. Her daughter, Olga Pantelaimonovna, and her husband and five adopted children shared the dacha with Lepeshinskaya. Dusya claims to have cared for the children, who were neglected by their mother, who nonetheless, as a fanatical opponent of genetic science, always expressed the desire to adopt more children to mould into perfect communists. When I looked through the card catalogue at the Lenin Library at all the titles of biological books and treatises by the now-forgotten Lepeshinskaya, I found an anomaly, a long novel called *Green Noise*, published by Goslitizdat, the state literary publishing house, in 1937. It was by Lepeshinskaya's daughter. (Librarian Fyodorov would not have approved of this mistake in the catalogue that made two distinct persons, however unworthy, into one.) Olga Pantelaimonovna, who worked in her mother's laboratory, had a feeling for nature. *Green Noise* is set in a sleepy Jewish village, inhabited by characters named Hirsh, Sara, Wanda, Sholom and Farshtein. The book ends lyrically, with the biblical saying, 'all is vanity': 'The sounds of a song, hardly audible, were carried from afar. The sound of the birch trees, rustling mysteriously in the cemetery, floated on the light warm breeze. The moon with its phosphorescent rays transformed the earth into a fairy tale . . .'

But let me return to the novelist's mother. Like her fellow charlatan, Trofim Lysenko, who consigned hundreds of scientists who disagreed with him to execution or imprisonment, Lepeshinskaya denied the 'bourgeois' axioms of genetics in favour of theories consistent with Marxist–Leninist dialectical materialism, in which 'being determines consciousness', and environment conditions everything. The power of Lysenko and Lepeshinskaya in the scientific establishment reached its peak in 1948, at the height of Stalin's purge of doctors, scientists and 'rootless cosmopolitans'. While Lysenko claimed that he could produce barley from grains of wheat, Lepeshinskaya boasted that soon

Soviet scientists would be able to create new forms of life, new species. At a conference on her theory organised by the Communist Party in 1950, she argued, amid innumerable references to Marx, Lenin and Stalin, that a living cell need not be produced from other cells, but may be formed new from noncellular matter. She claimed to have observed new blood cells forming from globules in the yolk of an egg. Other biologists, members of the 'old intelligentsia' who clung to the idea of the 'autonomy of science', had joked from the beginning of her career in the 1920s that Lepeshinskaya was an alchemist, a charlatan and an ignoramus. But her revolutionary credentials were tools enough for a great career in Soviet science. Konstantin Timiryazev (Stalinist son of the great Russian biologist who lived behind the Sheremetev palace on our street) had protected her from these 'idealist' enemies, and guided by the 'compass' of Marxist–Leninist dialectics, she had journeyed to the 'fountain-head of life'. Lenin had said that nothing could exist outside the world of matter, and she would demonstrate that there was no mystery about the origins of living matter. Her aim, she said, was to probe the very essence of the living organism, to delve into the question of life, '*convinced* that in this fundamental question there could be no obstinate secrets': 'Life itself will show us its ancient source and be a guide to its own profoundest secrets.' Lepeshinskaya found it easier, she said, to study 'noncellular living matter' in Lutsino. One day, she invited a delegation of leading scientists to her dacha and told them to look into a barrel of rainwater from the roof to witness the evidence for her theory. The scientists looked into the barrel and saw nothing but the darkness of the stagnant water, but fearing for their careers, if not for their lives, they marvelled aloud at her great discovery.

Unlike Alexei Balandin, whose background was remarkably similar to hers, Lepeshinskaya knew how to betray her social origins and shape a revolutionary biography. She traced her Bolshevism to an early disgust at her mother's successful capitalism. Lepeshinskaya was born in Perm (one of the cities known in the years of her greatness as Molotov). Like Balandin's, her mother was a businesswoman who made a fortune in coal mines and factories. Her mother took pride in the living quarters she had built for the miners, but Olga saw 'caves dug into the hillsides like tombs, with dense clouds of smoke pouring out of their tiny bottle-glass windows, and doors so low one had to enter on all fours'. In her mother's mines, 'deep under the earth, in stifling gloom, half-naked men lay in the water and hacked at the coal face with picks'. She rejected the gilt and stucco world of home, and went to St Petersburg to study medicine. She read Darwin and Marx, mixing with the same revolutionary-democratic female students – *kursistki* – as Vera Balandina. For the Red Cross, she visited imprisoned revolutionaries in the Peter and Paul Fortress, and followed the Old Bolshevik Pantelaimon Lepeshinsky into exile as his wife, sharing the romance of the underground, a life of counterfeit passports, coded telegrams, riding in freight-cars with false-bottomed suitcases, arrests and searches, and the certainty of ideological rightness that lasted her lifetime.

❧

At first Lutsino seemed clean to me, a refuge from the city filth. I loved the air, slept deeply. Women came up from the village at the end of summer to sell us good food: huge glass jars of brined cucumbers, marinated with oak and maple leaves and juniper berries; eggs from chickens fed on parsley, with dark yellow yolks and quivering whites. We sometimes met a goatherd on our walks, who hailed us as 'little son' and 'little daughter', and told us about the ruined collective farms in her native Mordovia and how it was better around Lutsino, where her goats ate so well they 'gave four glasses and some'. (She had heard that goats in Western countries gave more, but she did not think she believed it.) The customers at the village shop seemed gentle and familiar: Tajik construction workers who came for dried fish, bread and soap, 'the cheapest you have'; the drunkards with puffed-up faces who drank vodka all afternoon at the plastic table in the corner; the large gypsy family who tried to sell us tracksuits ('best quality, very cheap') from the back of a tiny old Zhiguli with blacked-out windows. The small church by the cemetery on the hill had recently been rebuilt, by a Zvenigorod mafia boss after the murder of his son. We watched the slow restoration, from dereliction to bright, orange-painted magnificence, of the larger church down in the village. In the early Soviet period, the church was used as a warehouse for a musical instrument factory; later it fell into ruin. On the day the cross was erected on its dome, Nina said, she was suddenly able to walk without her stick. The ringing of its bells came up the hill to the dacha, morning and evening, another of the day's few sounds, like the freight train passing through in the valley, the running tap outside Nina's house, the shout of a workman among the trees, the colony dogs on guard, birdsong and frogs in spring, teenagers from the village singing by their riverside bonfire on summer nights. I sensed the seasons again, whose rhythms of dormancy and exuberant vitality city life had blurred.

But later I began to be disturbed by Lutsino's history, its garbage. One winter I found some *Pravda*s in the woodpile: speeches from the XXth Party Congress, February 1956. I pondered what might be hidden, living or dead, in the raised foundations of the dacha. There was an animal in the roofspace who ran back and forth at night above the bedroom. When I went to look, I found the attic was a clutter of old science books, *Collected Lenin*, dirty rugs, useless broken junk. Though she used nothing, Nina kept everything. When the snow melted, vodka bottles and faded plastic reared up in the village gulch. There was no organised refuse collection. Nina said she was at peace here; she wanted nothing else. In September she knew which mushrooms to pick. I can name only the *mukhomor*, the deathcap. Nina remembered the 'Lutsino masquerades', her mother riding a lady's bicycle. She wrote poetry. In one poem she praised the Lutsino autumn. In another, she lamented that she could no longer see the world around her; her work as a computer programmer (a 'demiurge, creator of fleeting lives') had destroyed her eyes. She had a tic, an involuntary blink. In summer, mosquitoes settled on her big filmy face.

On Orthodox Christmas Eve in our last Lutsino winter, which was snowless and strange, I followed Nina to the church at midnight; out of the creaking back gate, over the foundations of the never-finished brick wall, through the scatter of pines under the pylon, along the edge of the cemetery, and down past the litter dump in the hollow. The graveyard at Lutsino, with its low iron boundaries, Orthodox crosses, communist stars and fluorescent plastic flowers, is the most tended part of the village. The frozen ground crunched, the melt patterns of ice on the slope were illuminated by the full moon and the electric glow from the village. There were car headlights on the road, torchbeams and voices on the paths on either side of the cemetery. Nina once told me that her spiritual guide, Father Alexander Men, said that sometimes, in graveyards, he could sense the ongoing dramas of the dead. I sensed them now, as though it were the graveyard in Dostoevsky's short satirical masterpiece *Bobok*, where the dead – generals, scientists, court councillors and society ladies – quarrel, chatter, philosophise and play card games under the gravestones, still able to sense the moral smell of their own lives and the lives of those close by.

Alexander Men, a Jewish convert to Orthodoxy, was a catacomb priest in the late Soviet period. 'He was the man sent from God to be a missionary to the wild tribe of the Soviet intelligentsia,' the scholar Sergei Averintsev once said. The elderly Nadezhda Mandelstam was baptised by him, and often came from Moscow to take communion at his little wooden church in Novaya Derevnya, the village, not far from the capital, where he was parish priest. Father Men's intellectual passion was natural science. As a young man in the late 1950s, he had hoped to study biology, but he was excluded from university as a Jew, and had to settle for enrolment in the Institute of Fur. 'From my early childhood, contemplation of nature has been my *theologia prima*,' he said. 'I used to go into a forest or a museum of paleontology in the same way I went into a church.' Nature was an icon of the first quality to him, and he believed that 'a religious outlook cannot be intellectually justified except somehow on the level of evolution'. Reflecting on the discoveries of his own times, he observed that science's penetration into the fabric of matter had made 'the scale of nature's destructive tendencies ever more apparent'. Thermodynamics, he believed, 'revealed a tendency in the movement of the cosmos *opposed* to the process of becoming'. Early one morning in September 1990, Father Men was murdered with a single axe-blow to the back of the head, as he walked alone in the mist on a forest path from his home towards the suburban train station. He was on his way to Novaya Derevnya to celebrate the liturgy at the church of the Meeting at the Temple. No one has ever been charged with Father Men's murder, but his many devoted followers in the intelligentsia believe that the crime was most likely the work of xenophobic elements within the KGB, afraid of his charisma, his Jewishness, his openness to other faiths and the wider world, his 'inner freedom'. 'Nothing can be ultimately proved,' Men once wrote; 'real scientists know that . . .'

The interior of the church at Lutsino, clean and newly painted, was decorated with bare fir trees, its concrete floor covered with plastic sheeting. The priest, Father Evgeny, in rich vestments of white and silver, anointed the congregation one by one, dipping a paintbrush into a small glass of oil held by a young acolyte. A man with drink-bloated features wiped holy oil over his face with a rough hand, and left the church, muttering. Anointed in her turn, Nina took her place among her friends at the front of the milling congregation, a lighted candle in her hand, her face, framed in its white headscarf, for once reposed, not twitching. (Just as Chekhov observed in his story 'The Steppe': the old 'are always radiant when they come back from church'.) She looked ready to stand all night on her lame leg before the saints, prophets and angels on the iconostasis, the screen of images of transcendent order and community which, according to her faith, brings the world of eternity directly into this world of time and matter. Nina's Siberian father and grandmother, a biochemist and a capitalist tycoon, are private icons in her life of devotion.

Alexei Balandin once described chemistry as the 'contemplation of the world of matter'. At a turning moment in his creative life, Chekhov remarked that 'the writer must be as objective as the chemist', and that 'for chemists there is nothing unclean on the earth'.

FIVE

Mozzhinka

... we should not minimise our sacred endeavours in this world, where,
like faint glimmers in the dark, we have emerged for a moment from the
nothingness of unconsciousness into material existence.

ANDREI SAKHAROV, Nobel lecture

The sun had set hours ago, but the moon still lit the river and the fields beyond. In the forest, occasional squares of electric yellow beckoned from dacha windows among the firs. Banks of shovelled ice sparkled in orange-pink pools under the lamps lining the straight road through the colony. We skied past the Academy of Sciences clubhouse on the creaking snow. A soft glow shone from inside.

A caretaker still lived in a corner of the palace built for Stalin's scientists, keeping the unused building fully heated through the winter. The white plaster on its neoclassical façade had crumbled and the wide steps were cracked and dislodged by underground plant life and frost, but red carpets ran the length of its parquet halls, and the spider plants in urns at the foot of the grand staircase were still green and moist. In the auditorium, the stage was set with a podium and hung with curtains of heavy brocade. On the upper floor, the banqueting hall and kitchen waited for some evening of pomp and glass-raising that would never come: ranges scrubbed, pots stacked, knives sharpened.

Earlier in the day, when the caretaker had allowed us to explore the clubhouse, I had studied the portrait on the wall of Sergei Vavilov, looking at his eyes. By the end of his life, other scientists recalled, those eyes were tired and empty. On one occasion, in 1943, the renowned physicist had been seen coming out of the office of the president of the Academy of Sciences in tears, after petitioning on behalf of his brother the biologist Nikolai Vavilov, a greater scientist, who was starving in a 'death cell' in a prison in Saratov. Vyshinsky had ignored all petitions; Molotov had said, with irritation, that he had no time for the matter, and Andrei Andreev told a petitioner that there were 'facts of which you are not aware'. Two years later, Sergei Vavilov sat up all night, as Andrei Sakharov writes in his memoirs, smoking through several packets of cigarettes, asking himself whether to accept the post of president of the Academy, or to allow the appointment of Stalin's favourite Trofim Lysenko and the further devastation of Soviet science and agriculture. Vavilov died in 1951 at the age of sixty, before the *Great Soviet Encyclopedia* that he was editing reached 'Molotov', the name of the man who had personally sanctioned the arrest of his brother Nikolai. Under the entry for Nikolai Vavilov, the encyclopedia informed that 'the scientific work of Vavilov was stopped in 1940', which was code for the fact that he was arrested and never returned.

I imagined Sergei Vavilov as I passed, in his honoured place in the almost-dark clubhouse, his faded eyes staring out from the wall. Vavilov had insisted that this dacha colony be built here, at Mozzhinka, just outside Zvenigorod on the Moscow side of the ancient town. It was a place he loved. During the war, he had worked on night-vision technology for the military. In discussions about where to establish a dacha colony for academicians who had contributed to the Soviet victory, he favoured Mozzhinka, with its dense firs and moist clay soil, over the sandy massif above the bend in the river at nearby Lutsino. A native Muscovite, descended from local peasants, he knew the area from summer walks and mushroom-hunting expeditions.

As a young man, struggling to free himself for physics from his preoccupation with art and beauty, Sergei Vavilov had written in his diary that all he asked from nature was its quiet. Yet Mozzhinka holds more than quiet. It is the landscape of the folk tales of magic and terror that he had loved as a child, of the imaginative worlds of Hoffmann, Afanasiev and Gogol, which first summoned him towards a vocation in the science of sight and light. Wood demons might hide in the shadows of the firs, Baba Yaga's house on chicken legs might appear in some clearing in the forest, or, in some deserted church on the river's edge, the goblin Viy.

Rest for a scientist, Vavilov said, should be regarded as another way of furthering creative work. Mozzhinka *dachniki* remember him sitting in the garden of his dacha, always with some antique volume in his hand. Bibliomania was an aspect of his youthful aestheticism which he had tried in vain to overcome. As a schoolboy he had browsed in the antique booksellers of Mokhovaya and the basements of old Sukharevka, finding gems in the dust, such as a seventeenth-century edition of Otto von Guericke's *Experimenta Nova* (*ut vocantur*) *De Vacuo Spatio*, a treatise on the physics of vacuums. 'The book is the "highest" thing in the world, because it is almost a person,' he wrote in his diary in 1913; 'sometimes it is even higher than a person (like Gauss, like Pushkin)'. Yet he longed for his passion to cool. He was not a 'novice' in the matter of books, he reflected; he understood their value, the difference between a book that was 'just for himself', like a first edition of Goethe's *Faust*, and one that merely had 'rarity' value. Yet he could not stop himself acquiring all kinds of trash and 'bricks'.

In the *ex libris* plate in Sergei Vavilov's books, a man stands behind a lamp, his face invisible, his hand reaching out to a bookcase. What value did Vavilov, who wanted to hide his face in books, place on the leather-bound 'brick', printed on the finest white paper, which he edited for Stalin's seventieth birthday? *To Iosif Vissarionovich Stalin* contains essays by his brother's killers: 'scholars' like Lysenko, who hails Stalin as the 'incarnation of the people's wisdom' and hymns the 'miracle' of the transformation, through 'progressive biology', of wheat into rye, and Vyshinsky, who describes the conditions for the 'withering away of the state', a process which can only occur when there is no further prospect of attack from without (in the meantime, the former prosecutor cautions, the struggle against espionage remains one of the Soviet state's most important functions). In Vavilov's own contribution, entitled 'The Scientific Genius of Stalin', he makes an 'ardent, heartfelt greeting to our wise teacher', the 'Coryphaeus of Science', because of whom 'history does not just happen, but begins to be consciously directed'. He rejoices in the Soviet victory over 'mechanistic and idealistic theories in the study of living matter' in the field of biology. With these words, Vavilov was 'rejoicing' in the dissolution of the All-Union Institute of Plant Breeding that his brother Nikolai had founded soon after the Revolution, and in Nikolai's arrest and eleven-month torture by the NKVD, and his death sentence, in a minutes-long trial without witnesses or lawyers, for Trotskyite wrecking and espionage.

ᑯᴥᑌ

It was hard to keep up with my companion on the downward incline towards the river. Before the road turned back on its long loop along the bank, he slid on to a narrow path into the forest, and I could not tell where he was going. He had skied this way in the morning and was all momentum and purpose, shouting back to me that we should cut through the forest and ski across the field on the other side, then back to the house for shots of vodka. I stopped to rest and lost him. The path was dim, the wind picked up, the treetops clawed the lilac moonlight.

From my first visit, Mozzhinka had seemed to me a secret place, outside the run of time, made for play: hide-and-seek, treasure hunts, night skiing. Along the Riga highway, which leads west from Moscow towards Zvenigorod, new dacha settlements appeared from week to week among the pylons in muddy fields, their names, full of the ersatz romance of modern Russian *marketologia*, advertised on billboards at the side of the road – 'Prince's Lake', 'Sherwood', 'Little Italy', 'Nest of Gentry', 'Europe' – but the turn-off to Mozzhinka remained unmarked. On our way to Lutsino we would take it sometimes to visit a friend, an English widow with four young children, who lived, under some fragile charm, in a house enclosed by a high wall. Her husband, a brilliant inventor from one of the Mozzhinka scientific dynasties, had just finished building their home when he died a sudden death. She ran a small school in the basement. There were climbing frames among the tall birches in the garden, sheds full of skis and sleds, and a banya. In winter she flooded the driveway to make an ice rink, and at Maslenitsa, the feast before Lent, she hired a horse and sleigh with bells and a driver to ride the children down to the river and back. She had an English governess, a Georgian nanny (who prepared feasts of *khachapuri* and *lobio*, cheese bread and stewed beans, fragrant with herbs) and the friendship of the local priest, Father Ion, whose own daughter had been killed by a drunken driver one night on the road through the colony.

I began to read about the place. Spider threads of meaning appeared, as though left by human observers among the trees, waiting for the light to touch them. Everything I read – about childhood, the quietness of bereavement, Italy, romantic poetry, fairy tales, and the physics of light and time – seemed to illuminate the mystery of Sergei Vavilov's life, the tragedy of his success. By chance, as I was researching an article on the allusions to English poetry in Akhmatova's *Poem Without a Hero*, I discovered that Claire Clairmont, sister-in-law of Shelley and lover of Byron, had found comfort in this landscape in 1825. Mourning the deaths of Shelley and her little daughter, Allegra (Byron's child), Clairmont left Italy and found work as a governess in the tumultuous household of a Moscow lawyer. The family and its retinue of servants and educators summered near Zvenigorod.

Clairmont sat through her first night in an armchair, to escape 'Bugs, the torment of Russia'. The moon shone from behind thin dark clouds. The next evening, she wrote in her journal that the rainsoaked landscape had delighted her the whole day long. The wind in the trees reminded her of waves breaking on the shores of Lerici, Shelley's last home. Church bells from far-off villages 'gave meaning to the scene' – 'village replying to village with intelligible language'. Drinking tea in an arbour, she watched the sunset beyond the river, lines of golden light piercing through the deep woods so that 'every opening between each leaf seemed to be filled up by a diamond or a gem radiant with every different hue'. She read Goethe, and took walks with the 'very sentimental' German tutor Chrétien-Hermann Gambs. They discussed poetry, philosophy, mathematics and the newest discoveries in astronomy regarding the multitude of solar systems and the immensity of the universe, whose centre, as Pascal said, is 'everywhere, but its circumference nowhere'. She noted Plato's remark that, if the colour of the sky had been scarlet instead of blue, the 'prevalent quality of man had been a sanguinary disposition'. She read Shelley's revolutionary verse and reflected on his 'rapid passage over the world': 'his whole existence was a striving after virtue and wisdom and he hurried on his course with such rapid eager steps he often overtook them. He tasted the Summer of Life . . . and took flight ere the arrival of its inevitable winter'.

The Vavilov brothers, the physicist Sergei and the biologist Nikolai, both looked for 'virtue and wisdom' in science. Perhaps it was their dispositions, as well as the different destinies of the disciplines of physics and biology under Stalin, that shaped their respective fates, a 'paradox', Sakharov says, that was 'extreme even for those times', but which, in a way, 'summed up the whole era'.

At Mozzhinka in 1949, Sergei began a private memoir. Perhaps he knew his own life was ending; his prose is unguarded, negligent of Stalinist pieties about science or the past, full of the spirit of Nikolai. He looks back on himself as a solitary child, a dreamer, a mystic, a coward. 'For me the world was divine,' he remembers. 'I firmly believed everything that Mama and Nanny Aksinya told me about heaven and hell and the white-haired god who lived behind the clouds.' He dreamed of the faces on icons, of miracles, sorcery, alchemy. Their father was a devout man, politically liberal and patriotic, with a complex inner life. He read Dostoevsky and tried to write poetry. Sergei read everything on his father's shelves, returning to Pushkin every day, believing everything. Religion and fantasy were one and the same. One year, on his 'angel day' in early March, after a Lenten meal and a prayer service for his health, he was given a copy of Alexander Afanasiev's magical tales, a fort with wind-up cavalry and a book about Aladdin and his magic lamp. At school, he remembers endless discussions about Darwin and God, in which the schoolboys would often outwit the priests. None of these discussions, he thought, had any impact on the boys' religious development. Sergei had few friends besides his elder brother, who was his opposite in character: outgoing, bold, a fighter. Nikolai often remarked that it was Sergei who had the better brain, but it was Nikolai who led the way in atheism, materialism and revolution.

Though in books that appeared under his name in the 1940s Sergei Vavilov set an adamant face against the paradoxes of quantum physics that threatened to undermine the determinism of Marxist–Leninist dialectics, his private memoir is guided by the principle of uncertainty. Images of revolution in the streets collide with images of the interior world of home. Everything is disconnected. Again and again, he says, 'I did not understand', 'it was all unclear', 'I had no understanding', 'it was a blur'. There is no sign in his arrangement of fragments of memory of the Stalinist who claimed that all the laws of history had been understood. The narrative ends at the threshold of his vision, and Nikolai, erased from his public works, stands clear in the foreground. Vavilov remembers the shock of the destruction of the Russian fleet by the Japanese at Tsushima as an awakening to history. 'The ghost of Tsushima's hell', as Akhmatova called it, was a portent for their generation. Vavilov sensed great waves of history breaking over the country, but understood nothing. He remembers marching in street demonstrations with his cousins after Nicholas II's October Manifesto of 1905, not understanding their cause. A man in worker's dress stood on Theatre Square in front of the Bolshoi, shouting, waving a knife. Cossacks rode past the Manège, whips in hand. Crowds gathered outside the governor's house on Tverskaya. At home, over tea, the family discussed politics. His father, a self-made textile millionaire and Moscow city councillor, was convinced by the promises of civil liberties in the Manifesto;

Sergei took the socialist part, following Nikolai. There were speeches and pamphlets: Marx, Engels, Bebel. He listened and understood nothing. He remembers in precise detail the furnishings of home, the feel of domestic interiors, their shadows and light. From the dark sitting room, with its red and gold divans, he heard Nikolai and his friends at their discussion group, and dreamed of leading an intellectual circle of his own. A red kerosene lamp illuminated coloured reproductions from the popular journal *The Meadow*, mounted in gilt frames on the walls. In the grand wooden house on Presnya to which they moved from their apartment on Nikolskaya Street near Red Square, there were indoor columns and murals, mahogany furnishings, a seventy-five-volume leather-bound edition of Voltaire and 'various other junk'. On Nikolai's name day in 1905, they played charades at home, while outside, barricades went up, factories burned and workers fought street battles with Cossacks and gendarmes. Classes were cancelled. Schoolboys joined demonstrations. Nikolai printed a school journal on a hectograph, filled with political proclamations; their parents did not intervene. The year 1905 frightened the fourteen-year-old Sergei. He buried himself in science, philosophy and art. He imitated Nikolai, building barricades, tearing up portraits of the Tsar, but it was no more than a child's game. Unlike Nikolai, he could not make the transition from thought into action. He was 'spineless', he says; no man of steel. Political lines blurred in his mind. It came naturally in his family to be 'of the left', 'for the people', a 'democrat'. Yet he could not translate these vague sensibilities into the hardness of real politics, or, he adds, its necessary cruelty.

For all his efforts to follow Nikolai into the flood of revolution, Sergei was closer in his tastes to the aesthetes of Sergei Diagilev's World of Art movement than to the Bolsheviks. While Nikolai studied the slugs and snails that attacked the fields and vegetable gardens of the Moscow region, Sergei toured Italy in search of illumination. Alexander Blok's *Italian Verses*, a cycle of poems about Italian towns infused with the writings of John Ruskin, had appeared in 1909. Pavel Muratov had recently published a translation of Walter Pater's *Imaginary Portraits* and a two-volume study, *Images of Italy*. Akhmatova and her husband, the poet Nikolai Gumilev, spent their honeymoon in Italy in 1912. Sergei Vavilov was not part of this creative elite, but he had aspirations. In 1914 he published a pair of essays on Verona and Arezzo in a journal for teachers of graphic art. However, his diary of 1913 records a painfully deliberated turn away from aestheticism. 'Diary of my last aesthetic wanderings,' he inscribed on its title page, 'or the Tragicomic memoria of a physicist, bound by the will of fate to the aesthetic yoke'. After visiting Santa Croce in Florence, he convinced himself that Italy's true greatness was not to be found in Giotto, Dante or Michelangelo, but in Galileo. 'Science, science is my business,' he told himself. 'Drop everything and concentrate on physics alone.' On his visit in the previous year, the beauty of Venice had provided him with a logical foundation for pure aestheticism; now, even as he turned away, the 'strange and wonderful city-paradox' beckoned him again: 'the grace and ease of Venezia stretch out to me. Even in the rain the Piazza is a fairy tale, an enchanted place. Luxurious, sweet, brazen, beautiful Venezia . . .' His diary ends on the train: 'So, home in two hours. I hope to God I will set out on a new road. – Finis'.

The tragicomedy of Sergei Vavilov's wanderings between art and science did not end. In the 1920s, he played his part in the great cultural project, led by Emilian Yaroslavsky, who called himself 'Yaroslavsky the godless', of replacing religion with science for a people who still venerated icons and relics. Now the people could read books on physics in cheap editions published by 'New Moscow' and 'Red Virgin Soil'. In the Lenin Library, wanting to understand the life of the man who had made the dacha colony appear in the forest, I read Sergei Vavilov's popular classics – *The Action of Sunlight, Sunlight and Life on Earth* and *The Eye and the Sun*. Printed on coarse paper, the books are disintegrating, their ochred pages corroded at the edges; but their words are still lucid, beautiful to read. Suffused with culture, Vavilov's writing beckoned me back to the magical light of Mozzhinka. *The Eye and the Sun* has Amenophis IV, founder of the cult of the sun, on its cover. Its epigraph is from Goethe: 'If the eye were not suited to the sun, how would we see the light?' The world, says Vavilov, is above all an object of sight, a picture. He illuminates his explanations with lines from the poems of Pushkin, Tyutchev, Fet and Esenin, from Plato's *Timaeus* and the hymns of the ancient Egyptians. What does the sun mean to the earth? Vavilov asks, illustrating Copernicus with lines from Lermontov. He describes Newton's experiments in his rooms in Trinity College, Cambridge, his colour wheel. How did the earth fall into such a perfect position in relation to the sun? Why are plants green? How is it that the curve of daytime sight coincides almost exactly with the average curve of sunlight dispersed by plants? What would the world be like if plants were black? Why do deep-water fish have eyes? Why do the sun and moon look bigger as they approach the horizon? We believe in what we can see, Vavilov explains, but our sight will only tolerate the weak light distributed by the matter that surrounds us.

The wave–particle duality of light is no enigma, Sergei Vavilov insisted in public in the late 1940s, for, as Stalin said, 'Marxist philosophical materialism holds that the world and all its laws are fully knowable . . . there is nothing in the world that is not knowable.' The 'new physics', Soviet ideologists feared, sought to dematerialise matter and resurrect 'idealism' on the basis of new understandings of radioactivity. In *Lenin and the Philosophical Problems of Modern Physics*, Sergei Vavilov praised Lenin for bringing light to the 'obscure and winding back alleys of the new physics in which idealism tries to hide'. There is much, however, that will never be known about the ways in which he worked in the shadows within the corrupted institutions of Soviet science, taking advantage of the state's interest in nuclear weapons to defuse the polemics about quantum physics that threatened to lead to another purge.

The main subject of Sergei Vavilov's life's research was luminescence, the science of the laws of transformation by matter of different kinds of energy in light. This too took him back to Italy, alchemy and fairy tale. The study of luminescence began in 1602, when a dilettante alchemist, Vincenzo Casciarolo, found a lump of barium sulphide on Monte Padermo outside Bologna. The material glowed in the dark, and he hoped it might be the Philosopher's Stone. Fortunius Licetus, professor of philosophy at Bologna, called it the Luciferous Stone, which 'absorbs the golden light of the sun, like a new Prometheus stealing a Celestial Treasure'. He argued that the source of moonlight was phosphorescence of the kind that lit the Luciferous Stone, but Galileo rightly held that the moon glowed with sunlight reflected from the earth. Vavilov, who had dreamed of alchemy in childhood, illustrated luminescence with a scene from the Russian magical tale *Konyok Gorbunok*, 'The Little Humpback Horse'. Ivan the Fool, the brother who never knows what is happening to him, succeeds in fulfilling the impossible tasks the Tsar sets for him, retrieving a lost ring from the bottom of the sea. On his journey, at the end of which he finds fortune, Ivan sees a 'miraculous light' in the forest, which gives neither smoke nor warmth. He thinks the light may be an evil spirit, but it is a plume of the Firebird.

Why did Sergei Vavilov, the aesthete physicist for whom the world was full of mysterious beauty, end his life hymning Stalin and writing his memoirs in the quiet of Mozzhinka? Why did his elder brother, the convinced materialist who poured all his bright energy into the revolutionary new society, die in prison?

'Our life is on wheels,' Nikolai Vavilov would often say in the years after the Revolution. If the new Bolshevik state was moving forward at speed towards the bright future, Nikolai was in the vanguard. Shura Ipatev, his nephew, remembers him as a giant personality, full of charm and radiant energy, absent-minded in all things but science; so different from Sergei, whom Ipatev recalls as a cautious, guarded man. Nikolai was one of the few people in the new society with a car of his own, which he loved. In 1920 he announced his 'Law of Homologous Lines', an ordering of vegetation analogous with Dmitri Mendeleev's periodic table of elements, a revolution in the science of botany which improved on the Swedish botanist Carolus Linnaeus's classification of plant species. He drove between Moscow and Leningrad in the 1920s, setting up botanical institutes, lecturing on Darwin, fruit hybrids and the geographical specificity of wheat genes. He had a protegé, the young peasant scientist Lysenko, who was always covered in mud and wore his cap askew on his head. Vavilov drove to Afghanistan in search of edible grains that might be grown in the USSR. Ipatev remembers him in a cream summer suit, with a field bag over his shoulder, tipping his 'hello-goodbye hat' as he set out on his travels. In Abyssinia, he was received by the barefoot regent Tafari-ras, who kept him up all night talking about life in the workers' state. He greeted people in eastern languages: '*Salaam aleikum*', '*Salamat bashid*'. He loved children and gave them exotic gifts: rings set with Afghan turquoise, a silk umbrella. He took his nephew to row on the pond at the Moscow zoo and observe sex transplants on chickens. Sometimes he allowed him to ride with him up to the Kremlin gates in Lenin's Rolls-Royce.

For Nikolai Vavilov, as for so many of his kind, the practice of science was an aspect of a wider commitment to social justice. In the new society, he wanted to use his extraordinary theoretical mind and his preternatural capacity for hard practical scientific work to improve agriculture, improve the quality of grain, make better harvests, feed the Soviet people. He had been taught by Moscow's great biologist Kliment Timiryazev, and conferred with the leading British geneticists in London and Cambridge. He believed in global research; he wanted to understand the plant world of the whole planet, the cultivation and migration of grain varieties – rye, wheat, rice and flax – with the movement of civilisation across the world, to learn from archaeologists about the seeds the dwellers on the Black Sea steppes had sown five thousand years ago.

In the 1920s biology, particularly the science of plant breeding in the style in which Nikolai Vavilov practised it, was a glamorous science, full of poetry and charm. 'A plant . . . is the envoy of a living thunderstorm that rages permanently in the universe . . . a plant in the world is an event, a happening, an arrow, and not a boring, bearded development,' Mandelstam wrote in his *Journey to Armenia*. He was devoted to scientists like his friend Kuzin. He declared,

> I don't know how it is with others, but for me the charm of a woman increases if . . . she has spent five days on a scientific trip lying on a hard bench of the Tashkent train, knows her way around in Linnaean Latin, knows which side she is on in the dispute between the Lamarckians and the epigeneticists, and is not indifferent to the soybean, cotton, or chicory.

Yet by the 1930s, those very disputes, on either side of which stood Lysenko and Vavilov, were becoming lethal. Lamarckians, also known as 'progressive biologists', held that one could change inherited characteristics by changing the external conditions in which a plant or animal lived. With his bogus theory of 'vernalisation', which he expounded without scientific terminology or reference to the works of other biologists, Lysenko promised that maize crops would grow in the far north, oak trees on the southern steppe. When applied on collective farms, Lysenko's ideas led directly to a crisis in Soviet food production.

One of the NKVD informers who had first begun to slander Vavilov (among others) was the plant breeder and professor at the Timiryazev Academy of Agriculture, Ivan Yakushkin, descendant of the famous Decembrist exile. As a gifted young professor at the Agricultural Institute in the southern city of Voronezh during the Civil War, Yakushkin had tried to escape to Turkey with the retreating White forces. He was arrested in 1930 and released the following year. 'Immediately after my release, I was recruited by the OGPU as a secret agent,' he wrote in a note found recently in Vavilov's secret police file. 'I continued in this job until I was discharged from it in Nov 1952 or 1953.' In 1931, Yakushkin was already reporting that Vavilov's institute was a centre of organised 'wrecking activities'. One day in 1935, Vavilov bumped into Stalin in a corridor of the Kremlin, and the tyrant, for a moment, looked afraid. Vavilov knew the collision was a portent. In the same year, Stalin shouted, 'Bravo, Comrade Lysenko, bravo!' at a congress of collective-farm 'shock-workers'. In 1937, by which time his secret police file was already bulging, Nikolai Vavilov was forced to resign as president of the academic institution that he had founded. Molotov, then Chairman of the Council of People's Commissars, dutifully imitated Stalin by supporting Lysenko's 'people's agrobiology', sneering openly at Vavilov. Molotov refused to allow an international congress of geneticists – which two thousand leading scientists were set to attend – to take place in Moscow. Two years later, Molotov, who was in charge of agriculture for the Central Committee, refused Vavilov permission to lead a Soviet delegation to a scientific conference in New York. Vavilov's own discoveries about hybridisation and plant genetics could have improved Soviet crops. Instead, the USSR ended up importing seed stocks from America. The great botanist was mocked and silenced; the institutions he had founded were taken over by Lysenko's followers, or dissolved.

After his arrest in 1940, Nikolai Vavilov was interrogated in an NKVD prison in Moscow, kept standing for twelve hours at a stretch till his legs swelled. Between August 1940 and July 1941, he was interrogated four hundred times. When Hitler's troops were close to Moscow, Vavilov was sent to a prison in Saratov. Molotov remembered how David Ryazanov, who had been exiled to Saratov, had once quipped that socialism could not be created in one apartment, let alone one town. By all accounts, Nikolai Vavilov created something fine in the way of society in the windowless 'death cell' in which he lived, starving, for a year, without bathing or exercise. The narrow overcrowded cell was in a basement, an electric bulb burned night and day, and in summer it was very hot. 'Vavilov brought a measure of discipline into things,' another inmate recalled. 'He tried to cheer up his companions ... he arranged a series of lectures on history, biology and the timber industry. Each of them delivered a lecture in turn. They had to speak in a very low voice . . .' Before he died in 1943, Nikolai Vavilov had delivered more than a hundred hours of lectures to his cellmates.

Decades earlier, at the age of thirty-three, Nikolai Vavilov had written to the woman he loved, 'I take love too seriously. I really have a profound faith in science, in which I find both purpose and life. And I am quite ready to give my life for the smallest thing in science.' He continued,

> It was my birthday yesterday . . . for some reason I keep recall-ing the opening lines of Dante: 'Nel mezzo del cammin di nostra vita' – 'Halfway along life's path . . . I strayed into a dark forest . . .' Now I have got to get out of that forest . . . It is a difficult forest, but is there any forest which does not have a way out?

I was learning about the lives of the Vavilov brothers while I was rereading Akhmatova, and, as sometimes happens, the books began to read each other. Akhmatova's *Poem Without a Hero* begins in the year 1913, the year of Sergei Vavilov's pilgrimage to Italy, and ends on the road 'to the east'. The poet, a bereaved and silenced survivor, sees a 'funeral course' in the 'solemn, crystalline silence of the Siberian Land'. The road 'opens' to her, a road 'along which so many have gone'. T. S. Eliot's line 'In my beginning is my end' is one of several epigraphs in the *Poem*. Accordingly, she sees the 'years of Yezhov and Beria' foreshadowed in the decadence of 1913, which comes back to her in the darkness of the Stalin era as a har-lequinade in an enchanted palace, a 'midnight Hoffmaniana'. The year 1913, in which Sergei Vavilov chose a 'new road', Akhmatova called 'the apotheosis of the 1910s in all their magnificence and all their flaws', 'the final year' before the onset of the 'real Twentieth Century'. In the secret world of magical tales, the poet found her own cryptic way of writing about 'the fate of a generation . . . about everything that befell us'; a way not to 'disappear into a state hymn'. *Poem Without a Hero* is full of mirror-writing, hidden drawers, flasks of poison, demons and curses. Towards the end of her life, Akhmatova sometimes saw the poem as 'completely transparent, emanating an incomprehensible light (. . . when everything shines from within)'.

⌁

Savvino-Storozhevsky Monastery stands on a promontory above the river, just beyond Zvenigorod. I visited with my family in late February, during Maslenitsa, the great feast that precedes the Lenten fast, stopping on the roadside to climb the ice-slicked steps to the Cathedral of the Dormition, a plain single-domed white-washed square building, which stands apart from the walled monastery. The roadside was busy. People came up and down from the cathedral, watching their feet; others had stopped their cars at the bottom of the hill to fill plastic flagons with spring water from a pipe that protruded from a bank of spattered snow on the roadside.

'The road is always mounting', wrote Claire Clairmont, who came to Savvino-Storozhevsky to hear a *Te Deum*; the monastery is 'half way up the hill from the road side and hid among the trees . . . surrounded by four white walls with a tower at each corner'. The monastery is the same now, though a Soviet-era sanatorium for the military is also hidden among the trees, advertising its amenities with large colour photos, mounted on a concrete wall opposite the monastery gates, of shiny-fleshed soldiers in a sauna. Perhaps they are not as out of place here as they look; Savva Storozhevsky, a disciple of St Sergius of Radonezh who founded the monastery at the end of the fourteenth century, took his name from the word *storozh*, which means 'guard' or 'look-out'. Zvenigorod had been ravaged by the Mongol Khan Tokhtamysh in 1382, and the monastery, with its view over the land around, was a look-out post for the church.

Savva continued to look out for his church in the face of invading armies. In 1812, Napoleon's stepson, General Eugène de Beauharnais, was taking a night's rest in the monastery with his men, when the door opened and a man in a long black robe came in and said, 'Do not let your troops sack the monastery or take anything from the church. If you fulfil my request, God will be merciful and you will return to your homeland unharmed.' The General went into the church next morning and recognised the face of his night-time visitor on an icon of the Venerable Savva. He bowed to the saint's relics in their silver shrine. In his many campaigns, Beaugarnier came to no harm, and his descendants returned regularly to Zvenigorod to venerate Savva.

The survival of Savva's relics in the Soviet period is a story of violence and secret deals. The saint's remains had been disinterred in the late seventeenth century in the presence of Alexei Mikhailovich, the second Romanov tsar, who built a residence in the monastery, surrounded it with high brick and whitewash walls, and added greatly to its power and wealth. Alexei's son Fyodor III, who lived in the monastery, commissioned a silver shrine for the relics, which, by then, the faithful believed to be imperishable. In April 1918, the Bolsheviks confiscated the monastery's fields, cattlesheds, stables, workshops, dairies, mills and beehives, its guesthouse and its grand Moscow hostel on Tverskaya. The priest Father Vasili fell on his knees in the Cathedral of the Nativity and begged the congregation to protect its sacred objects. The following month, a group of local Bolsheviks, led by a commissar named Makarov, came up the hill to requisition bread and take an inventory of the monastery's possessions. Father Vasili rang the bells, and peasants came running from nearby villages. A fight broke out by the walls. Makarov and another Bolshevik were killed and several others wounded. A revolutionary tribunal in Moscow convicted Father Vasili of organising an uprising against Soviet power, and sentenced him to an unlimited prison term with hard labour. The monastery's remaining property was taken, and most of the monks dispersed. In February 1919 the People's Commissariat of Justice issued a resolution on the unsealing of relics, and the Zvenigorod Soviet decided to expose the remains of Savva. As the last few monks held a liturgy, over a hundred men entered the monastery. They opened the shrine and cut away Savva's bindings, revealing a skull and thirty-two bones. Savva had decayed. The Bolsheviks jeered, rearranging the bones to make them look ridiculous. 'It was the Garden of Gethsemane,' one of the monks said later. Local people were summoned to look. Some mocked, others wept and venerated the exposed bones. Two months later, a group of armed men from the local Soviet took them out of the shrine, wrapped them in newspaper and tablecloths and drove away. A Moscow professor of ecclasiastical law, Nikolai Kuznetsov, led an appeal against the removal of the relics to the Council of People's Commissars. An investigation was launched, overseen by Lenin. The proceedings, conducted in the monastery, were led by a specialist in the 'struggle against religion' who concluded that the treatment of Savva's relics had been 'in conformity with revolutionary discipline'. Soon afterwards, Professor Kuznetsov was arrested in his apartment on Neglinnaya Street and sentenced to death by a revolutionary tribunal, a sentence later commuted to imprisonment in a concentration camp until the conclusive victory of worker-peasant power over world imperialism. (Kuznetsov was arrested again in 1924, and served a sentence of exile in Kirghizia. He was arrested a third time in 1931. There is no information about the date or place of his death.) The last monks were evicted from their cells, and the monastery was closed.

Yet even in his decayed state, Savva retained spiritual power. Sometime in the 1920s, Mikhail Uspensky, curator of the State Historical Museum and the Museum of the Revolution, was called in to the Lubyanka. A secret police officer pointed at a silver platter on a table and said, 'Take this dish and put it in a museum. Do whatever you think necessary with what is on it . . . the bones of Savva Storozhevsky.' The curator understood what the Chekist intended. Uspensky, who was from a well-established Moscow intelligentsia family, had married a Zvenigorod girl and built a dacha on a hill near the monastery. Their son, born in 1920, had been named Savva in honour of the saint; he grew up to be a polar scientist, writing books called *The Motherland of the Polar*

Bear and *The Birds of Novaya Zemlya*. The Uspenskys kept the relics in their Moscow apartment for a while, then buried them in a sealed container in the garden of the dacha. After the dacha burned down, Uspensky moved them back to Moscow, saying he could not die before he had dealt with Savva. In 1983, the Uspenskys handed the relics over to the newly reopened Danilov monastery in Moscow. In 1998, they were returned to Savvino-Storozhevsky.

On the day of our visit the monastery was busy. On the pathways of packed snow between the white monastery buildings, women in spike heels, tight jeans and short coats passed long-haired monks in black habits. In a *lavka*, a nun sold fresh bread, purple wine in plastic bottles, mead and soft *pryaniki*, honey cakes filled with plum jam. Outside the Cathedral of the Nativity, a notice advertised the monastery school. A mother, wearing a long dark skirt and headscarf in the Orthodox style, led her five young children into the cathedral ahead of us. Some of the frescoes had been repainted in bright tones. In the mottled dark gold and grey-black of the older frescoes were figures of bishops: Arseny of Tver, Dmitri of Rostov, St Pantelaimon, and the Venerable Savva in prayer before an icon on a rock in a desert. The colours in the unrestored parts of the church were most beautiful: powder blue, pink, dark green, held between the cracks and fissures. The gold paint, contoured on the rough plaster, took in light from many tapers that made its surface appear to be in movement. Lamps of swirling silver hung from the canopy with its five domes. From the ceiling among teal-blue vine tendrils, the faces of saints looked down, suspended in gold; so many faces, without bodies but with hands open, taking in grace, or closed in prayer. The interior of an Orthodox church is intended to give a sense of heaven, and heaven is crowded. Visitors crossed themselves in front of an icon of Nicholas II and his family. A young man kissed a case of tiny brass reliquaries, one of which contained a fragment of stone from Golgotha.

Savvino-Storozhevsky's most precious icons now hang in the Tretyakov Gallery in Moscow. Story has it that the three panels from an iconostasis depicting Christ, the Apostle Paul and the Archangel Michael, by one of the greatest of Russian icon painters, the early-fifteenth-century monk Andrei Rublev, were found under a woodpile in a derelict shed sometime in 1918 or 1919 and taken to the Kremlin workshops to be restored under the supervision of Igor Grabar, curator of the Tretyakov before and after the Revolution. Details of the story are obscure. The months of fear and anguish, when devout local Christians fought devout local Bolsheviks, were a time of rich opportunity for a canny aesthete like Grabar. He had been close to the World of Art movement in the 1900s, but chose to stay in Russia after 1917 and give his energies to the workers' power. Former associates in the art world called him a renegade, 'infected with the general psychosis', for his part in the expropriation of Botticellis from princesses.

In the summer of 1918, Narkompros (the People's Commissariat of Enlightenment) set up a commission for the preservation of ancient Russian art. As well as Grabar, the commission included the art critic Pavel Muratov. The chaos of 'war communism' worked to the advantage of the art historians, who had long revered Rublev's icons for purely aesthetic reasons. One of the commission's first moves was to send a group of restorers to Savvino-Storozhevsky, where the frescoes were crumbling and covered with candle grease and thick white secretions of lime. A local historian in Zvenigorod believes that the story of the discovery of the Rublev panels in the woodshed may be a cover for one of the more educated young priests at the Cathedral. Father Dmitri Krylov had known one of the restorers of Narkompros, the Byzantinist and art historian N. D. Protasov, since his student days. Fearing for the icons, he may have handed them over to the restorers without permission from his superiors at the monastery or from the local Bolsheviks. Protasov and Grabar then contrived the story about the woodpile for official reports.

Beside Rublev's icons, 'everything loses its lustre'; they 'do not yield even to Titian', Grabar wrote. He considered the Zvenigorod panels among the finest works of the fifteenth century. In his 1926 study of Rublev, Grabar described restoration as archaeological work, penetrating through layers of paint to find the secrets of colour and illumination, and gaze into the holy of holies of the creative process, where 'we unlock the mystery of his craft and comprehend the precious meaning of his art'. The fragments of paint on the panels now look like mosaic; the material is torn back so that one can see, revealed up close in the strong light of the Tretyakov Gallery, the linen cloth on the icon wood on to which the layers of colour, the softest earth purples, blues and pinks, have been applied, and the artistic miracle of these icons, the circles of black paint that Rublev has transformed into a human gaze, dynamic sightlines that penetrate outward into the room. How is it possible that the fullness of a human gaze, a divine gaze, an intelligence, should still be present in a small circle of black paint on this piece of cracked and abraded wood? Is this a question for science? Rublev demands an 'inward visit', Alexander Men said; 'mathematics cannot prove its beauty'. The features on the gentle faces are drawn as fine as incisions. There is no shadow in these faces, only a pervasive glow of gold, and, in the strong head of the Apostle Paul, occasional flecks of white, under the eye, on the earlobe, the brow, the back of the neck, the curling beard. The face of the Archangel is the most golden of the three, for Michael is made of light, the 'chief captain of the host', on whom Lucifer cannot bear to look. In Orthodox tradition, angels are 'secondary lights' that spread the fire of the divinity, defending earthly creation against the forces of ruin.

As president of the Academy of Sciences, Sergei Vavilov was actively concerned with the preservation of cultural monuments; Peter the Great's Kunstkamera in St Petersburg and many of the 'Pushkin places' were restored at his initiative. Yet there were places (as well as people) that Vavilov was powerless to preserve. In the late 1940s, a friend from Mozzhinka visited the Savvino-

Storozhevsky Monastery. By then, some of its buildings were warehouses; others had fallen into ruin. 'If you told Academician Vavilov, maybe he would help,' the guard on duty said. 'Do you think I don't know what is happening there?' Vavilov responded, with a rare show of vexation.

In the summer of 1919, the monastery was used as a home for mentally retarded children. The children lived here like wild animals, scavenging for food. Later it was used as a labour camp, then a sanatorium. The only part of the monastery to be preserved intact after 1918 was its museum, which for many years was cared for by Alexander Maximov, its first curator. A local historian and parishioner, Maximov had been called to Moscow for the proceedings over the 'uprising', and sentenced to hard labour for slandering Soviet power. Somehow, he avoided his sentence, and found work with the People's Commissariat of Enlightenment.

In the museum we saw the potsherds and flints of early man, found around Zvenigorod. 'What kind of people were they?' Sergei Vavilov asked in the first sentences of his memoir, thinking of his ancestors, 'here, near Moscow'. 'Nobody knows anything about them, and indeed they knew nothing about themselves,' he added. 'Peace be upon their dust and their souls.' In another display case, pieces of broken china, glassware, doorknobs and ceramic tiles were arranged on the felt. Mounted in the last room was a pamphlet by Grabar, published in 1919, on 'Why it is necessary to guard and keep the treasures of art and antiquity'. As we were leaving, the old lady guarding the room insisted that we watch a documentary film. She turned out the lights. In grainy black-and-white, we saw the cross pulled off the Cathedral of the Nativity, a bonfire, icons in the flames. Children grinned at the camera, and old peasant women looked into the hectic lens in terror, giggling horribly, sobbing into their shawls. It was propaganda, but all its meanings came out backwards now. Darker footage inside the cathedral showed the opening of Savva's shrine, the quick cutting of the bindings by a hand with a knife, bones in the dust. Then a cartload of dirty orphans arrived at the monastery gates, waving. At the end of the film came scenes of the 1930s sanatorium. Young men, with heroic communist bodies, exercised in perfect synchrony on the riverbank. Then a horde of young women ran on to the sandy shore, stripped naked and skipped into the water, laughing, splashing. Wearing identical white slips and shorts, the young men and women ran together up the hill towards the monastery; transfigured, indestructible, captured as light between the sun and the camera lens.

I looked out over the miles of white land from outside the monastery walls. The days were lengthening, there was warmth in the sun. Claire Clairmont admired the way this hill and its groves sloped in a gentle descent to the river, remarking on the 'little streams of light which the rays of the sun made through each line of trees'. In *The Eye and the Sun*, Sergei Vavilov related a story told by Gorky that illustrates how human beings unconsciously materialise light: 'I saw Chekhov, sitting in his garden, trying to catch a ray of sunlight in his hat and put it on his head.'

SIX

Novgorod

Preserve my speech forever for its taste of misfortune and smoke,
for the resin of mutual patience, for the honest tar of work.
The water in Novgorod wells must be black and sweet
so that in it, for Christmas, the seven-finned star is reflected.

OSIP MANDELSTAM, 1931 (dedicated to Anna Akhmatova)

The night of 3 January 2001 must have been a fine one in the village of Khotyazh—fine enough, at least, for Nadia and Kolya to have kindled a small fire of birch twigs and broken roof timbers to light their midwinter tryst in the ruins of the Klopsky Monastery near the ancient city of Novgorod. On top of the hillside of rubble that once formed the domes of the Church of St Nicholas, the lovers had left behind them an empty tin of sprats, a scatter of cigarette ends and a written record of their presence scratched in the soft frescoed plaster of the apse wall.

The wooded high ground above the river Veryazhka on which the monastery stands feels like an island, especially in winter, when the freezing air vibrates with the hum of open space. The surrounding expanse might not be a pattern of small winding rivers and collective farmland just three hundred miles north-west of Moscow, but limitless distances of ice. Only the hull of a rowing boat, half sunk in snow, marked the river's edge as we crossed from Khotyazh to Klopsky on foot, leaving our driver in his battered white Mercedes. He had wanted to drive us across the frozen river, but we left him, sitting disgruntled at the wheel with the engine running, incongruously urban among the green and yellow *izbas*, the wooden well-heads, rotting hayricks and wandering Alsatians of the village. 'How can anyone live in villages like that?' the writer Danil Granin exclaimed as he toured the

Novgorod area in a motorboat one summer after the end of the
Soviet period; 'such melancholy'. The Russian word Granin used
for the atmosphere of villages like Khotyazh was *toska*, which,
besides melancholy, contains shades of yearning, nostalgia, even
anguish. The cultural historian Dmitri Likhachev was in the boat
with Granin that day. There was no forest left, he observed. The
villages had been destroyed and all that remained of the churches
were scattered ruins. In 1937, Likhachev said, the landscape had
none of that *toska*.

Mikhail of Klopsky, the early-fifteenth-century saint to whom
the monastery on the hill is dedicated, was a *yurodivyi*, one of
Russia's 'holy fools for Christ'. Unlike other holy fools, anarchic
spirits who unmasked the falsehood of the world by breaking its
rules and mocking the powerful, Mikhail kept, in his own strange
way, to the order of life in the monastery, and many of his prophe-
cies had a precisely targeted political import, heralding and
endorsing the rise of Moscow. Likhachev described him as 'a well-
known supporter of Moscow'. Mikhail sometimes disappeared,
and seldom spoke; when he did, he would often mirror the speech
of others. 'Who are you, a man or a demon? What is your name?'
the monastery superior, Theodosius, asked Mikhail three times
when he appeared at its gates out of nowhere, and each time
Mikhail simply echoed the abbot's question.

In the various lives of the saint, written in the late fifteenth and
mid-sixteenth centuries, Mikhail's origins are hidden in mystery.
V. L. Yanin, the great historian of ancient Novgorod, recently
hypothesised that he had been born into one of Moscow's most
powerful princely families. Prince Dmitri Shemyaka, who had vied
for supreme power with his cousin, Grand Prince Vasili II of
Moscow, once visited the monastery, and Mikhail foretold his
imminent death, stroking Shemyaka's head and saying three times,
'Prince, the earth cries out!' He foretold the end of the independent city-state of Novgorod, greeting the birth of Ivan III – the
Muscovite Grand Prince who would finally subjugate the once-
flourishing republic – in a frenzy of ominous bell-ringing. In the

early 1990s, archaeologists working in the monastery uncovered part of his stone tomb in a side chapel of its Church of the Trinity, and chose to leave him undisturbed in the ruin. On the day of our visit, his burial place was piled high with freshly cut branches of pine. Still distinct, twenty feet above him, painted in the place where, according to Orthodox iconographic tradition, the earthly Church must be represented, were the dark outlines and quiet colours of a walled city of onion-domed buildings: Novgorod.

On the northern shores of Lake Ilmen, Novgorod once linked the great plain of Northern Rus with Europe, Byzantium and the Muslim East, across a pattern of deep lakes and wide rivers. At the centre of this feudal trading city was the magnificent white and gold Cathedral of St Sophia and, strung loosely around it, a chain of simpler churches and monasteries, visible on every horizon. A unique tradition of religious art developed here between the tenth and fifteenth centuries. And when Mongol horsemen burned their way across Rus in the thirteenth century, nature conspired in Novgorod's preservation; the surrounding forests and marshes proved impassable to the Khan's armies, a peace was settled, and the city's great libraries and churches survived. Unlike other once-abandoned churches in the area now being restored to bright perfection and ecclesiastical busyness, the Church of the Trinity in Klopsky still expresses the mystery of its destitution, a destitution whose circumstances are stranger than any of the regional power struggles that its patron saint foresaw.

There are fewer stories and more lies about the process of ruin around Novgorod than about its building and restoration. I sat with my travelling companion on the rubble of the church wall, sheltered from the wind by the branches of a tall sycamore, and read my guide to the Lake Ilmen region. She took out her sketch pad (she is a landscape painter). The guide book was dense and difficult to use, printed on bad paper in the last year of Communist Party rule. Its manic stream of undifferentiated informativeness made it a kind of late Soviet chronicle, gasping in the coils of Communist Russia's contorted doublethink about culture and value. The guide moved erratically between minutiae of architectural history, morose asides about the squalor of Soviet building, proud tales of military triumph and defeat, and random accounts of the achievements of local workers: the annual haul of the men of the Red Fisherman Collective Farm, or the heroic hands of Maria Nikolaeva of the Red Banner, which in 1972 succeeded in extracting 4,300 kilos of milk from the udders of a single cow. After several pages on Klopsky's construction over the course of three centuries, the guide related in its habitual passive voice that, in 1923, the monastery 'was handed over to the keeping of the Novgorod Museum, which was not in a position to provide for its maintenance and restoration', that 'it was taken apart little by little for its brick', and that 'the complex suffered greatly during the years of the Great Patriotic War'.

Though it has only recently been possible to give a precise account of certain categories of knowable fact about Russian history – we may now be told, for example, how many medieval icons were torched by the Bolsheviks of the region in 1927, as well as how many measures of milk its cows yielded in 1972 – more veiled forms of political and moral witness and betrayal have for centuries been inscribed in the study and contemplation of Novgorod. Medieval Novgorod was governed by a local assembly, the *veche*, which elected its own ruling Council of Lords. From the late eighteenth century and throughout the nineteenth, the city embodied the aspirations of democratic thinkers, indicating that Russia was not doomed to unyielding autocracy, but rather that a courageous love for ordered forms of freedom lay deep within the traditions of the people. 'Novgorod had a popular government,' wrote the Enlightenment thinker Alexander Radishchev, who was exiled to Siberia by Catherine the Great; 'the people in the assembly at the *veche* were the true rulers'.

> *That bell on the* veche *tower served freedom alone,*
> *Which tolled its destruction*
> *And how many proud souls were lost in its fall!* . . .

the Romantic poet Mikhail Lermontov wrote. A generation later, the Decembrists elevated Novgorod to a political ideal, using the *veche* as a model in their draft constitutions. Many of them wrote reverently of Novgorod, and Pavel Pestel, who was hanged after the failed uprising of 1825, made a study of the city. Later in the nineteenth century the anti-tsarist writer Vissarion Belinsky called the city a 'nest of Russian daring'. Before his arrest in 2003, Putin's political prisoner Mikhail Khodorkovsky invoked the Novgorod *veche* as a model of parliamentary democracy for post-Soviet Russia.

Just as the 'democratic' history of Novgorod was important for one way of looking at the Russian past and the possibilities for the Russian future, the story of its defeat by Moscow was important for those who valued, above all, the unity of the state, ruled from Moscow. In Molotov's library there is a book with a picture from one of the ancient Russian chronicles on its cover, showing the battle of the Muscovites with the Novgorodians on the river Shelon. Published the year before Stalin's death, *The External Politics of the Centralised State: Second Half of the Fifteenth Century* marks a time when Russian nationalism carried greater weight in official ideology than socialism.

Alexander Herzen, one of the revolutionary-democratic company in spirit, took a contrary view of Novgorod, which he called a 'wretched little town with a great historical name'. In one of its more subtle political punishments, Tsar Nicholas I's secret police exiled the anti-tsarist writer to Novgorod to work as a city councillor. In *Past and Thoughts*, Herzen remarks how funny it is to think of all the secretaries, assessors and provincial officials petitioning passionately for a post which, for a man of his culture and political sensibility, was imposed as a punishment. Until he walked out 'sick' in 1842, Herzen followed orders in the mindless 'signature factory' inside the Novgorod Kremlin, from which the Novgorod district was governed. He was 'fearfully bored'. In quiet, mounting disgust at the apathy, stupidity and cruelty of the provincial officials, he rummaged through files, discovering vivid testimony of the local nobility's debauchery and violence with house-serfs and peasants, and the brutality and degradation of the 'military settlements' near Novgorod, which had led to a murderous popular uprising during a cholera epidemic there in 1831. The 'military settlements', agricultural colonies run like army barracks, had been set up by Tsar Alexander I as a social experiment designed to bring rational order to the chaotic Russian countryside after the defeat of Napoleon. To Herzen, these insurrectionary events were ominous for Russia: 'In halls and maids' rooms, in villages and the torture-chambers of the police, are buried whole martyrologies of frightful villainies; the memory of them works in the soul and over the course of generations matures into bloody, merciless vengeance *which it is easy to prevent*, but will hardly be possible to stop once it has begun.'

Dmitri Likhachev revived the dream of medieval Novgorod as an emblem of civic justice in the twentieth century. In simple prose he explained the 'world significance' of this 'lecture-hall city' to which, he said, one may go to 'learn Russian history, and how to understand Russian art'. He even sensed the human contact of the past in the constant wind that blows off Lake Ilmen, piercing as a sea wind; he called it the 'wind of Russian history', as though the wind carried the sharp thrill of memories of fourteenth-century Novgorod's links with the Black Sea and the Caspian to the south, and the White Sea and the Baltic to the north and west, trade links that extended from Scandinavia to Byzantium, further than those of Genoa or Venice. The breath of Likhachev's own longing for freedom and world culture is perceptible in his work on Novgorod, a city he began writing about in Leningrad under siege. In his passages about the space and reach of medieval Novgorod, the very names of foreign places sing of open borders and free exchange: Denmark, Constantinople, the Hanseatic ports, Flanders, France, Persia, Arabia . . . The material of the city continued to work as the material of dissident political imagination, revealing more and more of its secrets throughout the twentieth century. The architecture and devotional art above the ground, and all the paraphernalia of medieval daily life that its clay soil had kept safe for nine centuries – wooden roadways, water pipes, amber beads, foreign coins and hand-scratched birch-bark documents recording mundane transactions and familiar emotions – bear witness to a past time of democracy, cosmopolitan culture, widespread literacy, civic order and digni-fied faith.

In the terrible year 1937, Likhachev spent a tranquil summer exploring Novgorod with his wife, Zina, then heavily pregnant with their twin daughters. Preservation and destruction were hap-pening simultaneously around them; some of the churches around the city were deserted, some had become fish factories, others were undergoing careful restoration or excavation, and a few, which they could not visit, were in use as NKVD prisons. Unable to afford a camera for visual record, Likhachev resorted to draw-ing on a Leningrad Academy of Sciences message pad. The *Novgorod Album* – his holiday sketches of monasteries, riverbanks, fishing boats and beloved people – was published in 1999, just months after his death. The long pencil strokes with which he caught the sloping profile of his wife's belly reveal how much the scholar had learned from studying the laconic lines of Novgorod's medieval icons. Zina's hands rest earthily on her hips, but the archangels and madonnas of the icon painter Theophanes the Greek are traceable in the poise of her head, the fall of her dress and the rakish halo-swirl of her sunhat.

I remember well the quiet authority of the tall leather-padded door of Likhachev's office in the dimly lit corridor of the Pushkin House, the Institute of Literature in Leningrad, where I worked in the archives during my graduate studies in 1990. Since then, in documentaries about Likhachev's life on the old-fashioned televi-sion channel Kultura, I have glimpsed the interior of that room: its soaring topography of crammed bookcases, desks piled high, icons and framed portraits of Russian writers. In his last decade, Likhachev, who died in 1999 at the age of ninety-two, was hon-oured as the embodiment of the best traditions of Russian intellectual life. Despite all the crimes and barbarities he witnessed during his imprisonment in the first Gulag on Solovki Island, he had come to love the place, just as he loved the whole Russian north, studying its ancient cities and monuments, campaigning for their preservation. Against the grain of official Soviet thought, which taught that everything was ultimately knowable with the aid of dialectical materialism, Likhachev saw the world as a riddle, a mystery. 'What is beyond the world, and can one not look into that part of the mirror world which is hidden beyond the edges of the mirror?' he wondered as a child.

The son of a Petersburg chemistry teacher, Likhachev came from a milieu which took thought seriously. Most of the boys in his class at school during the cataclysmic years of revolution and civil war shared his urge to work out for themselves a personal philosophy. One called himself a Nietzschean; another dreamed of government by an intellectual aristocracy; a third, who was a sceptic, was recruited by the secret police after leaving school and, at risk to his own freedom, warned Likhachev of his coming arrest. Likhachev's university days in the 1920s were a time of intellectual exhilaration for him. Until 1927, Leningrad was a carnival of 'humorous' philosophical circles. Likhachev joined the Cosmic Academy of Sciences, whose members greeted each other with the Greek word *khaire*, 'rejoice', presented playful scholarly papers and awarded one another 'chairs'. Likhachev was 'professor' of Melancholy Philology. A profoundly religious friend held the Chair of Elegant Theology, and two 'principled atheists' held Chairs in Elegant Psychology and Elegant Chemistry. The Academy proclaimed the principle of 'happy science', insisting that 'the world that science establishes by research into our surroundings should be "interesting" and more complicated than it was before it was studied'. Marxism, to Likhachev, was 'unhappy science' which diminished the world, made it dull and grey and monotonous, 'subordinating it to coarse materialistic laws which kill morality'. He was arrested in 1928 in front of his parents for having publicly criticised the Soviet reform of Russian orthography and, after nine months in prison cells, spent the rest of his sentence in labour camps. For Likhachev, who had seen beloved companions executed and thrown into mass graves, and known the anguish of betrayal by people he trusted, a sense of the relativity of time and the possibility of transcendent justice formed the foundation of a personal philosophy which pacified and consoled him, giving him what he called 'spiritual poise'. 'If time is an absolute reality', he reflected,

> then Raskolnikov was right. Everything will be forgotten . . . and all that will remain will be humanity 'which has been made happy' by crimes that have passed into non-existence. What is more important on the scales of time: a future that is actually approaching, or a past which is disappearing more and more, into which, as into the maw of a crucible, good and evil go in equal measure? And what consolation is there for a man who has lost his dear ones?

Dmitri Likhachev wrote a letter to Varlam Shalamov in 1979, when both were old men. They shared a knowledge of the Gulag that they still could not speak of openly. 'I had a period in my life which I consider to have been the most important,' he told Shalamov cryptically. He wanted to preserve through his writing the people he had known and who, once his memory died, would disappear without trace. He paid tribute to Shalamov for having given expression to his own experience, for unearthing the material that lay buried in his memory.

In the short idyll between imprisonment and war, Likhachev visited Novgorod several times, boating between monasteries with fellow academics from Leningrad, picnicking on riverbanks, making notes. At this time, Russian historians like him who had survived the first wave of purges and the institutional cataclysms of the 1920s and 1930s were quietly finding ways of evading the binds of Marxist–Leninist dialectical materialism, which subsumed the humanities under the heading 'material culture' and, in effect, transformed them all into branches of sociology. The State Institute for the History of Material Culture was founded in 1919 to replace the Imperial Archaeological Commission. Bolshevik contempt for leftover traces of the various 'stages' of pre-Communist society never succeeded in stifling the cultivated instinct to preserve and restore. In official publications in 1932, icons had been described as 'unnecessary and socially harmful junk', and the word 'archaeology' condemned as a 'senile bourgeois term'. At the same time, a commission of scholars and restorers set to work to examine the state of repair of the churches and their decorations in Novgorod and Pskov, neglected since 1917. In 1932, Artemy Artsykhovsky, the great archaeologist of Novgorod, organised the first excavation in the city under the aegis of the Institute for the History of Material Culture. In his free time he led his students around the region on local buses to admire the frescoes.

The day had begun in the dark with our arrival at Novgorod station. It ended in the wilderness beneath Klopsky, the sky darkening as we wedged pieces of the rotting wooden scaffold that held up the ruins under the front wheels of the Mercedes. Our driver, now a sweating wreck, was ready to dismantle what was left of the church in order to free the car which, fearing for us, he had gallantly driven across the river into a deep drift of heavy snow. Throughout that January day Novgorod seemed to stage a series of riddling tableaux about the cross-currents of preservation and loss that run through its own history, winding through human dramas, both public and hidden. As we walked down the straight boulevards towards the town centre in the flinty light and the grit and diesel smell of urban cold, the sun rose behind the five silver and gold domes of St Sophia.

In the nine centuries that have passed since St Sophia was founded, no building was raised higher than this central palladium. St Sophia, Likhachev said, was a meaningful reference point for the identity of the citizen of Novgorod; standing inside it, he would feel himself at the political centre of the powerful city-state.

The citizens called it 'Lord Great Novgorod', emphasising that the town, rather than any person in it, was head of the state. (This was a piquant historical observation in a state which named its cities after Lenin, Stalin and Molotov.) Looking up into the drum, the citizen would see the countenance of the *vsederzhitel'*, the 'holder of everything', holding Novgorod in his closed hand. In *The Cultural History of Novgorod from the Eleventh to the Seventeenth Century*, written during the three-year Nazi blockade of his own city, Leningrad, Likhachev relates a legend from the Novgorod Chronicle of 1045 about the painting of the image of God in the cupola. The icon painters, whose devotional work was to make sacred the contingent material of the world, painted the image of the Almighty with his hand open in a gesture of blessing. The following morning, the Archbishop noticed that the painted hand was clenched. The painters repainted it, but again and again the open hand closed in the night. On the fourth morning, the icon painters heard a voice coming from the image: 'Painters, painters, draw me with my hand clenched, for in this hand I am holding Novgorod, and when it opens, it will mean the end of the city.'

We spent the morning within the walls of the *detinets*, the kremlin overlooking the river Volkhov, at the centre of which St Sophia stands. Inside the medieval *detinets* were streets full of craftsmen: potters, smiths, icon painters, honey-makers. In this museum-sanctuary, everything was now ordered, labelled, in its place. The cathedral was again a place of worship. A *lavka* near the door sold tiny icons, beeswax candles and the diocesan newspaper (published, it said on the masthead, since 1875, with an interval between 1920 and 1995) with a Christmas message from Archbishop Lev of Novgorod and Staraya Russa, in which he talked of the thousands of newly canonised Orthodox saints, the martyrs of the twentieth century, and how the light of Christ enters a world accustomed to its own disfigurement. On a side wall were Sunday-school drawings in felt-tip pen of Adam and Eve's expulsion from Eden. In medieval Novgorod, churches were the centre of civic life, used for town meetings and elections, as the backdrop to feasts, and as warehouses and shelters for local people whenever there was risk of fire. The set pattern of their interiors depicted the earthly and heavenly Church, the whole of human history in all its populous riot and ultimate order, its highest reaches shining gold with the glory of God. Likhachev detected in the decorations of Novgorod churches an emphasis on social sins. In fresco scenes of the 'Terrible Judgement', as it is called in Russian, he found numerous depictions of the torments of the rich and powerful for wounding the poor and dependent. Admiring the free and flowing forms of Novgorod religious art, Likhachev noted that the earliest in St Sophia were very distant from Byzantine prototypes. They have their own distinct style, depicting the human form in peaceful poses, with sharply defined features, reddened cheeks and eyes directed straight at the viewer. He rejoiced in the preservation of a fragment of an eleventh-century fresco of Emperor Constantine and his mother, Helena, that the workers of the Novgorod Museum had covered with a thick layer of brick before the Nazis occupied the city.

We left the cathedral and wandered through the display of Novgorod decorative and applied arts in the fifteenth-century Palace of Facets. Beyond it was another long stone building. Searching for a few moments' shelter from the river wind, I pushed open the heavy varnished door, which opened into a warm foyer. Books and papers were arranged on a trestle table. A man in thick plastic spectacles and a worn sheepskin came in after us, with a gust of wind coming through the door behind him, which lifted the pages of the books and blew some papers on to the floor. We had coincided with the last day of the annual conference of the Novgorod Archaeological Research Centre. The man in the sheepskin coat went through the double doors into the auditorium. Go on, follow him, take your time, my companion said; she would go outside to watch the birds circling the domes and try to keep her cigarette alight in the wind. Thirty or so people were scattered around the immaculate yellow-painted hall, under a vast crystal chandelier. The man in the sheepskin sat down behind a colleague, picked a piece of lint off the back of his sweater and began to whisper loudly in his ear. I was at once lulled and stimulated by the atmosphere in the hall. On the stage, a man at a lectern was concluding a paper on the discovery, during last summer's dig, of eleven beads among the thousands of pieces of crystal opposite St Sophia and something I could not follow about the sewage system of ancient Novgorod. An older man took over the lectern, to soft applause. I looked down at the conference programme. It was Academician Yanin, elder of Novgorod archaeology, honorary citizen of the town, come to conclude the three-day proceedings. Yanin talked of the vital importance of the archaeologists' research, of the ongoing flow of cultural self-discovery, their movement forward into the past, about which there is always more to say, repeating and lingering on the word *raskrytie*, which means opening, unfolding, detection, exposure, revelation. As a schoolboy in the late 1930s, Yanin buried himself in the study of numismatics while his grandfather died in the Gulag and his father narrowly escaped execution. He graduated from Moscow University in archaeology in 1951, the famed year in which Artsykhovsky's expedition first discovered the birch-bark documents in the Novgorod clay. Yanin was thrilled by the texts on the bark, which hinted at the rich spiritual worlds of once-living individuals. Here were the voices of people who had been crudely stereotyped, stock figures in the theory of class war: merchant, peasant, feudal lord. The titles of his studies of the birch barks reflect his sense of the beguiling intimacy of these stilo-scratchings: 'I Sent You a Birch Bark', 'Love in the Eleventh Century'.

Yet, for all the warmth of Yanin's happy science, the story of Novgorod archaeology is no unbroken continuum of collective work, recovery and scholarly trust. In recent years, the work of *raskrytie* in secret police archives in Russia and museum archives in Germany has revealed collaboration inside Nazi-occupied Novgorod, what Russians call 'blank spots' in history, crimes that seemed to have long passed into non-existence.

Likhachev returned to Novgorod in May 1944, one of the first to arrive after its liberation. He recalls the collective wail that went up in his carriage as the train stopped at the empty place on the plain that had once been the city: What have they done to you? In the muddy edges of the melted river he could see the bodies of soldiers who had been blasted into the ice during the last battles of the winter. Church domes and bells lay on their sides among the rushes, stripped and gaping with holes, their lugs blown off. Frescoes had been shot away or defaced with pictures of naked women. Fresh Nazi graves, hung with swastika armbands, had been daubed with excrement. In the overgrown grass, Likhachev picked up the ball that had held the cross from the dome of St Sophia. The walls of the churches in the city were still standing, but the churches encircling the city, which had lain in the battle-field, had been devastated. The Church of the Dormition on the Volotovo field, which contained the finest examples of Russian pre-Renaissance fresco painting, carefully reinforced by restorers from Moscow in the early 1930s, was utterly destroyed by dynamite. (In 1912, the frescoes had been photographed at the behest of Igor Grabar for a book on Russian art, but the negatives, stored at the Jewish-owned Petersburg publishing house I. N. Knebel, were destroyed in 1915 in an anti-Semitic pogrom by the Black Hundreds.)

The museum workers were also among the first to arrive in Novgorod after the German retreat. They were like doctors, Likhachev said, come to heal the wounded city. He knew that some museum workers had never left, but could not speak of it. In 1994, two articles appeared in the weekly *Novgorod*, headlined 'The Wounded Traitor' and 'The Name We Are Supposed to Forget'. That name is Vasili Ponomarev, first military burgermeister of occupied Novgorod, later curator of St Sophia and valuer of art and antiquities for the Nazis. A native of Novgorod, Likhachev's contemporary, Ponomarev had studied in Leningrad, and participated in Artsykhovsky's archaeological digs in Novgorod in 1932, directing an excavation of Decembrists Street which uncovered traces of an ancient road paved with wood. Ponomarev was arrested later the same year in a purge known as the 'museum affair', and served five years in the Gulag in Komi in the north. His memoirs, discovered in 2004 in an archive in Marburg after a ten-year hunt by Russian researchers, reveal a man whose devotion to the remains of ancient Novgorod out-weighed his loyalty to the Soviet motherland. In his brief tenure as burgermeister, Ponomarev's only administrative decisions con-cerned the preservation of antiquities. Everything of value in the city passed through his hands. Objects of great worth became property of the Third Reich. Pieces of lesser value, including many icons and paintings, were handed out to German officers as booty. Ponomarev left Novgorod with the museum collections when the occupiers evacuated, staying with the precious freight until it came into the hands of the Allies. The Russian aesthete spent the rest of his life in Marburg, teaching and working on a catalogue of the antiquities he believed he had saved in the course of the cynical and pragmatic double game he played with the Nazi masters of his city. In Rome in 1955, Ponomarev encountered Artsykhovsky again at an international conference of historians and tried to shake his hand. Artsykhovsky judiciously refused to acknowledge him. The papers given by the Soviet delegation at that conference were pub-lished by the Academy of Sciences in 1956 and found their way into Molotov's library. Artsykhovsky's paper was called 'New Discoveries in Novgorod'. The volume also included an essay by Molotov's son-in-law, the historian (and secret police operative) Alexei Nikonov, on 'The Origins of the Second World War and the European Pre-War Crisis of 1939'.

The Third Reich had an ideological interest in local archae-ology. During the war, immense resources were devoted to the Ahnenerbe, a Society for the Study of Ancestral Heritages founded in 1935, which Heinrich Himmler had turned into an official organisation attached to the SS. The Ahnenerbe, which came into Russia behind Hitler's army, sought to trace the origins and migrations of the Aryan race, digging for remains of Germanic pagans with blood roots in the soil of the East. The organisation also made several journeys to Tibet in search of Vril, the spiritual energy centre of the earth. At the heart of the Ahnenerbe's pursuits was the idea of returning Germans to the Asian hinterland from which they had reputedly first come, to give them back their rightful *lebensraum*.

Several Novgorod intellectuals besides Ponomarev chose to stay in the city in 1941. Tatyana and Natalya Gippius (cousins of the Symbolist poet Zinaida Gippius) continued to work in the museum, but refused to help pack the collections to send to Germany. The St Petersburg poet Andrei Egunov (also known as Andrei Nikolev), who had once moved in the same circles as Mandelstam, also suffered arrest and Siberian exile in the 1930s. The Wehrmacht placed him in charge of propaganda and popular education, with a special focus, compliant with Nazi collaboration, on the history of trade between medieval Novgorod and the Hanseatic cities. The scholar and aesthete Boris Filistinsky, who had studied Mongolia at the Institute of Oriental Studies in Leningrad, also remained in occupied Novgorod. He wrote for a collaborationist newspaper named *For the Motherland* and was allegedly paid in icons and artefacts from the Novgorod Museum. Filistinsky was otherwise known as the poet Boris Filippov, in later life a distinguished literary scholar at a prestigious American university, who edited the collected works of Akhmatova, Mandelstam and Nikolai Gumilev. There is one small remnant of his Novgorod past in his archive in Washington, DC: an undated typescript of an article by Vasili Ponomarev entitled 'Pagan Prayers in the Novgorod Soil'.

⤜❦⤛

Contemplate the ice fisherman, hunched over his line, out on the blank place where the mouths of five rivers meet Lake Ilmen. He has not moved in the hour since we passed him on our way along the line of bulrushes that mark the frozen water's edge. I imagined that he must be a monk, gone out to catch food for his brothers in the *skit*, the hermitage; that his stillness in this burning cold was a kind of prayer.

The fish under this deep ice have long been famed: salmon, sterlet and pike; sturgeon so good that in the sixteenth century it was served at the table of the Tsar. Archaeologists have often turned up fossil nets in muddy clumps, and layers of medieval fish-scales packed in the soil. In Soviet times, the *skit*'s early-thirteenth-century church, the last built in stone before the Mongols invaded Rus, was put to use as a storehouse by the local fishery collective. After the Second World War, the Novgorod Archaeological Expedition turned up the earth and found traces of what looked like a shrine to the supreme deity of the ancient Slavs: Perun, god of thunder. In 1991, the hermitage at Peryn was returned to the Orthodox Church and reconsecrated. Within four years, monks had returned to the wooded hill.

On our second day in Novgorod, we had decided to abandon our driver and use the local bus service to get to Yuriev, Peryn's parent monastery. We came to the monastery through villages and fields, where faded scruff grass brushed through the snow. Likhachev described the way in which the architects of the twelfth century used the river as the axis of their town plan. The watchtowers of Yuriev in one direction and Antoniev in the other create a great symmetry in the landscape, which the churches built over the course of the next five hundred years (some in a single day, many over the course of a single summer) did not disrupt. As though all Novgorod were the work of a single architect, Likhachev marvelled, the city seemed to express a shared intention, a rare rhythmic integrity in space. A lay brother came out of a tin kiosk at the gate, an elderly man with beautiful grey-blue eyes who gave us, in welcome, a small icon of St Seraphim, and took us in to see the brightly restored frescoes in the church. The monastery seemed a busy, cheerful place that morning, resonant with the voices of daily life. A monk called out from the doorway of a low building by the monastery wall, pulling a hat over his long hair, asking for Nina and Tatyana. The lay brother told him that Nina and Tatyana were in the banya.

We left Yuriev on foot, taking the riverbend towards Peryn. Again, suddenly, we were in a landscape that felt desolate. It is the genius of Novgorod's geography to accommodate wilderness in well-populated space. For a few weeks in spring, when the snow dissolves and floods the road up to the hermitage, Peryn is an island. Despite the short distance from Yuriev, and the city of Novgorod two miles up the Volkhov from here, the place had an atmosphere of timeless calm. But around Peryn, we discovered, the semiosphere was buzzing.

The semiosphere – a concept that the twentieth-century cultural theorist Yuri Lotman worked out in the last decade of his life – is one of those capacious neologisms that characterise the Russian humanities. It denotes the 'vast intellectual mechanism' of which we are all 'both part and likeness', and which contains and brings together everything from the religious ideas of archaic cultures to the advertisements of our modern age. For Lotman, the 'universum of culture' is analogous with the 'biosphere' of the planet. 'Thought is within us,' he wrote, 'but we are within thought.'

In his essay, 'Symbolic Spaces', Lotman described the 'medieval thought-system', in which locality had a religious and moral significance 'unknown to modern geography'. Travel was a way to sanctity; to move from a city to a monastery or *skit* was, like pilgrimage or death, to unburden oneself of sin, to come to a sacred place. In the pre-Enlightenment semiosphere, says Lotman, countries themselves were classified as pagan, heretical or holy. Social ideals were imagined as existing in geographical space. 'Paradise is in the East . . . while Hell is in the West over the roaring seas, and many of my Novgorodian children will see it,' wrote the medieval Bishop Vasili. In one medieval Russian tale, Utopia is in India, and the traveller to that land will attain goodness as a prize. The Chronicles of ancient Rus also tell of Moislav, a sailor from Novgorod, who reached Paradise in his boat, a place of 'high mountains', where he heard 'much merrymaking'.

Nailed to the wooden gates of the Peryn *skit* was a notice in deep-pressed ballpoint, wrapped in polythene against the weather. 'Remember that you are entering a place of repentance and prayer,' it said. Then: 'Do not befriend your enemy, but pray for him unceasingly!' Leaning against a wall of the first building at the end of the long, ascending path was a pallet bearing a shining drum of 'USA OIL'. An Alsatian barked and pulled at its chain. A monk came out of the tiny whitewashed church. He turned to us as we came up the hill, then disappeared into one of the low red-painted cells that surrounded it on three sides.

From our north-east approach, on this monochrome winter day, the tiny Church of the Nativity of the Virgin, with its single cupola and corniced trefoil gables, looked just as it did when I first admired it in a black-and-white photograph taken in 1910 by the archaeologist, painter and guru Nikolai Roerich. The picture hung in the first room of the Roerich Museum, a palace (once a Marx–Engels museum) behind the Pushkin Museum in Moscow. Its serene monochrome geometry calmed the rampant swirl of Roerich's early paintings of pagan idols and solitary holy men alone in wild landscapes. Further along the wall, grainy photos of the Imperial Archaeological Society's 1903 excavations of Neolithic burial mounds around Novgorod, in which Roerich took part, broke the spell cast by the dioramas of his set-designs for the 'Adoration of the Earth' scenes in Stravinsky's 'stone-age' ballet, *The Rite of Spring*. It was the only corner of the strange exhibition that was not a shrine to its subject, giving refuge to a visitor like myself who found more to contemplate in the mess and precision of historical remains than in aids to cosmic under-standing like the immense, purple-lit crystal on the pedestal at the top of the stairs.

Roerich's archaeology, his painting and his travels all originated in a single impulse: to make Culture sacred, Science spiritual. The largest room in the Moscow museum was filled with mystical paintings of hermits and mountain peaks hazed in Indian-kitsch rainbow colours. Its centrepiece was a relief map, dotted with coloured lights, of the Central Asian Expedition of the 1920s, when, with permission of the People's Commissar of Foreign Affairs, Roerich led a caravan from Moscow to the Himalayas in search of the 'common source' of Slavic and Indian cultures and the legendary subterranean city of Shambhala. It is rumoured in Moscow – though no one can say it in print – that Putin, who takes an interest in 'Eastern wisdom' of this kind, has assigned money from the national budget to be spent on another search for the doorway to Shambhala in the Altai region of Siberia, a cosmic energy centre where he likes to pose for photographers, seated half-naked on a horse, like some latter-day Mongol khan. Like the Russian Theosophist Madame Blavatsky, who brought the symbol of the swastika into European culture, Roerich believed in a hierarchy of Hidden Masters living in Tibet, bearers of the ancient race wisdom of the Aryan tribes.

I knew some of this when I saw Roerich's photo of the little church. I did not know, though, until I came to the place, how perfectly the little hermitage at Peryn can be made to embody his guiding idea: namely, that pagan and Orthodox Christian Slavdom are a spiritual and cultural unity, whose primordial origins, in many contemporary books of popular history and archaeology, are openly called 'Aryan'. For Roerich, archaeology was not a secular science, but an ecstatic earth cult. In India in the late 1930s, he heard about the Novgorod digs organised by the Institute of Material Culture, and hailed the Soviet archaeologists as a vibrant young tribe, like the prehistoric Indo-Europeans who had migrated to Russia, bringing their gods and their cults with them. 'Every expedition, every dig, every act of attention to the national epic speaks of new possibilities,' he said. 'They are building a city that will have no end. Novgorod at its origins and Novgorod in its future have been winnowed by science and creative work.'

As we tried the church door, the young monk reappeared, pulling on a dirty black sheepskin coat, carrying a heavy key. He had a long beard and a square receded hairline, just like Dostoevsky in devout mid-life. Without eye contact, he gestured us into the church, where, with one finger raised, he related how, in the tenth century, Peryn was converted from a pagan to a Christian sanctum, and the wooden effigy of Perun thrown into the Volkhov. The Novgorod Chronicles tell of a passer-by who saw the sacrifice-hungry idol trying to reach the shore, and shouted, 'You have eaten your fill, Perun, now swim away.' (Herzen had his own wry liberal joke about the place, saying that his home on the Volkhov was 'opposite the very barrow from which the Voltaireans of the twelfth century threw the wonder-working statue of Perun into the river'.)

According to ethnographers who chart Russian *dvoeverie* (double-faith), Perun did not swim away. Instead, he blended in iconography and the popular imagination with the fiery-charioted prophet Elijah. Medieval amulets have been found in Novgorod with Perun on one side and a Christian saint on the other. Even now, apparently, when they pass Peryn, locals throw coins into the river to propitiate the pagan god. For the Roerich Movement, which has been active all over Russia since 1991, *dvoeverie* is a treasured sign of primordial Slavic 'spirituality'. Russian syncretic spirituality is the essence of race memory, harmony with nature and the 'energy of the cosmos', and freedom from the taint of Western urban 'civilisation' and the 'dollarocracy'.

The monk at Peryn was appeasing a deity more jealous than the thunder god. When I asked him whether the icons missing from the church were destroyed or looted during the war, he took the notebook from my hand. Jotting down dates and numbers as he went, he expounded a philosophy of history as Dostoevskian as his beard. For many in the Russian Orthodox Church, Dostoevsky is a kind of prophet, who revealed the underlying unity of papalism and socialism and foresaw their ultimate merger in the reign of Antichrist. In the eighteenth century, the monk said, Holy Russia was corrupted by the European Enlightenment and turned away from God. Socialism, another Western import, was precisely the metaphysical freedom which Russia had demanded from God two hundred years earlier. It led to bloody self-punishment. Of the 150,000 icons in Novgorod before 1917, he noted for me, the God-defying Bolsheviks left only a few thousand for the Germans to steal. His own monastic calling was to offer a lifetime's atonement for his nation's apostasy, and to help rebuild Holy Russia.

Despite their common view that the West has defiled Russia's sacred space and led her away from salvation (or her place in the 'vector of cosmic evolution'), the official Orthodox Church and the Roerich Movement spent their first decade of religious freedom engaged in a crackling row, conducted in books, pamphlets, cyberspace and the national press. In 1994, the Church anathematised the Roerich Movement as a 'totalitarian, anti-Christian sect'. A Moscow cleric, A. Kuraev, published a thousand-page denunciation of the Movement two years later, entitled *Satanism for the Intelligentsia*, in which he accuses Roerich of being an NKVD spy, a crypto-Nazi and a bad painter. To this, the 'well-known culturologist and politologist' Ksenya Myalo replied with a terrifying screed, rich in omens and pseudo-science, called *The Volkhov Star or Christ in the Himalayas*, in which she defended Roerich as a saviour of Russian cultural monuments, and, in his life and teachings, bearing wisdom from the ancient East, more Russian and more Orthodox than the Church itself. Now, she said, the Russian people risks being wiped out, becoming an outcast race, even on the territory of its own motherland. Among implacable enemies of the pure 'Russian soul' (of which Madame Blavatsky was another great and 'much-slandered' example) Myalo named Zbigniew Brzezinski, J. R. R. Tolkien, G. K. Chesterton, the 'judaic' media, the 'perestroika intelligentsia', Father Alexander Men, the Catholic Church, global capital, the 'bacchanalia of privatisation', NATO and the Internet. All of them fear paganism, she declared, and the great geographical space that the undefiled 'cosmocentric' Russian peasant, with his primordial race memory, instinctively senses as his natural element. Myalo noted in passing that the sun sets in the west, and that scenes of the Apocalypse always appear on the western walls of Russian churches.

The monk had been restoring the church at Peryn with his hands. The bare iconostasis was newly made in young wood; the stuccoed brick walls, to the very apex of the drum, were white. But soon, eloquent symbols of Russian faith would reappear. Roerich, who loved Novgorod for its 'buried secrets', said that if you press close to the earth, you will hear it speak. The voices at Peryn said that in this part of the semiosphere it was Lotman's 'scientific modern geography' that had yet to be discovered.

SEVEN

Staraya Russa

After all, an entire nation consists only of certain
isolated incidents, does it not?
DOSTOEVSKY, *Winter Notes on Summer Impressions*

From Novgorod, we took the empty road to Staraya Russa,
an hour's drive down the western shore of Ilmen, the 'lake of
weather'. Ancient and capricious, Ilmen is shaped like a heart.
Left behind when the prehistoric ice sheet drew north, its waters
ebb and dilate with the seasons. Winters are lighter in this part of
Russia, the frost less tenacious. Even so, the cold had erased the
lake's edge. The shore was traceable only from the scattered pattern of snow-dusted rushes. In the grey-white haze of the day,
when the many thousand interlinking veins of water that issue
from the lake were frozen and invisible, only occasional clusters of
low wooden houses on the plain hinted at the streams' south-
westerly meander.

On a bridge (designated a 'hero bridge' after some great
wartime battle) hung with dirty lamps roughly painted red, sig-
nalling roadworks, we crossed the salty Shelon that flows year-
round from the lake's westernmost edge. A flimsy sign pointed to
a Kombinat producing lubricants: *maslo* and *smazka*, oil and
grease. At Korostyn, the road came right up to the shore. This
'pearl in the princely lands of Staraya Russa' (quite without lustre
as we drove through it) was a wedding gift from Peter the Great
to his wife; an agreement was later signed in the village about the
creation of a unified Russian state. After Korostyn, we turned
south-east and passed Ustreka. *'Tiens, un lac,'* as the Frenchified fop
Stepan Verkhovensky exclaims on awakening from his delirium in
a hut in the fishing village; 'ah, my God, I did not see it before ...'

After Dostoevsky had landed at Ustreka on his first steam-paddle voyage across Ilmen, he reimagined the place as 'Ustevo', the accidental destination of Verkhovensky's final wanderings in *Demons*, the novel he came to Staraya Russa to finish in the dacha season of 1872. Verkhovensky's deathbed scenes at the lakeside are a comic-serious coda to the murder scenes in Dostoevsky's horror novel of ideas, his vision of unlimited despotism. The flighty mind of the 'scrofulous liberal' scholar (based on Timofei Granovsky, after whom Sheremetev Lane was renamed by the Soviets), father of a tyrannical political killer, finally unravels as he eats buttery peasant pancakes, attended by a doctor named Salzfisch. 'Historical knowledge heals,' Likhachev said, 'but laughter heals even more.' Likhachev considered Dostoevsky a remarkable humorist, and particularly appreciated the comedy in *Demons*, without which the novel would be 'unbearable'.

Stepan Verkhovensky is the apotheosis of the 'idealistic Westerniser', aimless, weak in his ideas, devoted to the notion that he is persecuted for his way of thinking. Dostoevsky wrote to a friend that benign liberals like Granovsky 'would not believe it if you told them that they were the direct fathers' of the radical 'demons' who were tearing Russia apart. It was the development of the line of thought 'from the fathers to the sons' that Dostoevsky wanted to explore in his political novel. In 1870 he begged his friend Nikolai Strakhov for a new biography of Granovsky by Alexander Stankevich, brother of the poet Nikolai Stankevich, saying that he needed the little book like he needed air, as soon as possible, it was indispensable material for his writing. As he developed the character of Stepan Verkhovensky, he continued to use the name 'Granovsky' in his notebooks.

Beset by money worries, ill health and family troubles, Dostoevsky arrived in Staraya Russa in May, hoping for a few months of rest and ordered domesticity. He had been told by a Petersburg professor of the tranquillity of the small spa town, where, for very little, one could rent a furnished house, 'even with kitchen wares'. He would seclude himself and write, while his two small children flourished in the sunshine and took mud cures. The family travelled by rail to Novgorod on a narrow-gauge track laid the year before, then took the steamer across Ilmen and down the winding Polist under a pale, cloudless sky. Their slow-rhythm journey was one of Anna Grigorievna's loveliest memories of married life. The domes of St Sophia shone as they pulled away from Novgorod. The lake was as still as a mirror; the scene looked Swiss. Anna absorbed her husband's tender mood; he loved and understood nature, she said. For the last two hours, as the paddle-wheel splashed down the lime-banked river, the domes of Staraya Russa seemed to come close and recede again.

My journey, on a day without radiance or colour, was at the urging of a friend in Petersburg, a Dostoevsky scholar of Slavophile persuasion, who had come to Staraya Russa one summer for a colloquium at the writer's house, and had been shown the way by an old local of such unalloyed simplicity and kindness of heart that he had held him in mind ever since as the perfect specimen of the Russian *narod*, the people. To encounter, in this of all towns, a man who embodied the pure and elusive spirit of the people seemed to my friend no accident. To him, Staraya Russa is a hallowed place. Indeed, Likhachev (who suggested the theme for my friend's doctoral thesis on Dostoevsky) once said that around Staraya Russa one can still sense the true Russia, breathe the sacred Motherland.

According to Orthodox tradition, the Apostle Andrew, the 'first called', came to these parts from Jerusalem in the first century, through Kherson on the Black Sea. The fisherman from Galilee is imagined passing through on his way north to the Volkhov and the island of Valaam, preaching Christ's gospel to the pagan fishermen of Ilmen. Staraya Russa is the only place to have preserved the name of the ancient Slavonic tribe, the Rusy. The legend of the town's foundation, a tale of family bonds, was written down at the beginning of the nineteenth century by Russia's first historian, Nikolai Karamzin. Two Slavic knights, the brothers Sloven and Rus, wandered north to these virgin lands from the shores of the

Black Sea, and named the lake after their sister, Ilmen. Sloven founded a town at the north end of the lake, where Novgorod now stands, and Rus founded another at the southern end, naming the two rivers that meet in its centre after his wife and daughter, Polist and Porusya. At the Church of the Resurrection on the headland where the Polist and Porusya merge, Peter the Great remarked on Staraya Russa's topographical similarity with Jerusalem, where, to the east of the temple, the sun rises over the salt sources of the Dead Sea.

I learned all these things from a creepy book I read in the Lenin Library after my visit. In the shiny pages of *The Formation of the Russian Character on the Example of the Historical Fate of the Staraya Russa Region*, published in 2003, I discovered that even now a mystique of Staraya Russa is being cultivated to serve Russia's new era of Orthodoxy, Autocracy and Nationality. This quiet place has become the symbolic heartland of a mythology of soil and tribe that has seeped from the works of nineteenth-century Russian writers into the sanctuaries of Putin's secret police. The book, which has multiple authors and advertises itself as a 'popular scientific publication for students of military academies', was published under the auspices of the FSB (as the secret police is now named) with a string of presidential and security organisations listed alongside the names of lieutenant generals and academicians on its title page. It is illustrated with colour plates of soldiers, ecclesiastics, tsars, monasteries and moody views of Ilmen, and begins with the announcement that, with the blessing of the Patriarch of Moscow and All the Russias (reputedly a man of the security services), a new chapel in honour of the miracle-working icon of the Staraya Russa Mother of God has been built on the territory of the Moscow Institute of Border Guards of the FSB. 'Symbolically', President Vladimir Vladimirovich Putin's 'epistle' to the nation in the 'transformative' year 2003 had been given on the eve of the feast of the miracle-working icon. And so it goes on, page after page, weaving the myth of Russia's primal supremacy, her God-bearing mission, superior soul, all proved by the presence of salt in the soil of Staraya Russa, the most ancient homeland of the Rus tribes, the 'salt of the earth', whose destiny has always been, as Dostoevsky preached, to unite and lead mankind. Like other pseudo-scholarly racial supremacist tracts, the book leans on bizarre etymological, and even biochemical, assertions, as though language itself were some cryptic guide to transcendent national destiny. *Rus*, I learn, was a Sanskrit root brought north by the Aryan tribes who settled here on the northern plain, associated with the sacred colour red (*'rush'*), 'the soul of the Russian soil', the 'talismanic' colour of Russian history. Every few pages, the name of Vladimir Vladimirovich Putin would appear, invoked in ever more cultish incantatory tones, each of his speeches, whether to the EU or the Ministry of Culture, a prophecy, his quintessentially Russian 'modesty' and 'humility' (attributes the media persuaded people to believe in before Putin's second election to the presidency) the very fulcrum of his patriotism and sincere love for the Motherland. Even Putin's name is 'euphonious with a good *energetika*' harking back to the roots of the tribe: 'the majority of Russian surnames with the root "Puti" are formed from the most ancient Slavic name Putislav,' which of course brings to mind the word *put'*, 'the way', which, in its turn, fans out into a dozen more good words pregnant with national portent. And in Church Slavonic, the authors remind us, the word *put'* is directly associated with Christ himself . . . *The Formation of the Russian Character* ends with the 'Staraya Russa Theses', a list of commandments about Russian national memory: 'Remember that when Dostoevsky writes about the universal responsiveness of Russians, it is not a metaphor . . .'; 'Remember that the epistle of the President was delivered on the eve of the feast day . . . that his innate modesty and humility help Our President to dedicate himself completely to the disinterested service of People and Fatherland . . . Remember!'

⊰✦⊱

What did Staraya Russa mean to Dostoevsky? And what does Staraya Russa remember about Dostoevsky, a writer who still looms so heavily over the Russian national imagination? 'Dostoevsky's Russia', Akhmatova's 'First Elegy' begins. Subtitled 'Prehistory', the poem conjures the historical landscape of Russia of the 1870s and 1880s, into which Akhmatova's own generation 'decided to be born'. Taverns trade, carriages fly, five-storey buildings rise on the streets of Petersburg. In the interiors, skirts rustle, armchairs are upholstered in plush, yellow kerosene lamps illuminate narrow wallpapered corridors, walnut-framed mirrors are 'amazed by the beauty of Karenina':

> And in Staraya Russa magnificent ditches,
> And in the gardens decaying summer houses,
> And the windowpanes are as black as an ice-hole,
> And one imagines that something has occurred,
> That it is better not to peep, let us leave.
> It is not possible to reach an understanding with every place,
> So that it reveals its secret . . .

As soon as Dostoevsky arrived in Staraya Russa to write the overdue final instalments of his prophetic anti-revolutionary novel *Demons*, he was placed under covert police surveillance on orders from the capital. The memory of the tsarist state was obstinate. Though he claimed to have been cured of what he called the 'psychic illness' of seditious thinking in Siberia over two decades earlier, as a once-condemned political prisoner who had almost faced a firing squad on Semyonov Square, Dostoevsky was still a man to be kept under watch. The police in Staraya Russa, who peeped in at his windows, informed the gendarmerie in Novgorod that the writer lived soberly in his rented house on the banks of the Pererytitsa, avoided society, choosing the quietest streets for his daily walks, and sat at his desk deep into the night. 'The country shivers, and the Omsk convict understood everything and placed a cross over everything', Akhmatova wrote in the last verse of 'Prehistory':

Look, now he shuffles everything up
And he rises, like some kind of spirit,
Over the primordial disorder. Midnight strikes.
The pen squeaks, and many pages
Have the smell of Semyonov Square.

The many pages of family correspondence that passed under the eyes of the local police during Dostoevsky's first Staraya Russa summer are all about illness, domestic disorder, the difficulty of writing, and cold. Anna had a nearly fatal throat abscess; Dostoevsky caught a chill and could not sleep for worry; little Lyuba fractured her hand; baby Fedya had diarrhoea and mosquito bites on his arms and legs. The doctor recommended mud baths, but it was not clear whether they made Fedya's itching better or worse. It rained endlessly, the windows let in draughts, the linen chest was disordered and the filth in the courtyard was unbelievable; everything soaked and rotten and wrecked. Work on the novel went badly; their 'gypsy life' was a dismal torment. 'There is nothing more unbearable', Dostoevsky wrote, 'than greenery and wooden houses in the rain under this horrible sky.'

And yet, Dostoevsky bought a family home in Staraya Russa and came back every year until his death. The layout and atmosphere of the town seem to work their way into the last chapters of *Demons*, where a night fire, set by arsonists, consumes the wooden houses in the poorer quarter on the far side of the river, exciting in onlookers those 'destructive instincts which, alas, lie buried within each and every soul'. His last novel, *The Brothers Karamazov*, is explicitly set in the town, though it loses its resonant name and becomes Skotoprigonevsk, which means Cattlepen. 'Though our town is small,' the unnamed narrator says, 'it is scattered and the houses are far apart.' 'Our little town', 'our district', 'the famous monastery in our neighbourhood', 'our town cemetery', the narrator says again and again as he relates his tale of metaphysical rebellion, murder and mental illness, moving freely in and out of the febrile minds of the Karamazovs and the whispering silence of the town's most hidden corners. Though Dostoevsky's characters have so much to say that there is scarce time for authorial descriptions of place, the atmosphere of the provincial town is vivid: its dreary streets and quirky houses, with their shaded gardens, banyas, dilapidated summer houses, courtyards, gates and fences; its squalid taverns and gold-topped churches; its marketplace, monastery, police station, courthouse and prison; its masters and servants, its shopkeepers, priests, landowners, doctors, beauties, widows, buffoons, fallen women, misers, debtors, gossips, gypsies, cripples, rakes, dogs and schoolboys; its smells, sounds and shared memories; its intrigues, crimes and neverending talk.

It was in Staraya Russa, in the summer of 1880, when, as Dostoevsky said, 'literally all the readers of Russia' were waiting for the conclusion to *The Brothers Karamazov*, that he wrote his 'epoch-making' speech for the unveiling of a statue of Pushkin in Moscow, which he gave in the building of the Noblemen's Club. Dostoevsky's words about the universal mission of the Russian people are saturated with the tribe-and-soil myth of ancient Rus. He found in Pushkin the expression of his nation's divine calling to unify 'all people of the tribes of the great Aryan race'. From Pushkin, Dostoevsky proclaimed, Russians could derive faith in their 'future independent mission in the family of European peoples'. Russia was impoverished, but 'Christ himself in slavish garb traversed this impoverished land and gave it his blessing'. Pushkin died young, Dostoevsky told the Moscow public, and 'unquestionably took some great secret with him to the grave. And so we must puzzle out his secret without him.' 'You solved it! You solved it!' voices shouted from the crowd. 'Prophet! Prophet!' However, Dostoevsky's 'solution' left latitude for interpretation. Konstantin Pobedonostsev, reactionary chief ideologist to the Tsar, thanked Dostoevsky for having 'uttered the Russian truth'. But the physiologist Ivan Pavlov heard the speech as politically radical. Unlike the rest of Russia's study-bound intellectuals, Dostoevsky really knew the people, Pavlov wrote to his fiancée, Seraphima Karchevskaya. His soul accommodated the souls of others. In prison he had lived as an equal with the people, and he stood with them still.

❧

We drove into town on Uprising Street, past the train station, across Klara Tsetkin Street and the bridge over the Polist. Turning down Mineral Street, we passed Engels and Karl Marx, cross-streets that lie parallel on the town's small grid, and stopped at the entrance to the health spa. We were stiff from the drive, and hungry. The forlorn Stalin-era pomposity of the main gates was a disappointment. Inscribed in granite above an empty urn on one side of the gates was a quotation from Pavlov: 'Mankind is the highest product of nature, not so that he can just take pleasure in nature's riches. Mankind must be healthy, strong, and intelligent.' Pavlov, who had won a Nobel Prize in 1904 for his work on digestion and the 'conditioned reflex', became a reluctant favourite of the Stalin regime. After the murder of Leningrad Party boss Sergei Kirov in 1934, Pavlov protested to Stalin about the sudden wave of terror, and Molotov twice wrote to the scientist, explaining that the attacks on 'malicious anti-Soviet elements' were necessary to counter the capitalist threat. Despite Pavlov's protests about arrests of intellectuals and the demolition of churches, Stalin tried to suborn him with gifts and favours. On one occasion, he told Molotov, who was organising a World Congress of Physiologists in Pavlov's honour: 'You must not think of Ivan Pavlov as just another of your 170 million citizens, but as Pavlov whose home is the whole world. Make sure everything is in the best of taste.'

My own taste is not Stalinist. I preferred the look of the spa as it was in Dostoevsky's day, when the waters were fashionable. I had seen how it was then in a tinted engraving in a book. It had delicately elaborate wrought-iron gates and looked like a European resort with the oriental touch of a romantic Caucasian watering place. Trellised walkways led to the Muraviev fountain, a soaring plume, set about with ornamental fruit trees and shaded seats, crowned with an octagonal latticework structure like a giant birdcage topped with Moorish spires.

We could see into the dimness of the park, where footpaths in the snow led through spindly trees towards five-storey dormitory buildings, mottled pink-yellow, the colour of the lichened bark on the birches. We asked the guard for directions to the restaurant, and he waved us into a building by the gate. We climbed the staircase and found ourselves in the anteroom of the spa director's office. I asked a woman leaving the room where we would find the restaurant, and she gestured benignly to a sofa by the door, telling us to wait for the nutritional technologist. In three corners stood wide desks scattered with files, cake boxes, telephones and empty tea glasses. The walls were decorated with faded photographs of spa therapies: stout women in white coats draping black mud over well-muscled men laid out in blue-tiled rooms, or adjusting dials on giant tubs of red-brown water.

I was familiar with the way time works in a room like this, suspended between torpor and the eternal possibility of sudden decisive action. The only thing to do was wait. I picked up a book from a side-table: *Virgin Soil of Staraya Russa*. Published in 1982, the book was a last exhalation of the Soviet Union's 'stagnation', when the Party tried to revive a tired, deprived society with decrees about the joy of communist work. I read of Brezhnev's decree on medical care at the XXVIth Party Congress, of the Party's grandiose and unprecedented struggle for the health of the people, of conscientiousness, initiative, drive, socialist competition, mass culture, Soviet duty, the Eleventh Five-Year Plan . . . Hunger and the grainy hum of the fluorescent lights were making my head ache. Women with large chests and back-combed hair came in and out of the waiting room, heels tapping on the linoleum. The pages of the book gave off a sickly plastic redolence of that medal-mad era of decline. I looked at pictures of heroic 'shock-workers' at the spa: Elena Alexandrova, 'Doctor of the First Category', a 'sweet angel, radiant with the joy of healing', and Nina Markvardt, the dentist with 'golden hands', 'Cavalier of the

Order of the Sign of Honour'. No patient would be left without ideological attention, the book promised. There are evenings of patriotic song, visits by heroes of labour, lectures on communist morality. To mould them into Soviet citizens who love work and are ready to defend the Motherland, adolescent patients are given an intensified programme of political enlightenment. There is a Lenin Room, and a library with tens of thousands of alluring titles such as *Urgent Problems in the Internal and External Politics of the Communist Party* and *Interpreting the Decisions of the Twenty-sixth Party Congress*.

There was no sign of any nutritional technologist. The hour of lunch slipped by. I had misplanned the day. I read aloud about 'rationalised nutrition': fruit and vegetables for vitamin cordials and salads from the spa's own hothouses . . . dairy products from its own cows . . . Master chef Zakhar Kistkin's secret recipe for meat cutlets stuffed with buckwheat kasha . . . Why had I proposed to my trusting friend that we come here first? The Brezhnev-era delicacies evoked in the book were a tormenting stimulus to 'psychic secretions'. The nerves in our cerebral cortices were delivering frantic signals to our digestive organs, but there was nothing to eat. Like Pavlov's laboratory dogs, his 'gastric juice factories' as he called them, we were becoming disoriented, anxious and sad.

Staraya Russa was quickly leading me to the view that there is far more in Dostoevsky about food and that powerful demon, hunger, and the intricacies of the relationship between the human stomach and the soul, than there is about Russian national identity. Pavlov was fascinated by Dostoevsky's questions about where the body ends and the soul begins. Food is central to the theological, political and psychological drama of *The Brothers Karamazov*. 'I can walk away from their bread, not needing it at all,' the crazy ascetic Father Ferapont declares. 'I can go into the forest and survive there on mushrooms or berries . . .' He regards the other monks, who cannot leave their bread, as enslaved by the devil. Ferapont has eaten almost nothing in years. The anorexic monk sees demons in coat pockets, behind doors, hiding in the guts of another monk, 'right inside his unclean belly'. Dostoevsky does not say whether Ferapont is a mystic or a lunatic, but when a superstitious little monk visits the old monk in his cell, he is filled with awe. 'You don't live by tea alone, I suppose,' Ivan Karamazov jokes soon afterwards, when Alyosha Karamazov, awkward in his novice's garb, arrives in the bustling Metropolis tavern, the first private encounter between the brothers. Praising the stinking tavern's 'first-rate' fish soup, Ivan reflects on his own indecent 'Karamazov thirst for life'. Their discussion over jam and tea dilates into Ivan's fierce case against a God who allows the torture and murder of children, and his recitation of his prose-poem 'The Grand Inquisitor'. Ivan's Inquisitor, who has 'vanquished freedom to make men happy', reminds the returned Christ of his three temptations in the wilderness, in which 'all the unsolved historical contradictions of human nature are united'. In the first, in which 'lies hidden the great secret of the world', the tempter invites Christ to turn stones into bread. 'The one infallible banner that will make men bow down is the banner of earthly bread,' the tempter says, 'for nothing is more certain. Grateful and obedient, they will lay down their freedom and say, "Make us your slaves, but feed us."'

As the last instalments of *The Brothers Karamazov* appeared, the young Pavlov worked on his doctoral thesis on the centrifugal nerves of the heart at a medical clinic in St Petersburg. Pavlov, who suffered from depression, found an emotional kinship with Ivan Karamazov, feeling his mind dominated by logic which seemed to freeze the impulses of his heart. And yet he feared solitude, suffered from terrible anxiety and longed to think his way to some science of life. Seraphima Karchevskaya, a devoutly religious student at a pedagogical institute, knew Dostoevsky, and turned to the writer with her own spiritual questions. As Pavlov confided in a letter to her, it was through reading Dostoevsky that he learned to appreciate his own melancholia as a form of privileged insight: 'a person has two opposed sides and is so constructed that at each moment he sees only one. If he is constructed well, he sees only the radiant side, if badly – only the grey. So the complete truth about oneself is presented only by the melancholic state.'

We shared a last stick of chewing gum. Almost an hour passed before the nutritional technologist arrived. A sweet woman with soft blonde hair, she told us that before we would be allowed to eat, we would have to be examined by specialists so that the food prescribed for us would be nutritionally correct. She would require samples for analysis, signed and stamped documents of all kinds. The process would take days, she smiled.

We wandered into the park, light-headed in the 'ionised oasis' by the fountain, to look at the brochure the nutritional technologist had given us, listing cures. The oriental birdcage and the trellised walks were gone now, and the mineral spring was clad in tilted slabs of rust-coloured marble, surrounded by broken benches with peeling paint and swing seats with green corrugated plastic canopies that creaked in the breeze. The brochure advertised cures for overwork, endo-ecological rehabilitation, tampons impregnated with Staraya Russa mud, and treatments for the kidneys, the nervous system, psoriasis, venereal disease, infections of the gums, the digestive tract, the gut . . . A woman in a worn fur coat and hat walked slowly round the fountain, closing her eyes occasionally, and raising her face to the sky.

A convent, dedicated to Saints Peter and Paul, once stood on this land, next to the salt works on which the high fortunes of Staraya Russa were founded in the fourteenth and fifteenth centuries. Later the salt works moved to the other end of the town, and the cherry orchards and kitchen gardens of the abandoned convent ran wild. Local people had always known of the curative properties of the salt springs, and used them to heal scrofula, backaches, asthma and broken bones. In 1815, the romantic age of the spa, word of 'miraculous cures' at Staraya Russa reached Fyodor Haas, a doctor who had published a treatise on the Caucasian springs of Essentuki and Zheleznovodsk. He studied the waters and talked to locals, but the medical establishment in Petersburg, fatigued by his idealistic schemes for improving the health of the Fatherland, met his findings with scepticism. In the mid-1820s, the mining engineer Ilya Tchaikovsky (father of the composer) took an interest in the mineral waters, and a doctor named Rauch came to take notes on the locals bathing in a mud hole. The first spa buildings went up in 1834, and for the next two decades soldiers wounded in Russia's frontier wars were sent to Staraya Russa to convalesce, while high society travelled to Europe or the Caucasus for cures. In 1858, a government minister named Muraviev ordered the digging of an artesian well, and the first steamboat sailed between Novgorod and Staraya Russa. The spa was imperial property, physicians with German names like Eikhvald and Veltz published learned articles on the mud, and thousands of visitors, from grand dukes to the exhausted anti-tsarist writer Nikolai Dobrolyubov, came for cures. By Dostoevsky's time, the town had been laid out for rest and pleasure: boating, costume balls in pavilions, theatrical performances, walks in the forest, excursions to nearby monasteries. Though the spa was reputed to be poorly maintained and the management corrupt, guards officers and society belles came for the summer season. One island in the Polist became such a favoured haven for romantic picnics that it was known as the 'island of love'.

At first the spa held no charm for Dostoevsky. He knew the resorts of Germany and Switzerland, where he had sought remedies for his epilepsy over the past decade. He found Staraya Russa society vulgar and pretentious, vainly aspiring to the glamour of the European beau monde. The women looked coarse and trashy in their extravagant couture, there were not enough cake shops in the town, the park was unimpressive, everyone spoke bad French and the waters were wretched. The only thing he valued was his subscription to the spa's library, where he was often seen in the afternoons, reading newspapers and journals.

Dostoevsky was sceptical about doctors, insisting that a modest German was usually superior to the grandest Russian physician. *The Brothers Karamazov* is full of jokes, burlesque and riddles about doctors and the latest enigmas of physiological science. The town doctor, who claims to understand epilepsy and uselessly medicates the dying child Ilyusha, is named Herzenstube, 'room of the heart'. The expensive Moscow physician, who heartlessly advises Ilyusha's indigent father to send the boy to Syracuse for climate, is a figure of bitter satire. In prison, Mitya Karamazov caricatures the behaviourist ideas of the famous French physiologist Claude Bernard, who died in the year that Dostoevsky conceived the novel. Dostoevsky's own most beloved physician, Stepan Yanovsky, described the writer as 'an insatiable analyst of moral chemistry', perceiving the kinship between his writing and contemporary scientific exploration of the relationship between the mind and body. Yanovsky's wife, the comic actress Alexandra Shubert, called the writer a *serdtseved*, a 'scholar of the heart'.

'I am not a doctor . . . I know nothing of medicine', the novel's narrator says as the devil appears, or appears to appear, to Ivan Karamazov. The narrator promises he will give some account of Ivan's 'brain disorder'. Instead he lets the reader eavesdrop on a dialogue between Ivan and the devil, who may or may not be a symptom of Ivan's nervous breakdown. 'Never for one minute have I taken you for reality,' Ivan shouts at the seedy gentleman who appears on the sofa opposite him. 'You are a lie, you are my illness . . . You are the incarnation of myself, but only of one side of me.' Then the devil says things that have never entered Ivan's head, remarking on the enigma of dreams, 'from indigestion or anything', in which the most ordinary people see artistic visions 'woven into such a plot, with such unexpected details from the most exalted matters to the last button on a cuff, as I swear Lev Tolstoy could not create'. The visitor is characterised in teasing detail. He likes to steam himself with merchants and priests at the public banya, and complains that, much as he likes 'being doctored', he can find no cure for his colds. The devil, whom the narrator calls the 'visitor' or the 'voice', is nothing like Ivan but knows the innermost workings of Ivan's mind. He mocks Ivan's philosophical writings but has no answers to the metaphysical and political questions they pose. Whether a supernatural being or the symptom of a brain disorder, the devil has no idea whether God exists or what history means. He too looks forward, he tells Ivan, to the end of all things, when the 'secret is revealed'.

A signpost under the trees pointed in four directions: to the library and entertainment complex, the main gates, the drinking gallery, the hydrotherapy pools. A tatty notice on the warped metal door of the pool building reminded bathers to present their dermatological, gynaecological, venereological and fluorographical certificates to the attendant on duty. Another advised swimmers to make 'subjective evaluations' of the health of their hearts. A list of eight possible physiological reactions to the waters ranged from 'a nice pleasurable feeling of tiredness' to acute fatigue, pain, dizziness, headache and nausea.

Pavlov advocated bromide and prolonged sleep for every variety of psychological stress or disorder. In 1921, Lenin signed a decree setting up a special state committee assigned with creating favourable conditions for Pavlov's work. Pavlov's materialist explanations of human behaviour were congenial to the ideologues of Bolshevism. (Later Pavlov would fearlessly denounce Lenin and Stalin, calling the Soviet government 'shit', and telling Molotov to his face that collectivisation would never work because it contradicted the psychology of the Russian peasant.) In the same year, Lenin commissioned a detailed report on the state and utility of the Staraya Russa spa. Four years later, it became the first health resort in Russia to work through the winter. In the late 1920s, when Lenin Corners were appearing in nationalised public buildings all over Staraya Russa, Dostoevsky was regarded as a potentially dangerous writer. Just as bromide and sleep inhibited the breakdown of the human machine, Dostoevsky's writings, which, as he once said, aimed to 'light up the dark sides of the human soul that art does not like to approach', threatened to excite internal disorder in Soviet man. The critic Vyacheslav Polonsky was involved in debates about the anti-revolutionary power of *Demons*, a novel which was never published as a separate volume in the Soviet period. People's Commissar for Enlightenment Anatoli Lunacharsky cautioned that Dostoevsky was a 'powerfully active substance which should not simply be placed in the hands of just anybody, especially the younger generation'. Dostoevsky contained too many riddles about the body and the soul, whose relationship the Bolshevik intellectuals were hoping would soon be reduced to a simple materialist formula. Among Molotov's books (bearing the stamp of a Communist Party Workers' Club and carefully recatalogued into his private library) is Lunacharsky's *Art as an Aspect of Human Behaviour*, published by the State Medical Publisher in 1930. Marked in the margin are the sentences 'Comrades, I think it very probable that in the very near future we will grasp the human soul and discover what it is. Why, indeed, is it so surprisingly mysterious?' Molotov admired Dostoevsky, despite the mysteries, and wondered why Lenin had hated the novelist. 'He was a man of genius, without question, that Dostoevsky,' he told Felix Chuev, adding that, like Tolstoy, Dostoevsky got things wrong, because the two nineteenth-century writers were stuck in a bourgeois point of view: 'We have risen above their level.'

It was getting colder as we walked out on to Mineral Street. Lights were coming on, easing the shadows of an early dusk among trees and buildings. We decided to take a long way round to Dostoevsky's villa on the banks of the Porusya, making a detour up to the corner of Engels Street, where our map indicated a big hotel called the Polist in one direction and the Sadko Cafe in the other. We cut into the small park set around the war memorial. We could see a cluster of bright lights at the end of the park, and imagined a cosy hotel dining room.

On the monument to the Glory of the Heroes of the Great Patriotic War there were effigies of soldiers, partisans and guns. Staraya Russa may have suffered more torture and destruction during the three-year German occupation than any town in Russia. 'We have all become landowners,' one Nazi lieutenant wrote home from here; 'we have acquired Slavic slaves, and we do with them whatever we like.' Before the guns had stopped firing, the heir to the once-German-owned 'Luther' plywood factory hurried to Staraya Russa to re-establish the family business. Expropriated after 1917, the factory on the edge of town had been renamed Proletariat.

Adolescent boys and girls joined the partisans in their 'forest republic', fortifying the swamps, living among the fat roots of pre-historic pine trees. Camouflaged in white, they blew up bridges and set fire to woodpiles bound for Germany. They stole into town at night to paste copies of their newspaper on walls and doors over Nazi commands, boasting of their victories: the ambush of a supply train, the detonation of a German car or the shooting of a 'fascist dog' on the highway. The town photographer collaborated with the Nazis, handing over negatives of active partisans. Locals suspected of helping them were hanged from the balcony of the House of the Peasant. When the Nazis evacuated, there were only 165 locals left, and four buildings standing. The spa had been turned into a cemetery. One German soldier sent a photograph of the ruins home as a postcard, captioned 'a town that will never be reborn'.

Unlike some of Staraya Russa's public institutions, reborn with all the classical pomp of the late Stalin era, the Polist hotel was a shabby *khrushchevka*, an angular five-storey brick building from the Khrushchev era, with a cursive metal sign, long gone to rust, pegged on flimsy struts on its roof, that rattled in the breeze. Mounted above the entrance to the hotel was an incongruously beautiful painting, three storeys high, in faded earth-golds, carmines, pinks and pale blues, depicting Sloven and Rus, the veneration of the sacred icon of the Mother of God of Staraya Russa, and other legends of the town's early history. The broken concrete steps were banked with ice. We stepped inside, leaving a dirty trail of slush on the new tiles. An old woman who had been sleeping near the empty coat pegs pointed angrily at our filthy boots and told us that the restaurant was closed.

We continued down Engels, across Herzen Street, to the Sadko Cafe. Another old woman in slippers and a woollen hat was guarding coats in the vestibule. Yes, the cafe was open, she said, but there was a private banquet taking place. Sounds of singing and clatter came from the dining room. I opened the door. Several pairs of expressionless eyes looked my way through the smoke. On either side of a red-faced man at the end of the table sat two middle-aged women in dresses of purple nylon velour and shimmering gold, each with a fleshy arm draped around his neck. A couple danced heavily in the corner, the woman's head resting on the man's shoulder, eyes closed. The table was a mess of half-eaten *zakuski*, ashtrays and cognac stains. I closed the door on the mournful bacchanal, and we walked out into the grey town.

Modern Staraya Russa came to an abrupt end where Engels Street met the river. Along either embankment of the wide Porusya stood low huts, some painted dull green or brown, others that looked as though their ornamented wooden frames had rotted through and were sinking into the dirty snow. Mitya Karamazov's run in the darkness to his father's house on the night of the old man's murder can still be traced on the street map. From the home of Grushenka, whose 'infernal curves' maddened both father and son to a pitch of rivalrous lust, Mitya crossed Cathedral Bridge, took the embankment to Dmitrievsky Street, then ran over the little bridge across a dirty stream called the Malashka, into a deserted alley at the back of Fyodor Pavlovich's house. Sexuality, as the librarian Nikolai Fyodorov thought, is 'the force which compels sons to forget their fathers, and which is responsible for the political and civil strife in the world'.

Dmitrievsky is now called Street of the Red Commanders. Almost none of the streets in Staraya Russa have kept their prerevolutionary names. They signal to each other like some revived underground of bomb-throwing assassins, communist internationalists, victorious proletarians, Chekists and commissars, as though the streets had been renamed after the revolutionary conspirators in *Demons*. One street is named for Vladimir Dubrovin.

An officer in a local regiment with links to revolutionaries in the capital, Dubrovin organised a radical circle of soldiers, merchants and peasants in Staraya Russa in 1878. After he was implicated in the assassination of a chief of police, Dubrovin was imprisoned in the Peter and Paul Fortress in St Petersburg. As he was dragged handcuffed into the streets and across Staraya Russa to the railway station, he cried out that Russia should do like France and rid itself of autocracy. The police investigation concluded that Dubrovin planned to settle in the town 'with the aim of inciting like-minded members of the peasantry to open insubordination against the ruling power'. He refused to give evidence at his court-martial, and was executed in the spring of 1879, still orating inaudibly through a roll of military drums. Even government ministers were grimly impressed by his steadfastness.

When Dostoevsky arrived in Staraya Russa later that month, the town was talking of nothing but the Dubrovin affair, and the 'moral abscess' in Russian society. The head of the local gendarmerie noted in his 'political survey' that the spirit of the people of Staraya Russa was 'rebellious' and could serve as 'ready material for anti-government ends'. In May, Dostoevsky wrote to Pobedonostsev saying that fanatics like Dubrovin are utterly convinced of their own rightness; they have 'their own logic, their own learning, their own code'. A few days earlier he had sent the manuscript of Book Five of *The Brothers Karamazov* to his editor, describing it as a 'portrayal of the extreme blasphemy and the grain of the idea of destruction in Russia in our time, among young people torn away from reality'. The convictions that Ivan Karamazov expounds to Alyosha in the tavern are a 'synthesis of contemporary Russian anarchism'. Ivan does not deny God, he denies the meaning of God's creation. 'All socialism began with a denial of the meaning of historical reality', Dostoevsky told his editor, 'and led to a programme of destruction.' *The Brothers Karamazov* reflects the ideas of Nikolai Fyodorov, in whom Dostoevsky became interested as he was conceiving the novel. Fyodorov's great theme was the 'fraternity of the sons for the resurrection of dead fathers'; Dostoevsky's novel depicts the fraternity of sons for the murder of their father.

One street, on the far side of town, is named for Stepan Khalturin, a member of the revolutionary movement People's Will with no connection to Staraya Russa, who succeeded in detonating a bomb under the Tsar's dining room in the Winter Palace in February 1880, killing guards and servants, and leading to panic in society and a declaration of martial law. Terrorists could be anywhere. The terrorist destruction that lacerated Russia in the last years of Dostoevsky's life convinced him that the apocalyptic vision of *Demons* had been justified; none of its characters had been in the least 'fantastic'. Revolutionaries were now openly committed to murder. Dostoevsky found their motivations and moral vacillations fascinating, noting the testimony of Vera Zasulich (translator of Marx's *Communist Manifesto*) at her trial for the attempted assassination of the governor of St Petersburg: 'It is terrible to raise one's hand against a fellow man, but I decided that this is what I had to do.' He continued to have close friends among materialists and progressives, even among old friends of Karl Marx, like the 'fine, intelligent woman' Anna Jaclard, who spent the summer season in Staraya Russa.

Footprints enticed us on to the frozen river. We took the steps down through the bare lime trees and walked towards Dostoevsky's house on the ice, a watery sky above us, our mood lightened almost to a dream-state by hunger. On the headland, where the Porusya met the Polist, the reaching spire of the cathedral was silhouetted against the darkening sky. Beyond the cathedral, the embankment is named after Dostoevsky. We kept to the river. A group of children had made a sled run where the embankment was steepest. They moved among the trees, calling, laughing. To the east, through a tumbledown fence, over low metal garages and wooden sheds that leaned at odd angles, we could make out St George's Church, where Dostoevsky worshipped, and where the Mother of God of Staraya Russa, now beloved of the FSB, hung until its disappearance in June 1941. Its single blue dome looked black on its round white tower. We climbed back up the slope and walked along the road past rusting Zhigulis.

On the windless night of his father's murder, Mitya Karamazov approaches the house from the lane at the back. He creeps past the banya to the elder and white hazel bushes under the window of Fyodor Pavlovich's bedroom. The old man leans out, beckoning lasciviously to his 'angel' Grushenka, gazing to left and right: the 'profile that Mitya loathed so, his pendent Adam's apple, his hooked nose, his lips that smiled in greedy expectation, were all brightly lit up by the slanting lamplight falling to the left from the room'.

In the last two years of his life, as emphysema choked him, Dostoevsky reimagined his home in Staraya Russa as the setting for scandal and murder within the 'accidental' Karamazov family. Local events served as material. Near the salt factory, a man called Peter Nazarov murdered his father. In a nearby street was the house of the debauched Major General von Sohn, one of a line of corrupt spa directors, who had been brutally murdered by a criminal gang not long before Dostoevsky's first visit, and lives on in local memory as a prototype for Fyodor Pavlovich. Likhachev loved the authenticity in Dostoevsky's novels, their truth to time and place. The writer's genius was not 'to structure a reality', he observed, 'but to structure his novels around reality'. He would 'catch hold of a fact, a place, a chance meeting or a newspaper report, and give it a continuation. He would populate the streets, open the doors into apartments, go down into cellars, make up biographies for the people he passed in the streets.'

Dostoevsky's house was made of narrow dark green clapboards, which were arranged in a zigzag pattern between the first and second floors. A sign saying 'Writer's Street' had been fixed to one wall. During the Khrushchev 'thaw', the embankment was renamed for Dostoevsky, and the decision was made to restore the house and rebuild the banya and the summer house. This was the refuge of Dostoevsky's last years, a time of 'hard labour' that he found more exhausting than his prison term in Omsk. 'What a fantastic and devious old man!' his friend Elena Shtakenshneider remarked of him then. 'Dostoevsky is himself a magical tale, with its miracles, unexpected surprises, transformations, with its enormous terrors and trifles.'

I had a picture of life in the interior from the memoirs of Dostoevsky's daughter, Lyuba. The house was small, 'in the German taste of the Baltic provinces', she recalled, 'full of unexpected surprises, secret wall cupboards, sliding doors leading to dark, dusty, spiral staircases'. In its narrow rooms, furnished in the empire style, mirrors with a greenish patina gave off frightening reflections. On the walls were pictures of 'monstrous Chinese women with nails two feet long and tiny feet'. Lyuba remembered long rainy days spent playing Chinese billiards in a closed verandah at the side of the house. Her father rose late, did gymnastics, sang when his mood was good, washed fastidiously and dressed in clean fine linen and starched collars. After his prayers, he drank two glasses of strong tea and took a third into his study, where everything was laid out on his desk in pedantic order. He rolled cigarettes and smoked heavily throughout the day. After lunch he dictated to his wife, who made a fair copy of what he had written during the previous night, and treated the children to sweetmeats from his desk drawer: figs, dates and nuts from Plotnikov's, a small shop in town that appears under its own name in *The Brothers Karamazov*. Then he read, often from the lives of holy men, before his afternoon walk. In the evenings, he ate early with the children, telling them fairy tales, or reading aloud from Lermontov, Gogol and Schiller, and said his favourite prayer over them: 'All my hope in Thee do I repose, O Mother of God, shelter me beneath Thy veil.' Late at night, as his son and daughter coughed in their sleep, he wrote, listening to the gale outside breaking hundred-year-old trees, testing how far he could go in the literary portrayal of child abuse. What kind of God allows children to be sadistically killed? Ivan Karamazov challenges the devout Alyosha.

We pushed open the gate into the back garden. Small piles of thin, fresh planks, lightly covered by the falling snow, lay scattered among the white-skinned birches. I had a handwritten scrap of paper, given to me by my Slavophile friend in St Petersburg, with the names on it of three curators of the house-museum: Vera Ivanovna, Natalya Dmitrievna, Natalya Anatolievna. He had assured me that the mention of his name would ensure us a warm welcome and an informative visit. The leather-clad door was locked. A sign said the museum was open. We rang, waited, and rang again. Last light was draining out of the day. The garden felt desolate. Should we go and sit in the summer house, where Alyosha waited for his brother Mitya and found instead his sinister probable half-brother, the epileptic household cook, Smerdyakov? 'I may be only a soup maker,' Alyosha heard Smerdyakov say, 'but with luck I could open a cafe on Petrovka Street, in Moscow, for my cookery is something special, and there's no one in Moscow, except the foreigners, whose cookery is anything special.'

I rang again, sensing movement inside the house at last, the sound of a door closing, footsteps. A tiny woman with nervous eyes looked out. I said my friend's name. Very pleased, very pleased, she nodded round the leather door. Yes, she was Natalya Anatolievna, no, we could not come in, no, the museum was under *remont*, there was nothing to see, all the rooms were locked up, everything put away.

We sat in the silent garden where Dostoevsky imagined Smerdyakov crooning to the strum of his guitar. The windows were dark, like an ice-hole. Not every place will reveal its secret. A light came on in an upstairs room. Stacked high against the windowpane was a loose pile of old books. Balanced on top of the books was a white porcelain soup tureen.

EIGHT

Rostov-on-Don

We both looked on the world as a meadow in May, a meadow across
which women and horses moved.
ISAAC BABEL, 'The Story of a Horse'

In the tumbledown backstreets that tip towards the Don, evening
had begun to unfold. Down here, 750 miles south of Moscow, the
spring was weeks ahead. Pop music and football commentary
spilled from radios and televisions inside small brick houses, all
built, said the brass fittings on their doors, in the 1870s. Doorways
lay open, revealing shadowed passages, bare and cool, with blue
tin letterboxes fixed to the walls. On wrought-iron balconies
above the pavement, laundry and gutted fish hung on lines above
a disarray of birdcages and broken furniture. A man with tattooed
legs sat smoking in a dirty armchair, watching us pass. 'Keep your
money in a savings bank', advised a new plastic sign on a grimy
shopfront. Below Stanislavsky Street, the buildings were smaller,
some no more than tin sheds. The road disintegrated into rubble
and dirt. Inside a derelict-looking nineteenth-century factory
building, men shouted over the grind and shriek of a machine
tool. Irises grew in clumps on a patch of waste ground, still
folded into tight green spears, lipped with petals of urgent purple.
A dog nosed the garbage sliding down the hill to the waterfront,
where the cherry trees were already in blossom.

A young woman in a belted black vinyl coat stepped out of a
corner door. She wore a wide choker and stilettoes strapped across
the ankle. An old man passed, leaning heavily on a squeaking baby
carriage filled with tightly stuffed plastic bags. Catching her long
hair in one hand, the young woman drew it across her shoulder,
dropped a diamanté cellphone into her bag, glanced at the little

boys scuffing up dust in the gutter, and turned away from the Don, up towards the centre of the town, her tread graceful and swift, despite her heels and the pocks in the asphalt.

Like Vassiliev, the Moscow law student in Chekhov's story 'A Nervous Breakdown', I know little of fallen women except from hearsay and books, but when I recognise one in the street by her dress or manners I remember stories I have read, and my imagination frets with questions, to which the answers are either jocular and cynical or bleakly tragic. 'They are alive! My God, those women are alive!' Vassiliev shudders after his first visit to a Moscow brothel. 'Doctor, tell me only one thing,' he demands when the student friends who had introduced him to the brothel take him to be medically treated for his ensuing spiritual agony. 'Is prostitution an evil or not? And if prostitution is truly an evil, then what?'

I walked with my companion along the embankment. Couples sat on blue wooden benches drinking Baltika beer, staring across the Don at the wild land on the opposite side. The waters flowing past had come over a thousand miles, moving south-east from near Tula where they rise, then south-west towards the Azov Sea. A short way along the riverbank was a row of new homes in smooth brick, bright with painted balustrades, security cameras and satellite dishes on their eaves. Signs on their iron gates warned of 'evil dogs'. With an electronic murmur, an underground garage opened to take in a silver jeep that had come silently up the road behind us. Commerce, for which Rostov-on-Don was founded in the late eighteenth century, had returned to the city, and its jumble of rich and poor had been quickly restored.

Rhoda Power, an Englishwoman who came to Rostov in 1917 as governess to the wealthy Sabarov family, found the city's appearance curious. In *Under Cossack and Bolshevik*, the memoir that she published soon after her escape through Murmansk from revolution and civil war, she describes Rostov's higgledy-piggledy appearance, in which 'next to some large and ornate mansion with statues at the door and twisted iron gates there would be a tiny wooden hut, thatched with straw and built half underground', where chickens, dogs and children crawled on the floor together. The river was fouled with factory waste in those days, and the water stank, but the main streets were paved, and electric trams ran along the Garden Ring, past banks, fashionable shops, clubs, insurance companies, cinemas and belle époque private residences like the mansion of the Sabarovs. Miss Power noticed that there were more Greeks, Armenians and Jews in the nouveau riche city than Russians and Cossacks. She was shocked by the open displays of anti-Semitic hatred among the local bourgeoisie and peasantry, who would spit at the mention of a Jewish name. Soon though, Beloborodov, Trotsky's future host at No. 3 Granovsky Street, would be ruling the city with Red Terror, and people like the Sabarovs would be on the run.

A barge passed with a cargo of sand. Trucks rumbled across the wide bridge that leads across the Don from Voroshilov Avenue. Beyond a lonely statue of Gorky, the embankment became a promenade, dressed with fairy lights, a spindly jetty, and pleasure boats in wait for the season, tied to iron bollards cast in the last year of the nineteenth century. The doors of a nightclub named Titanic stood open on the wharf, revealing the morose plush of its empty interior to the light air of the spring evening. A girl in a satin jacket and high boots hurried down to the waterfront from the town.

'I can accept the street as the multitude,' Tsvetaeva wrote to Pasternak in 1926, 'but the street personified in a single person, the multitude presuming to offer itself in the singular with *two* arms and *two* legs . . . oh, no!' Alone in Moscow in the heat of summer, Pasternak had hinted to Tsvetaeva of his temptations, the 'terrible truths revealed by the senseless seething of the dammed-up blood'. 'There is no masculine street, only feminine,' she told him in a fierce reply; 'it is the man who, in his lust, creates it. It exists in the countryside, too. Not a single woman would go after a ditchdigger (exceptions only prove the rule), but all men – all *poets* – go after street girls.'

The long friendship between the two poets, expressed in letters, poetry and dreams rather than actual meetings, began with an exchange of verse about the Don. They sought out in the history of the southern steppe mythical archetypes of companionship between men and women that seemed to answer the free and heroic measure of the soul; forms of relation more powerful and essential than the intimacy of husbands and wives. 'To the incomparable poet Marina Tsvetaeva, who is "from the Don, fiery and hellish," from an admirer of her gift', Pasternak inscribed in a book of his poems in January 1923, quoting a poem he had written in the last year of the Civil War:

> *We are few. We are perhaps three,*
> *From the Don, fiery and hellish*
> *Under the grey running crust*
> *Of rain, clouds and soldiers'*
> *Soviets, of poems and discussions*
> *About transport and art.*

Hungry in Moscow, Tsvetaeva had written verse about the warrior traditions of the Don during the Civil War, in which her husband fought for the Whites. She answered Pasternak's dedication with 'Scythian Verses', a cycle of three poems which take up his image of her as a fellow-warrior. 'Scythianism' was a form of self-stylisation for Russian poets in these years. 'Wide is our Wild Country,' wrote Tsvetaeva's poetic mentor Max Voloshin, 'deep is our Scythian steppe'. Blok's poem 'Scythians', written in the first months after the Revolution, hymned Russia's 'barbaric lyre':

> *Yes, we are Scythians! Yes, we are Asiatics,*
> *With slanting, greedy eyes!*
> *For you centuries, for us a single hour.*
> *We, like obedient underlings*
> *Held the shield between the two enemy races*
> *Of the Mongols and Europe.*

Now Tsvetaeva cast herself as an Amazon fighting on the ancient steppe, with an arrow instead of a pen. Scythia is the ultimate darkness: epic, magnificent, hushed. Its men and women live by different, more elemental, rules of conduct. Tsvetaeva invoked Ishtar, Babylonian goddess of fertility, sex and war, calling on the divine prostitute to keep safe from the marauding khan her 'tent of brothers and sisters', her cauldron, campfire and quiver.

Known to ancient Greek geography as Tanais, the Don marked the northern boundary of Scythia in the seventh to third centuries BC. According to Herodotus, the Scythians arrived on the northern coast of the Black Sea from some unspecified part of Asia, and had linguistic and cultural similarities with the nomadic Iranian tribes. Indeed, the name of the Don comes from the Scythian word *danu*, meaning river. The Royal Scythians, the 'most warlike and numerous', reached as far as the river Tanais, beyond which was a non-Scythian race called Black-cloaks, and north of them, an undiscovered region of lakes and empty country. A people without towns, the Scythians lived in wagons, herding cattle for food, every one of them accustomed to fighting on horseback with bows and arrows. Herodotus described how the landscape of river and watered plains favoured the Scythian way of life. The Tanais, the river that bounded the Scythian lands, had its source, Herodotus says, 'far up country in a large lake, and empties itself into a larger one still, Lake Maeotis', which is the ancient name for the Azov Sea. Herodotus did not admire the Scythians, save for the fact that they managed 'the most important thing in human affairs better than anyone else on the face of the earth: their own preservation'.

The Amazons, says Herodotus, washed up on Lake Maeotis after they had murdered the Greeks who had taken them prisoner. The warrior women made their way inland into the territory of the free Scythians and stole horses. When the Scythians discovered that the raiders were women, they wanted to get children by them, and soon the Amazons and the Scythians united, every man 'keeping as his wife the woman whose favours he had first enjoyed'. The women picked up the language of the men, but could never settle down as wives, accustomed as they were to a life of hunting and raiding. The Amazons wanted to venture beyond the Tanais, Herodotus relates, and the Scythians agreed, so they crossed the great river and travelled east for three days, then north for three more from Lake Maeotis. Ever since, the women have kept to their old ways, he adds, hunting on horse-back, sometimes alone, taking part in war, wearing the same clothes as men.

⤜⊹⤛

Though he had been sent down to the Don region in March 1930 to check on the spring sowing on the collective farms of the Russian south, Molotov never cut the pages of Boris Kushner's travel book *Southern Lights* (*Hot Dry Wind*). Kushner had inscribed his copy 'To dear comrade V. M. Molotov' in a generous looping hand in the summer of 1930. The few pages of the first chapter – 'Moscow–Don' – that I was able to read without taking a knife to the delicate volume (which I felt I should not do) made me want to follow his journey into the light of the south, from the capital to Rostov-on-Don. Kushner, whose life, like so many others, ended abruptly in the purges of 1937, was a member of the Party and a Futurist writer, actively involved, with Vladimir Mayakovsky and Osip Brik, in the journal *Lef*, whose purpose was to formalise an alliance between avant-garde artists and the Soviet state. The *Lef* writers, who wanted their work to serve the revolu-tion, elevated reporting – in particular travel notes and sketches – to the highest status among literary forms, because such genres served, and did not disfigure, the *fact*. The dominant spirit of Kushner's travel writing was his passion for technology, the fac-tory and the machine, which would at last overcome Russia's backwardness. 'Comrade commissars of trade . . . ! Study the organisation of the American private company Singer, which has seized the world market and penetrated into the most obscure places – a Russian peasant hut, an Abyssinian village, the home of a Chinese agricultural labourer,' Kushner remarks as his train passes the old brick Singer sewing-machine factory buildings at Podolsk, just south of Moscow. ('America is great nation!' a peasant on a train told Louise Bryant in 1917. 'Sewing machines come from America!') As the train to Rostov moves through orchards of white Antonovka apples into the sunny steppe lands, golden with wheat, his travelling companion tells marvellous tales of American harvests, and a 'giant complex machine', a 'miracle' known as the 'combine'. Kushner was writing rapturously of those 'oceans of wheat' in the year 1930, at the height of the First Five-Year Plan, when much of southern Russia was starving, as the state seized grain for export to finance its frenzied programme of industrialisation. A few months after Kushner inscribed his book, Stalin told Molotov, 'Force up the export of grain to the maximum. This is the core of everything.' In a speech lamenting Russia's history of backwardness, Stalin quoted from the poet Nikolai Nekrasov's folk epic, 'Who Can Be Happy and Free in Russia': 'You are wretched, you are abundant, you are mighty, you are powerless, Mother Russia.'

We turned away from the quiet of the Don, walking up into town on the curving side street down which the girl in boots had come, until it met Budyonny Avenue, a main road formerly known as Taganrog Street which cuts a dead straight line, parallel to Voroshilov Avenue, through the centre of Rostov. Like the granite plaques to Budyonny and Voroshilov on the façade of No. 3, these wide thoroughfares testify to the brilliance of their Civil War victories in Rostov and the Russian south-west, as well as to their unusual distinction in managing their own preservation (and the extinction of their enemies) throughout Stalin's tyranny and beyond.

Semyon Budyonny's life began in 1883, on a peasant farm on the Don. It ended ninety years later in the comfort of No. 3, in a panelled apartment overlooking the courtyard, among heavily framed oil paintings of himself, decorated with both tsarist and Soviet medals, astride a horse. In one room of his huge apartment, a visitor remembers, there was just one table on which were five telephones, one red, as though the Marshal 'were waiting for the call from the Kremlin to saddle his horses and storm world imperialism'. ('A benefactor and utterly devoted defender of the horse,' Valery Mezhlauk had labelled him in one of his caricatures, which showed him on horseback.) Budyonny and his devoted third wife had moved out of his original apartment in No. 3 to a different part of the building, to be free of all the ugly memories of the Marshal's first and second marriages. 'History belongs to posterity,' Budyonny wrote late in life in the journal *Don* (in an article that Molotov particularly admired and liked to quote); 'may it not be a distorting mirror.' Budyonny's great fear as he contemplated history's mirror was that it would give a distorted picture of Stalin, whom he had served with absolute loyalty since 1918. 'The veterans of the Revolution went through a great deal,' he reflected: 'they survived many a disaster, and stared death in the face more than once. But we suffered no worse misfortune than to see doubt cast on the revolutionary passion and revolutionary acts of the leader of our Party, Lenin's true comrade-in-arms, I. V. Stalin.' History's mirror was kind to Budyonny. As well as a main street in Rostov, the moustachioed cavalry general has a town in the south, a soldier's cap, a breed of horse and a children's game named after him.

By 1918, Budyonny had four St George Crosses, and the highest of tsarist military distinctions, a full ribbon of the St George Cavalryman. He had fought with distinction in a dragoon regiment in the Russo-Japanese War of 1903, studied at the St Petersburg Cavalry School, and served as a platoon sergeant in the Caucasus Cavalry Division during the First World War. He liked to tell his children that Tsar Nicholas II once extended his hand to him in St Petersburg. Budyonny exemplified a certain kind of military loyalty to political power, at once blind and cunning. After 1918, he calculated that it would be better to be a 'marshal in the

Red Army than an officer in the White' and returned to the Don, which quickly became the principal arena of the Civil War, to join local partisans fighting the Whites. The partisans became the First Socialist Regiment under Boris Dumenko. Budyonny served as Dumenko's aide. When the Socialist Regiment became the Special Cavalry Division, Budyonny was placed in command of a brigade.

The prosperous city of Rostov, the most heavily industrialised in the Russian south, with its intersecting railway lines, river links with north and south, and great trading port, was strategically vital, and changed hands six times between 1917 and 1920. 'Take Rostov at all costs, for otherwise disaster threatens,' Lenin declared in the spring of 1919, when the city had been taken from the Bolsheviks by German-backed White forces, swelled with Cossacks. 'Proletarians to horse!' Trotsky commanded, as he contemplated the success of the Volunteer White Armies in the south. Across the steppe, multiple armies clashed, conjoined and fragmented, taking turns at terrorising the local population, waging sadistic class war, assuaging every kind of hatred and bloodlust. Don Cossacks fought on both sides. As Trotsky observed, the allegiance of the Cossacks was, above all, to their own land, which they held on to 'with claws and teeth'. In 1919, Lenin gave written instructions to deport Don Cossacks – three hundred thousand were sent to concentration camps or forced labour.

By the end of 1919, Budyonny was commander of the First Cavalry Army, and had decisively retaken Rostov from General Anton Denikin's Volunteer White Army, which had made the city its organising centre. To commemorate the victory, Budyonny sent a signed photograph of himself to Lenin in Moscow. At first his forces contained only a small percentage of Don Cossacks, but when the White armies evacuated Russia for Constantinople by sea from Novorossiisk most of the Cossacks who had not left or been deported showed Budyonny's own flexible political allegiance. When his Cavalry Army entered Poland in 1920, as part of a Bolshevik attempt to push the Revolution westward, the fighting force was dominated by Cossacks.

Budyonny was not a Cossack, but he grew up on their land, loving their ways, aspiring to their skill in the saddle and with the sabre. In 1903, at the start of his military career, he married Nadezhda, a beauty from a farmstead in a local *stanitsa*, a Cossack settlement. She later ran a medical unit in the Cavalry Army. Like a Cossack ataman, Budyonny was known to his men as 'Batka Semyon', 'Little Father Semyon'. To be close to them, he had to look kindly on, even share in, their habits of plunder and insouciant brutality. 'The First Cavalry Army . . . destroyed the Jewish population as they went,' read a report to Lenin, which he marked 'for the archives'. As Stalin built his own power against Trotsky, consolidating a military faction loyal to himself in the aftermath of the Civil War, reports of looting and pogroms carried out by Budyonny's cavalry in Poland in 1920 were carefully suppressed. Like Voroshilov's, Budyonny's loyalty to Stalin was absolute. This seems to have created a lasting bond with Molotov, to whom Budyonny would always send greeting cards on national holidays, hailing his disgraced comrade in an ever more shaky hand from across the courtyard of No. 3.

When we moved into No. 3, one of the stories our landlord told me with the most relish was of how Budyonny's Cossack first wife had died in the house of a shot to the head, and how his second wife, a loose-living and beautiful opera singer named Olga (whom Budyonny met when taking a mineral water cure at Essentuki soon after his first wife's death), had been arrested in 1937 and sent to the Gulag. Before then, I had been more familiar with the Marshal's name from Isaac Babel's *Cavalry Army* than from history books. Like Kutuzov or Napoleon, kept for ever vivid in Tolstoy's *War and Peace*, Budyonny's image – white smile, trousers embroidered with shining silver, chestnut mare – is preserved in fiction.

An Odessa-born Jew, Babel moved from the south to Moscow with his family not long after 'Batka Semyon' and his Cossack bride moved into No. 3. In the summer of 1920, under the name Kiril Lyutov, the bespectacled writer had accompanied Budyonny's horseback army into Poland, watching the killing, asthmatically inhaling the dust of battle, sleeping in shtetls and Polish manor houses, writing in his notebook, true to the new aesthetic of the fact. In 1923, Babel's laconic and exquisite *Cavalry Army* stories were published, to immediate acclaim, in *Lef* and *Red Virgin Soil*. Budyonny reacted with hatred, threatening to hack the author to pieces with his *shashka*, his long sword, it is said. *Cavalry Army* was a libel against Cossacks, the Red General raged in a newspaper article of protest, whose title – 'The Womanishness ['*Babizm*'] of Babel in *Red Virgin Soil*' – punned on Babel's name. *Babizm* was the worst insult Budyonny could muster for the writer from Odessa who had become suddenly famous in literary Moscow by portraying him and his men as bandits, marauding Scythians.

Babel's prose is at once opulent and spare, intimate and detached. He sees war with the eye of an aesthete. Atrocity is set among the beauty of the landscape, described in imagery of extravagant violence. The orange sun rolls across the sky 'like a severed head'; the evening cool drips with the smell of 'yesterday's blood and slain horses'. Babel writes of the instinctive life of warriors from the fascinated perspective of the educated outsider, unable to ransack or kill. 'I'll never be a real Budyonny man,' he noted in his diary after watching the Cossacks loot a village. 'I took nothing, although I could have . . .' At the end of *Cavalry Army*, in 'Argamak', the writer's 'dream is fulfilled'. He has learned to sit in the saddle: 'The Cossacks stopped following me and my horse with their eyes.'

The critic Vyacheslav Polonsky suggested that Babel not only rode with Budyonny's Cavalry Army, but also served the Cheka. In the early 1930s, he was part of the Moscow elite, and lived in a favoured apartment with his common-law wife Antonina Pirozhkova, an engineer on the metro. He socialised with the chiefs of the secret police, Yezhov and Yagoda. Nadezhda

Mandelstam thought that Babel visited the Chekists in their own homes because he wanted to find out what they smelled like, what death smelled like. (He was arrested in 1939 and taken to the Lubyanka. In January 1940 he was shot, the day after his 'trial' for Trotskyite activities and espionage.) Polonsky considered that Babel's almost sadistic interest in blood and death and killing was a limitation of his writing. From the start, Babel had assiduously collected material about violence and attended executions.

In his 1920 diary, which could not be published until the end of the Soviet era, Babel made observations on certain 'terrible truths' about relations between men and women on the margins of battle. 'All our fighting men – velvet capes, rape, forelocks, battles, revolution and syphilis,' he noted, 'all the soldiers have syphilis . . . the scourge of the soldiery, Russia's scourge.' He expressed genuine admiration for the army nurses: 'It's a whole epic, the nurse's story . . . our only heroes are heroines.' In the city of Zhitomir, at night on the boulevard, he reflected on the fixed composition of the urban sexual chase, and its sadness: 'Four avenues, four stages: getting acquainted, chatting, awakening of desire, satisfaction of desire . . . I'm tired and suddenly I'm lonely, life flows past me, and what does it mean.'

Among the many voices in the *Cavalry Army* stories – of priests, rabbis, Bolsheviks, anarchists, plunderers, turncoats, a pregnant Jewish woman, giggling Cossack nurses, and Sashka, a stallion-riding Amazon – is the speech of Budyonny himself:

> Budyonny, in red trousers with a silver stripe, was standing by a tree . . . 'The scum will squeeze us', the commander said with his dazzling grin, 'we win or we die. There's no other way. Understood?'
> 'Understood,' answered Kolesnikov, opening his eyes wide.
> 'And if you run – I'll shoot you,' the commander said, smiling . . .

From the wide street in Rostov that bears his name, I imagined Budyonny, newly installed in No. 3 with his Cossack wife, when the row with Babel began. The premises of Babel's publisher were just around the corner, on Vozdvizhenka. The horseman from the steppe had settled in a nest of intellectuals, of alien codes, of *babizm*. It was in their new life as Bolshevik grandees in Moscow that the strain in the childless marriage began to tell. Many of the other Party wives were sophisticated intellectuals; many were Jews. Perhaps the city apartment building felt even stranger and more unsettling to Budyonny and the war-hardened Cossack wife who had shared his military campaigns than the battlefield had felt to Babel. Stories of her death vary. One says that the General had taken out his loaded pistol the previous night when he had seen a suspicious group of men in the courtyard. Another, that Budyonny had drawn his Walther and cocked the trigger when a gang approached him as he walked alone down Nizhny Kislovsky on his way home from a meeting. As he was undoing his shoes in the hallway, so the family story says, Nadezhda took the gun from the commode, held it against her temple, said 'Look, Sema,' and pulled the trigger.

⁓❧⁓

On our second day, in the sunny flush of morning, we drove out of Rostov towards the Starocherkasskaya *stanitsa*, the settlement that was once the capital of the Don Cossacks, who called themselves the Free Don Host. On the eastern edges of the city, among willows and birches, pricked green under a high sun with the first leaves of the accelerating spring, were elegant nineteenth-century houses, now dilapidated communal homes, painted in faded tones of mustard orange, pale yellow, green and blue. Just as the houses in the city had become diminished as the streets cascaded towards the riverbank, so here on its outskirts, larger buildings gave way to smaller and smaller houses, until we passed the tiniest dwellings I had ever seen, painted in colours that echoed the dusty steppe and the bright sky. This harmony of tonalities that moves across the great expanse of Russia is a lovely side effect of decades of central planning: trucks, fences, shutters, shops, cemetery railings, from Archangel to Kyakhta, all coloured in the same repertory of paints, at various stages of corrosion and distress.

The gravel road, which narrowed quickly as we left the city, and was full of potholes, took us some way south on to the steppe, then turned north again to meet the Don. Forsythia was in early bloom, and the grass was patched with brilliant green. We came up to a landing stage, jutting into the river at a narrowing bend. As a car ferry pulled away on the opposite side, we stood on the rush-clustered bank and waited. The sky clouded over and a wind blew from downriver, agitating the pewter surface of the water, lifting a chill into the air. In winter, cold from northern rivers courses deep through the underflows of the Don, freezing it, icing the Azov Sea. The ferry came slowly towards us, bearing a bright blue Moskvich (a vintage Soviet car) and a rusted three-wheeler with handlebars at the front and a trailer behind. A pack of wild dogs stopped to watch the craft approach, tails high, sniffing the breeze.

In Cossack songs about the Don, the river is always 'quiet', commanding the landscape through which it flows with its own glorious silence. The river is 'grey-haired', a *batyushka* ('little father'), or Don Ivanovich, a proud and generous provider, feeding the soft fields of 'Mother Donland'. Our turn came to cross the river, in the company of an old man and his stout wife with a motorbike and sidecar piled with garden rakes. I stood on the platform, leaning out over the water, as the wind blew back my hair. At the moment of equidistance from the shores, the wind dropped, and the low hum of the ferry engine seemed suspended in a deeper quiet, evoked by the unending flatness of the landscape. I wanted to stay out here, on the open vessel in the middle of the wide river, to ride its waters up towards the Volga, or follow their strong current down to the Don mouth at the Azov. As we drew towards the opposite bank, the dull green domes of a church could be seen among the trees. A group of young boys, dressed in camouflage trousers, trainers and tall Cossack hats made of black astrakhan sheepskin, stared at our slow-moving stage from the road, hands in their pockets, as it approached.

Cherkassk, as the Starocherkasskaya *stanitsa* was once known, was the Don Cossack capital for 150 years from the middle of the seventeenth century. In the days of Cossack autonomy, it was the seat of the *krug*, the Army Circle that was selected democratically but governed with fierce authoritarian discipline. In time, as the Cossack way of life became more settled and integrated into the institutional structures of the Russian state, the plenitude of the river in spate, which had once aided in the defence of the fortress at Cherkassk, made the place unsuitable as a capital. In spring, the Don would overrun its banks and wash up among the stone churches and wooden dwellings of the settlement. So in 1805, Ataman Matvei Platov, a native of Cherkassk and a national military hero, moved the capital to higher ground twenty miles up-country, and named the new administrative and trading centre Novocherkassk. Now Starocherkasskaya (Old Cherkassk) is preserved as a tranquil memorial to the culture of the seventeenth- and eighteenth-century Cossacks, who were, by turns, loyal fighters for imperial Russia and unruly rebels against the autocracy of the Tsar.

The Cossacks, a military caste described by Akhmatova's son, the orientalist Lev Gumilev, as a 'sub-ethnos', formed into a distinct people through their own wayward relation with the authority of the state. The first Cossacks appeared in the lower Don region in the fifteenth century. The word *kazak* (Cossack) is of Turkic origin and means 'free man'. Runaway peasants and other sundry fugitives from official injustice, taxation and conscription fled south and adopted a nomadic life on the ungoverned steppe. By the beginning of the seventeenth century, the Cossacks, with their unequalled horsemanship and fighting prowess, had become a powerful force in the wild lands on the edges of the empire, defending Russian territory against incursion by brigands or foreign states, leading the outward push of the imperial frontier to the south and east. Cossack autonomy gradually diminished, and by the middle of the eighteenth century, ministries of state in

St Petersburg were responsible for appointing atamans and military commanders.

Until the late seventeenth century, the Cossack way of life was strictly masculine. The first Cossack wives were captives, taken as war booty. Male authority was unconstrained. An unloved wife could be sold to another Cossack for cash or goods. A woman could be beaten, even killed, with impunity. Later, the Cossacks, who soon became, for the most part, Orthodox (many of them schismatics, Old Believers who had broken with the Church over liturgical reform in the seventeenth century), took on the marriage rites of the Russians. Don Cossack love songs are addressed not to women, but to eagles and falcons, horses, spurs, rifles and *shashki* (the long swords that had to remain silent as Cossacks rode into battle), to vodka, freedom, the greening steppe, the steep shores and braided yellow sands of the Don, and the joys of killing.

Life is a kopeck. Let's go to the border to beat the enemies of the Fatherland. Half of them we will hack to death, the rest we will take prisoner . . . We gallop forward, we cry, we hack. Surrender, or you will fall like grass in the field, we will cut you clean into firewood.

Tolstoy, who spent time with Cossacks as a soldier in the Caucasus when Russia was fighting rebel Chechens in the 1850s, was particularly intrigued by relations between men and women in their small rugged communities, which, for him, were a realisation of primitive innocence: instinctive, authentic, close to nature. 'A Cossack, who considers it improper to speak affectionately or idly to his wife in front of strangers, involuntarily feels her superiority when he is alone with her face-to-face,' he observed. Tolstoy greatly admired the physical strength and beauty of Cossack women. 'In general', he wrote in *The Cossacks*, they 'are stronger, more intelligent, more educated and more beautiful than Cossack men'. His hero, Olenin, a wealthy idler, 'what in Moscow society is called "*un jeune homme*"', leaves the city for the Caucasus, and falls in love with a Cossack girl, Maryana, who is strongly built, dignified and beautiful, with black-shadowed eyes. She walks with a dashing, boyish gait, works hard, and expresses nothing of her inner life. Olenin's main occupation in the settlement is gazing at her. '*La feel com sa say tray bya*,' thinks Olenin's citified manservant Vanyusha when he first sees Maryana drawing wine from a cask in her simple Cossack dress: 'Back in the servants' quarters at home they would have laughed if they had seen a girl like that.'

From the ferry, we walked the short way into Starocherkasskaya, passing a graveyard, at the gates of which an old man was selling worms for bait from a plastic bucket. We turned up the dusty road to the early-eighteenth-century Military Resurrection Cathedral, which stands alone on the edge of the town, surging upwards out of the raked-bare fields. Before the Cossack capital was moved, the cathedral served the entire Don Cossack region. Built in the Byzantine style by Moscow masters sent to Cherkassk by Peter the Great, the brick and whitewash cathedral, set in its own bare steppe landscape, was simple and strong. From a powerful lower mass, it soared into a jostle of simply decorated towers with long narrow windows and bulbed cupolas topped with green-patinaed metal and pink-gold filigree crosses that caught the sunlight. Gift of a tsar, the cathedral expressed Cossack allegiance to the centralised Russian state; inside, among the whitewash, baroque gold and polished slate, was a massive chain, said to have shackled the Cossack rebel Stenka Razin before he was quartered alive on Red Square. Stenka Razin's life of piratical raiding and rebellion had taken him to Persia and made him ruler of a Cossack rebel republic centred in Astrakhan, from where he aimed to dominate the Volga and advance on Moscow. From the place where the cathedral now stands, Razin, master of Cherkassk in 1670, once called the Don Cossacks to follow him north to unseat the Moscow boyars and subject the whole of Rus to their own violent, egalitarian principles of government.

Razin was a figure of enduring popular and artistic fascination. Pushkin (who later wrote a history of the Cossack Emilian

Pugachev's uprising against Catherine the Great) said that Stenka Razin had been his first hero, that he had dreamed of the rebel when he was only eight years old. On May Day 1919, Lenin unveiled a monument to Stenka Razin on the Lobnoye Mesto, the 'execution place', on Red Square, proclaiming the 'real freedom' that the workers' state would bring, and telling the young people in the crowd that they would 'live to see the full bloom of communism'. The folk ballad 'Volga, Volga, Mother Volga' sings of Razin's marriage to a beautiful Persian princess. 'He has changed us for a baba!' Razin's men complain in the song. 'Just one night he spent with her, and by the morning he had become a baba too . . .' The Cossack chooses his men, and the princess is cast into the river as a 'gift from the Cossacks of the Don, so that there will be no discord among free men'.

As the authority of the tsarist state broke up in 1917, Tsvetaeva wrote a poem about Stenka Razin. In 'Free Passage', a prose vignette that recounts her visit to a rural requisition station in 1918, she meets a handsome tow-headed peasant soldier – 'Two St George Crosses. A round face, cunning, freckles . . .' – and names him Stenka Razin: 'He's Razin – *before* the beard, but already with a thousand Persian girls!' Tsvetaeva trades stories and poetry with the young soldier, and they talk about Moscow, Marx, churches and monasteries: '"I wanted to say something else, comrade, about the monks. Nuns, for example. Why do all the nuns make eyes at me?" I think to myself: Sweetheart, how could one *help* but . . .' As they part, Tsvetaeva gives the blue-eyed soldier a signet ring, a tsarist ten-kopeck piece in a silver frame, and a little book called *Chroniclers, Travellers, Writers and Poets on Moscow*, 'a treasure house'. He stirs in her images of 'pretemporal Rus': 'I reach out to you! Straw-headed Stepan, listen to me, steppes: there were covered wagons and nomad camps, there were camp fires and stars. Do you want a nomad tent – where through the hole you see the biggest star?'

After visiting the cathedral, we climbed the eight-sided tent-shaped belltower, startling the pigeons. There was once a prison in

the cellar of the tower. Standing beneath the bells, among feathers, pigeon droppings and hunks of rotting timber, we looked
out of its portals, eye level to the cupolas. On the ground below
lay the iron yoke of a trading scale and the folds of the door of the
Turkish fortress of Azov, Cossack trophies of territorial wars long
past. From the other side of the tower we could see the ensemble
of Starocherkasskaya: the Don church, the Ataman's palace, the
whitewashed fortress-home of the Zhuchenkovs, an eighteenth-
century family of trading Cossacks, and the two-storey house of
Kondraty Bulavin, leader of another peasant uprising. Between
the cathedral and the old stone buildings, paled in by slumping
fences, was an untidy line of tiny wooden houses with hand-
carved eaves and shutters, some newly painted bright green. From
above, everything seemed to lean this way and that, vegetable
plots had been raked over, bathtubs and basins filled with soil for
spring planting, garden rubbish piled up. An old woman hoed,
small bonfires smoked, the skin of the dark earth greyed in the
sun. From afar, we watched two monks in long black robes walk
side by side across a field towards the village.

We wandered lazily through the Museum of Cossack Life. The
objects on display – eighteenth-century linen chests, lead weights
and accounts ledgers, orders and medals, books on the geography
of the Don, wine labels, buttons and lace, dainty pots of *theater
puder* and *blancheur de la peau* – told not of nomadism, wildness
and fratricidal war, but of domesticity, settled purpose, order and
measure, an austere and precise sense of the value of beauty. On
the walls were hundred-year-old photographs of Cossack families, with grave faces staring out from under their hats, posed
against the same slumping fences, on the same patchy grass.

Fiction can make innocent things sinister, and the yellowed
family portraits made me think of Babel's story 'A Letter', in
which Kurdyukov, a peasant soldier in Budyonny's army, writes
home to his mother. In filial tones, he tells her how, during the
Red advance on Rostov, his father, a secret medal-wearing White,
killed his own son Fyodor, calling him a 'mercenary' and a 'Red

dog', only to be killed in his turn by his other son, Semyon. Kurdyukov shows Babel a photograph of his family before the Civil War: 'Papasha' with a glazed stare in his colourless vacant eyes; Mama, shy and consumptive in a bamboo chair; and behind them, two lads, 'monstrously huge, slow-witted, broad-faced, goggle-eyed, frozen as if on drill parade, Kurdyukov's two brothers – Fyodor and Semyon'.

In the Don church opposite the museum, a liturgy was being sung. A sign told women to cover their heads, not to wear lipstick. The iconostasis was newly painted with bright medallions show-ing Adam, Noah, Cain, Abel, Abraham and Samuel. Outside, a war veteran who had lost both legs in Chechnya sat in the sun in his wheelchair, collecting kopecks in a sawn-off Pepsi bottle. Next to him, a bright green bicycle leaned against the church wall. Tulips were pushing through the packed earth. Dogs barked and a cockerel crowed. Sound carries far over the flat land. A voice called up the belltower, '*Komandír! Komandír!*', 'Commander! Commander!'

At a trestle table under a willow tree, a moustachioed man in a Cossack hat was selling books. I began to browse, and he told me, with a small bow, that he was Mikhail Astapenko, Cossack histo-rian. Each book was stamped with the seal of the Don Cossacks, a simple graphic depicting a happy warrior sitting on a barrel with rifle, sword, horn and cup. There was a school textbook by Astapenko on the history of the Don Cossacks; a book of Cossack recipes (fish and white cabbage pie, Rostov lamb, Antonovka apples in sour cream); an album of Cossack songs; *Atamans of the Don Cossacks from 1550 to 1920*, edited by Astapenko with contribu-tions from Cossacks in Rostov-on-Don, Paris, Yosemite and Buenos Aires; and Astapenko's literary anthology on the Cossacks from ancient times to the year 1920. I bought the anthology, and the bookseller signed my copy 'from the author' with a brisk flour-ish. It contained excerpts of poetry, novels, short stories, historical narrative and folk song: Karamzin, Pushkin, Lermontov, Tolstoy, Gilyarovsky, Roman Gul, Mikhail Sholokhov, no Babel . . . But there, to my happiness, in a section entitled 'Brother on Brother', was Tsvetaeva's poem 'The Don'. A 'rebel, gut and brow', she called herself. As the 'wife of a White officer', in Moscow's Polytechnical Museum at the end of the Civil War, Tsvetaeva recited her 'Don monarchist' poem to an audience of Red Army soldiers and communists. 'The passions of the stage', she said, 'are military.' She described her recitation that night as 'the discharge of a *duty of honour*':

> *And our descendants, remembering the past:*
> *'Where were you?' – The question will rumble like thunder,*
> *The answer will rumble like thunder: – On the Don!*
>
> *'What did you do?' – We accepted torments,*
> *Then grew tired and lay down to sleep . . .*

Son, the Russian word for both sleep and dream, rhymes with the name of the quiet river that runs through the wild country of the Scythian steppe.

⋘∻⋙

Not long after seven, we arrived back in Rostov, charmed and rested by the southern light after the long Moscow winter, wanting to wander the city streets again in the dry evening air and avoid, for as long as possible, the joyless precincts of the Intourist Hotel. On the Garden Ring trams swung past hives of kiosks, selling food and flowers, gaudy clothes, trinkets, underwear and plastic shoes, imported from Syria, Turkey and China. Set behind them, in the ground floors of mansions built in the proud years of Rostov's cosmopolitan prosperity, were sepulchral stores selling French and Italian designer clothes and handbags, and lingerie boutiques called The Pearl and Wild Orchid, with white headless mannequins in their windows, dressed in suspender belts and lacy negligées. Molotov married a woman from the south who had a certain chic: a tailor's daughter who (before the Revolution changed everyone's lives) had worked as a shop assistant. In his library I found an odd book called *Our Ladies*, the oldest of the books hidden in the bottom of the bookcase, published in 1891, when Molotov was just one and No. 3 not yet built. *Our Ladies* was a wry essay of social commentary (reminiscent of Sands's series of satirical prints, *The Gay Women of Paris*, in its mercilessness about the consumerist motives of women) about the art, the expense (silks and jewels, sweetmeats without end) and the woes of love among the *haute bourgeoisie*. Though it was out of place among all the books on central planning and diplomacy, the book was marked with numerous underlinings in a familiar purple ink. The marked passages pondered the arts of seduction, the ways in which women enslave and drain men with their beauty, their endless desire for luxury and amorous diversion, their faithlessness. 'A woman of contemporary upbringing will not sell her life away cheap,' warned the author (whose name was A. Dyakov), and his reader took note.

We came to the city opera theatre, a socialist culture palace of the 1960s, vast and white. Puccini's *Madama Butterfly* was playing, but we were almost an hour late for the start. A lady usher in navy blue, who was chatting to the elderly coat-check attendant in the marble foyer, told us to wait for the interval and then go in and find a seat. Upstairs, a thin man in a grubby waistcoat was arranging trays of Sovetskoe champagne and red caviar sandwiches on a table beside a white piano. The doors of the auditorium swung open, and the public emerged loudly into the chandeliered hall to queue and promenade. The women's evening clothes, as ruched and silky as the curtains on the marble staircase, glinted back from long walls of mirrors. When the third bell rang we took two seats at the edge of the hall. The red synthetic velvet gave off sparks as women brushed past, puffing, sighing and chuckling. As the curtain rose on a new set, the audience applauded, whispering loudly over the recorded overture. 'Oh, the bitter fragrance of these flowers,' sang Pinkerton, straining dryly for the high notes. As Cho Cho San ended her life with the blade of her father the Samurai, a mobile telephone played the Dance of the Sugar Plum Fairy in someone's handbag. 'To die with honour, when one can no longer live with honour,' the geisha sang, holding her father's sword.

We ordered a late supper of river pike and boiled potatoes in the bar of the Intourist. The music was hard to bear. Two women came to sit at the bar and smoke, lingering over a single cocktail. One was blonde and very young, and wore a mini-skirt and white platforms; the second was older, her Asiatic features blanked by make-up, her hair streaked with orange. Their minder, a heavy man with coiffed hair in a canary-yellow jacket and thin black tie, sat alone in a booth, his back to the mirrored wall, watching the room. A business traveller came in for a bottle of wine. As he waited for his change, the blonde caught his eye, then walked slowly out of the bar ahead of him, tossing her long hair.

The investigative journalist Anna Politkovskaya lamented the role that prostitution played in foreign perceptions of her country. I think of her now when I think of the south. In the last book she published before she was shot dead in the elevator of her Moscow apartment building in 2006, she listed those things that the West finds 'entirely to its taste' about Putin's Russia: 'the vodka, the caviar, the gas, the oil, the dancing bears, the practitioners of a particular profession'. As she was flying south to Rostov-on-Don two years earlier on her way to the school in Beslan in which terrorists from Chechnya were holding many hundreds of children hostage, Politkovskaya was served tea laced with poison (she was certain) by the secret police. Like Marina Tsvetaeva, on whom she wrote her graduate dissertation, Politkovskaya was one of a 'fierce few' who stood against a rising power. She wrote about the dirty wars in the south that people would rather forget. 'Behind Anna everything burns,' as one of her colleagues at the newspaper *Novaya Gazeta* said to me before her murder.

At the reception desk in the Intourist lobby, I waited for our room key. A young woman at the desk was slowly copying out the passport details of a man in a suit. 'Speak English?' he asked. She shook her head, smiled a feline smile, and bent over her writing again, long eyelashes resting on her reddening cheek. 'French?' She nodded. 'Tu est tray jolie,' said the traveller; 'tu as *tray* beaucoup de charme.'

NINE

Taganrog

I am not a historian; I am a man living in history.
FATHER ALEXANDER MEN

The steppe clarifies sight and focuses memory. On the drive along the old post road from Rostov-on-Don to Taganrog, it was the sign to the ancient city of Tanais that outlined itself in the foreground of my vision. As though we might turn off and find ourselves among busy traders in fish and slaves in this far colony of the Hellenic world; the small rust-pocked black letters TAHA-C pointed left across the stony grassland. 'In writings it is written that there is a lot of treasure here,' says the old shepherd in Chekhov's story 'Fortune', 'only the treasure has a spell on it, you won't get at it.'

A freight train rattled past, shaking me out of the moment-long spell cast by the ancient place name on the road sign. The railway marks the course of the Dead Donets, a tributary that slips out of the Don just beyond Rostov and dances its own way up country to flow into the northeastern tip of the Azov Sea, mingling with the marshes in the delta. Locals like to think that this white shoreline could be Lukomore, the enchanted land in Pushkin's *Ruslan and Lyudmila* which 'smells of Rus', where a green oak stands on the empty sand, a place 'where there are wonders'.

I had made this journey to the south with a friend who was writing a book on Chekhov's life. The year after he returned from Moscow to Taganrog, the town of his birth, Chekhov wrote a story set on this road. 'Beauties' is the recollection of a gymnasium student's drive with his grandfather on a parched August day. To shelter from the hot dry wind they stop in an Armenian village, Bakhchi-Sala, where the boy's grandfather knows a rich Armenian whose face is like a caricature. The man's daughter, by contrast, is the most beautiful person the schoolboy has ever seen. She is an 'authentic beauty' of the classical type. Every feature is correct in line. Nature has not made the slightest error in the composition of her face. The boy's appreciation of the Armenian girl is absolutely without desire, pleasure or joy. Instead her beauty brings on a heavy nagging sadness. In the second part of the story, at a railway station, he sees a beauty of an utterly different kind. She has fair Russian features, captivating in their disorder. He imagines the melancholy station-master in love with the careless laughing girl, living out his days by the train timetable, faithful to a plain wife, weighed down with the sadness and loss bestowed on him by his chance encounter with the beautiful. Wasted on this desert air, beauty seems all the more gratuitous on the part of nature; its only purpose, to mark the cruelty of time.

Beyond the sign to Tanais were a few trees, wind-hooped and bare, alone on the plain. A small herd of cows grazed among the artemisia, thistles and needle grass near the road. The morning was cloudless, the sky deep blue. As Chekhov observed, the distance on the steppe is lilac in colour. The furthest reaches are always empty, lines of sight extending into a beckoning distance beyond the point where the eye can make out any shape. This landscape is a place of privilege for the long-sighted, like Vassya, one of the briefly glimpsed characters in Chekhov's story 'The Steppe', who, beyond the world seen by others, sees another world all of his own, in which foxes, hares and birds of prey keep a careful distance from men.

In the decades before Chekhov wrote his steppe stories, historical periods floating far apart in time had gathered and come into view, as classical archaeologists, working with ancient Greek texts like the *Histories* of Herodotus and Strabo's *Geographica*, began to search some of the many hundreds of Scythian, Maeotian and Sarmatian burial mounds that had long grown into the landscape of the southern steppe, and to ask local shepherds for their legends of buried treasure.

Even now, this landscape, with its fallow collective farms grazed by small peasant herds, does not smell so much of Rus as it does of Royal Scythia and the seafaring Greeks. The story of the region is the story of the encounter between steppe and sea. The wonders concealed under the sandy shores of Azovia were left by Greeks and Bosporan kings: sailors, traders and colonisers who spread their civilisation to the north and east. After them came mounted 'barbarians' to lay that civilisation waste, followed by Turkic tribes. For centuries, the Polovtsians and Pechenegs lived in tents, and ate and slept by their fires, fighting battles and settling treaties with the princes of early Christian Rus. Peace was broken again by the Mongol armies of Khan Baty, who established the powerful state of the Golden Horde in the fourteenth century. The revenue-minded Mongol overlords allowed Genoese traders to build a *factoria* named Tana in the delta, where the city of Azov now stands. After the Mongols, the region was ruled by Crimean khans, vassals of the Ottoman empire, against which Russia struggled over four hundred years for control over the fertile steppe land, with its precious exit routes to the southern seas.

The ruins of Tanais lie a little way inland, on former Cossack farmland, near the settlement of Nedvigovka. Before it disappeared into the earth, Tanais had been a town for seven hundred years. It was once a Hellenistic emporium at the very mouth of the great river Tana, with its back to the nomad lands of the steppe, facing across the sea towards the Greek entrepôts spread along on the southern shores of Lake Maeotis, as the Azov was anciently known, and the wide straits that lead down into the Black Sea. It was a frontier city; the biggest bazaar for the barbarians after Panticapaeum, the geographer Strabo said, which (like Novgorod under Ivan the Terrible) had been devastated and burned at the end of the first century BC, as an insubordinate outpost, by its own ruler, King Polemon. Several hundred years later, marauders came again to these lands; not on ships this time, but on horseback: Goths and Huns, armed with bows and arrows. Houses burned, stone towers fell, and after their fires had gone out the wild grasses grew back over the hewn stones of Tanais. Earth, river and shoreline changed places.

Chekhov grew up in a landscape that had recently, in almost random fashion, yielded up precious antiquities to the imperial museums of the great northern cities. He was still a schoolboy at the classical gymnasium in Taganrog (remote in every way from St Petersburg and Moscow) when Friedrich Nietzsche characterised the 'age of historical culture' in his essay 'On the Uses and Disadvantages of History for Life'. The culture of the nineteenth century, the age of the archaeologist and the philological scholar, is not really a culture at all, Nietzsche said, 'but only a kind of knowledge of culture', an age of senile occupations, choking on sterile knowledge of the mightier civilisations of the past.

Yet here on the steppe, archaeological discovery took on something of the freedom and wildness of the place. The first archaeologists of the Russian south were military men like Colonel Ivan Stempkovsky, governor of Kerch, who used the intervals between fighting the French and the Ottomans to discover the 'fortune' that lay beneath the soil of the empire's contested borderlands. Though archaeology had been taught as an aspect of the history of art at Moscow University since 1809, the subject was not yet a distinct 'science'. Stempkovsky exemplified a new awareness of the past as treasure to be unearthed, collected, studied and domesticated. Amateur archaeologist, corresponding member of the French Academy, Stempkovsky presided over the founding of museums in Kerch (which was built over the Greek city of Panticapaeum) and Odessa in 1823, which displayed local finds not considered fine enough for the growing collections of antiquities in the Hermitage in St Petersburg. Though he and his kind were despised as dilettantes by the academics in the capital cities, Stempkovsky devised a programme for the archaeological excavation of the south, proposing societies for field and study work, and a chain of specialised archaeological museums. On his way to a military posting on the Volga, he traced this road between

Taganrog and Rostov in search of Tanais, the ordered polis that he knew had once existed on these empty or haphazardly settled spaces. From reading Strabo's enigmatic one-liners in French, he guessed that Tanais would be found close to the Don mouth. Near Nedvigovka, he unearthed ancient fortifications, discerning the form of a town, finding fragments of an amphora and coins marking the reigns of the Bosporan kings Sauromates and Cotys. Meanwhile, as Cossacks ploughed the landscape of burial mounds and ruins that the Tsar encouraged them to settle on this politically hot imperial frontier, they also chanced upon treasure, which they were free to dispose of as they wished.

Buried in the steppe, eye beads of glass and agate, bracelets and earrings of wrought silver and gold, mirrors made of bronze beaten into discs, arrow tips of iron and bone . . . all tell of trading cultures exchanging styles, the lines between them never quite clear. Not long after Stempkovsky's death, Pavel Leontiev, a young classics professor from Moscow University, came south to confirm Stempkovsky's conjecture. He found the remains of a later town, more crudely built than any Greek settlement, with shards of roughly made ceramics with no refinement of ornament, and coins no older than the first century. Disenchanted, he concluded that the place was not, after all, Tanais. In 1867, the Imperial Archaeological Commission, still searching for treasures to display in the exhibition halls of the Hermitage, renewed the excavation at Nedvigovka under the direction of the numismatist Baron Vladimir von Tiesenhausen. At the same time, workers breaking rocks to lay the railway track that skirts the seashore broke through to the buried city. The *Don News*, and even newspapers in faraway St Petersburg, talked of a gigantic underground passageway, a water channel from the Don to Tanais. There were seductive rumours of great stores of buried treasure, and Count Stroganov, head of the Archaeological Commission in the Russian capital, came south to discuss the matter with the Ataman of the Don Cossacks. No great treasure was found, and soon digging stopped at Nedvigovka, leaving local peasants to take what they wanted from the ruined city. More local rumours of treasure led to a brief dig early in the twentieth century, led by the archaeologist Nikolai Veselovsky, but it yielded little. It was only after the Second World War, when Soviet archaeology revived under men like Artsykhovsky and Yanin, that systematic excavation began and the boundaries of Tanais were confirmed. Digs unearthed traces of fishing and agriculture, of glass-making, smithies and large amphorae that had once contained oil or the bodies of children dead in infancy. Archaeologists identified a necropolis and ritual objects that suggested the worship of a supreme deity.

⁂

'There is treasure out there, but what use is it if it is buried in the ground?' Chekhov's old shepherd asks in 'Fortune'; 'it will just be lost, without any use, like chaff or sheep's droppings . . . not a soul can see it.' The shepherd believes that the treasure belongs to the peasants ('it's our treasure'), not to the landowners or the authorities. Full of new impressions of the Don steppe, which he loved and where he had once 'felt at home and known every butterfly', Chekhov wrote 'Fortune' (whose title, '*Schast'e*', also means 'happiness') as soon as he returned from the south in June 1887. The story became his favourite. He considered it the best thing he had written, '*quasi* a symphony', dedicating it to his friend, the poet Yakov Polonsky, 'with particular love'. 'Fortune' is filled with glancing references to the great historical events that touched the landscape of the Don steppe and the north shores of the Azov: the building of Peter the Great's navy; the fortress of Taganrog; the return of the Cossacks with silver and gold stolen from the French after the defeat of Napoleon; the sudden death of Tsar Alexander I in a palace in Taganrog; the liberation of the serfs in 1861. Yet the idle dialogue of the simple men standing like columns on the plain, and Chekhov's evocation of the landscape (which moved his friend Levitan to praise him as a '*paysagiste*'), drop these events on to the great expanse of time, archaeological time. Recorded history diminishes to a few specks, clearly outlined on a vast horizon. As well as enchanted treasure, the shepherds believe in pike that laugh, watermelons that whistle, rocks that hum and a hare that stops in its path and says in a human voice, 'Hullo, *muzhiki!*' The steppe itself breathes, thinks, sings; human thought moves across the brown land, among plants, rocks and animals, faint among other elements, unheard. The last words of the story are: 'the sheep were also thinking . . .'

If cities of stone transform time into rigid space in which we can try to orient ourselves within history, the unbounded steppe loosens time again, diminishing historical particularity to a whisper in the grass. In the spring of 1887 Chekhov absorbed again the unique time-patterning of the steppe. His acute perception of the way in which vast open space unshapes human time reshaped his own writing as he transformed himself in the course of that year from 'A. Chekhonte', scribbler of comic sketches for newspapers, into Anton Chekhov, writer of assured 'artistic' prose for literary 'thick journals'. There is so much space in Russia that 'a little human being does not have the strength to orient himself', Chekhov remarked in a letter to the older writer Dmitri Grigorovich two days after he finished his long plotless story 'The Steppe'. For Chekhov, Russian landscape creates a particular human plight, whose ardours are more spiritual than physical; the plight is in essence tragic. All the energies of the artist must be turned towards two distinct forces, man and nature, Chekhov told Grigorovich. In Russia, uniquely, these two forces are engaged in a terrifying struggle. Whereas in western Europe people perish because their living space is cramped and stuffy, in Russia people perish from an excess of space.

In the weeks of what he called his 'Kalmyk life' of nomadic travel on the steppe (which he crossed by train, looking out at the changing scene with a gentler eye than the machine-loving *Lef* writer Kushner), Chekhov collected a mass of material, filling himself 'to the gorge' on the poetry of the landscape. The train has its own poetry, the poetry of the fleeting apparition, and in Chekhov's letters there are lists of sights that blink past in the train window. 'Topknots, oxen, kites, white huts, southern streams, the branches of the Donetsk road with one telegraph wire . . . rust-coloured dogs, greenery . . . everything flashes past like a dream . . . it's hot,' Chekhov wrote. He had found a place, he said, as rich in seams of untouched beauty as it was rich in coal; a place that would show the Russian artist that 'it is still not crowded'. He was animated by the steppe, and in his turn he animated it so vividly that critics talked of his prose as 'pantheist'. He gave nature the power of mood, intention and play. A poplar tree is lonely, uprooted plants are frightened by a storm cloud, the grass sings and sorrows, a storm rages around a Cossack inn, trying to get inside the building with the unassuaged hatred of the once powerful, birds laugh and weep hysterically, the steppe sighs and smiles, and the sheep are stunned and depressed to the point of numbness by their own slow, drawn-out thoughts.

Chekhov's reflections on geographical space were imbricated with his fretful self-questioning about just how much space, and how much time, his own writing should occupy. He wrote to Polonsky about the difficulty of longer forms, and to Grigorovich about his inexperience at writing at length, his 'constant and ingrained fear of writing too much' (duly apologising at the end of his letter for its wearying length). Writing in longer form was something he said he simply '*did not know how to do*'. His motifs, he knew, were light and dry; pages turned out 'so laconic as to appear positively compressed, impressions piling up against each other in a great heap'. He was in two minds. 'All in all it's better to write small things than big things, they are less pretentious and the public likes them,' he wrote in a letter; three days later, he was talking again of his contempt for 'trivial pieces' and his desire to work 'on a bigger scale or not at all'. The year before Chekhov's return to the south, Grigorovich had told him to take more time over his writing, to find a different decorum, for he had '*real* talent' and should not write about dirty feet, twisted toenails and the deacon's navel, as he had in his bathhouse sketches. But to Chekhov the medic, nothing was unclean, and he carried on writing freely to his family from the south about the effects of travel on his gut and the ever-changing condition of the varicose vein in his leg.

From Taganrog, he continued to write small pieces as Chekhonte, sending them back to the *Petersburg Gazette* for money, which was short. 'The Cossack', a moral fable set on the steppe, in which one act of uncharity determines the course of a whole life, he found too 'Tolstoyish' for his liking. 'The Inhabitants' evokes the absolute laziness of a southern provincial town, and in 'Volodya' he addressed the recent spate of suicides among students at the Taganrog gymnasium, a strange epidemic that was read as a sign of 'sick times', for the political malaise that Dostoevsky diagnosed had reached the Russian south.

The change in Chekhov's writing came when he was back in Moscow, meditating on the landscape from afar. 'The Steppe', which narrates the wagon journey of a nine-year-old boy along the highroad from one provincial town to another, was Chekhov's debut as a serious writer. The journalist Burenin admired the plotless story, and told Chekhov that his description of a storm that gathered but did not burst was the 'height of perfection', adding that, though Chekhov did not know how to write long stories, 'The Steppe' was just a harbinger of the great works to follow. In all this anxiety about literary length, one senses the shadows of Tolstoy and Dostoevsky over Chekhov, who was a provincial schoolboy in the years of the two novelists' greatest fame and creative power. Chekhov told his publisher Suvorin that he had bought some Dostoevsky in a bookshop and found it 'good, but very long and immodest', with 'many pretensions'.

The superfluity of unbounded space summoned Chekhov to modesty. He sensed that to be laconic is ethically correct, that brevity in the temporal art of writing fits our place in the world, for we are small creatures and should not try to be bigger than we are, nor tire one another, for time and space are tiring enough. Yet his writing is full of time and space. His art is the art of making things rise in clear form out of flat space. As one critic said of his story 'On the Road' (which was greeted in the capital with a 'furore' of enthusiasm), the characters come out 'in relief'; their romance arises and is extinguished in the course of half a page. On his native steppe, a journey, however long and monotonous, traces only a negligible fraction of the map; the sound of a bucket breaking off in a coal mine resonates over miles of empty space; the cobweb railway route of his journey though Rostov to a Cossack wedding in Novocherkassk (a roundabout route which Chekhov drew humourously in a letter) involved nine-hour waits for connections, and every apathetic town and station looked like every other. In his short form, however, Chekhov magically created a sense of long duration. (Writing is 'just a conjuring trick', he told his brother, the essence of nonsense, prestidigitation pretending to be magic; 'you can write about coffee grounds and surprise the reader by conjury,' he said.)

In 'On the Road', Chekhov creates a vast character in a few pages. Likharyov is 'a giant rock', a Russian Don Quixote who has spent his life pursuing ideas. (The story, whose epigraph, from Lermontov, is 'a little golden storm cloud [*tuchka*] spent the night / On the breast of a giant rock', inspired Rachmaninov's symphonic fantasy 'The Rock'.) His voice is a deep bass, but Likharyov speaks in tenor from fear of his own loudness. Faith is a capacity of the spirit, inborn, like talent, he says; it is a capacity which Russians 'possess in the highest degree', living out their lives in an endless sequence of beliefs and passions. Likharyov first became a slave to science, then turned to nihilism, populism, a Slavophile passion for ancient Rus, Ukrainian nationalism, archaeology, folk crafts, and finally the renunciation of private property and Tolstoyan non-resistance to evil. His spirit is larger than all his intellectual passions; his eyes are constantly searching for something in the snowclouds. Now he is on his way to dig for coal in the mines on the bare steppe.

In Dostoevsky's novels (in which, as Shalamov noted, there is no landscape at all) ideas fill the scene, people talk endlessly, coiled and struggling inside thought. In Chekhov's steppe stories, people talk about ideas, but nature takes their words and muffles them, or diffuses them into the landscape, of which they are an incidental part. In 'The Steppe', even chauvinistic polemic of the kind that filled the pages of Dostoevsky's *Writer's Diary* during the war of faith between Russia and Turkey in the Balkans (which excited fierce patriotism in Chekhov's home town during his final years at school) is carried away, diminished. 'Our Mother Russia is he-ad of all the world!' the traveller Kiruha sings out, and the echo catches his words, and carries them onwards, 'and it seemed as though stupidity itself were rolling away on heavy wheels over the steppe'.

❧

After Tanais, we came to Taganrog. The tree-lined streets were empty, the late morning sun warmed the dusty pavements between clean-edged shadows, and everything was still. All the same, time, which had loosened on the steppe, immediately seemed to have twisted back into a ravel: taut, baroque and self-aware. Though Taganrog's name (taken from the headland on which it stands) is ancient, and no one is certain what it means, the city arose in an age which took history seriously. It quickly turned itself into a showcase of its own proud cosmopolitan past. The memorial museum to Tsar Alexander I (who died here, spirit-sore and weary, in 1825) was the first of its kind in Russia. Ever since then, Taganrog has been a town in which local history has been cherished with particular attention. A memorial museum to Chekhov opened just over a hundred years later. At a time when Stalin's secret police were going through the pre-revolutionary collections of caricatures of local personalities in the town museum in the Alferaki Palace as they drew up lists of local aristocrats and bourgeoisie in the hunt for class enemies, Chekhov was still easy to love, lightly accommodating Russia's new historical disposition. He was Molotov's favourite Russian writer. Molotov told Chuev that Chekhov was 'for socialism', which, 'as he expressed through one of his characters, he thought would occur in two hundred years' time'. Yet, Molotov added, there were times when he could not bear to read Chekhov, because for all the 'precision' of his writing, there was 'no optimism in him'.

Founded by Peter the Great as a base for his fleet five years before St Petersburg, Taganrog stands on a curving promontory where the steppe meets the sea. It was one of the first Russian towns to be laid out to a premeditated street plan. With his Cossack troops, Peter had at last taken the Turkish fort at Azov across the water. Taganrog's first mayor was Cornelis Cruys, a Dutch-Norwegian sailor and geographer, whom Peter had recruited on his self-improving visit to the Netherlands. Cruys made the first maps of the Don River and the coast, and, in collaboration with the Tsar, produced the first Russian atlas, published in Amsterdam. A fortress, named for the Holy Trinity, was built at Taganrog with its own stone-walled harbour. With its pentagonal geometry, the plan of the fortress resembles a military medal emblazoned on the soft flow of the shoreline.

Russia only held the headland for twelve years before another defeat by Turkey, which forced Peter to return the Azov fort and demolish his new town. Taganrog lay desolate for almost six decades, until Russia was victorious again, and mapped the place anew, drawing up administrative boundaries and dividing and distributing the steppe to landowners. This was wild frontier territory, virgin land that had never felt the plough, attracting ruffians, outlaws and rebels. No attempt was made to track down fugitives who fled south, and they settled on the fertile grassland, tilling and sowing for its new Russian owners. Meanwhile, the empire's military frontier moved south. With the conquest of the Crimea, Taganrog lost its strategic significance and became a place of peaceful trade. Catherine the Great, who cherished the talented and enterprising of every nation, invited Greeks and Italians to colonise the city. The beneficence, high-living sociability and easy-going corruption of the Mediterranean merchants gave Taganrog its style of ostentatious bonhomie, which even communism could not quite erase.

We found a cafe on Frunze Street, tucked into the shade of an acacia, and as we drank coffee we watched groups of young women come and go from a nearby institute, all in high-heeled black ankle boots and zippered jackets. A cook in a white coat with vast quivering arms came out of the kitchen every few minutes and set down a large tin tray of fresh-baked pastries on the counter. At tables piled with their English-language textbooks, the young women ate pastries and sipped hot tea off spoons, reapplying dark lipliner and face powder from mirrored compacts before going out again into the quiet of the streets. Many of them had lean Mediterranean features, brown-black hair and large dark eyes.

My companion studied the street plan. She had taken over the maps and the camera, full of clear purpose in her hunt for biographical treasure. I was glad to follow her passively through the warm day, sensing the writer's genial presence in every place we visited, just as one is meant to do in Taganrog. There is reciprocity in the fact that this town has become a museum to Chekhov, for he diffused his personality throughout Taganrog, helping direct it towards the kind of civic self-knowledge that is expressed in museums of local history, libraries and architectural conservation. As an established writer in Moscow, he sent many books to Taganrog's new library. He had dreamed of founding a museum of local personalities, reflecting their contribution to the development of the Russian south. When a local museum did open in 1898, Chekhov, now famous in Moscow, sensed that the walls of the Alferaki Palace in which it was housed now held in a powerful force: the life of past epochs, and those local individuals who stood out in high relief against the background of the centuries.

Unlike Olenin in Tolstoy's *Cossacks*, who gets free of his past as he travels south from Moscow on his uncomfortable train journey down through Tula and Kharkov, Chekhov was heading towards 'everything known and remembered'. On arrival, he found Taganrog so sleepy and antique-looking that it made him think of Pompeii. After eight years in Moscow, he looked on his new surroundings with wry snobbery mixed with simple affection; a city sophisticate come back to his provincial home town. Sometimes he writes his letters back to friends in Moscow in the voice of the tourist, describing Taganrog's superb climate, the food, the plumbing, the inadequacy of the beds and local service, and the looks and manners of the women, who, he says, are coarse, amorous and nervous, with good profiles and a taste for clothes in olive green. It 'smells of Asia', he writes, and 'Asia' was easy code for 'outside history'. The inhabitants of the town just eat, drink and reproduce, he complains; it is all eggs, *kulich* and bagels, Santorini wine and suckling babies, with not a book or a newspaper to be found. The lavatories are appalling, everything is grubby and tasteless, and the postman sits down to drink tea after every letter he delivers. In witty letters to clever university friends, Chekhov is droll and patronising about poor showy Taganrog. 'If I were such a talented architect as you I would knock it down,' he writes to his friend the architect Fyodor Shekhtel (who, like Isaac Levitan, was a model for one of the whoring students in 'A Nervous Breakdown').

Yet in another letter, Chekhov says that Taganrog 'smells of Europe'. He writes with affection of long-known people, recording who has grown fatter, who thinner, the thrilling electricity in his uncle's smile, and the ever more impressive civic schemes and luxuries of Achilles Alferaki, Mayor of Taganrog, scion of the wealthiest of the families of Taganrog tycoons, and civic benefactor. Alferaki shared Chekhov's spirit of gentle satire and acute attentiveness to the particularity of local people. At his home, the late-nineteenth-century beau monde of Taganrog, such as it was, would gather to dance, play music, cards and charades, do rebuses and *tableaux vivants* and write comic verse. It was Alferaki himself who drew the remarkable caricatures in which the NKVD took such an interest during Stalin's Terror. (On the back of many of the caricatures, the words 'taken during the search, 19/XI/-36' are written in the hand of Andreev-Turkin, curator of the museum.) His caricatures are of Duma members, customs officers, a schoolteacher, the chief of police, foreign consuls (of whom there were sixteen in Taganrog), gawky girls and shy youths, financiers like Negroponte, who ran the Azov-Don Commercial Bank, and Mussuri, head of the steamship company. The Alferaki Album is a necropolis, in which the curious faces of the city's dead are treasure.

Chekhov is now the public face of the town about which he was so droll and patronising when he returned from Moscow. We visited first the house in which he was born, and filed through its few low rooms with a party of deaf and dumb children, whose teacher told them all about the early life of the great writer in sign language. There were daffodils in bloom at the foot of a great tree. In the tangled shadows of its long branches, the little white house was tiny. We went then to his father's corner shop, on a dusty street that looked like a film set. On the counter in the reconstructed interior were old tea caddies, caviar tins and weighing scales; high in the corner hung a set of icons, the front-room furnishings of a life of diligent piety and unsuccessful trade, behind which the merchant Pavel Chekhov, who had been born a serf, beat his children sore. We visited the local theatre, all red velvet and gilded gesso, built with Italian money for the performance of Italian opera, and the library, designed by Shekhtel, whom Chekhov addressed as 'Dearest Maestro' in the letter which jokingly proposed the demolition and reconstruction of the whole town. It was the middle of the afternoon when we came to Chekhov's school, the Taganrog classical gymnasium, by far the most stately of the Chekhov places we had visited, its large windows looking out from austere high-ceilinged classrooms, across the town square to the sea.

As in so many Russian regional museums, the displays in the Taganrog museum in the baroque Alferaki Palace on Frunze Street rushed from deep to shallow time. Relics of the Bronze Age, the Ionian Greeks and the Scythians quickly gave way to medieval coins and weighing scales and armour and axe heads of the Polovtsians, and the feathered and beaded caps of the Kalmyks. In Starocherkassk, I had come to like the balance of opulence and simplicity of Don Cossack clothes, made up in orange, purple and yellow brocade, and the adornments set with tourmaline and mother-of-pearl. There were maps and muskets, finely worked and carefully preserved, displayed alongside rule books for good behaviour, health manuals and anthologies of spiritual readings from the Petrine era.

I cannot find an adequate English equivalent for the Russian word *kraevedenie*, which my dictionary translates as 'study of local lore, history and economy'. *Kraevedenie*, which blossomed in the 1920s, is a branch of scholarship devoted to the knowledge of place in all its particularity. The local museums that can be found in towns of every kind throughout this vast land are characterised by the tender attention of the *kraevedi*, professional devotees of local knowledge. In his introduction to the 1927 book on the Russian countryside in Molotov's library, Oldenburg praised the thousands of *kraevedi* of the 1920s as the people destined to bring the city and the countryside together, unify the culture through understanding. Gorky hailed the new science as 'work whose significance cannot be exaggerated', understanding that *kraevedenie* encouraged the 'growth of our sense of human dignity'. As the contemporary *kraeved* Sigurd Shmidt remarked in a recent essay (in which he lamented the systematic murderous purge of Soviet *kraevedenie* in the 1930s), it is a form of local love, of spiritual work. (Sigurd Shmidt, son of the polar explorer Otto Shmidt, was raised in No. 3. He edited the *Encyclopedia of Moscow* [1998] from which I have learned most of what I know about the city.) Here in Taganrog, *kraevedenie* reveals itself as distinctly Chekhovian in spirit, at once modest and profound, grand in vision and attentive to the miniature, alert to the quirks in history and human personality, long-sighted, all-forgiving. Chekhov observed people close up, but he also knew how to withdraw his gaze to the far distance from which human failings look smaller.

It was the light hands of the local historians that saved the things in these museums by hiding them in the first years of Soviet power, when treasure had a different meaning, and things of beauty and value had been revalued and placed in danger. Much of the porcelain, textiles and fine furniture in the Alexander I Memorial Museum went missing in that frenzy against tsarism and the Church, and icons were publicly burned. (Its collections had been prized also for their improving effect on the taste of the local magnates in interior furnishings, which tended to the vulgar.) At the end of the 1920s, however, there was saving work done on the necropolis of Beglitskaya Kosa outside Taganrog, which was threatened by the erosion of the shoreline.

One of the most treasured collections in the Taganrog regional museum is the archive of Pavel Filevsky, a local historian and teacher of history and geography who had studied at the gymnasium at the same time as Chekhov. Filevsky wrote a memoir of all the teachers they shared: the Russian teacher and the Latin teacher, the masters of divinity and literature and the 'pathologically irritable' Edmund Dzerzhinsky, who taught mathematics (and whose son Felix became the first head of the Cheka and worked himself to death for the Soviet security state, his statue standing outside the Lubyanka for decades until it was pulled down in front of a revelling crowd in August 1991). Filevsky was ardently Orthodox, and sympathised with the anti-Semitic Black Hundreds. From a Kharkov gentry family, he loved Taganrog, writing poetry in praise of the town and a learned article on Pushkin's one very brief visit. In Chekhov's lifetime Filevsky published a historical novel called *The Fall of Byzantium* and, as the First World War broke out, a universal chronology and conspectus of the history of humanity, its doings, its thoughts and its creative work from 5508 BC to AD 1910. He planned to write a full history of the region, beginning with a volume on the Scythians, taking in all aspects of its development – historical, biological, geographical and economic – just the kind of masterwork of positivist historical fact-accumulation that Nietzsche thought had exhausted European culture and made it senile. A portrait of Filevsky in old age shows him as the very image of the blood-drained intellectual, almost an ascetic in the style of El Greco. He had survived the Revolution, giving lessons in factories and technical colleges in the early 1920s. In 1927 he became a member of the North Caucasus Regional Society of Archaeology, History and Ethnography, and three years later a curator and archivist of old Taganrog. Through local history, he managed to weave his own work into the new system. There are letters in his archive from friends and colleagues who fared less well, museum workers, librarians and schoolteachers arrested and sent into exile in Kazakhstan and Siberia for imagined crimes against Stalin's state. 'I do not regard myself as guilty, but the inexorable Article 58 had stuck to me like smallpox,' the local teacher Vinnikov wrote with his sense of irony unbroken from 'not such a distant place, as we Russians like to say'. A letter from another teacher, trembling on the edge of despair, said that 'sometimes things are so hard, grief and mourning so profound that only deep faith sustains our weak strength and holds us back from taking a foolhardy step'. The librarian Edward Yurgens left his letter unsealed, knowing, he said, that his correspondence was 'of interest to other individuals'. In his Central Asian exile, the only thing that alleviated his sorrow was the knowledge that he had loved 'everything beautiful in mankind, in art, and in nature, and remained sure of the source of all beauty'.

In 1925, Felix Dzerzhinsky was on the verge of nervous collapse, after successfully laying the foundations of the Soviet police state. In that year, he had captured the political chameleon Boris Savinkov, ex-terrorist and collaborator of Sidney Reilly, and spent many hours in 'conversation' with him in a cell made comfortable in the Lubyanka. In May 1925, Savinkov, who had written letters to friends from the prison extolling the glories of the new Soviet state, died after a mysterious fall from a window. Reilly was regarded as the key to the British spy networks that still troubled Dzerzhinsky, and he conceived an elaborate 'sting', known as

'Operation Trust', to lure 'the ace of spies' himself back to Russia. Reilly was arrested in a Moscow apartment in September 1925 and taken to the Lubyanka for interrogation, labelled Prisoner No. 73. On 5 November, he was executed with a shot to the back of the head, allegedly on direct orders from Stalin.

The Party insisted that Dzerzhinsky take a rest, so he came with a small escort to Taganrog, where his father had once lived in a small house opposite the gymnasium. Dzerzhinsky requisitioned a suite for himself in the palace in which Tsar Alexander I had liked to rest his tired spirit. Insomniac, Dzerzhinsky prowled through its rooms and galleries by night. Rumours about some secret purpose for his visit spread through Taganrog, and parents kept their children indoors, made the sign of the cross when he drove past in his armoured car with the curtains open, and refused to open their doors to visitors. Living in his father's town did little to alleviate Dzerzhinsky's depression, and he soon left for Moscow on a special train. He died an exhausted man the following July, in the middle of a rambling speech to his comrades, 'punctuated by hysterical outbursts'. Molotov carried his coffin.

In the town's main church, the icons were draped in black lace: a Greek practice that I had not observed in any other Russian place of worship. Chekhov visited the cemetery when he came back to Taganrog, remarking that it was beautiful but looked as though it had been ransacked, with one of its memorials barbarously scratched. He walked among the tombs with a female friend called Monya Khodakovskaya, a freethinker who laughed at the dead and their epitaphs, as well as the living priests and deacons in the church. Chekhov was sensitive to the vulnerability of the dead to our slander and abuse. He witnessed a funeral in Taganrog, and wrote that 'it is not pleasant to see an open coffin, in which a dead man's head is shaking'.

We wandered through the cemetery. Demakos, Verazzi, Kleopatro . . . Russian family names on the tombs were scarce. There were many Marias. The usual fake flowers, in crazy colours gone dusty, decorated oversize metallic graves, some of which had broken apart and yawned a little like open coffins. A great many had crosses improvised out of scaffolding, set in place in the Soviet period, when tombs were adorned with red stars, signs of loyalty to the Revolution even in death. I wondered how archaeologists might interpret these scaffolding-crosses thousands of years from now, when the seventy-five years of Soviet communism were just a fleck in the great panorama of human time. Would they wonder and theorise about them just as archaeologists now wonder about the signs of ritual and belief in the stone catacombs of the barbarian burial mounds on the steppe? Why, archaeologists wonder, are the long bones from the left legs of horses always laid out from north-west to south-west in the inner chambers of Scythian tombs, sealed with shields and mats made of pebbles, where the dead always lie with their heads towards the entrance?

⚜

We went down the Depaldo steps to sit on the beach and feel the wind from the sea meet the wind from the steppe. Far out, the water was flat grey, lightless and filmy. Close to shore there were low white breakers, and the gulls wheeled and screamed. I threw my knapsack gratefully down on the sand; it was weighted now with books and journals that I had picked up in the museums of the town. Wherever I go, I buy as many local publications as I can fit in my bags. The random nature of this kind of dilettante collecting is the essence of its pleasure. This time, I had found several books on Chekhov and two issues of the 'literary-historical almanac' *Landmarks of Taganrog*: June and December 2001.

The first almanac was a special issue on the history and culture of the Armenians who settled in Taganrog and the Don region at the invitation of Catherine the Great. It contained an enchanting short article called 'Chekhov's Beauties', which identified the Armenian girl from the steppe. The real woman, whom Chekhov had encountered as a schoolboy, had lived to the age of fifty-six, her life taken up with children and domestic work. Her descendants still live in Rostov and Novocherkassk and in the village of Bolshye Saly (the Russian name for Bakhchi-Sala); to this day they celebrate Chekhov, the writer from Taganrog who hymned the extraordinary beauty of their babushka.

In the second almanac, besides essays on the history of the local library and bibliographical lists detailing Chekhov's close and generous interest in its acquisitions, was a set of recently disclosed archival documents about events in Taganrog and the Don during the Civil War. These dead, whose names and words, once lost like chaff or sheep's droppings, had been so recently disinterred in the archives, are not indifferent yet to what Budyonny called 'history's mirror'. Values have been revalued again, historical facts are collected and remembered, their 'uses and disadvantages for life' suddenly transformed. Full of blood and vengeance and competing claims of honour, the archival section included the memoirs of the anarchist Nestor Makhno, and the memoirs of the White General Anton Denikin and the Ataman of the Don Cossacks about their ill-fated attempt to create a free Cossack state in the Russian south, with aid from the British, in 1918. There were documents on the Red Terror – massacres of the local aristocracy and bourgeoisie – and the atrocities of the Whites, with grainy black-and-white photographs of the dismembered bodies of Red factory workers, twisted, mutilated, history's nameless dead, open-mouthed and heaped like broken dolls, eyes staring.

The wind ruched the white sand and flapped the pages of my almanac. I would have lost it had I let it go. I held down the corners and had begun to read when I came upon Budyonny's name in an open letter by a historian called Polikarpov. (I am always curious about the neighbours in No. 3.) Polikarpov's letter, which revised the official history of the Civil War in the south, had been published at the very end of the Soviet period in response to an open letter by Budyonny. Polikarpov challenged Budyonny's account of the trial and execution of the Red Cavalry commander Boris

Dumenko, once Budyonny's military superior, who was accused of organising an anti-Soviet mutiny in Rostov at a critical moment in the war during the spring of 1920. Polikarpov's historical argument had profound implications for Budyonny's reputation; the mirror was beginning to reflect a different image of the Marshal.

Dumenko's demise was an ominous sign of what was to come, of the nature and momentum of a Party purge that would soon take down so many. ('We had nothing to do with the shooting of Dumenko,' Molotov said later, when he heard that in the Central Committee someone had alleged that he and Stalin had acted not through the power of persuasion but with a revolver, with 'Trotskyite' methods.) Like Budyonny, Boris Dumenko was a George Cross cavalryman who joined the Reds at the Revolution. In a brilliant victory, he took Novocherkassk for the Bolsheviks in January 1920. Within a few months, however, he had been shot by his own side. In essence, Polikarpov alleged, Dumenko was sentenced without any evidence of treachery against the Bolsheviks. His trial turned on Budyonny's interpretation of the word 'stormclouds' (*tuchi*), which Dumenko had used in a tête-à-tête in Budyonny's apartment. 'I did have a conversation about stormclouds,' Dumenko admitted, explaining that all he had meant was that there were stormclouds gathering for the Bolsheviks that should be smashed. After Dumenko's arrest, Budyonny decided that his comrade had been inviting him, in hinting metaphors, to change sides and join him in some treacherous anti-Soviet adventure. The trial was a pure example of revolutionary justice, a model for the show trials of the 1930s. When challenged about the lack of any real evidence against Dumenko, the prosecutor Beloborodov replied:

> If we begin to sift through separate facts, then perhaps it will be possible to refute them . . . the defence invokes conscience. I would like, comrade judges, to draw your attention to the fact that now, under the dictatorship of the proletariat, in an epoch

in which all values have been seen to be dethroned, the appeal to conscience is useless.

This was Beloborodov, the man who had passed down the order to murder the dethroned Tsar and his wife and children, who would play host to Trotsky in No. 3, and who, as Molotov remembered, was heard not long afterwards crying out to the conscience of his comrades in the Kremlin from the corridors of the Lubyanka: 'I am Beloborodov. Pass the word to the Central Committee that I am being tortured.'

By the time he wrote *The Cherry Orchard*, Chekhov was no longer using gunshots to turn the action in his plays, breaking the scene instead with the 'dying away, sad' sound of a bucket breaking off in a distant coal mine, a distantly remembered note of the steppe. He mastered the art of the ending. He learned about the horizon of time from looking into the lilac steppe distance. When sight is keen, the end is revealed as just another beginning. Future time is aways a question, not an answer. I think of the endings of his stories: wind outside the door; the small-town station conductor lighting candles; sheep thinking; rain beating on the windows unheard; the question 'What would life be like?'; Likharyov's eyes searching for something in the clouds, snow covering him as though he is a rock.

Then there is that perfect ending, set in a Moscow hotel room: Chekhov's reply to the tragic picture of adultery in Tolstoy's *Anna Karenina*. 'The end was still a long way off', runs the last sentence of 'Lady with a Little Dog', 'and the most complex and difficult part was only just beginning.'

TEN

Vologda

The best defence for a person, just like an insect, is the ability to take on the colour of his surroundings.
SENTENCE PENCIL-MARKED IN MOLOTOV'S EDITION OF
RABINDRANATH TAGORE'S SHORT STORIES, ANONYMOUSLY
INSCRIBED 'To Molotov, 1925'

There has been a revolution – now we never need another revolution. Yeltsin's words had sedated the only other customer in the all-night bar, one of the men in pointy shoes who traditionally furnish the marble-clad lobbies of Soviet-era provincial hotels like the Spasskaya. His shaved head dropped on to the back of the sofa, his jaw fell open and his girth relaxed with sleep, pulling taut the leather of his jacket. It would be another twenty minutes before the restaurant opened for breakfast, and my companion, the painter, was out in the street smoking her second cigarette of the day. The state television *Farewell to Yeltsin* continued on its tense loop. Mourners stood in line outside the Church of Christ the Saviour to file past the open coffin of the man who had put an end to the rule of the Communist Party. The Channel One presenters wore black ties and grave expressions. Studio guests spoke of Yeltsin's human qualities. He was close to the people, he rode on buses, he was a real *muzhik*. 'We never need another revolution' were the only words the dead man was allowed to say, in a sixteen-year-old fragment of archival footage reeled over and over again. Yeltsin gave us freedom, everyone repeated. And now we are free.

Having released my coffee from the push-button machine on the counter and rinsed the sleeping man's empty beer glass, the barwoman settled on a stool, hooked one white stiletto into the chrome ring at its base, revolved away from the television and stared at the wall. Between the liquor bottles on the mirrored shelves behind the bar, her bleached hair and the brilliant green of her suit were reflected away, gleaming, into infinity.

From Vologda, on this cool, quiet morning, Moscow seemed far away. Yet the sense of remoteness in this town is an illusion, Shalamov says. Vologda is a night train's journey due north of Moscow. It is 'part lace and part exile'; but it is not Siberia.

Shalamov, the son of a philo-Semitic dissident priest, was proud of the history of opposition to state power in his native town. As he describes in his memoir *The Fourth Vologda*, in the years of his education he absorbed the long history of the 'liberation movement' from the air. Any individual who ever opposed the power of the state is likely to have passed through Vologda. Between the middle of the nineteenth century and 1917, around ten thousand exiles registered with the local police. Dreams of utopia and quarrels about the meaning of life became part of Vologda's spiritual climate, he said, turning it towards the West and the World, 'with a capital letter'. Though it is famed for its sixteenth-century stone churches and its exquisitely carved wooden houses, Vologda was not just an architectural chronicle of Ivan the Terrible's strengthening of the Russian state in the 'Great North'. The constant presence of political exiles disposed the whole town to look towards future time, beyond the indeterminate murk of the present towards the radiant dawn of hope. Russia's future was already present in discussions, disputes and lectures by rebels against the state, and in the books they gave, by exile tradition, to the local library when they left.

Vologda's exiles range from Avvakum, the seventeenth-century schismatic priest, to the serial allegiance-changer Boris Savinkov (who transformed himself from socialist assassin before the Revolution into monarchist adventurer and companion-in-arms of Sidney Reilly in the conspiracies of 1918); from the daughters of Field Marshal Sheremetev to the philosopher Berdyaev (whom Lenin later deported from Russia on a steamship in 1922) to

Lenin's sister, the dedicated but rather ineffectual revolutionary Maria Ulyanova, whom the tsarist secret police found ludicrously easy to follow. Vologda was a transit point in lives filled with tension. In truth, as Shalamov explains, it was a tsarist compromise on political punishment. The statistics calmed the regime and delighted the liberals. For after the railway line was laid in the 1860s, the dawn of an exile's most immediate hope came with a timetable. Vologda was only a night from the two capitals. From the exile's point of view, Vologda *is* St Petersburg and Moscow, Shalamov says, 'only be sure not to mention it within hearing of the authorities'.

Roused before dawn by the train conductor, I pulled aside the curtains of turquoise nylon lace to see the sun rise over the plain, as train No. 42 made its long decelerando through the allotments and semi-urban dereliction on the edge of Vologda. The birch trees which give rhythm to every Russian train journey grew more sparsely up here, the telegraph poles shone silver with age. Dead trees and fallen poles lay strewn and drying, their thin forms crisscrossed on the grey earth. (Trees in the north die lying down, Shalamov says in 'Dry Ration', just like people at the end of their 'broken northern lives'.) The few other passengers in *luxe* – a pair of giggling redheads in leather mini-skirts who drank beer in the corridor half the night long in the company of a *biznisman* with a fancy Italian briefcase – were staying with the train on its onward journey to Vorkuta. The conductor had changed out of her short nylon housecoat and slippers and, having cleaned out the WC with pungent disinfectant, stood ready by the carriage door, her chest straining at the brass buttons of her uniform, her weight rebalanced on her heels so that she looked like an entirely different woman.

Trotsky despised the word *luxe*, but, though I have sometimes travelled like a proletarian, I now relish without shame the privilege of travelling *en bourgeois* on Russian trains. 'The bourgeoisie must be preserved in its innocent aspect,' Mandelstam wrote in *The Fourth Prose*; 'it must be entertained with amateur theatricals, lulled on the springs of Pullman cars, tucked into envelopes of snow-white railway sleep.' Writing about comfort at the end of NEP, when everyone had felt homeless, he wondered about the origin of the 'fastidiousness and so-called decency' of the bourgeois. 'His decency is what makes the bourgeois kin to the animal,' he reflected; 'many Party members are at ease in the company of a bourgeois for the very same reason that grown-ups require the society of rosy-cheeked children.' The true bourgeois is more innocent than the proletarian, Mandelstam said, 'closer to the womb world, the baby, the kitten, the angel, the cherub'. But in Russia, he added, 'there are very few of these innocent bourgeois, and that has a bad effect on the digestion of revolutionaries'.

The precision of Mandelstam's image holds. Innocently tucked in *luxe*, in an envelope of snow-white linen, carried on my way with no power over the stopping or the going forward, I find the nature of railway sleep impossible to predict. Sometimes the springs of the train car will lull me quickly into the unconscious dark; sometimes they keep me half awake all night, stirring in the heat to the hard lights and shouting voices on station platforms as we pass, so that as we pull into some new town at dawn, I feel I have not slept at all.

The Russian railway system retains undiminished its power to stir a primitive geographical excitement in the traveller. Since the first rails were laid, passion and imagination have pulsed without cease along this circulatory system. Russian literature is full of trains, because (like prostitutes, who also populate the literature) they bring together places, social worlds and life stories that would otherwise never touch. Trains are vehicles of plot and destiny, adventure and tragedy, surprising thoughts and conversations, uniting the squalid and the sublime, iron and plush, making intimacy possible across the great reach of space. The architecture of Moscow's railway stations rises gloriously to this excitement. The night before Vologda we were in the halls of the Yaroslavl Station, a fantasy pastiche made up of motifs from the architectural style of northern Old Rus and from its fairy-tale tradition, designed by

Chekhov's friend Shekhtel, from where trains leave Moscow for the north and east. Beneath wall friezes conjuring primordial wildness and space – wolves, bears, walruses, Sami huntsmen and their sleds – the 'urban surf' (as Shalamov called it) kept up its neverending roar. Travellers hurried to their platforms past kiosks and beggars, laden with big sacks in laminated plaid in which small-time market traders carry their wares all over Russia and beyond. The departures board announced trains to Komi, Ulan Bator and Peking. We made our way down the platform, past the female conductors standing at the door of each carriage in full uniform, with their air of important expectation about the night journey ahead. They simpered mockingly when we showed our *luxe* tickets. On the neighbouring track was a train bound for Pyongyang. A set of knives hung in the window of the galley kitchen next to the dining car, silhouetted in yellow-grey light through a blind. Already sunk in the torpor of the long, enclosed journey ahead, the travellers bound for North Korea had changed into tracksuits and taken off their shoes; lying in long carriages of unpartitioned berths, four high, their limbs pressed against the grimy windows, among bundled blankets, they looked out with vacant eyes.

'Yaroslavl Station. The noise . . . of the city that was dearer to me than any city in the world,' Shalamov writes in the final sentences of his story 'The Train'. 'A ticket to Moscow . . . a ticket to Moscow . . .'; it seems an impossible thing. In Irkutsk, as he waits for the train, he sees books on sale for the first time in years: 'I wouldn't buy books until I got to Moscow. But to hold books, to stand next to the counter of a bookstore was like a dish of hot meaty soup . . . a glass of the water of life.' 'Prison car, prison car,' he repeats to himself as he jams himself into a narrow space between the middle and upper berths of the train. But by the end of the writer's long journey from Siberia, shared with a sad prostitute with bright painted lips, a grubby two-year-old sharing a bliss of love with his tender father, and a drunken vomiting lieutenant, the train car has become the 'unending happiness of freedom'. On the Yaroslavl Station platform he sees, at last, the dear face of his wife, come to meet him as she has many times before. 'This trip, however, had been a long one, almost seventeen years,' he writes in the last sentence; 'most important, I was not returning from a business trip. I was returning from hell.'

Very few passengers left the train at Vologda. We walked its length under the latticework of overhead wires strung between high metal towers, away from the pearly morning sky over the northern plain, towards the town. Workmen checked the heavy rusted wheels of the train with hammers, the deep sound ringing out like muted bells. When he was in exile here in 1910, Molotov would often come to the sidings and repair shops at the Vologda station to spend time with the local railwaymen, who, as poorly paid proletarians with terrible working conditions and no insurance or representation, were particularly receptive to his Marxist revolutionary message. Radicalised railwaymen were to play an important role in the drama of 1917.

After the Revolution, in 1918, platform five on the Vologda railway station was briefly the 'diplomatic capital of Russia'. The Embassy of the United States (followed by other nations of the Entente) had evacuated the capital for Vologda after breaking off diplomatic relations with Russia. They chose Vologda because it connected the Moscow–Archangel line with the Trans-Siberian. It was a crucial point on the map of anti-Bolshevik military intervention. Until the accommodating mayor found the Americans a residence in town, the Embassy was a train carriage. 'The railway station restaurant was ... the favourite haunt,' the Secretary of the Embassy recalled; 'there was a fair assortment of food to offer: big jars of dill pickles, black bread, kvass and hard-boiled eggs.'

In front of the station was a scruffy park, to one side a bus depot, and on the other a high building blazoned with the words GLORY TO THE COMMUNIST PARTY OF THE SOVIET UNION in faded mosaic, crusted now with dust. There was no trace of any station restaurant. Eight years before the Western diplomats fled from the revolution he and his comrades had made, Molotov, dressed as a minstrel, played the violin in the station restaurant for a rouble a night. The place was reputedly popular with travellers as well as with heavy-drinking local merchants and their beauties. The most popular song in his repertoire was 'Ah, why was this night so good?' During the two-year sentence of exile he served in the Vologda region, Molotov had met a troupe of musicians on one of the town boulevards and hired himself out for the summer. After he had performed, his friend Nikolai Maltsev would meet him at the restaurant and the two revolutionaries would stroll through the empty streets of Vologda, pasting slogans on the walls of buildings, sharing their dreams of humanity's radiant future. (Later Stalin enjoyed humiliating Molotov about his moonlighting in exile. 'You played for drunken merchants, and they smeared your mug with mustard,' he would mock in front of the Politburo.)

We left our rucksacks in a cage in a concrete cellar (the station's luggage store) under the tall building guarded by an old man with satirical eyes and, hoping for breakfast, made our way down the broken pavements of Peace Avenue, turning left down Chekhov Street and up Maltsev Street, then left again on October Street towards the Spasskaya Hotel. Overnight train journeys make one hungry, and in the large restaurant of the hotel, among hefty cooks in white coats and a mass of silent guests, we found a breakfast that outclassed our hopes: strong tea, black bread with curls of pale butter, kefir, boiled eggs and slices of cheese and ham. Vologda, Shalamov tells us, is renowned for three things: its lace, its prison guards ('The Vologda prison guard does not like to joke,' the saying goes) and its dairy products. The first of the four Vologdas that he identifies is the town of full-cream milk and grasping, godly peasants, with their own pronunciation, who will serve any regime with the same loyalty, and will not thin their milk even if the world is being destroyed around them.

The aged Molotov had wistful memories of his time in Vologda: vivid years of youth and hope, friendship, music and books. Though he admitted he had never experienced real hunger in all his long life, he remembered periods in exile when he had to go hungry: 'My friend Arosev, a writer, who was there with me would tell me, "Well, we have nothing left. Let's eat up the sugar! What's left of it . . ."' Molotov prided himself on his lack of bourgeois philistinism, his dislike of luxury. ('I am against the tranquil life! If I craved a tranquil life, it would mean I had been "philistinised."') Yet there is a distinctly bourgeois fastidiousness about his description of the domestic circumstances of his exile in a letter to Maltsev. He tells his friend how pleasant it was drinking tea on the journey, how his rented accommodation was 'cosy and bright with a mass of nice things and pictures', an icon and a lamp, and a separate guest room with a 'pleasant table'. A pitcher of milk was delivered every day for six kopecks, and their landlady made them dinners of cabbage soup with meat, and sometimes kasha. The beds were full of fleas, he noted, and there were no mattresses, so he slept on his coat, but he visited the local banya as often as he could and enjoyed free facilities in the local library, where he could read all the current journals and the local and national press. Molotov writes warmly of the contentments and satisfactions of exile, how it gives him time to read all the many books he longs to read. The government gave him a stipend of eleven gold roubles a month, and only three things were forbidden: to leave his place of exile, to serve in any official position and to teach (the last of these rules he disobeyed). All he really missed was the chance to hear serious music: Beethoven performed in a real palatial concert hall.

As for so many revolutionaries in tsarist Russia, prison and exile were an educational opportunity. Stolypin, the Tsar's Minister of Internal Affairs, is said to have declared that if the young troublemakers had been workers he would have let them go abroad, 'because it is hopeless to try to reform workers', but these students, 'members of the intelligentsia', he had sent into exile in the hope that the pure air of the 'quiet North' would cure them and they might still be of use to the state. In Vologda, besides minstrelling and cultivating the revolutionary sentiments of the railwaymen, Molotov devoted himself to his studies. He enrolled for Latin examinations in the local gymnasium. Like Stalin, who read dozens of books during his weeks of exile in Vologda, Molotov made good use of the local library. As we know, Molotov was an active, passionate and eclectic reader, a true bibliophile. He told Maltsev that he was always on the look-out for good editions, that books filled his nights and days. He read Darwin and the 'Russian Darwin', Kliment Timiryazev. He read Sidney Webb's *Trade Unions* and sat diligently over the volumes of Marx's *Capital* (not wanting to hurry, he said, over the 'theory of value'), and all the latest and best publications on literature, the social sciences and philosophy, littering his letters to friends with references to Pushkin, Tolstoy and Dostoevsky (in Vologda, he finished Dostoevsky's *The Insulted and the Injured*), as well as to numerous lesser-known literary critics, short-story writers and Symbolist philosophers like Dmitri Merezhkovsky and the future Commissar of Enlightenment Lunacharsky. 'They are all mystics. I don't understand how Lunacharsky compares his four steps of art and socialism and what kind of "god-building" he wants,' Molotov complained in a letter.

It was Chekhov (whom he had read 'from cover to cover') who most keenly engaged Molotov's moral sensibilities at this time, and became his favourite writer. He wrote to Maltsev about the delights of his literary arguments with his paradoxicalist roommate, who would accuse Chekhov of being a petit bourgeois (a *meshchanin*) and say that only bureaucrats and petit bourgeois should read him. For Molotov, by contrast, Chekhov's stories rang with the call to revolution. He was moved by the writer's concern for the 'little man', by his reflections on the pointlessness of lives crushed by poverty and bureaucratic arbitrariness. Chekhov made Molotov 'burn with indignation against the prevailing order', his grandson, the political commentator Vyacheslav Nikonov, writes in a recent biography of his grandfather as a young man. 'Millions read Chekhov and were indignant about the state of things,'

Nikonov comments with filial pride, 'but few were prepared to go through punishment for the sake of the bright future.'

It was in Vologda that Molotov first heard of Stalin. When he left, Stalin came to take his place. 'He was famous even then, in 1910, as Stalin,' Molotov remembered, 'that's what he called himself. And I called myself Molotov . . . You assume an alias, you change an alias. Stalin is an industrial name, apparently chosen for the same reasons as mine – Bolshevik reasons.' These were names for hard men: Stalin, 'man of steel'; Molotov, 'hammer man'. His first encounter with Stalin – the first leader of the Bolshevik underground he had met – was in 1912. They worked together on *Pravda*. At this time Molotov was a student in the Petersburg Polytechnical Institute. He and Stalin were bound by the fact that they had done time in Russian prisons and exile, unlike some of the 'softer' revolutionaries abroad in places like Switzerland. They always used the familiar '*ty*' form, and called each other Koba and Vyacheslav. Stalin had taken one of his girlfriends, Marusya, he said, noting without resentment that Stalin was very attractive to women. What distinguished Molotov in a Party that at the beginning was markedly un-Russian (full of Latvians, Jews, Armenians and Georgians) was that he was a pure Russian of the north. One of Stalin's nicknames for him, which he often used, was Molotoshvili, a Georgianising of his name. In one letter he hailed him as Molotshtein, a mocking Jewish variant. In his old age, Molotov told Chuev, 'I am a man of the north'. He took walks every day, even in the harshest frost. Churchill talked of the 'breath of cold' in his smile.

⚜

After breakfast, we turned towards the Vologda River, walking down wide, still-empty streets in deepening April sunlight to the house of the insane poet Konstantin Batyushkov. According to the prevailing wisdom of the 1920s, Shalamov believed that venereal disease had destroyed Batyushkov's mind. 'A great Russian poet, a crazy syphilitic,' he called him. More likely, Batyushkov suffered from inherited schizophrenia. Here in Vologda (where he had been born in 1787) his family created an elegant asylum for the poet, in which he spent three decades, suspended outside historical time, in ever-gathering psychosis.

During Shalamov's childhood in the 1910s, the beautifully proportioned yellow house curving round the corner opposite the Vologda Kremlin was a girls' gymnasium, the Marinsky (where Shalamov's mother and sisters were educated). Even then there was a memorial plaque to Batyushkov which Shalamov could read ten times a day, as his childhood home was only a few hundred yards away. 'Father never spoke to me of Batyushkov,' he remembers; 'from this I conclude that my father did not like poetry, feared its dark power, far from common sense.' It was only as an adult that Shalamov learned to repeat with his 'teeth and larynx' the line 'O, heart's memory, you are stronger than reason's sad memory' (a line that in Russian is full of patterns of compacted sound), and to understand what he called Batyushkov's power over the word, which was 'freer and more unbridled than Pushkin's . . . preserving the most unexpected discoveries'.

Now, Batyushkov's house is a teacher-training college, in which two rooms are made over to the poet's memorial museum. The woman at the coat-check raised an eyebrow as we passed, as though our visit was a comical event, entirely unexpected. Classes had begun. We looked into a hall in which rows of young women and a few men sat listening to a lecture. On the wall of the corridor was a brightly coloured frieze on lacquered wood, illustrating, with accompanying quotations from great Russian writers and painters, the pedagogical value of Russian fairy tales. 'What charm there is in these stories!' exclaimed Pushkin. 'Through the fairy tale the thousand-year-old history of the people is revealed,' wrote Tolstoy. 'In them, one can see . . . the cunning Russian mind, so inclined to irony, so simple-hearted in its cunning,' commented Belinsky. In one picture, a crow wearing an apron stirred a pot of soup as a mouse approached with a wooden ladle.

In another a fox in a *kokoshnik* and *sarafan* – a folk crown and pinafore – sat on a birch log laughing wickedly.

Batyushkov's sunlit asylum was like a room in a dolls' house. Russia's golden age, the Parnassus of the early nineteenth century when poetry was still an aristocratic salon pursuit, was figured here, as though for children, an idyll of lost refinement. In the Soviet gloom, this era made a radiant past, sanitised for reverence – a profusion of garlands, urns and lyres and curved Karelian birchwood; the svelte lines of quill pens and high-waisted nymphs – everything as fragile as gilded porcelain, and utterly sweet.

'He lived through three wars and was healthy in a bivouac,' Batyushkov wrote in a sketch about himself, 'but in peacetime he found himself dying.' What use was he? 'How should I occupy my spiritual emptiness? Tell me how I can be useful to society, to myself, to my friends!' he wrote to the poet Vasili Zhukovsky.

Once Batyushkov's world had been large. He served in campaigns against the Swedes and entered France with the Russian troops after the rout of Napoleon. He travelled to London, Dresden, Bessarabia, Vienna, Venice, Rome and Naples. He convalesced in Teplitz after a bad spell of depression, and in Simferopol burned all his books and tried three times to take his own life. He loved Moscow with particular tenderness. The sight of the city in ruins after the departure of Napoleon's Grande Armée (a 'sea of evil', he said) precipitated another spell of depression. 'Barbarians! Vandals! And this nation of fiends has had the audacity to talk of freedom, of philosophy, of love for humanity!' (Batyushkov understood the power and meaning of great cities. Before the Napoleonic wars, he had been preoccupied to the point of obsession with the poet Tasso's *Jerusalem Delivered*, written in the sixteenth century when Ivan the Terrible's Vologda was being built.) He worked as a librarian in the Public Library in St Petersburg, a place in which, to this day, whatever may be happening in the streets outside, the world feels wide and light and time nothing but a blessing. Later, he served as a diplomat in Italy, which he called 'a library, a museum of antiquities', and he called

Rome, a 'magical city', a book that could never be read in full. The poets in Batyushkov's own 'summer house of the muses' were Homer, Hesiod, Tibullus, Petrarch, Dante, Tasso (who also suffered from mental illness), Ariosto and Byron. Among his friends he counted Pushkin, Vyazemsky and Zhukovsky and the Decembrists Nikita Muraviev and Sergei Muraviev-Apostol (who was hanged); all loved his poetic gift and grieved as he lost his mind. 'What a miracle this Batyushkov is!' Pushkin scribbled in the margins of one of his books. Throughout his life, Batyushkov kept reworking the same poem, 'Dream', which begins, 'Dreaming is the soul of poets and verses'. His last lyric, written in Vologda in the year of his death, began: 'I awake so as to fall asleep, and sleep so as to awake for eternity.'

Batyushkov's name is one of those in the canon of Russian literature which I have often passed in the pages of books without stopping to pay attention. In Mandelstam's first collection, *Stone*, there is this defiant little lyric:

> *No, not the moon but a bright clockface*
> *Gleams for me, and what am I guilty of*
> *If I perceive weak stars as milky?*
>
> *And I find the arrogance of Batyushkov repellent:*
> *'What time is it?' they asked him here,*
> *And he made the curious reply: 'eternity.'*

Stone, which appeared in 1912, in a literary world accustomed to the mystical abstractions of Symbolists, is full of rebellion against all kinds of poetic arrogance. Mandelstam loved time and matter. 'I have been given a body. What should I do with it?' He wanted verse to shake off the weight of words like 'eternity'.

There were several bright clockfaces gleaming in Batyushkov's semi-circular room: an English grandfather clock with a gleaming face; a gold empire-style timepiece on a glass-fronted bookcase, its face borne on the wings of a cupid, and, under a portrait of Batyushkov as a young man, a clock mounted with urns, columns and babies with gilded wings. I studied a portrait of the poet painted two years before his death. By then, Batyushkov was a relic of his glorious past. He sits in a red velvet chair, arms crossed, with the pout of an angry child, his eyes resentful and confused. In his lapel is a small wilted yellow flower which, the museum attendant told us (as though she had been present at the difficult sitting), he had insisted on wearing. In another painting, set in this room, the poet looks through the window at the Vologda Kremlin, his back to the painter.

The attendant's voice faltered when she talked of Batyushkov's madness. She showed us a photograph of her own son and daughter dressed in costumes of the Napoleonic era: bonnet, fan, ringlets, brass buttons and epaulettes. She was grateful for our visit, and told us that once, several years ago, she had received some visitors from Italy. She loved Batyushkov's room; its curving wall and its large windows gave it a good *energetika*. When I asked about life in Vologda, she sighed: 'Yes, everything is changing, getting better, I suppose, now they teach Batyushkov in school. But this is a provincial town,' she added, looking through the window; 'nothing really happens here.'

❧

We crossed into a park beside the Vologda Kremlin on paths of broken asphalt, following the sightline in the painting of Batyushkov's back, towards Shalamov's house. Now that the last of the snow was gone, Vologda was preparing for summer: men were unloading timber from a truck, old women swept the paths with besoms. Restoration work was under way in the Kremlin, a pleasure boat was advertising disco cruises down the river from a loudspeaker and fairground attractions were being mounted in the park. Opposite a dusty shooting range decorated in camouflage colours, bright balloons in primary colours with mad smiling faces decorated a motionless carousel. Stacked against the brick and faded whitewash of the Kremlin wall were the red and blue carriages of a little train and a set of pedalos, turned on their sides in a rusty rack.

Over the wall we could see the domes of St Sophia, some regilded, some still dull pewter grey, birds wheeling in the air above. The soft silver blue of the aluminium drainpipes was webbed and mottled like a leaf. The English writer Arthur Ransome, who was a correspondent for the *Manchester Guardian* in 1918, was enraptured by the play of colours in the Vologda sky: 'white churches against the blue winter sky, churches capped with towers of intricate design, showing the great bronze bells hanging in their airy belfries of gold and green, of plain grey lead and of violent deep blue, thickly sown with gold stars'. In Molotov's library, with all its pages cut, was a copy of Ransome's book *Six Weeks in Soviet Russia*, translated by Karl Radek. The Russian edition was published in 1924 and in the introduction it said that, when the book had come out in 1919, it had 'played a large role against the Intervention, when Russia was cut off from the rest of the world by a wall of lies and slander'.

Varlam Shalamov's family called St Sophia the 'cold church'. It was gloomy, he said, with no spiritual warmth. We tried to go inside, but its heavy gold doors were closed, and a woman told us crossly to go away, the church was under *remont*. Legend has it that a piece of stone from the foot of an angel on its ceiling fell on the toe of Ivan the Terrible during the ceremony of its consecration; a sign, the Tsar decided, that he should not move his capital from Moscow to Vologda. Instead we wandered through the regional museum, laid out in an orange-painted side building inside the Kremlin. As always, the exhibits took us through local history, from fossils found in the Devonian layer of the local earth to a mounted quotation from Gorky about the great Soviet task of freeing the people from the past, and a public declaration of 1931 by Molotov on the social benefits of 'mass singing'.

The Shalamov house museum was, by contrast, a museum of a more contemporary style with passages of text mounted on bare brick walls. In 1918, Shalamov says, everything that had furnished his childhood was lost. He left Vologda in 1924, to throw himself into the new civilisation taking shape in 'seething Moscow', and never returned. To evoke the writer's distant past in Vologda, it is better to read *The Fourth Vologda* (its title a homage to Mandelstam's *The Fourth Prose*), which Shalamov composed in his mid-sixties, in the writing years in Moscow after his return from almost two decades in the labour camps of Kolyma. In *The Fourth Vologda*, which summons with vivid immediacy the texture of his childhood, the Gulag is a shadow falling back across the past. Shalamov wanted to bring together three times in his memoir – past, present and future – for the sake of the fourth, which is art.

He revisits the ice hills on the riverbank, built by his brother, a wild gymnasium drop-out famous for his hunting skills. He remembers his whole family out on the river on summer fishing expeditions in a pair of boats; the samovar and the kerosene lamp at home; his father's newspapers and his treasured American watch (which survived the Gulag in Shalamov's possession); his mother's poor cookery, her swollen body and her strange belief in the resurrection of the dead through the advance of chemistry, which she was convinced would soon find the way to refine people into pure spirit.

Like Batyushkov and the political exiles, Shalamov's father brought to Vologda the air of faraway places. He had been to New York, Hamburg and Berlin, and before Shalamov's birth served as a missionary in Alaska. In the hallway, he kept a black cupboard eclectically filled with prized exhibits. Father Tikhon Shalamov's private museum did not contain any copies of classical sculptures like those in the museum of Marina Tsvetaeva's father in Moscow, Shalamov remarks, but he had a ship in a bottle, a collection of Native American arrows, Eskimo cult objects, shaman masks, a walrus tusk and a picture of the boat on which he had sailed to America as a young priest. To the fury of the local Black Hundreds, his father would pray in front of a reproduction of a Rubens painting stuck on to plywood, instead of venerating icons painted in the local style of Andrei Rublev or Theophanes the Greek. His father was from a long line of northern holy men, Shalamov says; shamans who became priests when Christianity came to Russia, but kept their pagan depths. The name '*shalam*', he says, is a primitive word whose sound carries the word '*shaman*' as well as the word '*shalost*', meaning mischievousness. His father's sermons against the pogroms of the Black Hundreds led to a breach with the local church hierarchy, and he found work in the service of an anarchist millionairess named Baroness Des-Fonteines. The radical Baroness had been exiled to Vologda, and bought up vast forests and paper factories across the Russian north, building factory schools and a wooden church that looked like a toy, in which Shalamov's father celebrated the liturgy, attracting foreign employees of the paper business, English and Americans, who came to worship in winter, trudging through the forest on paths cut like tunnels in the deep snow.

Shalamov and his father came into conflict over books. Unlike his unruly brother (who caused Tikhon Shalamov another kind of paternal agony), Varlam was a prodigious reader. The speed of his reading unnerved his father, who kept the keys to the family bookcase, a massive glass-fronted piece of furniture with a deep bottom section in which nothing could be seen. Shalamov remembers with precision, as bookish children do, the sequence of books on the shelves: the gospels; the poetry of Heinrich Heine without a binding; Andrei Bely's novel *Petersburg*; works of contemporary Russian religious philosophy (some of the same writers that Molotov read in Vologda); and the journals *Family and School* and *Nature and People*. Marx stood on the shelves beside Tolstoy. There was nothing, though, that Shalamov considered real treasure: no Shakespeare, no Dostoevsky. His father wanted him to read German philosophy by the light of the kerosene lamp, but Shalamov preferred adventure fiction: Alexandre Dumas, Jules Verne, Rudyard Kipling, James Fenimore Cooper, Jack London and Sir Arthur Conan Doyle.

It was only in the house of a schoolfriend, one of the illustrious

Veselovsky family (in which, Shalamov remarked, there was a distinct literary-critical gene), that he encountered a real library:
'endless bookshelves, boxes, parcels of books, a kingdom of books
that I could touch'. Throughout his childhood, his father's cry resonated: 'Stop reading!' 'Put down that book!' 'Turn out the light!'
After decades of absolute hunger for books in the Gulag, he perceived the hunger for books as the condition of his childhood, the
condition of his whole life. His primal hunger was such that no
number of books could ever slake it. There is no sweeter thing, he
said, than the sight of an unread book.

Shalamov was expelled from Moscow University in 1928 for
'concealing his social origins'. For his blind clergyman father's
profession, he had put down 'invalid'. He was arrested for the first
time in 1929 and sentenced to five years on Solovki for his involve-
ment, with a group of female university friends, in a Trotskyist
underground printing press, illegally producing copies of Lenin's
'Last Testament' (in which the ailing revolutionary made critical
comments about Stalin). Shalamov was re-arrested for the same
crime (a common Stalinist practice) in 1937 and sentenced under
Article 58 to five years in Kolyma in the far north, a sentence
which was extended for a further ten years after stool pigeons in
the camp reported on various features of his conversation in the
barracks. On the Dostoevsky jubilee, Shalamov had laughed
mockingly about how all the novelist's works had still not been
published in the USSR. He had disparaged the Soviet writer
Konstantin Simonov (winner of five Stalin prizes) as a talentless
hack, and expressed admiration for Marina Tsvetaeva (the secret
police could not quite place her when writing up the protocols of
his case, and it was noted that she was just another of those female
poets whose subject matter is the bedroom and church who
hanged herself 'for personal reasons').

After Shalamov's house, we found a bench in the sunshine, below
an odd new statue of Batyushkov with a horse, and looked across
the Vologda River at the Sixth Army Embankment on the other

side. (Unlike Moscow, and long before St Petersburg, this city was originally laid out on both banks of the river.) Molotov once lodged on the embankment in the house of a merchant called Velikanov. My map indicated that the large classical building directly opposite was a Psychotherapeutic Centre. Further along the tree-lined embankment were barracks, and an eighteenth-century baroque church with elaborate tracery on its belltower and small ungilded fish-scaled domes. Leaning against its white plaster wall was a wrecked bus. A speedboat passed, splitting the water, driven by a man with three teenage girls in the back, mouths open, long hair flying, their voices lost in the wind. A private drama was unfolding below us: a couple arguing drunkenly across the bonnet of a Lada parked among litter on the grassy riverbank, the woman crying angrily, turning away, then going back for more.

Thinking about Shalamov had made me think about Mandelstam again. He is here in Vologda too: his style and spirit saturate Shalamov's writing. In his image of Mandelstam is Shalamov's sense of redemption. Vologda made me sense what Mandelstam meant when he talked about how Dante overheard the 'overtones of time'. Dante 'altered the structure of time', Mandelstam wrote, 'or perhaps to the contrary, he was forced to a glossolalia of facts, to a synchronism of events, names and traditions severed by centuries'. In *The Divine Comedy* voices from across historical time talk among themselves in synchrony, in sheer simultaneity. Lifted out of time and place, they are still preoccupied with precisely what has happened in time and place.

Shalamov's 'Cherry Brandy', whose title alludes to Mandelstam's poem about the Zoological Museum, imagines the poet's death from hunger in the Gulag. Mandelstam, who once called life 'a precious gift, inalienable', is lying in a cold barrack, his fingers – white, bloodless and swollen from hunger – lie on his chest; 'sometimes there would come, painfully and almost palpably dragging itself through his brain, a simple and strong thought – that someone had stolen the bread he had put under his head'. This acutely terrible thought, which makes him prepared to quarrel, swear, fight, search (if he had the strength), leads to other thoughts: a ship coming to take him away, a birthmark on an orderly's face, the sense that his past life had been a book, a fairy tale, the knowledge that only the present moment is real. 'Cherry Brandy' is a meditation on the dark power of poetry, the life-giving force through which Mandelstam lived. Everything – work, the thud of horses' hoofs, home, birds, rocks, love, the whole world – could be expressed in verse. All of life makes itself comfortable in words, and every word is a living piece of the world. As the poet eats his last bread ration ('a miracle – one of many local miracles'), pushing it past his bleeding gums with blue fingers, time floats and spins. The other prisoners tell him to save some of his piece of bread for later. The poet's last words are 'When later?'

In 1965, Mandelstam's widow wrote to Shalamov that she thought his prose, with its 'inner music', the best in Russian for many, many years; she thought it might be the finest prose of the twentieth century. Shalamov, who revered Mandelstam's Acmeism (to him it was not just another poetic movement, it was a lifetime's pledge, the heart of all courage, a means of existence), thanked Nadezhda Mandelstam for the compliment, saying that for him she was the 'supreme court'.

In May of the same year, Shalamov attended an 'evening of memory' for Mandelstam in Moscow. For the first time, the poet's name could be mentioned in public. When it was Shalamov's turn to speak, he looked pale, with burning eyes (like the seventeenth-century heretic priest Avvakum). His hand movements were clumsy and unco-ordinated, but he spoke beautifully. He said he would read the story 'Cherry Brandy' which he had written twelve years earlier in Kolyma, in a desperate hurry to record the life of Mandelstam. It was only when he returned to Moscow that he realised that Mandelstam had not been forgotten; he had never died. Shalamov began to read his story. 'The poet was dying. His hands, large, swollen from hunger with their white bloodless fingers and filthy overgrown nails, lay on his chest . . .' Soon a note was passed to him by the organiser of the event, asking him to stop, but Shalamov put it in his pocket and carried on to the end: 'The poet understood. He opened his eyes wide, not allowing the bloodstained bread to slip from his dirty, blue fingers . . .'

In Vologda, I heard again a glossolalia of facts about hunger.

It was Molotov who put men like Shalamov and Mandelstam on trains bound for hell. Molotov, who considered 'all talk of morality and humanism false through and through', and was always fastidious about not being 'bourgeois' or 'philistine', was asked by Felix Chuev at the end of his life what he thought about the fact that no one could find meat for sale anywhere in the USSR. 'To hell with the meat!' he replied. 'Just let imperialism drop dead!'

'In my youth, whenever I experienced failure I used to repeat the phrase, "Well, at least I won't die from hunger,"' Shalamov wrote in his story 'Dry Ration'. 'It never crossed my mind to doubt the truth of this sentence. At the age of thirty I found myself in a very real sense dying from hunger and literally fighting for a piece of bread.' Shalamov's Gulag stories, which are full of his hunger for the streets of Moscow and for the feel of books in his hands, give an account, rare in literature, of real hunger. He records how the human mind melts with the flesh, how when starvation is sucking the body dry, all human emotions disappear – 'love, friendship, envy, concern for one's fellow man, compassion, the longing for fame, honesty' – how 'camp hunger' makes people dream identical dreams – 'rye loaves flying past like meteors or angels' – how it can bring people to a level of indifference to the world that is as close to transcendence as it is horrifying, and drive them to mutilate their own dying bodies.

❦

We had tea in a riverside cafe with walls lined in shiny red vinyl. A large group of middle-aged men and women at a table laid with many bottles of vodka was drunkenly singing in loud exultant chest voices the Young Pioneer songs of their youth. We walked back in the direction of the station under a milky sky. The streets in Vologda are so wide that the pretty wooden houses seem to be sliding away from each other into empty space. Many are silver-grey with age; their origin as trees more striking after so many years in the sunlight and the snow. They seem gradually to be returning to their element; cracks and peelings run along their lines of growth, ferrous blackness seeped into the grain of the wood, as their fittings rust and are not replaced.

We stopped in on the memorial museum of Lenin's sister, the revolutionary Maria Ulyanova, to discover that its name had changed to the Samarin Museum of Daily Life. (Molotov had lodged with Ulyanova in Moscow when he moved his revolutionary activities from Petrograd in 1915.) I asked a white-haired attendant about Ulyanova, of whom there is now no trace in the museum. With a look of regret in her proud blue eyes at my asking about the revolutionary, she told me that Ulyanova had only rented a room in the house, and had nothing to do with its owners or its true history. The museum was now dedicated to displaying the innocent decencies of bourgeois life in pre-revolutionary Vologda: a family dining table with fine china soup tureens and a shiny samovar, icons and prayer books, white muslin dresses, sepia photographs of dacha parties and rows of school-children in pinafores and ribbons.

The Museum of the Diplomatic Corps on Herzen Street, which I had particularly wanted to visit, was similarly disposed to rearrange the facts of the past according to a new set of political and cultural values. Its two rooms were on the ground floor of a large house that the US Embassy occupied for five months after moving out of its train carriage on platform five. The diplomat and historian George F. Kennan, who believed the Allied Intervention of 1918 to have been a mistake, painted an idyllic picture of life in the quiet northern town. In the evenings, diplomats of several anti-Bolshevik nations gathered around a crackling fire in the large brick stove, telling jokes and playing

cards, with the ringing of church bells and the creak of sled runners coming through the calm air outside.

By the summer, the Bolshevik government in Moscow had
decided to drive the foreign missions out of Vologda, and Karl
Radek (who worked then in the Commissariat of Foreign Affairs)
ordered that guards be stationed around all buildings occupied by
diplomats of the Entente nations, and cut off their means of communication. In late July, the ambassadors withdrew to Archangel.
Left in charge in Vologda was the English 'mission secretary', a
mysterious figure named John Gillespie, a fluent Russian speaker,
who assisted the local anti-Bolshevik underground in an uprising
that quickly failed. The Cheka was, it seems, convinced that
Gillespie was just another alias of Sidney Reilly.

'In this town of uprisings, why was there no uprising against
the new power?' Shalamov wondered in *The Fourth Vologda*. The
single reason that he can find is the will of one hard man, the
commissar and Chekist Mikhail Kedrov, who came to Vologda in
1918 to break up the local authorities, declare martial law and
ration bread. Night and day the arrests went on, Shalamov
remembers; it was under Kedrov's terror that his family lost all its
possessions. Kedrov was 'bone of the bone, and blood of the blood
of the Moscow intelligentsia', Shalamov says, a lawyer and a fine
pianist, who impressed Lenin with a performance of the Bolshevik leader's favourite piece, Beethoven's *Appassionata*.

'What tense do you want to live in?' Mandelstam asks in
Journey to Armenia. 'I want to live in the imperative of the future
passive participle – in the "what ought to be".' It takes a certain
disposition, however, to have iron certainty, throughout a lifetime
of blood and loss, of what ought to be. 'If there is no primary
objective, then what is there to struggle for?' Molotov said at the
end of his life. 'If there are no goals, what are we struggling for?
Where are we going?'

The wheezing eccentric who showed us round the Museum of
the Diplomatic Corps lived in a more complicated tense: the 'what
ought to have been'. As we soon discovered, the strange museum,

with its small display of photocopied documents and photographs, was his creation, the fragmentary realisation of a lifelong
historical fantasy. Followed by two slender young women (his
graduate students, he told us), the heavy red-faced man explained
in intricate detail, with the aid of many flourishing rhetorical
questions, the diplomatic delicacies of 1918, and the spy intrigues
and international love affairs – Reilly, Lockhart, Savinkov, the
international femme fatale Moura Budberg – that may or may not
have played a role in the destiny of the Revolution. He had written a doctoral dissertation on the story of the Vologda missions,
and tried, without success, to travel to London to follow up the
story in the declassified British state archives. Living in Vologda
in the Soviet years when Russia was closed to the outside world,
he had found a hidden burrow in history, tuning his ear to its facts,
putative facts, lost possibilities. After the end of communism, he
had spent years petitioning the local authorities (whom he
despised as old communists) for the use of the building. They all
wanted to forget that the Allies had ever been here, he said. Now
his museum memorialises a moment when Vologda was the stage
for what he believed ought to have happened; if the people had
risen up against the Bolsheviks with the aid of the Allied armies
that landed in Archangel, if those armies had been stronger and
had pressed down to Moscow, if the Tsar had not been murdered,
if the 'conspiracy apartment' in No. 3 'Cheremeteff' had not been
raided, if Lenin and Trotsky had been paraded through the streets
in their shirt-tails in the summer of 1918.

The anteroom to the museum was a shop selling all kinds of
bric-a-brac, icons and cheaply produced polemical pamphlets,
several written by the curator himself. One, by the dissident priest
Gleb Yakunin, denounced the Orthodox Church for its close
dealings with Lenin, Stalin and the secret police. Its cover showed
a blotchy photograph of Patriarch of Moscow and All the Russias
Aleksii II (also known as Drozdov, KGB General) at a lectern
beneath a statue of Lenin. The curator offered to sell us a lovely
icon of three northern saints; when we explained that we would

not be allowed to take it out of the country, he sighed: 'It is only Russia that still does not understand that the world is round.' The building was dilapidated; he needed money for repairs. Communists, he huffed, they let everything fall to ruin except their own palaces. It was as though this affable man's lifetime of obstinate dislike for the ruling power had intensified the pressure of his blood, making his body push angrily at the seams of his clothes. In the great Vologda tradition of patriotic opposition that Shalamov describes, his mind was turned towards the World and the West (with a capital letter).

I told the curator we had come from Moscow on our way to Archangel. He warned us about the harsh wind that blows off the White Sea. Then he laughed. 'Moscow, eh?' (He made it seem so far away.) 'Another of them died down there yesterday. Now he's lying in the great cathedral . . . just another communist!' It took me a moment to realise that he was talking about Boris Yeltsin.

ELEVEN

Archangel

> For a person who has had the experience of living in Russia,
> who has experienced the metaphysical Russian roller coaster, any
> landscape, including an other-worldly one, seems ordinary.
> JOSEPH BRODSKY, 'Footnote to a Poem', *Less Than One*

Down on the waterfront, where we wandered late, the floating nightclub *USSR* was straining to create its own aura of night. Even this early in the northern spring, there was little way of telling the time from the light in the sky, which changed according to signals more mysterious than the hour of the clock. From his pedestal, Otto Shmidt, the 'ice commissar', should have been looking out from the prow of the city towards the throat of the White Sea, across the scatter of islands that flood and change shape in the violence of the snow-melt. Instead his granite gaze fell on a stack of stereo speakers leaning against a rusted iron door at the back of the club. The red-and-blue wooden structure throbbed so frantically in its solitary rave that it seemed ready to shake off its moorings, to be caught up in the pull of the ice floes that rushed past the curve of Archangel towards Molotovsk at the river mouth, turning and disintegrating in the seaward flow of the Dvina.

Monuments are so vulnerable. History drifts off and leaves them stranded. The statue of Peter the Great on the embankment was unveiled in the patriotic year 1914. When the Bolsheviks finally broke the White hold on Archangel, the Tsar was pulled down and left lying face first on the steps of his own house. In his place, the Party erected a monument to the victims of the Allied Intervention of 1918 (whose 'greatest inspirer', as Molotov underlined in one of his history books, was Churchill). Whenever centralised state power and national borders are at stake, the image of Peter I comes out, as it did in 1941, in a book in Molotov's library by Academician M. M. Bogoslovsky called *Peter I: Materials for a Biography*. After the 'Great Patriotic War', at the height of Stalin's own reign as 'tsar', Peter, the personification of Russian maritime power who dreamed at the end of his life of an Arctic sea route from Archangel to the east, was restored to a new position on the waterfront.

For decades, all across the Soviet empire, in the bleakness of town squares cleared to make space for them, giant statues of Marx and Lenin declared in stone that they had determined the course of history and pointed the way. The Lenin in Archangel's main square was the last to be erected in the USSR, in place of a fountain that the local Party boss had tired of seeing from his office window. Its sculptor, Lev Kerbel, a Politburo favourite, said his conception was an 'Ilyich' that local people would want to approach for solitary contemplation, perhaps to ask advice. The bust of Shmidt – hero of Stalin's 'age of discovery' – was chiselled in the same genre. He was the Soviet state's 'honorary walrus' (as Valery Mezhlauk had caricatured him in one of the weird drawings in the Party archives). On the dirty grass by the Maritime Museum – long closed for *remont*, with cobwebs furring its windows – the adamant jut of his beard looked peevish, thwarted.

In my first sighting of him, in the diary of the Soviet playwright Alexander Afinogenov, Shmidt had been similarly diminished by the realities of daily life crowding in on him. Afinogenov visited him at his Moscow home in No. 3 in 1937, the year in which Shmidt would plant a flag bearing a portrait of the Great Leader on the North Pole and declare it Soviet territory. 'Two other families live in his apartment,' Afinogenov recorded, noting the large sad eyes of Shmidt's wife, Vera, and her aura of sickness. 'He has three rooms, the stuffy front hall smells of dinner from the kitchen, the study is tightly packed with furniture and books.' 'Why do we live here?' Vera said. 'Otto is used to it. It's close to the food store and the hospital, close to the Kremlin and work.'

Afinogenov rejected the title 'Drifting People' for the essay he was writing about Shmidt's polar research station: the word "drifting" had too much shadow in it. Shmidt told him that he had fallen into the Arctic by chance, through mathematics, philosophy and history, and his fascination with the physics of the sea and the 'white spots' on the map. Now Shmidt was 'master of the Arctic' in the same way that a writer should be master of his craft. Shmidt embodied the Soviet virtues that Afinogenov was struggling to cultivate in his writing: self-criticism, fellowship, dedication to the collective, energy, happiness.

He watched Shmidt's flight for Archangel take off from a Moscow airstrip, his heart pounding when the motors of the heavy aircraft faltered. Shmidt's feats brought Stalinist tears to Afinogenov's eyes, giving him the sense that the full flowering of happiness on earth was just around the corner. It had something particular to do with the conquest of the Arctic and the miracle of radio contact across the expanding reach of Soviet space, which made the Pole seem as close as the writers' colony at Peredelkino just outside Moscow. 'When communism has triumphed all over the world . . . our planet will turn into a flowering paradise,' Shmidt orated from the Pole, 'rivers will flow in the direction in which men point them, oceans will give up the strength of their waves to the service of humanity.' Afinogenov imagined Soviet flags being planted on the Pole every year, and the sea ice, always on the move, carrying them off around the globe on floating mounds, meeting ocean liners with their show of communist power. He had been reading *The Brothers Karamazov* all summer, 'living' in the novel. Yet Shmidt's feats made his soul light. His inner life conformed. He turned away from Dostoevsky's anti-utopian vision of sickness, doubt and shadow, rejoicing in the bright autumn of 1937, the great twentieth year of the Revolution, when it was good to be alive, and the streets of Moscow were hung with banners, full of smiling faces and young love.

Our conductor on the train from Vologda the night before was a native of the communist north. Her eyes sparkled and she retained the same bustling dignity whether she was swabbing the lavatory with a frayed rag and a pail of cold water, or bringing glasses of tea to her passengers in *luxe*. A burly man, waved off by a weeping babushka, blundered up and down our carriage for the first hour of the journey, demanding a drink. Uncowed by his bulk and inebriation, the conductor pushed him back into his compartment. 'How much do you get paid for this?' he mumbled, lurching past our open door. 'Not enough to make it worth putting up with you!' she answered with another shove. At Kharovsk, she resorted to the highest measures and called up two militiamen, who marched the alcoholic (now limp with need) down the corridor and off the train. 'Arkhangelsk!?!? What are you going there for?' the conductor asked us as we left him sitting head in hands on the edge of the track. 'It's not like abroad, you know.' She mimed a spit over one shoulder. 'Arkhangelsk, phoo! Poverty! Filth! Slush! *Plague!*' I asked her where she liked best. 'Egypt,' she answered without missing a beat: '*Egipet.*' She had been to 'rest' – twice – at Hourghada on the Red Sea. 'Next time, Tunis!' she announced, turning down the corridor, chest upraised. 'Sophia Loren's favourite!'

Until after midnight, I read about the legendary northern kingdom of Biyarmia in a *Guide to the Russian North* that I had found in the antiquarian section of House of the Book, on the Arbat. Published in 1899 by the Archangel–Murmansk steamship company, 'at the request of the Ministry of Finance', the small red morocco book still conveyed the style and entrepreneurial exuberance of the late-nineteenth-century travel industry, the sense of what travel could do to civilise and extend the reach of the Russian state. In that year, the Moscow–Archangel railway line, financed by the great art patron Savva Mamontov, had just been completed, and a hostel had been built to accommodate the large numbers of pilgrims on their way to visit the monastery on the island of Solovki. Railways and steamships were opening undiscovered country to the 'scholar, the naturalist, the ethnographer, the artist, the professional traveller, the hunter, the pilgrim, the entrepreneur and the simple tourist', all of whom the guide invited to discover 'our mysterious north', the vast Archangel region, where only 350,000 people, almost all of them peasants, inhabited a region of virgin tundra and swamp, of rivers and lakes, one and a half times the size of France. The original owner of the guide (whose name was Konstantin Belyachevsky) had pencilled 'NB' beside the price of a second-class fare from Archangel to Suma, where 'Suomi' (Finns) still lived, and an exclamation mark beside a passage about the delightful islands and villages in the Dvina delta where indigenous wooden 'tent' churches rise up from the landscape like creations of nature. I envied Belyachevsky his journey, the excitement of seeing the brand-new electric lighting at the stations along the line.

I did not tell the conductor, when she came to wake us in her brass-buttoned uniform and fresh lipstick, that it was the words 'Archangel 1944', written in faint blue ink in the set of Pushkin I took from Sands, that had given her city its gravitational pull. I wanted a clearer picture of the young officer in the indigent bombarded city, where the people who had not starved had lived on wild food foraged in the woods, before the ships came in from Scotland and Iceland, bringing chubby tins of Spam, jars of sausage, and Quaker sugar in sacks labelled 'Pennsylvania' and 'Buffalo'. Did Sands find his Pushkin at some impromptu roadside stall, where the sorrowful people of Archangel sold broken crockery, children's toys and precious books, while loudspeakers in the street played martial hymns and speeches calling them to fight to the death? Did he make his learned annotations on the text of *Eugene Onegin* here, I wondered, in the British Mission on Trade Union Street when the nights were white, or years later, in a pool of lamplight in his Cambridge rooms after dinner at High Table?

'The time has not yet come to count the lives saved by this wheat from beyond the sea,' Shalamov wrote in his Kolyma tale 'Lend-Lease'. Then the time did come. I had brought with me to Archangel another of Sands's books: *The Northern Convoys*, published in 1991 in commemoration of the arrival in Archangel fifty years earlier of the first of the aid convoys, code-named Dervish, which the editor called the 'first friendly handshake between Great Britain and Soviet Russia since 1918'. Folded inside was a typed letter. 'Respected Dr Sands,' it began, 'the historians of Archangel, together with colleagues from Norway, England and America propose to publish a series of memoirs under the working title *War in the North*.' Their aim was to clear away some of the one-sidedness of Soviet historiography, which had diminished the significance of Allied aid. The historians from the Lomonosov Pedagogical Institute on Lomonosov Avenue asked the now dying Sands (who never wrote for publication) for a memoir of his war: ten to fifteen typed pages, 'photographs (glossy) would be especially appreciated'. Through the long decades of the Cold War, the heroic story of the convoys had been out of bounds, but the historians on Lomonosov Avenue had kept their records, awaiting the day when they could ask for memories and images from beyond the sea.

One British naval lieutenant (who, like Sands, went on to become a Russian fellow in an Oxbridge college) remembered the tact of the local authorities in wartime Archangel, who, before the British came ashore, had boxed up in wood the captured British tank that had served since 1918 as a monument to the failure of the Intervention. He shared his impressions of what Churchill had called the 'sullen sinister Bolshevik state', describing a 'Lenin evening' in Archangel. 'The spirit of Lenin is everywhere,' a speaker had intoned, convincing the lieutenant that the Lenin cult was essentially religious, an insight that directed the course of his research at Oxford after the war.

❧

In our days in Archangel, we gravitated towards the waterfront – like everyone else, it seemed, in the pale, quiet city – to watch the swirling ice. Space and distance are even more of a riddle here than time. It was impossible to get one's bearings. What are the physics of the river in spring? Sometimes the water rushed with ice all morning, then cleared into an ice-free flow of muscular brown water. By evening, the ice was back. One moment the industrial vistas across the water seemed close, the next, far off. By morning, washed in a deeper light, they had moved to another place altogether, as though the ice had shunted them out of the way. What looked a hundred miles away suddenly pulled close, and I could pick out the monuments of the Soviet industrialisation of the north: smokestacks, cranes and pylons in the grey-brown tableau of Kyarostrov and derricks on the quays of the shipbuilding island of Solombala. All this metal abrading the softness of the sky signalled at once the filthying of the air and the diminution of the human, and the transformation of cold dark geological matter, coal, into warmth and light.

Lenin and Stalin saw nothing in the north but savagery and empty space in which 'cultured states' could quickly be established. The Northern Region, a vast area stretching from Novgorod to the White Sea, was Molotov's first bureaucratic responsibility after the new Soviet state moved the seat of government from Petrograd to Moscow in 1918. It was in this position of responsibility for production, factories and nationalisation that he was able to see how much the reality of 'expropriating the expropriators' differed from Marx's idea on the page. During the First Five-Year Plan, for the anniversary of the Revolution, an obelisk of the north was erected in a square behind Archangel's waterfront, declaring in granite that the will of the proletariat, and its power and vigour, would 'transform this dark and backward region into a new industrialised north'. The power that industrialised the north combined the energy of genuine ideological and patriotic love with the power of the state over its slaves. The obelisk had taken the place of another vision of light in darkness, a statue of Mikhailo Lomonosov, the intellectual luminary from the north who transformed the culture of eighteenth-century Russia. The Lomonosov statue is famous in Archangel as a monument with no fixed place. Inspired by his own ode, 'Evening Thoughts on the Greatness of God at the Happening of the Great Northern

Lights', the bronze luminary has an expression of awe on his upturned face. Lyre in hand, dressed in Roman sandals and a toga, he stands on the northern half of a globe; on it is the word 'Kholmogor', the humble place where Lomonosov was born, son of a northern fisherman, in a village which is almost washed away each spring. If Archangel could be compared to a person, it would be Lomonosov, Dmitri Likhachev said: a poor boy raised in the rich soil of his native culture, educated first by the Church and then in Germany, in the centres of the European Enlightenment. Lomonosov, who was sure that the Russian future lay in the exploration of Siberia and the Arctic, educated himself to endure the cold too, not by wearing a toga in winter, but by sleeping with his windows open through the coldest nights.

A group of runners in thin tracksuits and woollen hats came out every evening, running past the Arcades and the Palace of Culture, where the Trinity Cathedral stood before it was disassembled during the First Five-Year Plan and its materials recycled by Severoles, the northern forestry company. A loudspeaker is still rigged up on the Palace of Culture to broadcast into the street. The *subbotniks* of spring, days when people come out voluntarily to clean the city, happen at the same time as the ice-flow. Within a few hours, every concrete litter bin along the embankment had been repainted lilac, and the black and yellow beach umbrellas on the dark sand of the beach were restored to apiary brightness. Mothers walked their babies, moving slowly, stopping often to watch the ice. From the open windows of an old wooden mansion, School of Music and Performing Arts No. 42, came the sound of three pianos and a cello and the voice of a teacher, counting time. Seagulls called. Down below the embankment, in the broken hulls of abandoned rowing boats, there was still clean white ice, and driftwood so warped by the sea that it looked like dirty cloth. In the frozen puddles, the melt was grimed, oily substances blending in the ice, creating rainbow slicks. Every colour, whatever its source or substance, seemed precious in the pallor of this place. Parts of the promenade had slipped unchecked into the Dvina, forming little pools dammed with broken concrete where cigarette ends, fish cans and beer bottles swayed in the lacy foam. Outside the Hotel Pur-Navolok, the pennants of the oil company Rosneft and the diamond mining company Alrosa flapped in the wind beside the Russian tricolor.

Of the grand and melancholy neoclassical buildings that faced the Dvina, my favourite was the derelict Girls' Gymnasium, founded in 1811 for the centenary of Lomonosov. What a sign of enlightenment, this magnificent white neoclassical building, straddling the street corner with such proud symmetry, in which young girls were educated on the classical German model. Its windows were dark now, many of their panes broken. Graffitied in English on a wall were the words 'Know Your Rights!' If I were the mayor of this city, I thought, at this precarious moment of opportunity, when financiers in Moscow say that Russia is 'afloat on a sea of liquidity', I would ask Alrosa or Rosneft to fund the restoration of the school. But Archangel's popular mayor was in prison, having been arrested on corruption charges soon after announcing his plan to run for the presidency against Putin's appointed heir.

This waterfront with its once wooden embankments was built to greet foreign ships, to display their comings and goings as the very pride of the city, water showing itself to town and town to water, in the manner of a seventeenth-century engraving of Antwerp, Dresden or London. The Arcades, built when Arch-angel was Russia's only seaport as the architectural centrepiece of the city, now stand alone on the headland. Though most of the vast original structure of the Arcades has been demolished or crumbled into ruins, a small inner section has recently been exquisitely restored to house part of the regional museum. In it is a 'Lomonosov room', displaying the school workbooks of Archangel's greatest son, and an ingenious splinter lamp by which he studied at night. For the second half of the seventeenth century, before Archangel yielded its place to St Petersburg as a cosmopolitan 'window on Europe', the brick Arcades showed the foreign merchants who came to deal in linen and fur the power and solidity of the Russian state, and its love for trade.

It was here, in 1553, that Hugh Willoughby and Richard Chancellor of the Mystery Company and Fellowship of Merchant Adventurers for the Discovery of Unknown Lands 'discovered Russia' as they journeyed on their ship, the *Edward Bonaventure*, in search of the north-east passage to India and Cathay. With all the recording passion of nations in their prime, Willoughby and Chancellor logged each day and night of their voyage, noting lands, elements and tides, the moon's course, the arrangement of the stars and the height of the sun. Their log-book was the first of its kind. The English seafarers weighed anchor opposite the fifteenth-century monastery of St Nicholas (where the nuclear-submarine works at Severodvinsk, formerly Molotovsk, now lie), naming the White Sea 'St Nicholas Bay' on their maps. Chancellor went south to Moscow and met the Ivan 'the Terrible', who quickly became an Anglomane and gave exclusive trading privileges to Chancellor's company, the Muscovy Company. Willoughby continued his voyage, reaching the long narrow island of Novaya Zemlya just above the Russian mainland before dying with his crew as they wintered in Lapland.

The effect of Archangel on the imagination is almost clinical. It is a place for stowaways and adventurers, locals say, for people who long for freshness, to see the way the sea bleaches rock and wood, to imagine making voyages of their own to the summit of the planet. At this latitude, the North Pole itself exerts a powerful gravitational pull. When Mamontov built the railway, his pro-tégés, the painters Valentin Serov and Konstantin Korovin, came north to paint the landscape and the people. But the dreams of their contemporary, the painter Alexander Borisov, were of venturing further north, of going 'up' from Archangel. We were the only visitors in the city's small, lovingly tended Borisov Museum, an old timber house where fishing nets and plastic seagulls have been hung on the ceilings, and a tape plays the calls of Arctic birds. The son of a peasant from the North Dvina, Borisov took a rocking chair, a bearskin and a chestful of brushes, canvas and paint, and went to live in a hut on Novaya Zemlya. (My painter companion was enraptured by the story of this adventure for art's sake.) His boat, the *Mechta* ('Dream'), was a copy of the *Fram*, the ship the Norwegian explorer Fridtjof Nansen had built for his journey to the Pole, with an egg-shaped hull that levitates evasively in the moving ice so as not to be crushed. The Moscow journalist Vladimir Gilyarovsky found himself staring at Borisov's vast polar landscape *Kingdom of Death* for over an hour. Gilyarovsky, great connoisseur of human character, was amazed by Borisov's daredevil toughness for the sake of art, his ability to keep a paintbrush in his grip at forty degrees below zero. Once, after watching his dogs die in the freezing sea, Borisov spent nine days and nights on a broken iceberg, spreading his body weight so as to keep the ice intact. In 1907, in Paris, Vienna and Berlin, he exhibited his sublime images of ice and snow in all their infinite coloration, of wrecked boats, lurid Arctic skies and the huts of the Samoyeds on Novaya Zemlya. Before the Revolution, Borisov was involved in a plan to build a railway linking northern Europe with Siberia, along which the station buildings would be designed by well-known artists.

After the Borisov Museum, we ate in a log-cabin restaurant in the restored hostel of the Solovetsky Monastery: salmon and cod baked in clay pots with potatoes and sour cream, buttery blini with honey and curd cheese. Then we went to the old Lutheran church which now houses the local Philharmonia and spent the evening watching old ladies in *sarafans* and golden *kokoshniks* singing northern folk songs and dancing with vigorous old men in knee-high chamois boots. Before each song a statuesque announcer in a black-and-silver evening gown and elbow-length gloves delivered a short lecture on its regional pecularities, extolling the oral village culture which had kept the songs alive. In the interval we bought their homemade *kazuly*, spice biscuits in the shapes of reindeers and bears.

Were these songs that Likhachev heard when he first visited the north on a month-long school trip in the summer of 1921 and decided that this must be the most beautiful part of the planet? People should travel to the Russian north, he wrote, to experience its healing moral strength just as they travel to Italy to experience the healing moral strength of the European south. In the way that water, earth and sky combined with the terrible strength of stone, storm and cold, he perceived an encounter, whose drama astonished him, between past and present, man and nature, contemporaneity and history. And of all histories, Likhachev believed Russia's to be the most significant, the most tragic, the most philosophical.

The schoolboys in Likhachev's party travelled by rail from Petrograd to the just-built city of Murmansk, then by steamyacht around the Kola Peninsula on the Barents Sea into the White Sea and down the Dvina Lip past Severodvinsk to Archangel, from where they took a river steamer down to Kotlas, before returning to Petrograd by rail. Sunset turned instantly into dawn, the colours of the water and the sky changed with every passing minute, there were virgin forests and tundra and waters that ran with strong fish. The scene was made sacred with churches and hermitages and shrines, filled with signs of the prayerfulness of the ascetics who had made the landscape itself their cathedral. Likhachev loved the trace of human touch in the wild, the sense it gave him of what his own tortured nation could create.

The city children visited Pomors in their huts, listening to their songs and fairy tales. The hunters and fishermen were beautiful, Likhachev remembered; their way of life seemed uniquely authentic: measured and light, a rhythm of labour and the simple satisfactions of labour, the comforts of houses made of wood, and bedcovers of eiderdown. Later, Likhachev came to see the far north as the most Russian part of Russia. Slavs had arrived from the west and south at the end of the tenth century, settling along riverbanks, mixing with more ancient peoples: Nenets and Sami. Under the Mongols, more Russians drifted north from Novgorod.

There was less serfdom than further south, and the fairy-tale landscape of dark, endless forest invited the possibility of disappearance and escape. The north had preserved a tradition of freedom for Russia, Likhachev believed, and had saved the nation in its most terrible times: during the Polish-Swedish intervention of the early eighteenth century, and during the two world wars of the twentieth. The region also saved from oblivion the culture of Novgorod, whose colonies extended into the Archangel region, preserving the oral culture of folk epics (*bylini*), fairy tales and song, as well as wooden architecture, handicrafts and the skills of boat-building, fishing and polar exploration.

Likhachev perceived the northern landscape as otherworldly, just a step from paradise or hell. When in 1929 he returned to the north as a political prisoner in the first Soviet Gulag on the Solovki archipelago in the White Sea, he found himself sitting on a rock in the sun, sensing God, present but unknowable. At that moment, a camp guard who would, in the ordinary course of things, have shot the stray prisoner, lowered his gun.

Shalamov spent much longer than Likhachev in the hell that the Soviets created in the Russian north, in the infinitely crueller Arctic landscape of Kolyma over three thousand miles to the east. (On the mineral wealth of Kolyma, Molotov commented to Chuev, 'We found just the country for socialism. Everything is here, you just have to look for it! And you can find whatever you want.') 'I gave away twenty years of my life to the north,' Shalamov told Pasternak in 1956; 'for years I never held a book in my hands, nor touched a leaf of paper or a pencil.' He turned away from the God that Likhachev shared with the medieval ascetics, perceiving the landscape itself as filled with spirit and intention. 'Even a stone did not appear dead to me, nor the grass, the trees, the river,' he wrote. 'The river was not only the incarnation of life, not just a symbol of life, but life itself. It possessed eternal movement, a calm, a silent and secret language of its own . . .' He turned the landscape that tortured him into something he could love: a book. The permafrost and the stone, he wrote, will never forget. Shalamov reduced the understanding of self until there was nothing left in it but the idea of writing, the trace. Even the name tag on a prisoner's foot in a mass grave was a kind of literature. In the north, he found substances that last longer than the ink with which death sentences are signed by men like Molotov, whose own initials 'V.M.' were the same as the acronym for the death penalty: *vysshaya mera*, highest measure. Graphite, the only writing instrument the *zeks* (the convicts) were allowed, is 'eternity, the highest standard of hardness become the highest standard of softness', Shalamov writes; graphite is a greater miracle than a diamond, whose chemical make-up is identical.

Four-hundred-year-old memories of welcoming ships from abroad, ancient northern memories of freedom and the sensibilities of quiet scholars like Likhachev combine in this poor city's particular tact about the past and other foreign places. It was tact which made the city authorities box up its captured British tank in 1941 so as not to offend men like Sands. It was tact which led the city's historians to ask him for his memoirs fifty years later. The historical tact at work in the exhibition halls of the regional museum was of a far more costly kind. With a frankness and inventiveness that I have not encountered in any other Russian city, the museum laid out the story of the forced resettlement of the kulaks (46,261 families deported north to hellish 'special settlements' along the railway line) and the Gulag camps where slaves logged the forests till they died of hunger, disease and exhaustion. 'We have never refuted the fact that healthy prisoners capable of normal labour are used for road and other public works,' Molotov told the Congress of Soviets in 1931; 'this is very good for society. It is also good for the prisoners themselves . . .' In that year, almost two million peasants were deported to 'special settlements'. Lining the walls of the main staircase of the museum at eye level were photographs of local victims of 'repression': Anton Minaev, from the Department of Finance of the Northern Region, repressed in 1937, died in Magadan in 1940; Vasili

Gorokhov, first rector of the Technical University, shot on 22 April 1938; Dmitri Nikitin, Tolstoy's personal doctor, and Professor Boris Rosing, 'inventor of the television', deported to the Archangel region, died 1933. 'In late 1937 and early 1938', a small notice says, 'there was an almost complete purge of the leadership of the Archangel region: many honest workers were condemned; thousands of people who were guilty of nothing were repressed.'

As I looked at their blotched black-and-white faces, I thought of Shalamov's 'Lend-Lease', in which, near some Arctic mine hidden in the folds of a mountain, in the landscape that can hide and reveal so much, an American bulldozer appears (bringing a new word into the Russian language) with the tractors and Studebakers and spam 'from beyond the ocean . . .' Planes and tanks and machines were of infinitely greater importance to the state than people, Shalamov writes. While the camp authorites fought over the food, the convicts were so hungry they ate the machine grease from the bulldozer, convincing themselves it was American butter: 'foreign joy that tasted like a young stone'. (The taste of young stone? Is there comfort to the senses in thinking in geological time?) And this particular 'symbol of victory, friendship and something else' had a blade like a mirror, which was used efficiently, driven by a common criminal ('a parricide, to be precise') named Grinya Lebedev, who was proud to fulfil his duty to the state, to scrape the bodies of Gulag prisoners into a mass grave: a 'stone pit filled with the undecaying corpses of 1938 . . . sliding down the hill, revealing the secret of Kolyma', thousands of bodies, which the unforgetting permafrost resisted 'with all its strength', bodies frozen and preserved, 'curled fingers, rotten toes, turned to stumps by frostbite, eyes still burning with the gleam of hunger'.

❧

On our last day, we drove out of Archangel, past rotting log houses on muddy streets with wooden pavements, to Malye Korely, an outdoor museum of wooden architecture, and walked in the sunshine among churches with fish-scaled tent roofs and carved log houses brought here for preservation from all over the Russian north. A bride and groom in a horse and carriage were driven several times around the circular road through the forest as bells rang from one of the old churchtowers. The bride's veil blew back in the wind, she laughed, her wedding party cheered and held out plastic cups of champagne, and the chimes sounded mad with nuptial glee.

Our train was to leave around midnight, so we went to eat baked fish and blini at the Solovetsky Hostel and wander on the waterfront again. A small group of young clubbers was waiting for the *USSR* to open, boys in their mid-teens with mulish laughs, smoking and drinking Baltika beer, leaning on the busts of Otto Shmidt and the pre-revolutionary seafarer Georgy Sedov. In 1936, Shmidt's words reached as far as Trotsky in exile. '"The better part of our youth", the well-known polar explorer Shmidt said recently, "are eager to work where difficulties await them,"' Trotsky wrote in *The Revolution Betrayed* in 1936. 'This is undoubtedly true,' he continued. 'But in all spheres the post-revolutionary generation is still under guardianship. They are told from above what to do, and how to do it.'

The busts of Shmidt and Sedov made a poignant ensemble. The ship in which Shmidt sailed from Archangel to Franz Josef Land on his first great navigation to declare the island a forepost of the USSR was named the *Georgy Sedov*. On one of his Arctic navigations, Shmidt had hoped to bring Sedov's remains back to Archangel. The son of an Azov fisherman, educated at a naval school in Rostov-on-Don, Sedov had tried to reach the North Pole overland with three dogsleds. Having miscalculated the distance by a factor of ten, he died on the sea ice. His *Travels to Kolyma and Novaya Zemlya* were published after his death in the year of the Revolution. In the Soviet era, Sedov's tragedy was used to illustrate the cruelty and chaos of capitalism. When he had tried to finance a voyage in search of a northern sea-route to the east, the Archangel merchants had double-crossed him (selling him a ship sabotaged for insurance fraud), and the state treasury had refused him funds. 'All the Russian people have to give is a little money', Sedov pleaded, 'and I will give my life.' The collectivist society would not have betrayed such dreams of discovery and conquest. Shmidt could not find Sedov's body; his burial place had been washed away.

The old system may have failed Sedov, but what did it really mean for a polar explorer and scientist like Shmidt to live so 'close to the Kremlin', so close to Stalin and Molotov? In old age, when Molotov used to like to draw floorplans of Stalin's dachas, he reminisced about the maps lining the walls of the corridor of his dacha at Kuntsevo. 'He liked wall maps,' Molotov said. 'Here was Asia. Here was Europe. We spent a lot of time there . . . he was interested in how to make use of the Arctic Ocean, the Siberian rivers, the treasures of Siberia . . .'

I had looked into Shmidt in the Lenin Library before coming to the north, and as the descriptions of his navigations led out into thrilling uncharted vistas of white space, they simultaneously seemed to lead into a dark tunnel. One of his books was an address of 1937 on Soviet plans for the Arctic, which talked of the conquest of the northern sea-route, the need for heavy industry in the far north, the necessity of gaining access to the mouths of the northern rivers, the new industrial centres at Kolyma and Norilsk, the ship-building feats at Murmansk and the success of the mines at Barentsburg on Spitsbergen. Yet, he said, there is no need to resettle millions in the north. It is harsh. Just enough to do the work. And they must be fed properly, the people in the north, with the freshest food, or they will not be able to work. Vegetables, he said, have a huge psychological significance. Anyone who has worked in the north knows the joy that every single leaf can give. We must have collective farms, hothouses near Norilsk. What was he really saying? In another of his books from the late 1930s I recognised an *ex libris* plate that I had seen before, in one of Vyshinsky's works on Soviet jurisprudence. From the library of the 'bibliopsychologist' Nikolai Rubakin (who must have bequeathed his books to the Lenin Library), the plate showed a Gothic arch at the end of a book-lined room, a book on a lectern and a human figure with arms outstretched to the sun, and said, *Long Live the Book, the most powerful weapon in the struggle for truth and justice!* The struggle for truth and justice . . . 1937 . . . the far north . . . What did the brilliant and courageous Shmidt know about the ways in which the unconquered Arctic was to be turned into a source of raw materials for the USSR?

I read the transcript of a 1938 radio show for children, set to Beethoven and Tchaikovsky, about Shmidt's heroic explorations, and leafed through a two-volume book, published in the same year, on the doomed voyage, four years earlier, of the *Chelyuskin*, on which Shmidt had set out from Murmansk to navigate the northern sea-route in a single summer. Data accumulates, page upon page: the number of fur trousers and undergarments each crew member took on board, the co-ordinates of every moment of the seven-month drift in the sea ice, every cloud that passes, every temperature change, and the endless motion of the ice in the Kara Sea that eventually crushed the ship and sunk it in the space of two hours in February 1934. The Arctic was an arena for politics. The *Chelyuskin* story signified the great humanity of collectivism. Every head was counted, even the dogs were saved – they were 'Soviet' dogs – and only one man died as the 101 survivors unloaded the ship. Shmidt's ice camp, in which the survivors lived until their heroic rescue by Soviet pilots, was a model of Soviet society: co-operative, optimistic, built on common labour, organised to perfection under a benign leader, who even stenogrammed a daily paper and lectured the shipwrecked on the poetry of Heinrich Heine and dialectical materialism.

Shmidt called revolutionary Marxism a 'living fire' which burned inside him. He wanted to fill in 'white spots' in science, to do away with the mysteries. He devoted the last years of his life to cosmogony, developing his own theory of the origins of the universe out of solar dust. He tried to reconcile Marxism with the theoretical challenges of quantum physics: the theory of relativity and the discovery of the 'inner freedom' of the electron. Matter can no longer be seen to act against the backdrop of space and time, he explained, for the 'new physics' reveals that time and space are interdependent, that time is altered by what it flows through, that time can alter the characteristics of space. How should a Marxist counter the 'pure idealists' who say that time and space exist only in our observation of them, and that there are as many worlds as there are observers? There was no experiment that would prove the truth of Marxist dialectical materialism, he concluded, unless it was the success of the workers' paradise that the Communist Party was trying to create on earth.

❧

When the recording mania of nations falls apart in wreckage and doubt, another search begins: the search for the places where the bodies lie buried, for a record of their names. After the fall of the USSR, in the heady years of Yeltsin's presidency, questions about the voyage of the *Chelyuskin* floated up from the undertows and conspiracy theories appeared in national newspapers and television shows. What had been the real purpose of the hastily prepared, ill-equipped expedition? Why were there women and children aboard? Why had Stalin refused all offers of help from abroad? Why was it never said that the *Chelyuskin* had been built in Copenhagen? Why had the two attempts to find and raise the wreck found no trace of the ship? Had a second ship sailed in convoy with the *Chelyuskin*? In 2004, after another attempt to find the *Chelyuskin*, the head of the Russian Submarine Museum, Alexei Mikhailov, concluded that the recorded data about the whereabouts of the ship were false. The conspiracy stories suggested that the *Chelyuskin* had been bound for Chukotka to prospect for minerals, accompanied by a slave ship, the *Pijma*, loaded with Gulag prisoners: kulaks, former NEP men, 'saboteurs', 'learned double-dealers', priests and Jewish radio-enthusiasts (foreign spies by definition), under guard by members of the NKVD following orders from the Lubyanka. In 2006, divers from an expedition led by Mikhailov, and partially sponsored by Roman Abramovich, billionaire governor of Chukotka, finally discovered the wreck of the *Chelyuskin* fifty metres deep; they raised a few fragments of the ship, and the memory of the Soviet Union's 'happiest year'.

⤜⤛

I returned from Archangel to Moscow to banners across Vozdvizhenka commemorating Shmidt's drifting polar research station: '1937–2007 – the North Pole!' Not long afterwards, the Russian government announced to an astonished world that it had dropped a flag on to the seabed under the Pole and declared it Russian territory, on account of a ridge on the seabed – the Lomonosov Ridge – that is said to connect the mainland with the Pole. If the polar sea ice does retreat, the colossal untapped stores of oil, gas and minerals below present the prospect of riches unimaginable for the Kremlin. There were incidental rumours about a more cryptic geopolitics floating among journalists at Moscow dinner parties, claiming that President Putin had asked to have a piece of the polar seabed brought back for him, as one of the entrances to the underground kingdom of Shambhala in the hollow earth is believed to lie beneath the Pole.

TWELVE

Murmansk and Barentsburg

Draw the blanket of ocean
Over the frozen face.
He lies, his eyes quarried by glittering fish,
Staring through the green freezing sea-glass
At the Northern Lights.
CHARLES CAUSLEY, 'Convoy'

There was a time in the history of the Arktika Hotel when a drunken Russian could be taken outside and shot for assailing the honour of the British. Back then in 1942, not long before the hotel was blitzed to rubble by the Luftwaffe, its dining room was filled with Soviet naval officers and voyage-worn Allied servicemen come ashore from the convoy ships. The summary execution, one evening, of the Russian sailor who had jeered at the loyal toast to King George VI must have seemed to the subordinates of Generalissimo Stalin no more than an appropriate token of respect, bound to please their new comrades-in-arms. But for my companion and me, nearly sixty years later, the only recourse was a quick retreat from the Arktika's otherwise empty dining room as the larger of the two men at the next table, registering that the slurred proposition he had advanced had been met with an impregnable wall of ice, bent forward, and with the slow delibera-tion of the deeply drunk, spewed a lump of chewed fish on to the white linen cloth, laid down his head and fell asleep.

I suppose two white nights and a day spent reading memoirs of the convoys on the train from Moscow (which was also called the Arktika) had disposed me to think and dream about the war, to find in even a sordid encounter in a run-down hotel some hidden reminiscence of the years when the city showed the outside world its most sinister and heroic front. And after all, I had been drawn

[297]

to the Kola Peninsula by the black-and-white wartime picture, an image of austere gallantry, labelled 'Murmansk 1942' in copperplate hand, words charged with the excitement of far distance, that I found that hot afternoon at the bottom of an old box, its cardboard sides weakened and bloated by decades' worth of governing body minutes and university bulletins, in the college rooms of Sands.

In the tundra of the Kola lurks the world's greatest concentration of military and naval forces, and in its waters, battleships and ballistic nuclear submarines capable of sending missiles across the North Pole to annihilate large areas of the United States. Murmansk is a city built and rebuilt in a spirit of battle, a community whose memory and imagination were formed when enemies were real and present: over the Norwegian border – just a few minutes' flight for a Heinkel 111 – or slinking invisibly along the Barents seabed, loaded with torpedoes. Sculpted bodies of young men killed in uniform, images of the Russian soldier crucified and resurrected, are the icons of this city. One block down Lenin Avenue from the Arktika is a dynamic bronze of Anatoly Bredov, seconds before his sacrificial death, pulling the pin from the grenade that will blow him to pieces along with the German troops who surround him. And massive on a hill above the city stands 'Alyosha', an unknown soldier in moulded concrete. Looming in and out of view in the sea mist, he stands guard, pantoscopically gazing down at the rusting fishing and cargo ports, at the red-and-black nuclear-powered ice-breakers in their graving dock, and the passenger ferries plying back and forth to the closed town of Abram-Mys on the other side of the inlet.

Places disperse in images that come to form their identity. I had first seen concrete 'Alyosha' from another angle, in a monochrome photograph taken from a hill above Murmansk by the great Tass war photographer Evgeny Khaldei. I visited the retrospective exhibition of his work in the House of Photography on Moscow's Nikitsky Boulevard soon after we moved into Romanov. Khaldei's genius was to find composition in scenes of fear and destruction. He caught the tension in the faces of a group of people on a

Moscow street listening to Molotov announcing the Nazi invasion through a loudspeaker – 'a perfidy unparalleled in the history of civilised nations' – just as he caught the fear in the turn of a reindeer's head. His most famous image is the Red Army soldier planting the Soviet flag on the Reichstag, planting his own straining form among the stone statues still standing on the fire-blackened roof, as the rubble of Berlin smoked in the background. (It is said that Khaldei had to doctor the picture before it was published, as the soldier was wearing several watches.) Khaldei's pictures record, and are part of, the process by which Soviet consciousness was formed out of the epic of the nation's near-destruction and astonishing victory. Khaldei began his photographic record of the war in Murmansk in the June weeks after the German invasion, experiencing his first aerial bombardment on the rail journey from Moscow. At the exhibition I bought an album entitled *From Murmansk to Berlin*, and on my way home I stopped in at Intertour Luxe, the travel agency in the basement of our building, to ask for the times of trains to Murmansk, a city whose mere name had stirred me so powerfully in Cambridge.

Khaldei's Murmansk photographs are images of terrible beauty. His lens absorbed the strange mineral gleam of the Kola in the shimmering reflections of seven caped and helmeted soldiers trudging past a pool of still water on the rocky shore. Light catches the dark skin of the Jewish submariner-poet Israel Firsanovich, and his brow and cheekbones in burnished profile like the medals on his chest and the gold band around his tobacco-pipe, a portrait in the open air, the iridescent air of the Arctic circle. A close-up, taken from a gundeck, stills a plume of exploding water, as the Soviet star strains against the force of the blast on a flag in the foreground, and the snow-webbed hills of Kola behind, under a layer of low clouds as black as the sea, in which the bombers hid. The Kola hills, formed two or three billion years ago, are some of the oldest on the planet, but the scars of war became part of their geological composition. War discomposes nature as it destroys cities. On Fisherman's Peninsula, the granite outcrop that juts into the Barents just above the Norwegian border, Khaldei caught the moment when a reindeer, its antlers in perfect silhouette beside the last branches of a scorched tree, turned its head towards the five planes in the sky behind, alert and frozen in confusion, against a backdrop of shattering rocks, deciding which way to run. (He later admitted that this photo was a montage.) There was nowhere on Fisherman's Peninsula for the troops to dig in, Khaldei remembered. He photographs a group of soldiers clambering up a lichened rock face, absolutely exposed to the menacing clarity of the sky. As his fellow war reporter, the Stalinist poet Konstantin Simonov, wrote in one of his patriotic Murmansk war lyrics, 'the fighters, pressed against the ice and the rock breast, / Spend the night in the crags of Musta-Tunturi'.

And there, in Khaldei's collection, was Murmansk in 1942, where Sands had come ashore from his ship bearing Lend-Lease matériel just as the Nazis decided to obliterate the city with their incendiary and high-explosive bombs. Built of wood, half the houses in Murmansk burned immediately to ash, leaving nothing but their slim brick chimneys, forming a smoking landscape of solemn vertical structures. An old woman carrying a wooden suitcase on her back made fierce eye contact with the lens as she crossed the scene of ruin. She put down the wooden suitcase, Khaldei recalled, and said, 'Why are you taking pictures of my grief and our misfortune, little son?'

❦

Even in the years between 1916, when Romanov-on-the-Murman was founded at British request as a military supply port, and 1941, when the city, long since renamed Murmansk, became one of the most crucial fronts of the war, the Kola Peninsula had little sense of peace. 'We always felt we were at the front in this city of endless day and endless night, of strange snowstorms and startling colours,' remembered the poet Lev Oshanin, who travelled north from Moscow during the First Five-Year Plan to join in the construction of a chemical-mining plant at Apatity in the Khibin Mountains. His Stalinist hymn, 'Comrade Apatit', is addressed to that 'stone of fertility', an ore used to produce phosphorous fertilisers. Apatit takes its name from the Greek word *apate*, meaning 'deceit'; it is a fool's gold. Oshanin's poem imagines the creation of a new world, built and settled 'in our own way' on the 'naked earth' of the Russian north, setting the energy of socialist man against the inertia of nature. In place of the rawhide tents of the hunter-gatherer native tribes, the Sami and the Pomors, the Young Pioneers will build 'palaces' of stone. Exulting in the power of the ammonal explosions that 'tear at the rock' and 'destroy the terrible peace of the Khibin Mountains', they will take the virgin Kola by storm,

> *ploughing up the breast of the earth,*
> *Carrying the name of Kirov,*
> *Like blood in our hearts . . .*

Like the vengeful anti-Nazi war poetry that Simonov and Ilya Ehrenburg composed a decade later, Oshanin's verse is instinct with the slogans of state propaganda and the hot blood of mass rape.

Landscapes rarely express the moral experiences that have shaped them as starkly as the gouged mountains and poisoned tundra of the Kola. Occasionally, we passed an old woman at work on a vegetable plot, or a group of blond children in grubby clothes, leaning over a fence to watch the train pass. We stopped at Apatity, and women on the platform offered dried fish hung on wire coathangers. Freight cars lay in the sidings, loaded with rocks. Seagulls walked the telegraph wires. We sat all that June evening in the restaurant car; the train was, by now, a relaxed society, overwarm and smelling of tinned meat, axle grease and socks. After we had eaten, my companion moved the vase of plastic chrysanthemums to the edge of the table and took out her sketch-book, seeking form in the dissolving landscape of sky, water and trees, while I stared out of the window at the telegraph wires reeling away into the swamps. At around midnight we reached Belomorsk at the mouth of the White Sea and the sun rolled slowly across the horizon from west to east.

The Murmansk line 'was born in the smoke and fire of world war', the reporter Zinaida Richter wrote in her NEP-era travel-ogue, *Beyond the Arctic Circle*. Its first passengers were troops, its first freight, heavy weapons and explosives. It was built at great speed by Chinese migrant workers from Vladivostok, workers from Archangel and prisoners of war. Already in 1925, it was said of the Murmansk line (as is said of St Petersburg and Stalin's White Sea Canal) that there were bodies in its foundations, pris-oners and workers, that the edifice is also a tomb. Richter thought it looked unfinished compared to the other railway lines, quite unlike them. The railway buildings looked as flimsy as dachas, and there was no electricity on the platforms. The stations in the tun-dra were lit with kerosene lamps that made them look mysterious. After the Leningrad station, all the passengers were business people, NEP men: industrialists, traders, co-operative men, in-spectors, merchants, factory owners. She wondered what the railway workers made of the restaurant car of the train as it passed, with its white linen, flowers, bottles and stacks of pies, coming shining out of the snowy tundra and disappearing again, the train as a herald, a carrier of distant civilisation into the wild. She tried to compare the sky colours of the Arctic with daybreak over the Kremlin, but quickly turned away in contempt from all the 'iris, mother-of-pearl and such-like literary requisite'. The biggest new population along the way was in a town named after the recently deceased 'Comrade Dzerzhinsky', she noted with pride. Now the railway line clings to the route of the White Sea Canal, another triumph of Stalin's will, celebrated by Soviet writers, led by Gorky, in hyperbolic propaganda, built by Gulag slave labourers so that a submarine assembled in Leningrad could, without leaving Russia, travel by water to join the Northern Fleet.

Richter's travel writing, which took her in every direction across Soviet territory, is like Kushner's report on his journey south: part of the work of making Soviet space come together, of telling people in Moscow how people in the far reaches live and think. Richter talks proudly about the colonisation of the region, as yet in its early days, which is transforming the tundra, still the home of Lopars and Samoyeds, with their witch doctors and shamans, into a Klondike. Murmansk is a young town, she says; it 'arose only ten years ago because of war'. She describes its little tin houses, known as 'food boxes', left over from the years of the occupation, and the new bright green premises of the Fishing Trust. The main pastime in Murmansk used to be drinking at home, Richter says, but now that restaurants have opened under NEP people drink in public. (In the north, people have always drunk to oblivion, she notes.) The people she talks to in Murmansk all hope that the railway will mean that outsiders no longer look at them through a telescope. The locals do not wear fur because the Gulf Stream makes the winters mild. The 'Romanov half-fur' which Richter bought for her visit to Murmansk might just as well have stayed in the Leather Trust on Tverskaya Street. She meets Professor Kluge, a 'hero of labour', who runs the Murmansk Biological Station, and he goes round all year in a sea raincoat over a leather vest. (Professor Herman Kluge, an expert on bryozoans, ran the Biological Station, turning it into a prestigious research centre, until his arrest in 1933, when the Biological Station was broken up by the secret police. At the time when the physiologist Ivan Pavlov was petitioning Molotov for the release of intellectuals arrested in the aftermath of the Kirov murder, Professor Kluge was suddenly released from prison and exiled from Leningrad. He made his way up to the island of Novaya Zemlya, where he lived for eighteen months, close to the bryozoans, remote from the purges.)

Two months after my rail journey to Murmansk, in the company of a press pack, parents of seven of the submariners already dead inside the *Kursk* would take this same route towards the Arctic to be closer to their sons. The news photos of those men and women and the fragments of their speech reported in the papers are mixed now with my own incidental memories. The *Kursk*, a ballistic nuclear submarine the length of two Boeing 747s, designed to elude detection in the complex acoustic theatre of the Arctic seas, dived uncontrolled to the seabed during war games in August 2000, after two massive internal explosions. Its 118-man crew perished. For many days it was believed that a few might have remained alive in the aft of the submarine. It was on the Kola Peninsula that President Putin first turned his rage on a critical press, which was seeking the reasons for the disaster and the truth behind the official dithering, cover-up and possibly fatal delay in accepting offers of foreign assistance. These particular unnecessary deaths, widely seen as the nemesis of a superpower, seem also to constitute an exemplary tragedy for this remote city, a place at once dignified and seedy, whose public expressions are tugged between, on one side, xenophobic paranoia, pride in a violent past and the numerical manias of propaganda-tuned patriotism and, on the other, openness, ecological humility and genuine civic hope.

Regional museums in provincial Russian cities are not arranged for occasional foreign visitors so much as for the pallid teenagers who are always shuffling in sullen groups one hall ahead of you. These account for the 120,000 visitors who, as the guide will relate, annually come to observe its 140,000 exhibits. The Murmansk version of this model follows a standard teleology from mollusc to Marxist man. In the twilight of the first room, branches of soft coral and hairy sea-worms glow in jars of formaldehyde around a contoured plaster model of the bed of the Barents Sea. The other halls on the ground floor display specimens of the 600 mushroom genera and 540 varieties of moss that grow among the 2,700 million-year-old granite boulders of the Kola.

Past glass-eyed Arctic foxes, gulls and storm-petrels perched on plaster cliffs, visitors are led upstairs through rooms decorated with replicas of Sami wigwams, bearskin overalls and woven willow cradles, into the sudden drama of the Revolution Room with its red banners, guns and scenes of surging proletarians. Then a wide corridor leads on to the Great Patriotic War, evoked by anti-aircraft guns, framed billets-doux, stilled black-and-white footage and the demob papers, signed by Stalin and Marshal Zhukov, of one Ivan Ivanovich Shumilov, one of the millions of 'Ivans', who fought his way from Murmansk to the Reichstag. The only snag in the thread of this narrative of natural selection, human progress and patriotic sacrifice occurs in the space between these last two rooms: a tiny typed list on yellow paper, like an old train timetable, of the locations of Kola's twenty-three Gulags: Kandalaksha, Khibin, Apatity, Kirovsk . . .

The Naval Museum of the Northern Fleet is less generic, more dashing and elegiac than the Regional Museum, and there is more to buy: such as an anthology of local 'artistic-marinistics' – quatrains about flotillas of ice-breakers 'cutting the hard breast of the sea like brontosauri of the stone age'. For five dollars, we had pressed on us from under the counter a photo of a vast metal slug called the *Kursk*, lying in berth against a backdrop of snow-seamed grey hills, and the now famous snapshot of a stern Putin in the astrakhan shapka of the Fleet. And, for as many roubles, I picked up a special issue of a 'scientific and practical' local magazine called *Learning and Business on the Murman*, filled with factory-to-seabed biographies of Second World War submariners lost in action, and heroic captains such as the Dagestani Magomet Gadzhiev, or Israel Firsanovich, the Jewish submariner-poet with the pipe and the beautiful profile, who, before his sub was hit by British friendly fire in 1944, wrote that

> *There is no higher happiness than the struggle with enemies,*
> *No fighters braver than submariners,*
> *And no firmer soil beneath our feet*
> *Than the deck of a submarine.*

Now, it seemed, the only enemy in the sights of the Museum of the Northern Fleet lurked three thousand miles to the south, in a landlocked mountain republic. The final cabinet in the museum displayed a torn fragment of unrecognisable script which, the curator informed us, was a terrorists' scorecard, seized in Chechnya, of Russian soldiers mutilated and killed in captivity; an anticipation, I guess, of one of the many Russian rumours about the role of 'enemies' in the sinking of the *Kursk*, that it was the two Dagestanis on board who sabotaged the submarine. But allies past and present also had a place here. There was no hint, in the pictures of them sitting smoking on the granite hills of the Kola with their Soviet counterparts, of just how squalid and strange the British servicemen found Murmansk when they finally arrived with their shipments of matériel. And now again, as plankton seethed through the bodies of its sons, Murmansk waited for technology from abroad that would raise them into the air and bring them home.

There was no night in Murmansk, so after we had eaten in a louche restaurant in the ferry port overlooking a passenger boat called the *Anna Akhmatova*, we walked back through the town under white cloud, following the line of the waterfront. We wandered into the docks, past the Fish Kombinat, unremarked by the guard in his metal booth. Once part of the commissariat of Molotov's wife, Polina Zhemchuzhina, the fisheries buildings in Murmansk were now in a state of utter dilapidation, most of their plaster come away from the brick walls, patched with corrugated tin, grass growing through holes in the concrete, windows broken.

I looked past the rusted fishing trawlers at the keen black prows of the nuclear-powered ice-breakers, and imagined voyaging north across the Barents Sea.

❧

My daughter went down to the ship ahead of me, running down the wooden steps, calling, afraid that before the set hour the ice-breaker would weigh anchor and leave us stranded, seventy-eight degrees north, in this improbable settlement on the Gronfjorden.

We passed a landing where four men leaned on the railings, smoking and looking out to sea. I lost her when I stopped halfway down to the quay; the man with the postcards looked so sorry to see us pass. His seven views of what Russians call Spitsbergen, printed in sallow colour in Moscow in 1976, were priced at one krone each. One showed miners 'relaxing in the new Palace of Culture': weightlifting, performing Cossack dances. In another, 'Barentsburg keeps building', a brick hostel was going up, high against a white hill. A close-up showed chives growing under glass: 'fresh greens all year round for the miners' *stolovaya*'.

There was a sunset over the Barents Sea: 'across it lies the way to Spitsbergen', and a view of a ship loading in blue polar night. I felt in my pocket, found a single krone, and chose a picture of reindeer grazing on moss and purple saxifrage under a bare mountain. The miner took my coin and asked where we came from. When I told him Moscow but really England, he laughed sadly, gathered up all his cards and handed them to me as a gift. Well, perhaps cash has little meaning, I told myself in my embarrassment, in the strange world of Barentsburg.

In the world outside, dealers in rare coins pay good money for the illegal kopecks of the state mining trust, Arktikugol. There are even forgeries of the trust's currency issue of 1946, which marked the USSR's return to the coal seams after the German occupiers left. (In November 1944, as soon as the Red Army had driven the Nazis out of a small part of Norway, Molotov had laid full claim to Spitsbergen, stubbornly refusing to concede until well after the end of the war.) Recently, when Norway, whose laws have governed the *terra nullius* of Svalbard since 1920, called for the withdrawal of the trust's 1998 illegal coins, the collectors' market was flooded with Arktikugol money. The trust's postage stamps of 1995 feature ink drawings of lounging walruses and polar bears roaming the pack ice, sights I had brought my ten-year-old daughter this far north to see. It is not the Russians, however, but the Norwegians, who portray wilderness and its creatures as the true worth of this archipelago. Touch little, take nothing, leave no trace, the Governor tells visitors. In Barents-burg, the mining settlement purchased by the USSR in 1932 from a Dutch coal company, the Arctic desert is still valued in the rhetorical currency of the Five-Year Plan. 'Men wage a struggle against nature', Stalin said, 'and exploit nature for the production of material values.'

'The miner's labour powers space rockets,' declares a violently coloured agit-prop placard on the face of the Pomor Museum. 'Rock Miner! With your well-toiled hand, you give heat and light to everyone!' A miner stands in the foreground, white light exploding from one raised hand. With the other, he points to a backdrop of pipelines, power stations and pylons. According to Marina, who showed us around Barentsburg and told its stories with mercurial emotion, the display of hero-workers in the town centre is a Soviet tradition recently revived to motivate the flag-ging miners. But they no longer carry the Stalinist title *udarniki* (shock-workers, from the verb *udarit'*, to strike a blow or to attack). The faces on this screen are gentle and tired; no fire in their eyes.

In *After the Future*, the cultural critic Mikhail Epstein explores the 'frenzied erotics of labour' that drove Soviet civilisation from its beginnings to its desolate end. 'We will go into the earth in thousands,' the proletarian poet Alexei Gastev promised in *Poetry of the Worker's Blow*, 1918.

> We will not come back . . . we will perish and bury ourselves in the insatiable rush and the labouring blow . . . the earth will be transformed . . . when she can bear no more and rends her steel armour, in an ecstasy of labour's outburst, she will birth new beings whose name will no longer be man.

(Gastev was arrested for 'counter-revolutionary terrorist activity' in 1938, and shot in 1939.)

To Epstein, Soviet 'labour-lust' is promiscuous, oblivion-seeking, 'indifferent to its object so long as you can get into it, work it over, and lose yourself in it'. When the miner in Boris Gorbatov's novel *Donbass* got down on his knees before a wall of coal and switched on his hammer, 'a familiar tremor of joy rolled over his hands . . . the body of coal lay before him submissively as the miner was free to let himself go . . . the solid wall of untouched black forest moved excitingly close to him, enticing . . .' Epstein sees the Russian landscape as the victim of violent rape: 'its traces remain on the faces of our cities and villages . . . in the gullies and potholes on the body of our exhausted land'.

Marina came back in 2000. Productivity slumped when the women left after the catastrophe of 1996, so Arktikugol ordered their return. She did not want to dwell on the plane crash in which ten per cent of Barentsburg's population, mainly miners' wives and children, had died. It made her eyes fill. Or on the methane explosion a thousand feet down in the shaft the following year, which burned for four months. She wanted to show us little miracles of fertility and nurture: the fuchsias and parsley in the damp heat of the greenhouse; Yasha the bull, and Daybreak the sucking calf in the cowshed. Barentsburg's first baby, 'our baby', had been delivered premature a few weeks ago by the dentist before its mother could get to the nearest Russian obstetricians in Murmansk, whose direction is signposted, but which is much further from here than the North Pole. As we approached the wooden chapel, newly built to commemorate Barentsburg's recent dead, four miners walked slowly towards us in the afternoon sun, eyes on Marina's brightness. After sixteen hours underground, they like to attract our attention, she said with a shrug; it's life, what can you do?

Miners from Donbass in Ukraine compete to come to Barentsburg for the wages and conditions: $300 a month (when Arktikugol pays) and three meals a day in the *stolovaya*. They mark time in winters, which last eight months. Russia keeps these men working Svalbard's unprofitable seam for territorial reasons. A treaty signed in Paris after the First World War gave sovereignty over the former no-man's-land to Norway, and equal access to its economic and scientific assets to all thirty-nine signatories, many of whom had rushed on its mineral resources in the 1900s.

The treaty forbids any military activity. But Russia, whose Bolshevik leaders' concerns lay far from this barren *terra nullius* in 1920, has long considered its claim primordial.

Rival discovery stories vie in the naming of the place. The word Svalbard, 'cold land', remembers the Vikings, whose annals suggest that they sailed this far north in the tenth century, though Russian scholars, with their narrative of Russian primacy, think that the land the Norsemen saw was only Jan Mayen Island, half as far from Iceland. The western coast of the largest island, Spitsbergen ('Sharp Mountains'), was first named and mapped in 1596 by the Dutch navigator Willem Barents, on an expedition funded by Amsterdam merchants hoping for a northern route to China. Throughout the seventeenth century, the sea-trading nations sent adventurers north to map the bays, name the glaciers and nunataks and battle the ice pack in their 'shalops', slaughtering Svalbard's 'great stores of whales', 'sea morces' and polar bears. Sailors from England's Muscovy Company lit fires under great copper vats on the seashore, and feasted on the eggs and flesh of barnacle geese while their hauls of blubber boiled down, then set their ships for London, loaded with oil and bone.

Russian archaeologists, citing the remains of inscribed crosses and chessboards found on Svalbard, claim that before the existence of a centralised Russian state or fleet, before merchant corporations or cartographical societies, the Pomor trappers, dwellers by the northern seas (*po more*), had been sailing their boats – *lodyas* and *koches* – up to the land they called Grumant for reindeer hides and fox pelts, and wintering in moss-caulked driftwood *izbas* on its icebound shores. Tales of their battles with scurvy in the Arctic darkness became fashionable reading in Europe in the eighteenth and early nineteenth centuries. By the light of fish-blubber lamps, the Russian trappers knotted and unknotted rope to keep their blood moving, and tried to resist the 'witch-sisters' who roamed the islands for prey. 'The old trappers relate', says one account, 'that scurvy goes about there ... in human form', as an old woman with eleven sisters of dazzling beauty who chant an 'awe-inspiring song', enticing hunters to their destruction. 'Here are no Church hymns, no ringing of bells. Here everything is ours.' The last man to die would confess to the earth: 'Mother, moist Earth . . . Receive my sinful body into thy keeping.'

There was one Pomor peasant who, though he had sailed *lodyas* as a boy, chose to turn south overland for Moscow, where in 1731 he enrolled in the Slavo-Greco-Latin Academy, claiming to be the son of a priest. Polymathic in the sciences and humanities, Mikhailo Lomonosov was sent to Marburg by the Imperial Academy of Sciences to study mining and chemistry. In 1738, he read Swift's *Gulliver's Travels* in German, noting the book in a report on his foreign studies to the Academy. Even when he had become one of the intellectual luminaries of eighteenth-century Russia, Lomonosov was faithful to his origins. The first geographer of the northern ocean, he classified icebergs and studied how the sea melts and freezes. Fascinated by the role of maritime trade in making the great imperial nations, he imagined Russia's northern shores full of busy ports, and a route to the East that would fulfil Peter the Great's dreams of power at sea. In 1765, the year of his death, a scientific expedition to the Arctic inspired by Lomonosov reached Spitsbergen. By this time, English travel fiction – *Robinson Crusoe, Gulliver* and Captain Brunt's Swiftian imitation, *Voyage to Cacklogallinia* – was, at last, appearing in Russian translation. But more remarkable than these fabulous tales, said the head of the Archangel whaling company who had first heard the story, was Pierre Louis le Roy's popular *Adventures of Four Russian Sailors Washed Up by a Storm on the Island of Spitsbergen*, which was published in multiple editions in French, German and English in the 1760s and 1770s. Unlike the Englishman Crusoe, le Roy wrote when the first Russian version appeared, the 'Russian Robinsons' were real and, unlike Crusoe's, their desert island was infertile and cold. For six winters in the 1740s, while Lomonosov was composing odes in Moscow about how Russian toughness would overcome the Arctic, the stranded Pomors survived on reindeer's blood, scurvy grass and prayer.

We sailed slowly up the west side of Svalbard, in and out of fjords, for four days until we came to the ice sheet. When we were not hanging over the deck watching the sea ice roil and grind as the ship split it, we had fun reading scientific romances about the adventures of mad palaeontologists, like Jules Verne's *Journey to the Centre of the Earth*. When all the earth's surface had been discovered, popular travel writers invented fantasy worlds beneath its crust. 'We have made a magnificent discovery, my boy! We have proved that the earth is hollow,' says Perry in Edgar Rice Burroughs's *At the Earth's Core*, when his mechanical prospector, the 'iron mole,' lands in Pellucidar. 'We have passed through its crust to the inner world.' Then the macho hero, David Innes, son of a rich American mine owner, follows a 'tantalising, prehistoric girl' called Dian the Beautiful through the Land of Awful Shadow and the Mountains of the Clouds, observing the struggle for species dominance among evolutionary freaks by the seas of the Lural Az.

The light over the sea was intense, as though the weeks of unbroken day had gathered into one deep light. Marina was at the gangplank, holding my daughter's hand while they waited; her hair gleamed, her anorak was red as the icebreaker's hull. 'Don't judge us,' she said as we parted. 'We want this. We are equal in the permafrost – no money, no police – there is no equality left anywhere else.' For geopolitical reasons, Russia is strengthening its presence on Svalbard again, marking out national territory, bringing more men up to work the mines. Meanwhile, Norway, NATO member since 1949, would like the rusting Soviet settlements to disappear. Russian fishing boats feud with Norwegian coastguards. And the white spherical objects visible on the mountains when the clouds lift are, Russia believes, something to do with the US Missile Defence System. As we drew out, we looked back at the miners just emerged from the hollow in the earth; they smoked, watching our southbound ship and the sharp mountains, in endless regress on the other side of the fjord.

THIRTEEN

Arshan and Irkutsk

What would you and I do in Moscow, Boris (or anywhere else in life)?
A person's essence cannot be broken down into pieces of daily life.
Being a hero doesn't get you an apartment . . .
MARINA TSVETAEVA, letter to Boris Pasternak, 10 July 1926

I awoke from a brief jetlagged sleep at Tunka, where on moonless
nights cosmic rays are caught in metal boxes. Patterned like giant
beehives across the dry grass of the Buryat plain, the traps
are mounted on ungainly struts of wood standing on pads of
rough concrete. Inside the boxes are 'Cherenkov light detectors' –
phototubes named after Sergei Vavilov's most brilliant student,
Pavel Cherenkov – that measure the energy of cosmic rays as they
fall to earth in showers of charged particles. Bearing traces of cosmic
time, signs of the interstellar gases they have passed through and
collided with on their high-energy journey from black holes and
unknown distant galaxies, the rays penetrate our atmosphere,
participating in the evolution and mutation of life on earth.
Physicists study them for insights into the structure and workings
of the universe, the mystery of its origins.

The Tupolev landing at Irkutsk had made death seem close.
Hours later, my spirit was blank and I still felt nauseous. Along
the roadside, arrangements of dirty plastic flowers commemorated fatal car wrecks. The bereaved had bandaged the trees
around each shrine with rags, shamanist prayer ribbons. Did these
dirty scraps appease the spirits of the dead for the insult of a
pointless end?

In the Baikal region, which Chekhov crossed on his way to visit
the penal colonies on Sakhalin, he found all the landscapes he
loved: the Caucasus, Zvenigorod, the Don. 'Get the prosecutor to

send you here,' he wrote home, signing himself 'your Asiatic brother'. He complained that Siberia was just too spacious to fit into a letter; it was a place to be felt rather than seen. After Zun Morino, where the land flattens out and the snow-covered peaks of the Sayan come into view, the arrhythmic wheezing of the Zhiguli calmed at last, the mid-morning sun warmed my face, and my eyes closed gratefully on the changing view.

Vanya, the Russian driver my friend and I had hired in Irkutsk, was taking us on a detour to the village of Khurai-Kobok to visit the shaman who had recited a charm over his new Zhiguli. For miles we had followed the steel-blue waters of the Irkut, which flows out of the Angara and courses west through the Tunkin Valley to the border of Mongolia. The rocks on its shallow bed looked like boulders of snow. From Tunka, through which thousands of political exiles have passed after their collisions with the authority of the state, we took the smaller road which runs north straight to the foot of the eastern Sayan mountains, towards Arshan, whose name means 'sacred spring'. Buryats call this the 'land of Geser'. In one of the countless variants of *Geser*, the oral epic that Buryats share with Mongolians and Tibetans, the stone peaks of the Sayan that rise to over ten thousand feet at the north end of the valley are thirty-three celestial knights who decided not to return to the skies after they had cleansed the world of evil spirits, but remained on earth as faithful guardians.

Geser is the *Iliad* of Central Asia. It is traditionally recited by *gesershins* only after dark, over the course of nine nights. The exploits on earth of its heroes are the overspill of adventures and contests in the night sky. Khan Kurmas clashes in heaven with his enemy Altai-Ulan, carelessly chopping him into tiny pieces which fall to earth and become evil spirits. The petty demons pollute the earth with every kind of uncleanness and misfortune: darting about, crawling like worms, buzzing like flies, poisoning rivers at the source, making the earth barren and insects venomous. They bring sickness, poverty, hunger and ruin; they make men forget love and pity. At last Bukhe-Beligte, the middle of Khan Kurmas's three sons, who is born as an earthly boy in a poor hut, takes up the challenge of ridding the earth of the plague of fiends.

Before Kultuk, on the westernmost tip of Baikal, we had filled up at a lone pump, visible from far off, which cast a stately shadow on the wide strip of sun-weathered asphalt under the dry blue of the Buryat sky. The pump, the gas station and the broken-down truck in front of it were all painted the same blue, in different stages of fade and corrosion. We stopped at a signal and watched a train pass on the Trans-Siberian Railway line carrying newly made tanks, hundreds of gun barrels rushing along the curve of the track into the purple haze of a cleft between birch-covered hills.

We stopped again at a bend in the road high above Baikal to buy beer and smoked omul, the trout of Siberia. The gutted bodies of the fish were laid out on oilcloth, their wrinkled pewter sides held athwart with toothpicks, revealing gelatinous vertebrated flesh, whose pale pink fatness Vanya reckoned with sunburnt hands. At the lake shore, where we lingered to eat the fish that he had chosen for us with such pride, the ground was dry but still too cold to sit on, so we rested on our heels, looking across the slag heaps and rusted derricks on the wharf at the hills behind, where a fine mist plumed into the sky. Though it was late May, the thick pelt of crumbly ice on the lake had drawn back only a couple of feet from the rocky shoreline, so we had to imagine the fabled clarity of this great bow of fresh green water in which the omul swim.

'Sacred sea, free Baikal / Sacred boat, an omul barrel', run the first lines of 'Thoughts of a Runaway' by the mid-nineteenth-century district school supervisor Dmitri Davydov. Set to music by nameless prisoners working the silver mines of Nerchinsk, the poem soon became a folk song that everyone in the region can sing. The historical (as distinct from prehistorical) voice of Baikal is the voice of the runaway, attuned to every possibility of liberty in the natural environment, as well as every cruelty. With its mists and cliff-sheltered bays, from which a fugitive, unseen by any mountain patrol, might set out on the water in an abandoned fish barrel, this landscape has endeared itself to prisoners. And in the culture of the Baikal peasants, descendants of Cossacks, escaped convicts have long been held in reverence, given bread as they pass and *makhorka* tobacco to smoke on their way.

'The Irkutsk administration is repulsive . . . without morals or sense,' Molotov wrote to his friend Alexander Arosev, when he was exiled to a remote village called Manzurka in 1915. He had been in Moscow founding Bolshevik cells in factories until he and his comrades were denounced by an *agent provocateur* and arrested. As he liked to remember in his old age, he had travelled some of the Siberian journey shackled and on foot. He spent several months in the Irkutsk region, drinking heavily, eating little and reinforcing his Bolshevik credentials. It was in Manzurka that he made friends with the Bolshevik Alexander Shcherbakov, who would later live in No. 3 in Moscow and is said to have begged Molotov to take over the leadership of the USSR from Stalin after the Nazi invasion, and Martin Lacis, one of the cruellest fanatics in Dzerzhinsky's Cheka. 'Regarding books,' Molotov wrote to Arosev from Siberia, 'if you can send anything substantial, especially Marxist, I shall be extremely grateful . . . I am desperate for books . . .'

The lineaments of past time are sketched lightly around Baikal, which was discovered late by the outsiders who record events as history and place as geography. The Siberian past falls quickly into prehistory, in which the world is explained through the myths and cosmologies of small groups of hunter-gatherers, for whom geology is the family drama of Father Sky and Mother Earth. In local legend, the Angara, the only river among Baikal's many thousands that flows out of the lake, carrying its waters to the Arctic Ocean, is a rebellious daughter in love. The tall rock, known as the Shaman Rock, that rises above the village of Listvyanka at the headwaters of the Angara is the stone that Father Baikal threw into the swift run of his beautiful river-daughter when she defied him and broke through his shores to rush to the mountains to meet her betrothed, the Yenisei.

Unlike the southern steppe, this landscape has natural defences. Russians only reached the shores of the lake in the mid-seventeenth century, several years after they had arrived at the Pacific Ocean, thousands of miles further east. The Evenks, reindeer-herders whom the Russians called 'Tunguz', told the Russian explorers that the lake was called 'Lamu' and the people who lived on its shores 'Bratsky', Buryats, who called it 'Baigal'. For thousands of years, shamans had revered Baikal, which is the world's largest reserve of fresh water, for its spiritual powers. Olkhon Island, a centre of shamanism, is said to be the burial place of Genghis Khan, the 'World Conqueror', whom the Buryats worshipped along with the mythical Geser, as an unconquered hero who would one day return to liberate his people.

Cossacks built the stockade town of Irkutsk and soon afterwards the fortress at Tunka, the first place in the Tunkin Valley where Russians settled among the roaming Soyot. The Cossacks took tribute from the Buryat tribesmen in 'soft gold', the fur of the Barguzin sable, and on its profit the state grew strong. And to this day Moscow extracts from Siberia the flow of treasure that makes the city glow at night: gold, silver, diamonds, uranium, natural gas and oil. Siberia is a place for men of energy. 'You will hasten to me from Siberia,' the wealthy Madame Khoklakova exclaims to Mitya Karamazov in a maddening non sequitur as he begs her for the three thousand roubles that will save Grushenka from his father's lust. 'I have been watching you for the last month . . . saying to myself: that's a man of energy . . . that's a man who would find mines.' But like his creator and so many before and since, Mitya was sent to Siberia by the prosecutor instead.

Recently, the Buryats of Tunkin have resisted the founding of mines in their valley, believing that it will disrupt the sacred energies of the landscape. The mines in the Sayan angered the local spirits, they say, and created sickness. Until Putin vetoed the plan in the name of the environment, an oil pipeline, to be jointly built by BP and the Russian oil company Yukos, was to have run through the Tunkin Valley. Now the founder of Yukos, Mikhail

Khodorkovsky, another man of energy, was sitting in a prison in Chita in eastern Buryatia, arrested in October 2003 on his way to Irkutsk to give a lecture to students on democracy, and found guilty of fraud and tax evasion eighteen months later by a Moscow court.

We passed the entrance to a collective farm named Proletariat. Waiting at a bus stop was an old woman carrying a bag labelled in English 'Born to Shop'. My Soviet-era guidebook said that the Tunkin Valley was famous for the energy of its labourers, like the Stakhanovite shock-workers of the 1930s, Stepan and Anna Baiborodin. We stopped to drink at a roadside spring on the edge of a forest. Tunkin, the 'land of arshans', is rich in mineral springs. On the arid pasture on the other side of the road, the chimney of a rusty iron field oven smoked, tended by two stout Buryat women in headscarves, who stoked it with fresh birch. We leaned on the fence and watched the women ladle potatoes out of a vat for the labourers in the adjoining field. Soyot nomads grazed their pale long-horned cattle on these aromatic silver grasslands, still living in yurts made of reindeer hides, felt and birch bark, until they were forced into collective farms in the late 1940s. Three fine-limbed children cantered up on ponies to look at us. The youngest, a boy of about seven, with only a folded blanket as his saddle, pulled his horse's head so that it reared, higher and higher, his laughter carried away on the wind.

Just before Khurai-Kobok, death taunted us again. Vanya accelerated to overtake a small truck. His sudden rush of driverly will seemed more an aesthetic instinct than anything else, an urge to risk everything for the sake of a moment's unbroken view down the avenue of pines that led to the foot of the Sayan. The oncoming bus seemed to accelerate too. And I am sure that when Vanya pulled out he had not seen the motorscooter with its sidecar that took up the whole lane in front of the truck, whose driver proved unwilling to yield an inch of road to anyone. The faces of my children flashed before me in the fraction of an instant in which a gap opened between the bus and the sidecar, into which Vanya (who

like every other man in Russia eschews a safety belt on philosophical principle) swung the screaming shaman-charmed Zhiguli.

We stopped in the village to buy vodka for the shaman's ritual.
Besides vodka, the shop sold nothing but beer and *stakanchiki* of
clean white ice cream, which we ate on the dusty roadside, savouring it as the taste of life itself. ('There is vodka,' Chekhov wrote
from Baikal. 'If you ask why they don't eat meat or fish they
explain that there is no transport, roads are bad and so on, but
there's as much vodka as you like even in the remotest villages.') I
asked Vanya why the shaman needed the vodka, and I think my
laughter displeased him when he told me that after I had been
carrying it in my hand for a few minutes it would begin to reflect
my spiritual state. He would spit the vodka at my chest, Vanya
warned. With a lurch of unease, I asked Vanya if he was sure that
the shaman would not say anything about my future. I disdain
auguries; I want no clouding of the vodka. No, Vanya said, the
shaman only takes on minor disorders easily dealt with in the
spirit world. He will call down spirits to dispel bad energies in
your family, and sort out problems of sleep and digestion. (And
also, perhaps, those mighty spirits who protect feeble Zhigulis
whose drivers are possessed by a random death wish.)

The Tungus word *shaman* first appeared in print in the
self-written hagiography of Siberia's first political exile, the
seventeenth-century schismatic Archpriest Avvakum. In Avvakum's
sophisticated work of confessional literature, which introduced
the Russian vernacular as a written language, he described the
landscape and wildlife of Baikal, and the performance of a
shaman, who screamed, danced and flung himself to the ground,
foaming at the mouth. To Avvakum, the shaman was either a
charlatan or a 'devil', possessed of dark supernatural energy.
Catherine the Great's German botanist Peter Simon Pallas, who
came to Tunkin a hundred years later to record the wildlife, saw
the shamanic ecstasies as elaborate trickery, fake terrors that kept
the natives in thrall.

Mircea Eliade, the twentieth-century scholar of comparative

religion, classified the shaman as a 'specialist in the human soul', who 'alone "sees" it, for he knows its "form" and its "destiny"'. In *Shamanism: Archaic Techniques of Ecstasy*, he gathered ethnographers' accounts of shamanist beliefs and practices from around the world. A native Siberian told an ethnographer that

> everything that exists is alive. The lamp walks around. The walls of the houses have voices of their own. Even the chamber-pot has a separate land and a house. The skins sleeping in the bags talk at night. The antlers lying on the tombs arise at night and walk in procession around the mounds, while the dead get up and visit the living.

The Buryats believe, Eliade says, that the soul of the hereditary shaman is carried off by spirits on ecstatic night flights, to the east if he is destined to become a 'white' shaman, to the west if he is to become 'black'. On these night journeys the shaman learns the forms of the gods and spirits and their names. People have animal doubles who come to their aid. Illnesses can be caused by spirits that wander away as a person sleeps, and get lost or captured on their night journeys.

While Eliade was compiling his findings in Paris, the shamans of Siberia were living underground, having been cruelly persecuted in the 1930s, many shot or dropped under the Baikal ice with weights on their feet. On their collective farms, the Buryats were taught to worship and propitiate Lenin and Stalin, heroes and deities of a new occult.

The shaman's house of sun-burnished wood lay close to the road, surrounded by a paling fence, its shutters freshly painted white and trimmed in blue. A telegraph pole stood in the garden, its wires slung low over the roof. Behind the house, against the gleam of the Sayan, was a small hill, perfectly rounded like the hills in Roerich's mystical paintings. A sacred hill, Vanya told me casually. According to shamanist belief, the three realms are linked by sacred rivers, trees or mountains. This was all as it should be. The shaman set apart from his community; the landscape conforming.

Vanya's shaman was taught the arts by his shaman grandfather, out of sight of the Soviet authorities. As his collective farm disintegrated at the end of the Soviet period, he began quietly to practise, and people began to come to him from far about. Across the road were the ruins of the collective farm, a necropolis of wrecked, scavenged agricultural buildings and machinery. At the door of a half-burned barn filled with boulders and incongruous columns of carved stone, the teeth of a broken plough curled into the dry earth.

A little cross-eyed boy in a stripy sweater stood in the middle of the road, grinning at us. As the shaman opened the door at the back of the house, the boy followed us in, smiling rapturously. Inside, in typical Siberian fashion, three rooms, their walls lined with wood, were arranged around a large stove. There was almost no furniture and everything was scrubbed clean. The shaman received us in the kitchen, by the mouth of the stove. He had no ritual paraphernalia: no feathers, no tambourine, no pendants or ceremonial dress of animal skins. He wore a suit jacket over a zip-up tracksuit, and kept his peaked leather cap on. We sat opposite one another at the table, on which lay an open polythene bag of dried herbs. I passed him the bottle that I had been piously holding for the past twenty minutes. He poured some vodka into a tin cup and looked into it. 'Your blood is not pure,' he said, regarding my face for the first time. Did the vodka tell him that? I noticed that the nail on his right index finger was black and so long that it curled right over the top of his finger. In the front room, the shaman's grandson knelt on a chair, looking through the window at occasional cars passing in the bright sunshine, waiting for the ritual to end so that he could turn on the television. The shaman pinched some herbs into the cup, closed his eyes, and began to chant: '*Hondolo, hondolo, hondolo*'. He looked at me again and announced that some of my ancestors, long ago and far away, had been good souls and done good magic. Then he tipped the vodka into his mouth and spat it, not at my chest, but back into the tin cup. 'I have done good blessings for your children and for your bad sleep,' he said. The sun from the side window warmed the oilcloth and raised gentle scents of dried herbs, vodka and old wood.

⌘

In Arshan, we stayed in a tall forest of rock cedars and pines at a small guest house close to the Kungarga River owned by a woman named Agafya. We soon began to refer to her as Baba Yaga, which was unfair, as she bore no resemblance to a fairy-tale witch, but had a straight back and a ruddy, smiling face, and the white kerchief she wore on her head made her look like the Cossack matrons of Siberia from whom she was, no doubt, descended. It was just that her fingernails were long and grimy ('*kogti-nogti Baba Yaga*' – 'Baba Yaga, talon-nails'), and after we had eaten the omul cutlets she prepared for breakfast, lunch and supper, she had a way of putting her arms around our waists and pinching our ribs to check that we were plumping up as nicely as she thought we should. 'You don't get anything to eat,' Chekhov said of Siberia, 'and you end up feeling you have wings.' If only it were still true.

On the long drive, Vanya had told us that Agafya's house was the most restful and cleanest place he had ever known. (Pushkin fantasised in *Eugene Onegin* about a Russia filled with cosy inns for the weary traveller, and the dream has not died.) Cleaner than clean, Vanya said, the best place in the whole world to clean your soul. To reach the house, we had followed the course of an overground gas pipeline girdled in scruffy insulation that loops through the small scattered town of Arshan, passing the high walls of the Sayan Sanatorium. Chickens strutted freely at the entrance to Agafya's yard, which was a mess of timber and rubbish scattered between corrugated-iron sheds. Large cedars spread their shade over the whole property, on which were two houses and several outhouses: a banya, a kitchen with a brick-and-whitewash wood-fired stove and a gas ring attached to a canister, a WC (a broken-down hut enclosing a hole in the earth) and odd storage sheds. The guest house was her pride. She and her husband (who never emerged but occasionally spied on our comings and goings from the window of their house) had built it with their own hands, using timber of every age, so that some walls were close-grained light gold and others made of cold-blackened planks whose grain had roughened and wrinkled like weathered skin. Our room was furnished with two low wooden beds made up with clean linen sheets and blankets redolent of guests past. There were two other guest rooms in the one-storey building leading off a dark corridor.

Three pails of water drawn from the Kungarga were lined up outside the kitchen. As she showed us around, Agafya ostentatiously unwrapped a new bar of soap and laid it in a small contraption that hung beside the door: a wide dish with a long plug which, when pushed from below, released, like a tap, a trickle of water. The soap, we soon learned, was a gesture of hospitality intended for our exclusive use, for Agafya never touched it herself, preferring to wipe her hands on her apron after she had patted our cutlets into shape. Steaming in the dusty banya was rather like sitting in the smoking hollow of a burned-out tree. It never became truly hot like the stone banyas of the city, so we found it hard to bring ourselves to rinse off with the cold river water in the bucket beside the stove.

We ate on the verandah, and a little Buryat boy who lived next door would come barefoot through a gap in the fence to sit on an abandoned hubcap and watch our meals. Our first day in Arshan was hot, and by the evening midges had filled the yard and flies had gathered on the verandah, agitated by the sugar bowl and the remains of our omul, which Vanya had given to Agafya to lay out in a dish. On the second evening we suggested to Agafya that our smoked fish were finished, but she protested that there was still good flesh on their bones, and proceeded to pick them clean, dropping shreds on to our plates and swaying gently as she sang 'Sacred sea, free Baikal' with a cunning glint in her eyes. After supper, we took the path down to the Kungarga to step through the fast-running water on its marble stones. Sitting on the roots of a cedar on its banks, in the lovely freshness of the evening air, I took up my companion's smoking habit to kill the taste that lingered in my mouth.

Soon after we had fallen asleep on our first night, we were awoken by male voices on the verandah. There were sounds of bottles clinking, and Agafya setting out crockery. The noise kept up till around five, the men's voices growing louder as they drank. (Agafya happily told us next morning that they were workers renovating the sanatorium who had come round unexpectedly for her food.) We envied Vanya his room at the back. I had with me a book from Sands's library (which he did not appear to have read), a heavy volume appropriate neither for travelling nor for insomniac diversion, but I took it out and browsed in its pages by torchlight, slitting open the odd uncut pages with my fingernail.

The book, which was published by the Academy of Sciences two years before Stalin's death, was a volume of letters and other occasional writings by the Decembrist Ivan Yakushkin, sentenced to hard labour in eastern Siberia, like so many of the most educated and civic-minded men of his generation, for his part in the uprising against tsarist autocracy of 1825. 'In the depths of the Siberian mines, keep your proud patience,' Pushkin hailed his banished friends from Moscow. 'Your bitter work is not in vain, and the high striving of your thought.' I noticed that the series in which the book appeared was edited by Sergei Vavilov, who died in the year of its publication, so his name in the cover was cased in black. From its pages emerged a vivid geography of friendship, familial affection, sickness, endurance, loathing for slavery and injustice, and political hope: a geography traced across the towns of Siberia – Chita, Selenginsk, Kyakhta, Yalutorovsk, Tunka, Irkutsk – where Yakushkin and other Decembrist exiles spent thirty years of their lives, first in prison, later, under surveillance, in homes of their own. Some Decembrists had wives from their own class who followed them to Siberia. Others married local Russian, or even Buryat, women. The exiles set themselves to enlightened work: studying, educating local children, developing horticulture, drawing and cataloguing the flora and fauna of Siberia, and making watercolours of one another. They were touched by the landscape and they touched it in return. Were there comforts hidden in a book about these men (who were held up by the Soviet regime as proto-revolutionaries) for an intellectual like Vavilov, who lived so close to power under an infinitely more terrifying regime?

One of the longest of Yakushkin's letters was written to his mother-in-law, Natalia Sheremeteva, from the 'admirably well-built' prison fortress near Chita, which the Tsar had commissioned to keep the politically dangerous noblemen together, and apart from everyone else. Yakushkin's letter, perfectly uncomplaining and generous with simple detail, was the first and fullest account of the conditions of the Decembrists' incarceration, and manuscript copies of it circulated among relatives and friends in Moscow and St Petersburg. Addressing his mother-in-law as 'dear friend', Yakushkin tells of his sometimes acute anxieties about the wife and children he has left behind, but confesses that in prison, when he sits alone in the evenings, thinking of the people he loves, he sometimes feels as happy as he has ever felt. Older in body, he is younger in spirit, and most importantly, free for his studies in natural sciences and the development of the classical school curriculum. In that classic genre of prison writing, he describes the interior of the room in which he is incarcerated. He familiarises Natalia Sheremeteva with his daily routine and the small room, warm and light, in which he has the solace of his own furniture (dark wood, which reminds him of his mother-in-law's house), a samovar which he takes pride in cleaning almost as well as Stepan (one of the serfs he once tried to free), a porcelain dinner service, portraits of his wife and children, a crucifix and his books.

A few pages on was another remarkable letter; this one written to Yakushkin by the philosopher Pyotr Chaadaev in 1837. In it, Chaadaev wryly describes for his faraway friend the scandal surrounding the publication of his 'First Philosophical Letter', when the editor of the journal in which it appeared was exiled to

Vologda, all Chaadaev's papers seized, and Chaadaev himself declared insane. Chaadaev's letter, Herzen famously commented, 'rang out like a pistol shot in the dark night' of Tsar Nicholas I's reign. It set the terms for the polemics between 'Slavophiles' and 'Westernisers' that preoccupied educated Russia for the rest of the nineteenth century and beyond. In it, Chaadaev lamented that Russian culture was 'based wholly on borrowing and imitation'. 'And yet,' he mused, 'situated between the two great divisions of the world, between East and West, with one elbow leaning on China and the other on Germany, we should have . . . united in our civilisation the past of the whole world'. In his letter to Yakushkin, Chaadaev commends the Decembrist for his courage in adversity and for the fact that he has set to serious intellectual work in his exile and imprisonment. With a hint that he has seen a copy of the letter Yakushkin wrote to his mother-in-law. Chaadaev immediately engages his exiled friend in high-level intellectual conversation, apologising for the fact that his first letter should be so full of *préoccupations*, but he is such a person of ideas that he cannot liberate himself from their influence; they are the whole interest of his life and the foundation of his existence. He wonders about the state of Yakushkin's religious sentiments, lamenting his former 'frozen deism' and hoping that his current studies will lead to serious contemplation of the most important questions of the moral order, and that Yakushkin will have parted with the 'small-souled doubt to which deism tends', noting that the latest science is not at odds with religious belief, but rather that new discoveries in the field of electricity support the cosmogony of the Bible. Thinking of Yakushkin's current location on the map, so far from the sources of current intellectual movements, Chaadaev comforts himself that the times they live in are so saturated by the *fluide régénerateur* that, given Yakushkin's cast of mind, he will not be far from their influence however far away he may be in body. Ideas, Chaadaev writes, observe the law that everything flows towards the centre.

*

Next morning we walked a small way from Agafya's back gate through the forest, along the river, under another turn of the gas pipeline and down towards the Khongor Ula spring in its grove of a thousand beribboned pines. We passed the Buddhist datsan in the forest at the foot of the hill with its brightly painted yellow, red and blue pagoda roof. Tall silver birches rose up behind the lamas' tombs in the grassy grounds; pink azaleas, *bagalnik*, bloomed in the edges of the dark forest. The datsan in its wide meadow presented the only neatly organised scene in this town in which everything else seemed disarranged, frayed and flapping. The air was warm. The light touched the mountains, and the arrangement of vast shadows made them look perfectly regular in size and shape.

Kneeling on a small wooden platform beneath a concrete bridge, people took turns to fill plastic bottles with spring water flowing from a rusted pipe. Since the 1830s, these 'geomagnetic' waters have been used for healing by the Russians of Siberia. Some of the waters give new energy; others bring on sleep. In the last years of his Siberian exile, Yakushkin was in Irkutsk, being treated for a painful and disabling swelling of the legs by a doctor named Dzhibovsky, who advised him to come to the Tunkin waters for a cure. The doctor treated his legs with a herbal essence so pungent that Yakushkin hesitated about visiting his old friends the Volkonskys and the Trubetskoys at their homes in the town.

Beyond the spring were the structures of a Stalin-era spa resort: an avenue lined with plaster statues of athletic workers, urns and a crumbling ceremonial staircase that led to a balustrade at the foot of a forest pathway leading up through the falls to a cascade. At a kiosk I bought a twenty-year-old brochure about the Sayan Sanatorium, which claimed that most visitors to the resort are suffering from nervous-psychological exhaustion, adding that for many this condition is made worse by the great sufferings associated with their journeys to Arshan. On the dusty edges of the avenue, resting their heavy legs in the morning sun, old women sat on fold-out chairs, selling dried herbs from open plastic bags. I bought a handful of what I understood to be dried chrysanthemum petals from a sweet woman who told me she had recently retired from a career spent driving coal trucks to sell her herbal remedies in Arshan. 'Good air,' she said, waving her hand at the mountain and the sky, 'good ecology.' She told me to drop a few petals into my tea each morning to 'freshen my head'. I wish now that I had bought the whole sackful of her magical blue-grey splinters.

⋙⋘

'If someone tells me a tree is sacred, I will touch it,' Vanya told me, summing up his religious philosophy. At the last place of healing to which he took us, a spring of 'living water' on a bend in the wide Irkut, even the wire fence had been sanctified with knotted scraps of cloth and plastic bags. We paid a man in a hut, and changed into our bathing suits. We were the only visitors. Further along the riverbank, close to the forest edge on the empty field, was a lone tent, its canvas so rough and faded that it seemed a natural feature of the landscape. The mineral water, which poured thickly out of a wide shower head piped from the ground, came out of the earth at the precise temperature of the human body, smelling power-fully of iron. Its properties had transformed the concrete pad on which we stood into a satiny carpet of electric-green moss. It was hard to step out of the radius of the water into the cold wind that blew across the field, and I think I must have showered for too long in that blood-warm *fluide régénerateur*, for after a few miles on the long road back to Irkutsk, I felt weak and tremulous, close to that state of 'nervous-psychological exhaustion' for which Arshan boasts the cure.

Every traveller arrives in Irkutsk exhausted, Chekhov wrote home. For us, fatigue was a mercy, as the one-room apartment on the outskirts of the city which Vanya's cousin had vacated for our use that night was a desolate place and we were glad to fall asleep. The next morning it was raining heavily. We drank tea infused with chrysanthemum petals in the tiny kitchen, and looked out through the branches of still leafless birches at the squalid ranks of Khrushchev-era apartment buildings outside the window. It was not hard to imagine why this city, which is a nexus on the heroin route from Central Asia to Europe, has such a high rate of drug addiction and HIV.

Perhaps my sensibilities were still saturated with the active minerals of Tunkin, but Irkutsk on that wet morning seemed a place of almost unbearable pathos. Alexander Men was sent here in 1955, when the Institute of Fur was moved from Moscow to Irkutsk. It was here that he shared a room for three years with Gleb Yakunin, who converted from atheism to Christianity and became a dissident priest who denied the authority of the Moscow Patriarchate. As we boarded a bus for the city centre, a man running down the street dropped his briefcase. As he brushed the briefcase off, the bus that he had tried to catch accelerated into a large puddle, spraying him with filthy water. Before visiting the Decembrist houses, we stopped at a little cafe and ordered tea with lemon from the menu. 'Net limona' – 'There's no lemon' – said the woman at the counter. 'Isn't that lemon?' I asked, pointing to a saucer of lemon slices on the shelf behind her. She narrowed her eyes, sullenly dropped a slice into each cup with bare grimy fingers, and pushed the tea across the counter so hard it almost spilled.

Maria Volkonskaya's house was a sudden revelation of enlightenment and style: a pale grey two-storeyed mansion, with many large windows and an entrance from a large courtyard surrounded by stables and outbuildings. It is a historic work of reconstruction. In the First World War the house was used as a barracks by Cossacks. From the 1920s until the 1970s, it was divided into communal apartments. Moving to Irkutsk from the village of Urik so that her son could attend the gymnasium was the closest Princess Maria Volkonskaya ever came to returning to the rich European civilisation she had left behind when she followed her husband Sergei Volkonsky into Siberian exile. Her fine house of larch was transported here from Urik, and, as she was not allowed to appear in public places, Irkutsk society came to her, making her home the centre of local cultural life. (The Tsar and his agents still believed that the energy of certain individuals should be carefully contained, not understanding how containment only intensifies its force.) She would hold balls and masquerades for the young people of Irkutsk, and many famous musicians passing through would give performances in her home.

Maria Volkonskaya came from a distinguished line. The polymathic scholar Mikhailo Lomonosov was her great-grandfather. Her father, General Nikolai Raevsky, was a hero of the Napoleonic wars. In her teens, she had visited spas with Pushkin. 'Just for amusement', as Pushkin recounted, Maria and her sister bathed in warm sulphur-acidulous and cold ferruginous springs at a fashionable resort in the Russian south, where in the evenings she would win at card games and lottery. Staying with the Raevskys, Pushkin rejoiced in a 'carefree life surrounded by a dear family'. He loved and admired the simplicity and beauty of soul of General Raevsky, as he loved the 'gay southern sky'. Walking by the Crimean seashore, he read Byron, Voltaire and André Chénier. In the margins of a draft of *Eugene Onegin*, he sketched the *jolie laide* Maria with errant curls and a determined chin.

General Raevsky opposed his daughter's decision to follow her husband to Siberia and, on orders from the Tsar, she was forced to leave her baby son, Nikolino, with her parents in the capital. On her way east, Maria stopped in Moscow at the home of her sister-in-law Princess Zinaida Volkonskaya on Tverskaya Street. Zinaida arranged a concert in Maria's honour, which Pushkin attended, at which she performed an aria from Paer's opera *Agnese* in which a daughter begs forgiveness from her father. Zinaida's voice gave way before she finished the song, and Maria began to weep and had to leave the room. Pushkin, for whom Decembrism was above all a matter of personal friendship, was so stirred by the encounter that he began work on the poem 'Deep in the Siberian Mines', hoping to finish it in time for Maria to take it on her journey. When little Nikolino died at the age of two, Pushkin composed his epitaph: 'At the throne of the Eternal Creator, he looks on earthly exile with a smile, blesses his mother and prays for his father.' Unsure of whether she would 'give pleasure by reminding others of herself', Maria conveyed her thanks to Pushkin for the words he had found 'to console a mother's love'.

Almost two centuries later, at the tender place where the personal and the political meet, reminders of Maria Volkonskaya still give not just pleasure but consolation and courage. As I stood outside in the corridor of the Meshchansky Courthouse in a tight crowd of journalists and well-wishers in the summer of 2005, Mikhail Khodorkovsky gave, from an iron cage, his final address to the court that had pronounced him guilty of fraud and tax evasion at the end of a false trial which concluded with the judge reading out, over the course of nine days, expressionlessly, at the speed of a racing commentator, a virtual facsimile of the prosecutor's case. 'This was not a trial,' Khodorkovsky said, and then he thanked his wife, Inna, for her love, calling her a 'true *dekabristka*', a Decembrist wife.

In what may have been intended as mockery, the Kremlin or the Lubyanka (from whence, it would seem, all orders relating to Khodorkovsky's case emanate) took up the historical thread of the oil tycoon's heroic self-fashioning, answering his signal with a gesture of particular cruelty. In October Khodorkovsky, without being told where he was going, was covertly transported, alone in a sealed train carriage, to a prison colony in Krasnokamensk, six hundred miles from Chita, four thousand miles from Moscow, at the far eastern edge of Buryatia. A week later, through an advocate, he sent a message to his 'friends':

> Since 16 October 2005 I have been in the land of the Decembrists, political convicts and uranium mines.
>
> The Kremlin has tried to isolate me completely from the country and the people . . . they have tried to destroy me physically . . . They are hoping that Khodorkovsky will soon be forgotten. They are trying to convince you, my friends, that the

fight is over. That one has to reconcile oneself to the rule of self-serving bureaucrats in Russia. That is not true. The fight is just beginning . . .

The time of conformists is passing – the time of Heroes is coming.

Khodorkovsky has not been forgotten. Through him, a public conversation that began with the Decembrists has continued into the age of Putin. Three years after Khodorkovsky's first letter from Siberia, Russian *Esquire* magazine asked the writer Grigory Chkhvartishvili (also known as Boris Akunin, creator of the super-sleuth Erast Fandorin) whom he would most like to interview. Without hesitation, Chkhvartishvili replied that he wanted to interview Khodorkovsky, whose fate 'gave him no peace'. In a lengthy interview, conducted by letter, the detective writer and the political prisoner discuss, among other matters, the reasons for Khodorkovsky's arrest; the significance of his show trial (which Chkhvartishvili calls 'the most shameful page in the history of post-Soviet justice'); corruption at the very highest echelons of power; the attitudes to his plight of his wife, his parents and his children; the nature of true freedom; the burdens of property ('drowning in things'); his philosophical and religious convictions ('if there is no God, and all our life is just a moment between dust and dust, then what is it all for? What are our dreams, our sufferings, our strivings for? What is knowledge for? What is love for?'); the lasting impact of the Mongol yoke ('from the moment the "march to the east" began, the state has treated the population the way an occupier treats a conquered people'); and (with reference to the Decembrists, Herzen, Pushkin, Chaadaev, Sakharov and the poet Joseph Brodsky) the poignant history of Russian liberalism.

No thinking person, Chkhvartishvili says, seriously believes the official version of Khodorkovsky's downfall (that his company was a 'criminal group' whose business was fraud and tax evasion). Was he arrested because he broke a spoken agreement between Putin and the 'oligarchs' of the 1990s that they would keep out of politics? Was it (as women of a certain age tend to believe) that Khodorkovsky was too beautiful, and taller than Putin, and once dared to turn up for a presidential audience without a tie? Was it because Putin believed he was planning to use his money to stage an 'orange revolution'? Or was it, as Chkhvartishvili believes, because, having achieved his ambition to become the most successful entrepreneur of the new Russia by the age of forty, Khodorkovsky realised that 'happiness does not lie in money', and decided to devote his energies to helping Russia to become at last a civilised and competitive nation – a determination that gave someone in particular serious cause for anxiety?

Chkhvartishvili thinks about questions of legal justice. Why, he wonders, did the judges and the prosecutor go along with the farce? It is not like the days of Stalin's Great Terror when people within the legal system lived in fear of their lives. It is not like the Brezhnev era, when those who would not condemn the dissidents themselves risked prison or psychiatric hospital (the *psikhushka*). Khodorkovsky replies that, like so many in the *nomenklatura* and the bureaucracy, the judge and prosecutor in his case were probably motivated by *kompromat*, the fund of 'compromising materials' with which individuals are intimidated and coerced into corruption and conformity. He prefers to think of the hundreds of individuals who, he says, refused to give false evidence against him and his associates, even under threat of their own prosecutions. He names two: Anatoly Pozdnyakov, former director of the company Apatit, and Evgeny Komarov, former governor of the Murmansk region, who 'under the most severe pressure, refused to act against their consciences'.

⥀

When Yakushkin visited the Volkonskys in Irkutsk in 1854, he found Sergei older-looking but still in vigorous good health. (Unlike Yakushkin, Sergei Volkonsky would live to see the liberation of the serfs in 1861.) At their home they discussed current affairs (the Crimean war against the 'redheads', as they called the English), and the terrible story of Pyotr and Andrei Borisov. The Decembrist brothers had devoted themselves to botany and to painting the birds of Siberia. In that year, Pyotr had died of a heart attack, and in his grief Andrei had set fire to their house and hanged himself.

We arrived as the rehearsal for an afternoon concert was about to begin. A thin soprano, in a synthetic evening gown, false eye-lashes and elaborately dressed and lacquered hair, was swallowing nervously in the anteroom to the main salon, goosepimples appearing on her shoulders from the draughts that came in with the opening and closing of the doors. The attendants told us the museum was closed; when I explained how far we had come, they told us to hurry round its rooms without tickets and make sure we were out of the way before the audience arrived. Perhaps it was better to take in at speed its carefully composed exhibits. The story they told – of European high culture struggling to take root on the frontier of the Asiatic steppe – grew richer under Stalin and is still vividly active under Putin. The museum has a replica of the Viennese piano that Maria Volkonskaya had sent to her in Siberia; an aquarelle (by the Decembrist painter Nikolai Bestuzhev) of the Volkonskys in their room at the prison-fortress near Chita, with its empire-style birch seats; glass cases displaying the manuscripts of poems written to the Decembrists and by them, including Pushkin's salutation from Moscow. I found myself gazing fixedly at the fine stitching on a tapestry pipe cover, for a long oriental-style pipe, that Maria Volkonskaya had worked for her husband in her early years in Siberia. In the next room, the soprano warmed her voice with ascending arpeggios. As I came on to the landing, I could hear through the door the opening measures of 'Porgi Amor', the Contessa's long, drawn-out sigh of sorrowful wifely love from Mozart's *Marriage of Figaro*.

FOURTEEN

Ulan Ude and Kyakhta

Our thoughts are ours, their ends none of our own.
PLAYER KING, *Hamlet*

Near the Blue Buddha, seated in adamantine pose on his lotus throne, were the 'five long-lived sisters'. 'In Buryatia we love the sisters,' our guide, Lida, said, pointing her folded spectacles at the sinuous candy-coloured figures high above us on the wall of the Buddhist datsan. As she leaned against the car smoking a Vogue cigarette after our drive to Ivolginsk across the littered steppe, Lida had said with a low chuckle that she was both a Buddhist and a shamanist, and that she gave thanks to Lenin for the fact that she did not have to live in a yurt.

'The wise men and gods of Asia, unlike the terrible figures in the Old Testament, are familiar with irony,' the French communist Romain Rolland wrote in his introduction to the edition of Rabindranath Tagore's short stories in Molotov's library. It was one of the most beautifully made of all his books, a classic of NEP publishing, with a graphic on its cover showing a yogi and a serene Buddha in the lotus pose. 'Tagore's voice is the voice of the brahmin – the Buddha's smile,' Rolland wrote. But the only words of Rolland's marked in Molotov's copy, in unsteady purple ink, were the words 'our silence signified much more than we ever said'.

Lamaist Buddhism spread through Mongolia to Siberia from Tibet as Russian explorers were arriving here from the west. The Cossacks were more interested in receiving taxes from the natives in sable fur than in saving their souls through missionary activity, and by the early eighteenth century, when the border with Manchu China had been established, most Buryats had adopted Buddhism, which blended easily with their shamanist beliefs. In

1741, Buddhism was recognised as an official religion by Tsarina Elizabeth (she of the sugary baroque palaces, who would soon expel António Sanches from her empire on suspicion of being a Jew). By the middle of the nineteenth century there were scores of monasteries across the steppe, their brightly coloured temples, known here as datsans, rising in rich painted colour out of the scrubby sun-faded landscape. The monasteries were places of education where young men were initiated into the 'inner sciences', as well as the 'secular sciences' of grammar, medicine, logic and technology, and the 'minor sciences': poetry, metrics, music, astrology and dance. When the American explorer George Kennan (a distant cousin of the diplomat George F. Kennan) visited the lamasery at Gusinoe Ozero (Goose Lake) south of Ulan Ude, he was received by the chief lama, who asked him whether it was true, as Russian officers had told him, that the world was round, for such a belief was contrary to the old Tibetan books.

In 1945, when Stalin relaxed constraints on religious practice, the datsan at Ivolginsk was established as the only Buddhist spiritual centre in Russia, and to this day it is the residence of the Pandido Khambo-lama, head of the Russian lamas. In the new freedoms of 1991, a Buddhist Institute was founded here, and now the novice monks study old Mongolian, English, ethnography and information technology, as well as the ancient discipline of *choira*, or philosophical dispute.

Inside the Sogshin Dugan, as the main temple is called, everything was silken, richly dyed and painted gold, red, yellow and blue. Lida guided us through the pantheon and the symbolic landscape on the walls: paradise in the east; the syllable 'OM' (which we had seen painted on rocks along the road) on the orb of the sun; a cup and a rosary of skulls; green Tara, goddess of devotion, mother of the Buddhas, and symbol of their enlightened deeds. In one corner were the Dakinis, who travel through space and guide practitioners of Buddhism towards enlightenment; they are also known as 'space travellers' or 'sky walkers'. And further along was Dalha, the warrior or enemy god, who rides a white horse and is often shown in Buryat temples with his eight brothers, for there is a local cult of the Nine Brothers of Dalha, who distribute wealth unequally.

After the night train from Irkutsk to Ulan Ude, which runs eastward around the southern shores of Lake Baikal, we had breakfasted in the Hotel Geser (the finest example I had yet seen of the morose aesthetic of late communist privilege), and then wandered through the streets of the city in the quiet of Sunday morning. In the main square, a group of Chinese travellers asked if we would allow them to take our picture in front of the massive head of Lenin, the largest representation of the Bolshevik's cranium in the world. Plaques on the walls of the 'Red baroque' government buildings commemorated the hard-fought local victories of the Red Army in the Civil War, which led to the creation of the autonomous republic of Buryatia, with the former Cossack garrison town of Verkhneudinsk as its capital. Living under felt tent roofs was officially regarded as 'backward', and Buryats began to flood into Verkhneudinsk to live in buildings. More Russian 'specialists' arrived during the First Five-Year Plan, and the construction of the city began to follow the 'genplan', with suburbs of apartment buildings appearing around industrial projects. In 1935, as part of the Soviet nationalities policy, which was based on ethnic principles, the name of the city was changed to Ulan Ude, Red Uda, for the wide river Uda that flows here into the southbound Selenga.

We had met Lida in the ethnographic museum. With her witty eyes and her slick red manicure, she stood out vividly from the dozens of eerie Tungus cult objects she was curating: *ongons* or family spirits, with scratchy hair and crudely carved blank eyes, and no home or property left to protect but their glass cases. When I asked Lida about life in Ulan Ude, she replied with a snoring noise: 'Ulan Ude is asleep. Always has been, always will be.'

On the far side of the main square, out of sight of Lenin, is the old town, a few streets still laid out on its eighteenth-century grid pattern, with single-storey log houses, trading arcades and fine churches, now in decay. When Kennan came here at the end of the nineteenth century, he found the town little more than a fortress. He had come to study the penal system in Siberia, and found himself admiring the newly built prison in Verkhneudinsk, which convinced him that the Russian government was 'not entirely indifferent to the sufferings of its exiled criminals'.

Kennan met exiles who had served in the mines and had then been allowed to settle in wretched Siberian towns, living in simple wooden houses, whose stories seemed 'to furnish a very instructive illustration of the complete disregard of personal rights that characterises the Russian government in its dealings with citizens who happen to be suspected, with or without reason, of political untrustworthiness'. He found his interviews with the political exiles to be a bracing tonic after the illnesses he had suffered on the journey, meeting a Swiss-educated lady exile who declared, 'We may die in exile, and our children may die in exile, but something will come of it at last.'

We stopped in the Univermag, the department store that took up one side of the old trading arcades. In a corner that also sold linen and Tungus ornaments made of bone was a shelf of reading matter for the people of the sleeping city: popular histories of the Scythians and ancient Rus; works of Theosophy by Roerich and the Russian-born Madame Blavatsky; an anthology of spiritual masters of the East; and a book called *The Secret of Russia*. I chose two books by Akhmatova's son, Lev Gumilev, and a new book, published by the Institute of Oriental Studies, which gave a reinterpretation of the story of the 'mad baron' Ungern-Sternberg, who believed he was the reincarnation of Genghis Khan and brought terror to these parts in the four years after the fall of the Romanovs.

Roman Nicolaus Fyodorovich von Ungern-Sternberg, who claimed descent from Attila the Hun and the medieval Teutonic Knights who settled in the Baltics, was a seasoned fighter of thirty at the time of the Revolution. Like Budyonny he had fought with Cossack regiments and had been decorated with the

George Cross during the First World War. Fascinated by the Mongols and their landscape, he went east to Baikal after the Tsar's abdication, and adopted lamaistic Buddhism and the practices of the occult. Across the landscape of the failed empire, new ethnically based polities were being imagined. The Buryat intelligentsia was taken with the idea of a pan-Mongol kingdom. In late 1918, after Trotsky's Red Army had drawn back, a conference of Buryat-Mongols was held in Verkhneudinsk, financed by the Japanese, with a view to the creation of a Greater Mongolia, independent of both Russia and China. Baron Ungern, who dreamed of re-creating the Mongolian empire of Genghis Khan, recruited a volunteer army of many nationalities: Buryats, Mongols, Cossack remnants of the fallen White armies, Tatars, Japanese and Chinese. Qualifications for recruitment were a fur coat, a horse and saddle, *ichigi* Mongol-Buryat shoes and a *papakha* hat. His troops were paid through Cossack atamans. The company of men immediately around Ungern was reputedly made up of cocaine addicts and alcoholics. The unlimited use of narcotics and vodka fuelled his army's spectacular atrocities, rapes and the foulest imaginable mutilations, directed systematically, and with particular cruelty, against Jews, Bolsheviks and any person with a physical defect. (Believing in reincarnation, the baron claimed to be doing such people a favour with his slaughter.) Travelling with his personal Buddhist soothsayers and seventy bodyguards sent by the Dalai Lama, Ungern led an army of six thousand men into Mongolia in the autumn of 1920. 'The tribes of Genghis Khan's successors are awakened,' he said; 'nobody shall extinguish the fire in the hearts of the Mongols. In Asia there will be a great state from the Pacific to the Indian Ocean to the banks of the Volga . . . it will be a victory of the spirit'. Promising that he would make an avenue of gallows from Mongolia to Moscow, Ungern declared himself Emperor of Russia.

The Baron's adventure came apart in May of the following year, when his army was routed by the Bolsheviks near Kyakhta-Troitskosavsk and he was found by a Red Army patrol, alone and wounded, writhing in the dust as ants crawled over his body, screaming, 'I am Baron Ungern-Sternberg.' One of the Red Cavalry commanders facing Ungern was Konstantin Rokossovsky, whose horse died under him in the fighting. The report of Ungern's first interrogation at a barracks in Troitskosavsk was sent immediately to the Commissar of Foreign Affairs Georgy Chicherin in Moscow, and became known among scholars as the 'Ungerniad'. At his second interrogation in Irkutsk, the Baron again expounded his belief in monarchy and aristocracy, describing the authoritarian Nicholas I as the ideal ruler, a tsar who understood perfectly that without the stick people turn into moral and physical rubbish. After a secret trial in a theatre in Novonikolaevsk (now Novosibirsk), at which Emilian Yaroslavsky and Ivan Maisky acted as prosecutors, the Baron was shot in September 1921. 'For thousands of years the Ungerns have given orders,' the Baron told the court; 'we have never taken orders from anyone. I refuse to accept the authority of the working class.' For Yaroslavsky, Ungern epitomised the class enemy who hated Soviet power because all his property had been distributed to the peasants. He described the sentence against the Baron as a sentence against the whole nobility. 'The tragedy of Baron Ungern', he said, 'is that he could not match his feeble powers against the huge strength that he rose against.'

What refined torture, to make the Baron face Emilian Yaroslavsky as his prosecutor. A man of exactly Ungern's age, Yaroslavsky (born Minei Izrailovich Gubelman into a family of political exiles in Chita), for the Baron, was the worst kind of Bolshevik, a bespectacled Jew with thick hair. The unwitting creator of this piquant ideological *mise-en-scène* in the theatre in Novonikolaevsk was Molotov, who had persuaded Lenin to send Yaroslavsky back to Siberia after the Civil War. 'Of course it was my doing, but I don't regret that he was sent,' Molotov said to Chuev many decades later, recalling the events with clarity. Yaroslavsky, who had participated in the difficult Bolshevik takeover of Moscow and been first commissar of the Moscow military district, had become preoccupied with trifles, Molotov said: 'One moment he would request trousers for one person, another time it would be shoes for someone else . . .' After Lenin's command that he be sent east, Yaroslavsky rushed up to Molotov in their offices opposite what is now the Voentorg, shouting, 'You careerist! Your hands are all over this affair! You are a schemer!' 'What are you scolding me for?' Molotov replied. 'I just want you to work somewhere else.' (Molotov's driver once amused him by remarking how great it is that Russia has a Siberia to which all the human scum and rubbish can be sent.)

For the other prosecutor, Ivan Maisky, the Siberian steppe was a source of communist inspiration. In his memoir *Before the Storm* (written in London, it was the only book I found in the libraries of both Sands and Molotov), the Soviet ambassador to the court of St James recalls how, in Mongolia after the Revolution, he found himself overwhelmed by a sense of the possibilities of Siberia and wrote a poem which began, 'I believe in man! Mother Nature bore him in inspired passion as the pearl of creation and gave him immortal reason and power over himself . . .' Through the darkness of the centuries, mankind had been marching towards communism. Man would even change the climate. 'There is no limit to his imperial will!'

Evgeny Belov, author of the book I had bought in the Univermag, suggests that there was far more at stake in Ungern's cruelties than Yaroslavsky touched on in his crude Marxist prosecution speech. Belov took a 'revisionist' view of Ungern, traditionally dubbed 'Dictator of Mongolia' and an agent of the Japanese. (As Molotov said of Hitler, Baron Ungern was not a maniac, he was 'an idealistic man'.) Belov argues, citing previously unused letters from Ungern to his supporters in Mongolia, that he was not a degenerate lunatic nor a dictator, and that, contrary to the claims of the Comintern, he had no connections with the Japanese. For all his sadism and ultimate failure, Ungern was a brilliant man, Belov writes, whom the Mongolians looked to as a genuine national leader. The Baron was erudite. He knew several

European languages well and learned Chinese and Mongolian. He was conversant with contemporary scholarship and science, and could quote at will from Buddhist sacred writings and from Scripture. His ideas were based on deep comparative study of religion. He knew a great deal about Christianity and Buddhism, as well as communism and Judaism, which he hated, believing that the Talmud contained a plan for the destruction of nations and states.

Ungern divided the world into East and West, 'yellow' and 'white' races, fated to clash. The sacred culture of the East had been preserved untouched for three thousand years; therein lay its power over the culture of the West, which had declined, leading to the downfall of the aristocracy, bourgeois democracy and finally workers' revolution. He hated bankers and financiers as the greatest abomination of all. He revered the rigid hierarchies of Eastern cultures, and their conceptions of racial superiority. The phrases 'light from the East' and 'the rotten West' occur in almost all the letters he wrote to Mongolian princes, monarchist Chinese generals and his agents in Manchuria and Peking. 'My conviction has always been to await light and salvation which can only come from the East, not from Europeans who are corrupted down to the very roots.' Ungern's 'Middle Kingdom' would defend the East against the evil of the West; it would include the Mongol tribes and the nomads of Siberia and Central Asia, Kazakhstan and Tibet. One day, he promised, a new conqueror would arise, greater than Genghis Khan, who would rule until 'from his subterranean capital, the King of the World arises', bringing happiness to all humanity.

❧

On the belt-clasps and strap-buckles of the ancient Huns, wild horses are often fastened in struggling pairs, their necks locked in a single taut curve of bronze. The living horses feeding now on the dry grasses of the Selenga River Basin reached into each other's

hollows without the stylised passion of the zoomorphic ornaments that connoisseurs characterise as 'steppe baroque'; at the
crack of our tread the lazy intimacy of the grazing huddles among
the spindly trees broke up, and the horses cantered out of sight
across the plain.

We had been tempted to digress and delay on the southbound
road to Kyakhta. Our Buryat driver, Protas, was tired of our forever 'seeing beauty', as he said, and asking him to pull over so that
I could gaze and take pictures and my companion could smoke
and make quick sketches of the landscape; he was anxious that the
best highway shack-cafe this side of Mongolia would close before
he got to his plate of steamed meat *pozy*. Just south of Ulan Ude,
to save time, he boldly drove across a potato-field whose soil con-
ceals an ancient settlement of the Hsiung-nu; and then on, with a
few shrieking revs of the Zhiguli, up the arid hill where royal
members of this nomad people were buried with their treasure.
The Hsiung-nu, pronounced *Sunnu* or *Khunnu*, are the Huns who
crossed the Gobi Desert from northern China three thousand
years ago to extend their empire across the Siberian steppe. By the
third century BC the colonising Hsiung-nu tribes had united
under a royal clan. They traded in furs from the Siberian forests
and metals, taking tribute and controlling trade routes.

While we walked among the flat unhewn rocks that sealed the
emptied tombs in this wild garden of the dead, Protas left an
offering of kopecks at an upright shaman stone. The wind was so
loud that our voices barely carried. Before we left, he tied a scrap
of polythene to an outer twig of the solitary 'old man tree'. It
would flutter, he said, with the other rags on its branches, and the
friendly spirits of the place would hear of all his fears and wishes.

Before the discovery by Russian archaeologists in the 1890s of
the cache of 'Scythian-Siberian' bronze animals in the burial
mounds around Kyakhta, these Huns were known only from
Chinese written sources. The Han Chinese hoped that they
would eventually soften the tough pastoralist nomads with the
luxuries in which they traded. They sold them silk in the hope that

their skills on horseback would decline if they no longer dressed in felt and leather. They treated the Hsiung-nu who surrendered to them to fine clothes and carriages, delicacies to eat and soothing music. The findings in the tombs in Buryatia support the claim of Herodotus that the Scythians came from east to west across the steppe to settle north of the Azov and in the delta of the Don.

Since these discoveries, the prestige of this extinct people has been in steady ascent. In 1938, at the height of Stalin's Terror, the twenty-six-year-old Lev Gumilev, only child of Akhmatova and her first husband, the poet Nikolai Gumilev, was arrested for a second time and sent to Siberia. He had worked on geographical expeditions from Leningrad University in the western Sayan Mountains as a student in the early 1930s. He laboured in the Gulag mines at Norilsk as a technical geologist, contemplating the punishment systems of the ancient world, and secretly working on a history of the Hun people.

Meanwhile, in Leningrad, Akhmatova continued her own secret work on *Requiem*, the cycle of poems she had begun after her son's first arrest in 1935, in which private maternal loss is crafted into a monument to collective anguish. The secret police file on Lev Gumilev had apparently been opened after Mandelstam recited his satirical anti-Stalin poem to him and Akhmatova in 1934. It was in the Stalin epigram that Mandelstam made his allusion to Molotov's neck, and called him a 'half-person':

We live, not sensing the country beneath us,
Our speeches at ten paces cannot be heard,

And where there is enough for a half-speaker, –
There they recall the Kremlin mountain-dweller . . .

And around him is a rabble of thin-necked bosses,
He plays with the services of half-people.

By the time Gumilev's monograph, *Khunnu: Central Asia in Ancient Times*, was published in 1960, Gumilev had endured a third eight-year sentence in the camps, fought in the Battle of Berlin, and stopped speaking to his mother altogether, their relationship tortured to destruction by the mechanisms of the Great Terror.

Fabulous Scythian hordes to Herodotus and Pliny, barbarian aggressors beyond the Great Wall to the ancient Chinese, and an obscure adjunct to the name Attila in the mind of Europe, the nomad horsemen of Central Asia re-enter history in Gumilev's work as cultivated inhabitants of a distinct geographical region – a 'dry Mediterranean' – to which their art, culture, religion, and political and economic systems were subtly adapted. The Huns become the foundational example of Gumilev's 'scientific' theory of ethnogenesis, which explains the rise, flowering and vanishing of peoples as a 'biological' process. Landscape and climate, for Gumilev, are the determining elements in the formation of ethnicity; peoples are 'anthropofauna'. For Gumilev, ethnic phenomena are material, objective facts. 'There is not a single person on the planet without ethnicity,' he declared. Though he was of mixed blood himself – Akhmatova was proud of her Tatar blood and Gumilev shared her Asiatic features – he despised exogamy, which he believed destroyed nature and culture.

In his major work, *Ethnogenesis and the Biosphere of the Earth*, Gumilev accounts for the historical flourishing of human collectives with the concept of *passionarnost'*, 'passionarity' – a neologism for creative drive, the 'anti-entropic impulse', which bursts out during the creative period of an 'ethnos' and later ebbs. The approximate duration of an ethnos, which lies at the 'boundary of the biosphere and the sociosphere', is 1,200–1,500 years, which cover its creative period, the time of its actualisation and its inevitable decay. Passionarity is a biological attribute, 'an inborn capacity of the organism to absorb external energy and give it out again in the form of work'. Alexander the Great, Joan of Arc, Archpriest Avvakum and Napoleon were all great 'passionaries'. Culture can be deceptive, Gumilev believed. What we call 'flourishing' should really be seen as 'squandering', when people use up the great heritage accumulated by their ancestors, which creates an impression of abundance. Comparisons that measure non-European peoples by European culture and talk of their backwardness or stagnation are meaningless, Gumilev argues, because each cultural region has its own path.

Since his death in 1992, Gumilev has become a cult figure. In bookshops all across Russia, his works occupy large sections of the history shelves. In 2005 a monument was erected to him in Kazakhstan, and a university has been named in his honour in Astana, the Kazakh capital. Gumilev's work can easily be read to assert the great future for Russia–Eurasia which so many Russians believe they are owed by history. He suggests a geopolitical identity based on the heritage of the steppe. Arguing repeatedly against eurocentrism, Gumilev depicts both China and the West as predatory aggressors, insisting that Russia 'may only be saved through Eurasianism'.

Ignoring the historical evidence of the ravages of Khan Baty, who destroyed thousands of Russian towns in the thirteenth century, Gumilev denied that the Mongol presence had been a 'yoke'. (For scholars like Dmitri Likhachev, the arrival of the khans on horseback from across the steppe was a defining disaster for Russia, which had previously been among the most culturally and economically developed nations in Europe.) Gumilev talked instead about the fruitful saving character of Mongol rule – a symbiosis of Rus and the Golden Horde – which established the first pan-Eurasian state: a model for the Muscovite tsars. For Gumilev, the 'Jewish–Khazarian' yoke (a novel concept he developed) was far more deleterious than the Mongol invasion, for the Jewish 'behaviour stereotype' does not match with the behavioural stereotypes of the Eurasian ethnicities. For disciples of this mysticism of race, some of whom organised into a 'political social movement' in 2001 under the leadership of a clever demagogue in good standing with the Kremlin called Alexander Dugin, Eurasianism is a cultural antidote to 'Atlanticism'. The Atlantic powers are sea powers, and Eurasia is a land power, built on the conquest of the dry routes, the rectangle of the steppe, which is the equivalent of the Mediterranean for the West. The geopolitical force of maritime civilisations has always stood in opposition to Eurasian civilisation. In the sphere of foreign policy, 'Eurasia' pledges to 'support forces which act against the process of "American-style globalisation"', envisaging a Turkic–Slavic merger, and possible anti-Atlantic alliances with Islamic countries.

Selenginsk, which lies eighty miles south of Ulan Ude, where Pushkin's African great-grandfather General Gannibal once protected the imperial border, was once the most important stockade in the region. Later Udinsk was strengthened, and became Verkhneudinsk. In the nineteenth century, though, the most prominent town in this border region was Kyakhta-Troitskosavsk. Together, the Selenga River and the old post road to Kyakhta describe a long figure of eight, snaking southwards and crossing once at Selenginsk near Gusinoe Ozero. The geological and botanical features and shamanist lore of the 'Goose Lake' were carefully documented by the Decembrist Nikolai Bestuzhev in the latter years of his Siberian exile. After serving thirteen years' hard labour, Bestuzhev and his brother Mikhail were allowed to settle in Selenginsk in the 1840s. Their house stands tall among the wooden huts on the main street of this ramshackle outpost, close to the terra-cotta plaster and white Doric columns of the local library, once home to the merchant who adopted the illegitimate children of Bestuzhev and his Buryat common-law wife. The stone ruins of the baroque church opposite hint at the glamour of Kyakhta, fifty miles on.

Nikolai Bestuzhev had noted the strata of brown coal around Gusinoe Ozero. A power station, constructed under Stalin, still churns beneath the railway line on the north shore, sending electricity to Mongolia. In *The Decembrist Nikolai Bestuzhev, First Explorer of Siberia* (1950), the writer Lydia Chukovskaya contrasts the dark industrial scene with the primordial tranquillity that Bestuzhev experienced as he studied the lakeshore a century earlier, suggesting that he would have delighted in a future measured out in Five-Year Plans. But then, Stalin was still alive when her innocuous monographs on the activities of the Decembrist exiles appeared under the imprint of the State Publisher of Geographical Literature. Quoting Lenin and praising collectivisation must have seemed a small price for the freedom to describe the civilising energy, the distinctly European *passionarnost'*, which sustained the Decembrists in this alien place. Still locked away in the future dissident's desk drawer was *Sofia Petrovna*, the novel she had written in 1939 about a mother who loses her son to the Gulag, and secreted in her head were the lines of *Requiem* that she had memorised for her friend Akhmatova before the manuscript of the poem was burned. Decades later, when she was able to tell the story, Chukovskaya wrote:

> Suddenly in mid-conversation, she would fall silent, signalling with her eyes at the ceiling and walls, to get a scrap of paper and pencil; then she would loudly say something very mundane . . . cover the paper in hurried handwriting and pass it to me. I would read the poems and having memorised them, hand them back in silence . . . then she would burn the paper . . .

Chukovskaya's studies of the Decembrists (like the Yakushkin book I inherited from Sands) were published when Lev Gumilev, the son of her beloved friend, was back in the Gulag. These books are a kind of secret writing, the writing with a false bottom and secret drawers of the kind that Akhmatova alludes to in *Poem Without a Hero*. To write about Tsar Nicholas I and the Decembrists, even in sentences walled in by pious quotations from Lenin, was to write about tyranny, and the hope for justice and political freedom. If Stalin, Molotov and Vyshinsky could use words like 'democracy' and 'humanism' as they did, then Chukovskaya could use those words too. Her small book on Herzen's *Past and Thoughts*, which appeared fifteen years later, still has the same pathos. She talks of how difficult it was that

Herzen's friend Granovsky had held on to his belief in a life after death, and not become a true materialist. In tightly pencilled exclamations, Sands had pedantically corrected the distance Chukovskaya had given from Primrose Hill to the centre of London, and objected that the service in the Kremlin at which Chukovskaya claimed that Nicholas I and his priests thanked God for the hanging of the five Decembrists was in fact a service of thanksgiving for the preservation of the Tsar's life. Chukovskaya's dissidence was still buried then in the 1950s. In his Cambridge rooms, Sands could not have known that when she wrote about the cruelty of the Kremlin she was writing code. There were decoys on every page of her book. Perhaps, though, his pedantry had more love in it than spite. And how Chukovskaya would have loved to know that her little book had travelled so far, that a don in Cambridge was correcting her on the geography of London, a city she would never see.

Chukovskaya tells of how, despite the attentions of the police, Bestuzhev and his fellow-conspirators established peasant schools, compiled dictionaries of Buryat, painted the rare birds and butterflies of the steppe, built forcing-frames for melons and Chinese cucumbers, and sowed potatoes, asparagus and kohlrabi in a land that had only ever known onion and cabbage. They collected specimens, dried plants, insects, flowers and stuffed birds, and sent them back to the botanical gardens and the Moscow Society of Naturalists. Sitting in torn silk dressing gowns, their fingers dry, the Borisov brothers painted orchids and Venus flytraps. In the mid-nineteenth century, just as in the mid-twentieth, historical and geographical knowledge of Siberia was enriched by the attentions of tyrannised intellects. The Decembrists' letters and memoirs compose a single love poem to Siberia, Chukovskaya writes; under their pens, its wastes become rich and fruitful, full of promise.

Lev Gumilev was stirred by the idea that nature 'waits for the death of things (of the technosphere)', waiting to recapture the material that has been stolen from her by humankind. This steppe grass, the twitch grass whose Buryat name gives Kyakhta its name, stretching to the horizon in every direction, makes the 'technosphere' seem trivial, destined to be overcome. Yet humankind is tenacious in preserving the things it has made. From Siberia, Nikolai Bestuzhev wrote to his family in St Petersburg, asking for paints. He asked for 'Lake' and 'Prussian Blue' from a particular shop on the corner of Gorokhovaya and Bolshaya Morskaya Streets, remembering precisely how many colours fit into a box. The seventy or more aquarelle portraits of Decembrists that Bestuzhev painted in Chita had been discussed in the Russian press since the 1860s. 'Ask about the drawings,' Tolstoy wrote in his notebook when he was contemplating the novel *Decembrists*, which evolved into *War and Peace*. In 1921, when the family who had been keeping them left Russia, Bestuzhev's work disappeared. In 1945, the aquarelles were traced by a scholar named Zilbershtein to the home in Kuntsevo of the Old Believer family servant into whose safekeeping they had been given. Spread out on a velvet cloth under a lamp, not far from the dachas of Stalin and Molotov, were Bestuzhev's portraits of his friends: Maria Volkonskaya, not long after she had spent the evening with Pushkin in a salon on Tverskaya Street, her cheek resting on her hand, the guard tower and the spiked log walls of the Chita fortress in the window behind her. After his twenty-year search, Zilbershtein called this the happiest day of his life. It was a spiritual moment, he said, when he touched the past.

The last miles towards Kyakhta led over a sandy hill, through low evergreen woods. The forest floor was festive with dense *bagalnik*, the lambent pink globe-flower that grows beneath the pines. The Bestuzhevs enjoyed driving along this road in the opposite direction. Though they were always honoured guests among the liberal and high-living magnates of this city of stupendous and evanescent wealth, the exiles regarded it as a 'miniature Babylon': noisy, chic and exhausting. After champagne and fireworks, charity balls with the bons viveurs at the Merchants' Club and literary soirées in millionaires' salons, Mikhail Bestuzhev was relieved to return to 'blessed Selenginsk'. Nikolai would visit Kyakhta on request: to paint portraits of the tea-barons and their wives, assist on the local paper, restore the Italian icons in the cathedral and join in amateur dramatics on summer nights in the park.

Before the opening of the Suez Canal, much of the tea that Europe had come to desire arrived here on caravans from Kalgan in China to be sold to Russian wholesalers. Kyakhta's great rival for the tea trade was the East India Company; when England was fighting China in the Opium Wars of the 1830s and 1850s, the city's fortunes soared. Even the English drank Kyakhta tea then. At first, tea was bartered for lynx and sable furs, or Prussian wool cloth in fancy Russian packaging; then, in the 1850s, to the spectacular profit of the Kyakhta merchants, already masters of every kind of contraband and fraud involving promissory notes and paper *assignats*, the state lifted restrictions on the export of gold and silver coin. Now, carriages marked 'sables' no longer crossed the border with secret bottoms stuffed with silver and gold, the dignitaries riding in them wondering why they felt so heavy.

Contraband literature likewise flowed through Kyakhta. Decembrists could smuggle out their writings, and merchants and civil servants coming into Russia through China would bring in copies of Herzen's anti-autocratic journal *The Bell*, carried all the way from London. At the end of the century there were still surprises for travellers in Kyakhta's second-hand bookshops. Finding a copy of Charles Dickens's *All the Year Round* during an afternoon's browsing was George Kennan's only pleasure in this part of Buryatia, where he complained that 'sleeplessness, insufficient food and constant jolting' left little capacity for enjoyment of anything.

Crossing the border at Kyakhta, Kennan said, was like a ride on the magic carpet in the *Arabian Nights*: one moment you were in Russia, then you passed through a screen into the middle of the

Chinese empire. In Maimachan, the town just across the border, the tiny houses had dragons and gold balls on the roofs, merchants with long thin beards walked about in robes of embroidered silk, and the air smelled powerfully of garlic and Chinese pipe tobacco. The Russian and Chinese merchants even shared their own strange language of trade, full of English-influenced words like *pakgaus*, 'packing house'.

The Kyakhta Museum was full of nature made into things, the 'domination of dead matter by living man', to turn Marx's phrase on its head. Case upon case of stuffed birds and butterflies: Mongolian larks and nightjars with glass eyes and dusty feathers, and a wall of gaudy butterflies from South America, all of which, the museum attendant told us with pride, had been exchanged with a museum in Buenos Aires for a single, 'a *single!*' Buryat specimen, a small dull-brown butterfly called *Fedra*. On the walls was a series of virtuoso bird drawings by the neurotic Borisov brothers (men destroyed by the Tsar and his secret police, Chukovskaya writes), which, the attendant insisted, throwing off her knitted lace shawl and rising to guide us round the display cases, captured 'so perfectly' the particular *manera*, the manner, of each bird: the kinglet and the bullfinch, and the golden-crested wren, 'like a beautiful woman', showing its tail plumes, its head tilted at a coquettish angle, eyeing the viewer. In the next room were more of the artefacts exhumed from the steppe by the archaeologist Y. D. Talko-Grintsevich in the 1890s, pieces of metal shaped by the ancient Huns, which the 'technosphere' will not give back to the silence of nature. We were the first foreign visitors in a long time, the attendant sighed. The only outsiders who ever came to Kyakhta were parties of birdwatchers, she said, come to follow the migrations.

The Suez Canal had already drained much of Kyakhta's trade by the time the Trans-Siberian Railway was routed twenty miles to the west in the 1890s. The last of the merchants moved on, leaving their mansions and clubhouses to the learned societies of orientalists that had colonised the city. The Hun antiquities that the archaeologists discovered in the sands of the steppe may be the pure expression of Eurasian 'passionarity', but the Kyakhta Museum which they founded to preserve them – the last viable institution in this beautiful, dead city – is the creative work of traders' money, which mixes and scatters people – Gumilev's anthropofauna – without regard. And people are also scattered by the force and movement of ideas, like the ideas that brought a Jewish Bolshevik and a proto-Nazi Baltic baron face-to-face in a theatre in Siberia. History does not move forward. It moves not in a straight line, or a circle, but in an arabesque, which is not always a line of beauty.

No pictures of the border, Protas said. So I took one of the cathedral, with peroxide-blonde prostitutes and Buryat soldiers dealing on its broken steps. Then I turned to the frontier, and pressed the shutter with the camera at my chest; the loaded trucks at the checkpoint came out at an angle, sliding towards a Procter & Gamble mini-van, a vodka kiosk and a silver-painted statue of Lenin. He stood at the gates of the run-down knitting factory that occupies the grand neoclassical packing house in which China tea was once graded and sewn into sacks of skin.

Epilogue

I want someone to make me a gift of a whole day to myself . . .
Write to me about Moscow in Summer. My favourite thing,
to the point of passion.
MARINA TSVETAEVA, letter to Boris Pasternak, 1 July 1926

I am tired of the Reading Room. It is hot outside, and I can see the Kremlin towers through the dusty panes of the side windows. The sky is true Byzantine blue, made for the shine of gold domes. Open before me is a 1953 hagiography of the Stalinist pseudo-biologist Olga Lepeshinskaya. 'Was it not a city like this that loomed before the visionaries of the past when they dreamed of the future of mankind?' the Party hack-writer begins, picturing Lepeshinskaya, kept ever young by her daily soda baths, standing on a balcony in the House on the Embankment on the other side of the Moscow River. She sees 'the towers and domes, the graceful columns and lancet balustrades, the buildings crowned by turrets and spires like exquisite statuary . . . beauty created by millions of human hands', and so on and on. On a summer day like this, it seems ridiculous to be reading about such a vicious, justly unremembered fraud.

Dostoevsky was right when he observed in his notes on London that what the traveller craves is a bird's-eye view of a city. In Menippean satire, in which the Soviet literary theorist Mikhail Bakhtin saw antecedents for Dostoevsky's fiction, there are examples of the observation of the life of a city from a very great height. What if one could see into every room for a few seconds, as though in a diorama, to try to work out where history was being made? Most of what happens is not seen; hardly anything is written down.

'I would have liked to read out all their names', Akhmatova

lamented in *Requiem* for the millions of victims of Stalin and his men:

> *but they took away the list, and there's nowhere to find out.*
> *For them I have woven a thick cover*
> *Out of the poor words I have overheard.*

As Shalamov stood in the permafrost wilderness of Kolyma, and watched the bodies of the victims of 1938 being shovelled into mass graves by an American bulldozer, he had a revelation about the architecture of Moscow. The high buildings of Moscow are like watchtowers, guarding the prisoners of the city, he wrote in 'Lend-Lease'. Which came first, he wondered, the Kremlin towers or the watchtowers? The watchtower of the Gulag zone, he decided, was the architectural symbol – the principal idea – of his time.

The elfin old man whose hair stands on end has come around to my side of the desk again. Since the day he caught my eye in the queue for the coat-check last spring, he thinks we have a special understanding, and any second now he is going to leer and bow. '*Kto perrrvyi?*' – 'Who is firrrst?' asked the coat-check man, who loves to observe rank of any kind because it is something beyond the money economy that has left him behind. In front of me an old woman in a red velveteen dress, long golden plastic beads and a lamé collar adjusted her wide red belt. She had on matching red trainers and her hair was dyed orange. She comes to the library to read. In a city dizzy with fashion, this library is a carnival of anti-fashion. I was looking at the picture of the Communist Party of the Russian Federation candidate Zyuganov – wearing a fine suit, just like all the other candidates – that the coat-check man had put up on the marble pillar between the racks of coats. The old man, who had a little medal pinned to the dirty knot in his tie, was combing his sparse greasy hair back into its odd little quiff and, as he slid his little plastic comb back into his jacket pocket, he said, 'What is the point of voting for any of them? It's not a real election,' at which remark I was still nodding knowingly when he added, 'Gorbachev, Borya, Putin, they're all just as small and petty as one another. We haven't had a true leader since Stalin.' What does the old man do here all day every day with his piles of books and folders? I never have the chance to peep at what he has ordered lying on his desk, because he always seems to be at his desk or to appear beside it out of nowhere just as I pass.

I am going out to take a walk. In my jacket pocket I have the heavy brass keys to our apartment in No. 3. In a couple of weeks we will hand them back to Alexander Alexandrovich and close the door. He is thinking of selling. The apartment on the fourth floor is still for sale with a price in millions. It has been advertised as 'General Rokossovsky's apartment'. The real-estate agents believe that the connection with the Soviet hero will add half a million dollars to the value, but the Rokossovsky family claims to find this approach vulgar, for memory should have no price. Rokossovsky met his wife in Kyakhta after he had fought Baron Ungern; she was the daughter of a local official who initially opposed the match. The General was arrested in 1937 and tortured for weeks in a prison in Leningrad. He was released in 1940, and, after his distinguished service in the Great Patriotic War, moved into apartment 63.

I stand on the granite paving slabs beneath Dostoevsky. He has his back to the library. This mausoleum of thought looks just like a building from the Third Reich: a suitable resting place for Hitler, an odd place for a statue of Dostoevsky. As Likhachev once said when there was discussion of a monument to Dostoevsky, 'there are no positive heroes in Dostoevsky'. But Molotov thought that Russia itself was Dostoevsky's positive hero, and that Russia's 'God-bearing' role in history was one thing about which that difficult writer was correct. That was something Stalin also understood, Molotov said: the 'great historical destiny and fateful mission of the Russian people – the destiny about which Dostoevsky wrote: the heart of Russia, more than that of any other nation, is destined to be universal, it is the all-embracing humanitarian nation of nations'.

I came down here late one night before the presidential election, and there was a convoy of Icarus coaches coming round the corner under police escort, dirty coaches with the word *Deti* – 'Children' – written in their windscreens. The next morning, the children, who had been bussed into Moscow from schools and institutes in the provinces, appeared wearing identical white baseball jackets with the word *nashi* – 'ours' – written on them, waving placards in support of Putin and the United Russia Party. They stood on the square long enough to be filmed for the evening news, and then got back in their buses to be driven away from the city.

Above me, standing high on the balustrade of the building, are the heroic hypertrophied statue bodies, their wonderful heads bent over books, and below them in bas-relief on the library's granite and black marble side wall are the faces behind which were the greatest minds of humanity: Plato, Darwin, Copernicus and, last of all, the Russians, Dmitri Mendeleev and Ivan Pavlov. This library is so many libraries. The library of Nikolai Fyodorov, who believed that one day we would resurrect every body and every thought out of the vibrations of molecules in the secret depths of matter, beginning with the dust in books. The library of Vladimir Nevsky, who believed that public enlightenment would be the foundation of the great communist future. And then there was the library of the bibliopsychologist Nikolai Rubakin, who pioneered a 'psychology of reading', using reading therapy to promote mental health. As I was reading books published in the mid-1930s – Vyshinsky and Otto Shmidt – I kept coming across Rubakin's *ex libris* plate, which showed the words 'Truth and Justice' at the centre of a book-lined room flooded with sunlight.

Marina Tsvetaeva was proud of the fact that her father, Ivan Tsvetaev, one of the great historians of the city of Moscow, as well as founder-curator of the Pushkin Museum of Fine Arts, had left to the Rumyantsev Museum every last volume of his own vast library. Her mother also 'gave her library and her father's library to the museum. So from the Tsvetaevs, Moscow received three libraries.' 'I would give my own', she added, 'if I had not been forced to sell it during the years of revolution.' She remembers a bookcase in her childhood home not far from here, up the Arbat off Sivtsev Vrazhek Lane, in a house which is no longer there. 'In the second cabinet there lived the pathfinder, who led us far off into the very thickets of good and evil, to that place in the thickets where they are inescapably entwined together and, in the intertwining, make the shape of real life.' Tsvetaeva knew in 1912 that none of the reality of her childhood would last, and she wrote delicate short lyrics that the critics found too intimate and domestic, in which she addressed her mother, her sister and her home, and the streets of Moscow. The 'little houses of old Moscow . . . disappearing from the modest little lanes . . . Little houses, like ice palaces, where the mirrors reach up to the painted ceilings . . . these houses, with their portraits and clavichords are being replaced by six-storey buildings, because it is the "right" of the "house-owners".' Tsvetaeva asserts her own right to memorialise them with a nostalgia which, within five years of her writing, would become troubling and potent, forbidden. Her second collection of verse, *Magic Lantern*, in which these lyrics appeared, was not much liked by critics. She dedicated the book to her husband, Sergei Efron, who would fight for the Whites, spy for the NKVD and be driven from the Lubyanka as the Germans approached Moscow in 1941 in a truck marked 'Meat' or 'Bread' to be shot. 'Everything will flash by in the space of a minute,' she writes in the epigraph, 'the knight and the page, the sorceror and the tsar . . . Away with cogitation! After all a woman's book is only a magic lantern!'

I go down the treacherous granite steps into the underpass that leads, in one direction, towards the Alexander Gardens, takes you down to the metro the other way, and by which you can cross under Vozdvizhenka and come up underneath the old Peterhof Hotel, the Fourth House of the Soviets where President Kalinin once had his offices. Now half the building belongs to the Duma, and another part of it is a gleaming office complex for international accountants and lawyers. A low metal door is open inside the underpass just beyond a kneeling man with his books. This is the first time I have noticed that door. Through it I can see into the workings of the metro: walkways, thick wires snaking endlessly, lamps, metal ladders and railings, a whole underground world. The bookseller is here again today. He comes down with his bagful of old books and lays them out on a sheet of dirty plastic among the pigeon droppings and spit globules on the gritty floor of the underpass. What has he got for me today? Something curious. A little pamphlet, yellowing at the edges: Stalin's discourse 'On Dialectical and Historical Materialism', and some even older treasures: a book of *Songs of Prison and Exile*, published in 1930, songs the Old Bolsheviks used to sing to keep their courage up in the long years in Siberia before they came into their kingdom. And another curiosity: a polemic of 1899, re-covered in brown packing paper, by the great zoologist Timiryazev, called 'The Feeble Spite of the Antidarwinist', a polemic against the Slavophile conservative Nikolai Strakhov, author of *The Struggle Against the West in Russian Literature*, associate of Sands's Apollon Grigoriev, one of Tolstoy's only close friends, and biographer of Dostoevsky, with whom he had a spite-filled friendship. (It was Strakhov who passed on to Tolstoy in a letter a creepy rumour about Dostoevsky and 'a little girl in a banya'.) The title of Timiryazev's pamphlet, felt-tipped in purple on its brown-paper packaging by one of its previous owners, down here in the underpass, is still redolent of the intellectual fury in which it was written. Why am I buying it? I may never read it. Father Men used to say that books found their way to him, like relatives and friends arriving at a birthday celebration. I have far too many weird books, and I would do better to come down here and set them out for sale, but I will not leave Timiryazev here on this plastic sheet among the alcoholics and the impudent teenage buskers. Its fate is to come back to Cambridge in my luggage. Timiryazev lived opposite No. 3 in a small detached house behind the Professors' House, where, until it was shrouded for *remont*, his book *The Life of the Plant* was laid open on the desk at the page on chlorophyll.

As I was on my way across to the library this morning, camera crews were just leaving through the gateway behind the Professors' House, down from the entrance to the Kremlin Hospital where Polina Zhemchuzhina once lay dying of cancer, visited each day by a loving Molotov. Because it was hot, the windows of the hospital were open, the row of deep windows that were once the windows of the young Count Sergei Sheremetev. A young female doctor in a white coat looked out. The palace is now the tattiest building in the street. I wonder when it will get a renovation. The glass-fronted bookcases in the room behind her will soon be thrown out and and replaced with some new imported storage system in white and chrome. I almost bumped into the court artist, who, according to the nannies in the courtyard, has found another woman, younger still. He was in his summer outfit: crocodile-skin brogues, a red shirt and a Burberry-check jacket, his long hair wild, a manic look in his eye. Last week I heard the *komendantka* call him *kotik*, which means 'kitten'. The artist is rich and famous, but he always looks startled and lost.

The sun shone on Dmitri Manuilsky's plaque and for a moment cast his name in mirror writing on to the pavement. The cameras had been recording another historic set-piece: the gold cross had just been mounted on the highest dome of the half-restored Church of the Sign, which for so long had been falling into ruin as the kitchens of the hospital. The baroque church was inspected by the new regime in 1920. Its treasures were removed in 1922, a great weight of silver, which was handed to the Kremlin Armoury. The church was closed in 1929, and the proposal to make it into a sports hall for university students was dropped in favour of the plan to make it the kitchens of the Kremlin Hospital. Today the mayor had attended the ceremony with the highest ecclesiastics of the Orthodox Church, who walked out on to Romanov in the sunshine smiling and laughing, with their long beards and heavy gold crosses coming down to the middle of their ample chests.

'We don't need churches in the centre of Moscow,' Molotov

said when asked what he thought of the dynamiting of the Church of Christ the Saviour; 'it's wrong.' 'It is hard to change one's gods,' Shatov says to the murderous brainwasher Stavrogin in Dostoevsky's *Demons* as they discuss the Slavophile idea of Russia as the 'one and only "God-bearing" nation on earth'. Father Men called the Stalin era the 'polar night' of Russian history. He saw Stalinism as a religious phenomenon, which 'drew all the people's atavistic and spiritual drives into a common cause, made the figure of the leader the "measure of all things", gave him the attributes of a divinity, a limitless power'. 'Do you ever dream of him?' Felix Chuev asked the elderly Molotov. He did. 'I'm in some kind of destroyed city, and I can't find any way out,' Molotov replied; 'afterwards I meet with him.' The dream seems the closest he ever came to a real insight into his part in history. In some deep furrow of his terrible mind, Molotov sensed that what he and Stalin had done together had something to do with destruction. Dream life is part of the life of the city. Yet though life is like a dream, it is not a dream. In the dungeon of the world we are not alone.

In the 1960s, when Molotov and Khrushchev were both living in No. 3, Polina Zhemchuzhina met Khrushchev in the street. (Khrushchev had taken over Molotov's dacha as soon as Molotov was expelled from the Party and, as Stalin's daughter Svetlana Alliluyeva remembered, planted corn in the place of the magnificent roses the Molotovs had cultivated in its large grounds.) Zhemchuzhina begged him to have Molotov reinstated in the Party. Instead, Khrushchev took her to see the lists in the archives on which her husband had written the words 'to be shot' alongside the names of their old comrades and their wives, including the Ukrainian Party boss Stanislav Kosior and his wife, who had also once lived in No. 3. Chuev remembers Molotov's body in its coffin, his head shaking on its wrinkled neck as the catafalque was moved. In none of the pictures of Molotov that I have seen does his neck look thin or his head small, as Nadezhda Mandelstam said it was; though I suppose those wide-set features and penetrating, satisfied eyes might possibly remind one of a sleek tomcat.

On the other side of Mokhovaya, at the back entrance of the renovated Manège, crates are being unloaded from a pantechnicon with a foreign licence plate. Later this week, the Moscow Fine Art Fair will open in the Manège, full of Old Masters, Picassos and flawless diamonds brought to Moscow by merchants from Geneva and New York. This grand 'exhibition house' close to the Kremlin wall was built to commemorate the fifth anniversary of the Russian victory over Napoleon's Grande Armée, which entered Moscow in 1812 to find the city destroyed by fire. From the Revolution until Stalin's death, the elegant empire-style building was used as a garage for government cars. A few years ago, on the March night of Putin's second election to the presidency, the Manège caught fire. (No one thought the catastrophe was accidental. The Mayor, Yuri Luzhkov, produced plans for a renovation – complete with three floors of underground parking – the very next morning.) The wind blew pieces of flaming roofbeams from the Manège across Mokhovaya, over the University buildings and the Kremlin Hospital into Romanov, where they dropped, burning, on the asphalt, and smouldered into ash beneath our windows.

I walk past the Corner House on Vozdvizhenka and along a wooden walkway under the scaffolding. The Military Department Store was demolished a couple of years ago, and a new building is going up in its place. Mayor Luzhkov has promised it will be a replica of the Voentorg, which Muscovites had come to love (they come to love all the buildings in their city in the end), but nobody believes him. Luzhkov follows his own taste, which he calls 'imperial'. The new building is still under its vast green shroud, which is now in tatters. They will face it in polished granite, which the city planners favour because it looks so rich. The faces of Central Asian workers, who squat high on the scaffolding, stare down at the passers-by. The sounds of our heels are amplified; we make way for one another as we pass, without smiling.

Gusts of warm summer wind blow grit from the building site on to my legs. On the corner of Povarskaya Street, just beyond the church where Count Nikolai and Praskovia were married, there is a huge advertisement for an Italian jeweller, which asks, 'What is the secret of luxury?' For a few weeks this year the billboard said, 'Moscow Votes for Vladimir Putin!' but the regime is business-like about propaganda: business comes first. On the Hotel Moskva before the presidential election, for a few days, there was a gigantic image of Putin and his chosen heir, Dmitri Medvedev, in matching leather bomber jackets. As soon as the election-show was over, a Rolex advertisement went up, displaying a rugged man's hand with a beautiful gold watch on its wrist above the slogan 'All Power Is in Your Hands'.

On the corner of the Boulevard Ring, old women from the country are selling bouquets of pink peonies from plastic buckets. I walk up Nikitsky and Tverskoi Boulevards towards Pushkin Square, past the house where Herzen was born, in which Osip and Nadezhda Mandelstam lived in the early 1920s, and again in the early 1930s, before the poet's first arrest. At his speech in the Noblemen's Club for the unveiling of the statue of Pushkin which now stands on Pushkin Square, Dostoevsky told a nation terrified by bomb-throwing terrorists that Russia would save the world. Ivan Turgenev, who (like the historian Granovsky) had been thoroughly satirised in *Demons* as a self-regarding and pompous Europeanised writer, watched Dostoevsky's 'mean little eyes' and marvelled at his dangerous brilliance. Yet only the imagination of the writer of *Demons* could take in what would happen in the building of the Noblemen's Club (floridly remodelled by the architect Meisner) less than sixty years later – the show trials of the Old Bolsheviks, with Vyshinsky screaming for the blood of his blank-eyed tortured comrades, and Karl Radek, the star witness, playing cynical games with the lies written for him by his interrogators in the Lubyanka: 'For nothing at all, just for the sake of Trotsky's beautiful eyes – the country was to return to capitalism.'

Tsvetaeva loved the statue of Pushkin for its iron blackness. She called the monument to the Russian national poet with the African great-grandfather a monument against racism, a monument to the mingling of bloods. There was once a rambling monastery on the square, where now there is a cinema and the Shangri-La Casino, faced in swirling multi-coloured plastic. 'The Strastnoi Monastery pinkens, rising over the grey square', Tsvetaeva wrote in her early poem 'Tverskaya', in which she imagines walking along Tverskaya Street with her teenage sister on a spring day. Tverskaya is the 'cradle of their youth, the cradle of their half-adult hearts'. They take everything in: the shining shop windows full of diamonds, sunset, traffic lights, the voices of the passers-by.

Molotov came to Moscow for the first time in the same year, after his exile in Vologda. He remembers Tverskaya banked with snow. And Varlam Shalamov remembered his impressions of Tverskaya when he was new to Moscow in 1924, and watched the Revolution Day parade, led by Trotsky in his Red Army uniform, short with a wide forehead, walking alongside Bukharin, Yaroslavsky and Kamenev. Tverskaya is wider now than it was then. Its tall apartment buildings were rolled back on subterranean castors in the 1930s to make it better suited for parades. But the diamonds – Tiffany, Chaumet, Bulgari – are back in the windows of shops that used to be labelled 'Fish' or 'Cheese' or 'Milk' or 'Bread'. This year was the first time in decades that ICBMs were driven on to Red Square for the Victory Day parade on 9 May. From Romanov, we could hear them rumbling down Tverskaya in night-time rehearsals.

There is a new hotel where the Intourist used to be, the Ritz-Carlton, with a wide space into which large cars can sweep and a roof terrace with white leather sofas that looks down over Red Square and the Kremlin. The bar serves a martini cocktail called 'Casino Royale'. 'Tower upon tower, wall upon wall, palace upon palace! A strange blend of ancient and new architecture, poverty and wealth, European manners and the manners and customs of the East,' Konstantin Batyushkov wrote in his 'Walk Around Moscow', 'a divine inscrutable flowing together of the emptiness of vanity and true glory and greatness, boorishness and enlightenment, humanity and barbarism.'

I turn down Gazetny, 'Newspaper Lane', past the Telegraph Building and McDonald's, past the small pale blue church, in front of which almost every passer-by stops to bow and make the sign of the cross, past the House of Composers and the Ministry of Internal Affairs. Outside the Conservatoire, on the summer verandah of Coffeemania, beautiful people are drinking cappuccinos and smoking. Music comes from the rooms above: an opera singer practising *La Traviata*, her cadences mingling with Beethoven on a piano from further back in the courtyard. Marshal Budyonny's second wife, the lovely contralto Olga Mikhailova, daughter of a railway worker from Kursk, studied here in the late 1920s, before joining the Bolshoi Opera as a soloist. She was arrested in August 1937 for attending receptions at foreign embassies. After nineteen years in prison and the Gulag, she returned to Moscow, her physical and mental health broken, with stories that no one wanted to hear of her repeated gang rapes in the camps.

The latest fashion in chic Moscow eating places is to order numerous elegant dishes and leave them on the table hardly touched. Almost everything on the menu costs a week's pension. Three of the luxury cars parked outside Coffeemania have FSB plates in their front windows. I pass the hair and beauty salon where last week I was kept waiting because my stylist, Natasha, said one of her male clients had come for a cut and a manicure without an appointment, and as he is a general in the FSB she felt obliged to give him mine. It is just as Nikolai Bestuzhev said nearly two centuries ago: the 'outward brilliance of the court has been taken for the true happiness of the state, the extent of trade, the wealth of the merchant class and the banks for the well-being of the whole people'. Putin's courtiers are more interested in their jackets, their watches and their coiffures than in any God-bearing mission of the Russian people, whatever they may say to 'the people' each night on the TV. Outside the Ministry of Internal Affairs building, militiamen are waiting in the sun with their car doors open, their radios on. The doors of the Zoological Museum on the corner lie open to the darkness within, where a whale's jawbone rests on the tiles under the staircase with yellow-eyed Siberian wolves and bryozoans from the Barents Sea, and Mandelstam once walked the wrought-iron galleries with poetry flowing in his head. Outside the office building at No. 4 Romanov the guards move back the traffic cones for a hovering Mercedes. How many people in this city spend their working lives standing in the street to guard some favoured piece of the pavement for the comfort of the powerful?

I came home late last night after an evening with friends in No. 5. On the way downstairs from the top floor, I looked in at the progress of the renovation of the last communal apartment in the building. The Tajik workers invited me in as though they were the owners and I was an honoured guest, showing me the new gold gesso-work on the cornice mouldings. Outside in the street the wind was high. I went into No. 3 through the 'black entrance'. Behind me, the torn green wrappings on the new Voentorg flapped like the sails on a storm-lashed ship, light from within coming through the tears in the fabric.

There is never a right time to leave a city. 'Everything was very ordered and dignified,' Akhmatova wrote in 1939, 'Moscow, the beginning of spring. Friends and books and sunset in the window.' That is how it is. Order, friends, books. 'In Moscow without me' is now my favourite chapter title in Herzen's *Past and Thoughts*. Very soon I will no longer live above a *luxe* travel agency in which I can buy a train ticket to the end of Siberia. I gave back the key to the Molotov apartment a while ago. The banker forgot to ask me for it when he left, and I kept it in my desk drawer for many months, listening to the footfalls in the corridor above of the shy couple from Dresden who had moved in after the banker and who, the concierge told me, represented the Adenauer Foundation, which supports the development of civil society in Russia. The German couple never came to say hello and I never met them on the stairs, but once in a while they would hold a formal reception, and from the open door of the apartment would come the music of a string quartet. The morning after one of their soirées the concierge told me that Mikhail Gorbachev had been among the guests, but she was not particularly stirred by his visit, as, like most of her generation, she has nothing good to say about the man who brought democracy to Russia and gave away the empire.

I went up one day to give back the key and the German woman, who was very gentle and polite, gave me tea and let me look around. The magic lantern was gone – she did not remember seeing it – and so was the Shah of Iran's carpet, which Molotov's granddaughter (who calls herself 'Skryabina') had told her was worth sixteen thousand euros. The books were still there when I opened the lower bookcase, but the bookstands in the corridor had gone, with Winston Churchill and Dante. After the Germans left, the concierge was sad. The German woman used to go down to sit in her basement room and listen to the concierge's tape recordings of herself singing patriotic songs. Her love for the woman from Dresden was historically momentous for the concierge, for her greatest living year had been 1941. She reminisced every day about how, as an eighteen-year-old girl, she and her comrades – 'all young and strong and patriotic' – made barricades against German tanks in the Moscow streets.

Apartment 61 was recently sold by Molotov's heirs to the TV producer who already owned apartment 62 – Trotsky's last Moscow home – on the other side of the landing. For weeks the sounds of renovation came from above. This is my last torture by Moscow *remont*, I told myself as the drill sounded above my desk. One night water began to pour through the ceiling into my daughter's bedroom, and I went upstairs again. The producer's wife had come back from Tuscany. The fine lines of her beauty had coarsened. She had grown larger in the years since I used to see her regularly, unsmiling and perfect in her black mink, on the staircase. Now she wore flip-flops and a shapeless grey silk smock, her blonde hair a mess, her pouting face newly bruised with beauty injections. She took me to the bathroom, much less interested in the flood in our apartment than in what I thought of her taste in sanitary ware and marble tiling. She showed me through the rooms. The wood panelling was still in place, but the synthetic wall coverings in the bedrooms were gone, and so were the bookcases in the corridor. In the corner where the magic lantern once stood was a lavish purple velvet divan with an asymmetrically curving gold-painted frame. There were rows of photographs mounted in polished wood and silver on the window ledge in what was once the study where Molotov 'dug into everything from dawn to dusk', seeing bad tendencies take shape, which, he said, 'began, unfortunately, back in Stalin's time and mine'. My neighbour caught me looking at a picture of her, captured in a shining moment of absolute glamour, arm in arm at a party with the Italian designer Miuccia Prada. 'Shoes!' she said, breaking into English with a lovely smile.

NOTE

INDEX

Note

I have referred in the text to many of the books I read and drew on as I was working on *Molotov's Magic Lantern*. These brief bibliographical notes are for English-speaking readers who may wish to explore further.

In 1991, Osip Mandelstam's centenary year, his first collection, *Stone*, was published in an elegant edition by Collins Harvill, with facing-page English translations (and an introduction and notes) by Robert Tracy. New York Review Books recently republished the thirty-year-old *Selected Poems of Osip Mandelstam*, co-translated by the Mandelstam scholar Clarence Brown and the American poet W. S. Merwin (New York, 2004). Translations of Mandelstam's prose, including *Fourth Prose* and *Journey to Armenia*, may be found in *The Prose of Osip Mandelstam*, translated with critical essays by Clarence Brown (North Point Press, San Francisco, 1986), and *The Collected Critical Prose and Letters*, edited by Jane Gary Harris (Collins Harvill, London, 1991). Collins Harvill published Nadezhda Mandelstam's two volumes of memoirs, translated by Max Hayward, in 1971 and 1974, with the titles *Hope Against Hope* and *Hope Abandoned*. She herself requested these English titles, punning on her name, Nadezhda, which in Russian means 'hope'. The second volume ends with a love letter she wrote, and could not send, to her husband in October 1938, when she did not know where he was or whether he was alive or dead. 'Only now is it possible to illuminate that dark section of Mandelstam Street', Vitaly Shentalinsky remarks (referring to a poem by Mandelstam about his own name) in *The*

KGB's Literary Archive, which came out in an abridged English translation by John Crowfoot in 1995 (The Harvill Press), introduced by Robert Conquest. Shentalinsky had been demoted as a journalist in the Soviet period for repeatedly referring to Pasternak and Tsvetaeva in his writing. When Shentalinsky took advantage of 'glasnost' and went into the Lubyanka (quietly supported from the Kremlin by Mikhail Gorbachev's adviser Alexander Yakovlev) to petition the KGB for the hidden files on Russia's suppressed writers, he was told that he was the first writer to come into the building of his own free will. His researches raised many atrocities to the light, including details of Mandelstam's death and burial in a mass grave, the protocols of Isaac Babel's interrogations, and a letter to Molotov (as head of the Soviet government) from the theatre director Vsevolod Meyerhold (who was arrested at the same time as Babel), in which Meyerhold described the beatings that produced the 'confessions' so prized by Andrei Vyshinsky: 'the intolerable physical and emotional pain caused my eyes to weep unending streams of tears . . . "Death, oh most certainly, death is easier than this!" the interrogated person says to himself'. Alexander Yakovlev's *A Century of Violence in Soviet Russia* was published by Yale University Press in 2002, translated by Anthony Austin. (Under Gorbachev, Yakovlev had been head of a commission on the rehabilitation of victims of political repression.) 'Papers are not destroyed; people are', Yakovlev writes. 'More and more of the bloodstained documents pile up on my desk . . . If only the files would burn and the men and women return to life!' I read Yakovlev's remarkable book in the Molotov apartment, where the banker had left it out one day on the desk in the study.

Jonathan Brent's *Inside the Stalin Archives* (Atlas & Co., New York, 2008) gives a very readable account of the challenges and excitements of bringing to light archival materials from the Soviet period, as well as on how 'perplexing and often sad' such work can be. For the past seventeen years, Brent has collaborated with the Russian scholars Oleg Naumov and Oleg V. Khlevniuk, among others, on the Annals of Communism series for Yale University Press. *Stalin's Letters to Molotov, 1925–1936* (1995) was one of the first books published in this invaluable ongoing series. The caricatures of Party leaders that I mention in *Molotov's Magic Lantern* can all be found in *Piggy Foxy and The Sword of Revolution: Bolshevik Self-Portraits* (Yale University Press, 2006), edited by Alexander Vatlin and Larisa Malashenko, with a foreword by Simon Sebag Montefiore.

Lydia Chukovskaya's *The Akhmatova Journals*, translated by Milena Michalski and Sylva Rubashova (Harvill, 1994), relates how Chukovskaya preserved Akhmatova's *Requiem* in her memory. A less hagiographical picture of great poets comes through in the literary critic Emma Gerstein's fascinating and controversial memoirs of her troubled friendships with the Mandelstams, Akhmatova and Lev Gumilev, which appeared in English in 2004, translated and edited by John Crowfoot (The Harvill Press). (For some Russian readers, Gerstein shed far too much light on 'Mandelstam Street'.) Nancy K. Anderson's *The Word That Causes Death's Defeat: Poems of Memory* (published by Yale in the Annals of Communism series in 2004), which includes verse translations of Akhmatova's *Requiem* and *Poem Without a Hero*, as well as a biography of the poet and critical essays on her poetry, is a most valuable resource for English-speaking readers.

Carol J. Avins's long introduction to her annotated edition of Isaac Babel's *1920 Diary*, translated by H. T. Willetts (Yale University Press, 1995), gives a vivid portrait of the writer and his life. There are several editions of his short stories in English translation, including David McDuff's for Penguin Books (revised edition, 1998). Some of Marina Tsvetaeva's prose appeared in English in *A Captive Spirit: Selected Prose*, edited and translated by J. Marin King, published by Ardis (Ann Arbor, 1980) and by Virago Press (1983). *Earthly Signs*, Jamey Gambrell's translations of Tsvetaeva's Moscow notebooks of 1917–22 (Yale University Press, 2002), gives a fine sense of Tsvetaeva as a prose writer and includes a valuable biographical and critical essay by the translator. A new

English edition of the extraordinary three-way correspondence among Pasternak, Tsvetaeva and Rainer Maria Rilke of 1926 was published by New York Review Books in 2001, translated by Margaret Wettlin, Walter Arndt and Jamey Gambrell. *Selected Poems* by Tsvetaeva, translated by Elaine Feinstein from literal versions by Angela Livingstone, has been published in several editions by Oxford University Press, and most recently by Carcanet in 2004. The terrible end of Tsvetaeva's life is recounted in Irma Kudrova's *Death of a Poet: The Last Days of Marina Tsvetaeva*, translated by Mary Ann Szporluk, with an introduction by Ellendea Proffer (Gerald Duckworth and Co., London, 2004). Varlam Shalamov's *Kolyma Tales*, translated by John Glad, were published by W. W. Norton in 1980, and by Penguin Books in 1994. Looking further back in Russian literary history, English versions of Chekhov's short stories 'Fortune', 'On the Road' and 'The Lady with a Little Dog' appear in *About Love and Other Stories* (Oxford University Press, 2004), a collection of fine new translations by Rosamund Bartlett. Dostoevsky's story 'Bobok' can be found in *Russian Short Stories from Pushkin to Buida*, edited and translated by Robert Chandler (Penguin, 2005).

Among many historical sources, I have drawn particularly (and gratefully) on Derek Watson's *Molotov: A Biography* (Palgrave Macmillan, London, 2005) and on Larissa Vasilieva's *Kremlin Wives*, translated by Cathy Porter (Arcade, New York, 1992). I have also made extensive use of the conversations with Molotov recorded by Felix Chuev between 1969 and 1986. Chuev's *Hundred and Forty Conversations with Molotov* (*Sto sorok besed s Molotovym*) appeared in 1991. Albert Resis edited an abridged collection of these conversations in English, *Molotov Remembers: Inside Kremlin Politics* (Ivan R. Dee, Chicago, 1993). In 1999, Chuev published a fuller, corrected edition with the resonant new title (hard to render adequately in English), *Molotov: The Semi-Powerful Ruler* (*Molotov: poluderzhavnyi vlastelin*). As well as a number of interesting photographs – Molotov at his desk, with Stalin's young daughter, eating jam off a spoon, arm in arm with Hitler –

Chuev's book contains some evocative verbal pictures. On a 'white fairytale winter day', as they walk through the village of Zhukovka, Chuev and Molotov encounter Shostakovich outside his dacha. As they walk away, the composer stands and 'looks long after Molotov'.

Chuev claims that Molotov knew he would write a book about him. Molotov's grandson, Vyacheslav Nikonov, says this is a lie. He calls Chuev's *Hundred and Forty Conversations* a 'pirate book', whose publication came as a great surprise to the family. Though the authenticity of the conversations is not in question (and Nikonov was present at most of the meetings), Chuev's secret recording of them was, he says, 'dishonourable'. While Nikonov is ambivalently grateful to Chuev for the preservation of historical details that might otherwise have been lost, he regrets that the elderly Molotov comes across in conversation as stupider, less intellectual, than he was in reality. Nikonov, a political scientist and specialist in American history, is working on a multi-volume biography of his grandfather, a task for which, he says, his whole life has prepared him. The first volume (Moscow, 2005) takes Molotov as far as the year 1924, drawing on family and state archives. Nikonov gives his chapters epigraphs from Pushkin and Mandelstam; he discusses Molotov's views on Tolstoy, Dostoevsky and Chekhov, and quotes from Tsvetaeva's notebooks on the hungry Moscow winter of 1918–19, when 'we learned to love: bread, fire, wood, sun, sleep . . .'

Index

INDEX